How the Body Shapes the Way We Think

How the Body Shapes the Way We Think
A New View of Intelligence

Rolf Pfeifer and Josh Bongard

with a contribution by Simon Grand
Foreword by Rodney Brooks
Illustrations by Shun Iwasawa

A Bradford Book
The MIT Press
Cambridge, Massachusetts
London, England

This book was set in Syntax and Times Roman by SNP Best-set Typesetter Ltd., Hong Kong.

Library of Congress Cataloging-in-Publication Data

Pfeifer, Rolf, 1947–
How the body shapes the way we think : a new view of intelligence / by Rolf Pfeifer and Josh Bongard ; with a contribution by Simon Grand ; foreword by Rodney Brooks ; illustrations by Shun Iwasawa.
    p. cm.
Includes bibliographical references (p.   ).
ISBN-13: 978-0-262-16239-5 (alk. paper, hardcover)
978-0-262-537421 (alk. paper, paperback)
1. Artificial intelligence. 2. Cognitive science. I. Bongard, Josh. II. Grand, Simon. III. Title.

Q335.P445   2006
006.3—dc22

2006044919

To my friends in Japan (R. P.)
To Toby, Carol, and Ralph (J. B.)

Contents

Foreword

The great revolutions in science come about when what was formerly thought to be true and unassailable is both assailed and shown to not be true after all. Sometimes the assaults are brutal and front on, and sometimes they are gentle over a long period of time, gradually creeping up on the soon to be discredited truth.

This book is a gentle assault on some of the collateral tenets of modern rationalism; not an assault on rationalism itself, but an assault on many of the things that are commonly assumed by rationalists. Rolf Pfeifer and Josh Bongard question whether our nervous systems compute, whether they are separate control systems for our bodies, and even whether there can truly be disembodied reasoning. These three ideas are so ingrained in our computational metaphors that they usually go unquestioned— they make no sense within our normal frameworks of thinking in the fields of computer science and artificial intelligence, and even neuroscience. Beyond the mere technical these questions challenge the intellectual father of rationalism Rene Descartes and his "Je pense, donc je suis" (I think, therefore I am) from his *Discourse on Method* (written in French, not Latin, in 1637).

While such questions can be seen as a challenge to the very underpinnings of the scientific world view, they really are not. Pfeifer and Bongard are not suggesting throwing out the scientific method and replacing it, as some might fear, with postmodern relativism. Rather they are assaulting certain metaphors that have perhaps gone haywire in their influence on how we approach the study of intelligence, the study of us.

In modern times there have been two important and perhaps underestimated influences on our view of intelligence.

1. As Alan Turing described in his 1950 paper "Computing Machinery and Intelligence," his earlier and today still dominant model of

computation came from considering the externally observable behavior of a human computer, a person who carried out computations with pen and paper, and "is supposed to be following fixed rules." It is worth noting here that Turing modeled what a person does, not what a person thinks.

2. Ever since the human brain has come to be considered as the seat of our thought, desires, and dreams, it has been compared to the most advanced technology possessed by mankind. In my own lifetime I have seen popular "complexity" metaphors for the brain evolve. When I was a young child the brain was likened to an electromagnetic telephone switching network. Then it became an electronic digital computer. Then a massively parallel digital computer. And delightfully, in April 2002, someone in a lecture audience asked me whether the brain could be "just like the world wide web." Even otherwise serious scientists have become enamored of their own complexity metaphors declaring for instance that quantum phenomena and the brain are both so complex that they must be about the same thing.

Turing's metaphor has become the very definition of computation, and he points out in his 1950 paper, using Babbage's unrealized mechanical engine as the exemplar, that such computation is independent of the medium in which it is expressed. The metaphors for the brain (except for the quantum speculations) have entrenched it as the equivalent of Turing's form of computation, and thus rationalism largely assumes that the human brain is a Turing machine, carrying out Turing computation, and controlling its periphery, the human body.

But when we consider the evolutionary history of nervous systems we are faced with a dilemma not unlike one that is so often used to challenge evolution itself. How could evolution have incrementally produced the components of an eye—the lens, the pupil, the retina—when all are necessary, fully formed, to enable the other to carry out its function within the ensemble? When we turn that skepticism on its head we are left to ask what roles earlier versions of nervous systems played, before they became fully functional control systems, like Turing's "control" component which he talked about along with the "executive" and the "store."

Metaphors are useful in science as a way of understanding systems we wouldn't otherwise understand—metaphors can suggest appropriate questions to ask about a system, they can provide intuitive models about how things might work, and they can bridge gaps as a more explicit theory is being formed. But they can also lead to ways of thinking about problems that may be more complex than needed. Gravity can be viewed as a medium for conveying information about one body to another, but the information metaphor is not as useful as classical mechanics for computing the orbit of a planet around the sun. Likewise, metaphors about computation and information may not always be the most useful metaphor for understanding intelligence.

Pfeifer and Bongard provide another way of looking at intelligence, more in line with the evolutionary history of organisms, and less influenced by computational metaphors than most contempory work in artificial intelligence, cognitive psychology, and neuroscience. The viewpoint espoused in this book considers the physical manifestation of the body as primary. The stuff of intelligence has evolved in conjunction with that body and is more a modulator of its behavior rather than a primary and central control system. Such an inverted viewpoint is perhaps not so radically controversial when applied to "low-level details" like how an animal or robot might locomote. But it is truly an affront to the modern viewpoint when it is applied to perception and even more so to thought itself. And make no mistake, this is the direction of the authors' assault.

It is much easier to critique an existing approach to an area of scientific research than it is to create such an area. But this book is more than just a critique. It reports on wide varieties of experiments, many by the authors themselves, which start to provide an alternate framework within which further research can be carried out, and not incidentally, within which practical robotic artifacts can be built.

Suspend your preconceptions. There may be less to intelligence than meets the eye.

Rodney Brooks
Director, MIT Computer Science and Artificial Intelligence Laboratory
Panasonic Professor of Robotics

Preface

Embodiment, the idea that the body is required for intelligence, has been around for two decades, but an awful lot has changed since then. Research labs and leading technology companies around the world have produced or are developing a host of sometimes science fiction-like creations: almost frighteningly realistic humanoid robots, robot musicians, wearable technology, robots controlled by biological brains, robots that can walk without a brain, real-life cyborgs, robots in homes for the elderly, robots that literally put themselves together, artificial cells grown automatically, and simulated genetic regulatory networks for growing virtual creatures. This new breed of technology, along with many significant theoretical advances, is the direct result of the embodied approach to intelligence. Along the way, many of the initially vague ideas have been elaborated and the arguments sharpened, and the diverse outcomes are beginning to form into a coherent structure. Thus, it seemed like a good opportunity to work out the first steps toward a theory of intelligence and write a book about it.

From a personal perspective, I (Rolf) have given many seminars and lectures to nonspecialized audiences, and many of them were able to relate in very direct and natural ways to the ideas presented: the ideas I talked about seemed to hold relevance for their own interests and specialties. What most people found intriguing was that this research demonstrates how things can always be seen differently. We all have our strong prejudices and often think, "It's got to be like that, there is no other way!" For example, if you want to build a fast-running robot you must have fast electronics; an object-collecting robot must have a means for recognizing the objects it is supposed to gather; or an insect with six legs needs a centralized control program somewhere in its brain to coordinate all its legs while walking. Surprisingly, it turns out that none of these are true, as we will see later.

So, I felt that rather than writing another specialized textbook like *Understanding Intelligence*, co-authored with Christian Scheier in 1999, a popular science–style publication accessible to a wide readership might be a more suitable undertaking. Science and technology are no longer isolated fields. They closely interact with the corporate, political, and social aspects of our society; and that interaction, among its other effects, increases the need to justify basic research. Convinced that we might be able to provide a novel perspective not only on artificial intelligence but more generally on how we view ourselves and the world around us, we took up the challenge of trying to translate the scientific results and insights we have gained into everyday language. The result is this book.

Aims and Scope

The goal of this book is twofold: on the one hand it is to explore the implications of embodiment (how having a body affects intelligence), to work out the first steps toward a theory of intelligence, and finally to demonstrate the wide applicability of these ideas. On the other, we will try to show that things can always be seen differently. So, the book is conceptual, and is geared toward a broad audience in education, business, information technology, engineering, entertainment, the media, as well as academics from virtually all disciplines and levels, but especially those involved in psychology, neuroscience, philosophy, linguistics, and biology. And last but not least, this book is also intended for anyone interested in technology, its future, and its implications for society. No special training or education is required for understanding the ideas presented: we have tried to provide background information, examples, and pointers to further reading for the more difficult-to-grasp concepts.

The core of the theory consists of a set of "design principles for intelligent systems." The reason for choosing the form of design principles for our theory is that they are a compact way of describing insights about intelligent systems in general and they provide convenient heuristics for actually building artificial systems, like robots in particular. And actually building systems is crucial because we want to design and construct intelligent artificial systems so that we can understand intelligent systems in general: this is the synthetic methodology—the basic methodology of artificial intelligence—which can be characterized as understanding by building. As we will show with many examples, by building artificial systems we can learn about biology, but also about intelligence in general. An exciting prospect is that this enables us not only to study natural forms of intelligence, but to create new forms of intelligence that do not yet exist; "intelligence as it could be," to adapt a quote by the founder of the field of artificial life, Chris Langton. Thus, by building robots, our intention is to learn something about intelligence, and not so much to build technologically sophisticated robots. So, the book is not so much about the intricacies of the engineering process or the details of how to build robots, but rather about the basic insights that arise as a result of building robots.

We have tried to support our claim that the ideas developed in this book have broad applicability beyond the field of artificial intelligence proper by providing illustrations from the fields of ubiquitous computing, strategic management, human memory, and robotic technology in everyday life. We hope that the reader will enjoy these case studies and will feel encouraged to apply the ideas to areas of his or her own interest.

We should perhaps briefly comment on the term *artificial intelligence* here before continuing. With the introduction of the notion of embodiment about 20 years ago, the field has undergone fundamental changes, so that sometimes the term *embodied artificial intelligence* is employed, and we even published a book with precisely that title (Iida et al., 2004). In this book we will avoid that usage, because it somehow suggests that there is the "real" field of artificial intelligence—the overarching, encompassing discipline—and then there is this small subarea called "embodied" artificial intelligence. We feel that this perspective is somewhat inappropriate. As we will elaborate later, there are essentially two directions in artificial intelligence: one concerned with developing useful algorithms or robots; and another direction that focuses on understanding intelligence, biological or otherwise. In order to make progress on the latter, an embodied perspective is mandatory. In this research branch, artificial intelligence *is* embodied.

One last comment is necessary before we turn to the contents of the book. In spite of the fact that the materials presented are often a bit theoretical and require concentration on the part of the reader, we have tried to make the book fun to read by providing many examples. Also, the web site for the book (www.ifi.unizh.ch/groups/ailab/HowTheBody) contains many links to videos and other supporting material, as well as a discussion forum. To make the book even more appealing, we have engaged an artist and computer scientist, Shun Iwasawa of the

University of Tokyo, who, with great talent, technical skill, and understanding of the subject matter of the book, created Japanese Manga–style illustrations that, we hope, will stimulate the reader's interest and communicate the fun, forward-thinking style of this field of study.

Road Map to the Book

There are three parts to this book. Part I is introductory, familiarizing the reader with the contents of the book and the basic concepts. Part II, the core section, summarizes our attempts to develop a theory of intelligence. Part III applies the theory, in particular the design principles developed in part II, to a number of case studies beyond the field of artificial intelligence proper. Finally, part IV provides a summary of the major points made in the book.

In the first chapter we will introduce what the terms *thinking*, *cognition*, and *intelligence* mean, discuss why intelligence has fascinated people from all walks of life throughout history, and introduce the field of artificial intelligence and the embodied view of intelligence. Chapter 2 presents an overview of the intellectual landscape of artificial intelligence. This should give the reader a flavor of the kinds of research questions that are out there, as well as the fascination, but also the difficulties, of navigating and actually doing research in this highly rugged interdisciplinary field.

Part II is an attempt to formulate the first steps toward a theory of intelligence. It is the central part of the book, and so it is a bit on the heavy side, conceptually speaking. But we have tried to include many examples to illustrate the abstract ideas and to support our arguments. Chapter 3 outlines what type of theory we are looking for and introduces a general framework provided by a number of important notions such as diversity-compliance, frame of reference, the synthetic methodology, time perspectives, and emergence. This chapter contains a bit of philosophy of science, which we use to outline the nature of the theory, and describes what it means to make progress and to do work in the field. Just to take one example, there are three time frames at which we can study behavior: "here and now"; learning and development; and evolution. Chapters 4, 5, and 6 are organized around these time frames.

Chapter 4 first describes properties of real-world agents and then sketches a set of design heuristics—what we call the design principles for intelligent systems—that can be used to guide us in engineering such agents but also to help us understand biological ones. These design principles mostly concern the "here-and-now" time frame. Chapter 5 explores design and analysis issues from a developmental perspective, and asks how high-level cognition can emerge during a process of ontogenetic development; how cognition emerges as the agent matures into an "adult." For example, how is it possible that something discrete, such as abstract symbol processing, can arise in a completely continuous system—and we are all continuous systems—over time? A specific, somewhat provocative instance of this question is what walking—or, more generally, locomotion—has to do with thinking, which we will explore in detail in that chapter. The chapter concludes with a set of design principles at the developmental time perspective. Chapter 6 looks at how we can harness ideas from biological evolution in order to design agents—complete with bodies, sensors, motors, and brains— from scratch. Here, we as designers step back and let simulated evolution do the work for us. The point is to let evolution design virtual agents that perform increasingly complex tasks, so that at some point we might be inclined to use the term *cognitive* to characterize their behavior. One of the goals of this chapter is to demonstrate the power of artificial evolution. Specifically, we will give some impressive examples of where it has outperformed humans. While chapter 5 focuses on the lifetime of an individual, in chapter 6 we extend the time frame to encompass many generations of agents, and widen our view to consider not just single agents but populations of them. Again, we summarize the main results as a set of design principles, this time for evolutionary systems.

The implications of considering populations rather than individuals are discussed in chapter 7. There, we look at emergent phenomena that arise in populations of agents; that is, phenomena, or global behavioral patterns, in the group that come about as the agents interact with each other without knowing about the global pattern. These kinds of emergent behaviors are often referred to as collective intelligence. We will also introduce another kind of collective intelligence, namely modular robots: i.e., robots that are composed of many modules, which, as they interact with each other, can achieve interesting collective behaviors. In modular robotics, the modules can be viewed as agents, in addition to the robot itself. The main points in this chapter are also captured in a set of design principles for collective intelligence.

Part III discusses a number of case studies demonstrating the application of the concepts and design principles developed in part II to problems that lie outside the area of artificial intelligence proper: we will look at ubiquitous computing, management, the psychology of human memory, and robotic and artificial intelligence technologies in our everyday lives. We will show that the perspective of embodiment can shed new light on these topics. The case studies are self-contained and can be read in any sequence after the reader has finished chapters 1 through 7. In chapter 8, we discuss ubiquitous computing, a rapidly expanding discipline in informatics which in fact shares many ideas with artificial intelligence. In this new field, the goal is to explore the potential of "putting computing everywhere": into cars, clothes, cups, shoes, buildings, appliances, mobile phones, consumer goods in general; and embedding them into communication networks of ever-increasing size and complexity. Chapter 9, written by Simon Grand and Rolf Pfeifer, is an initial attempt to apply the perspective of embodied intelligence to the business world, and in particular to the design and construction of new products, businesses, and companies in an intrinsically uncertain, complex, and unpredictable world. That chapter is meant to demonstrate that the design principles indeed have wide potential applicability. Chapter 10 presents a case study on human memory that illustrates on the one hand how embodiment provides a new perspective on old problems, and on the other how it can be employed to better understand recent trends in memory research. Chapter 11 tries to assess the feasibility, desirability, and economic reality of developing all kinds of robots, and in particular humanoid robots, that could enter and participate in the everyday lives of humans and our society.

Part IV, the last part of the book, will summarize the main points of our theory and provide a review of the design principles in a single chapter, chapter 12. There we also present a list of selected highlights that sum up what we feel are the key insights gained throughout the book. In conclusion, we will return to one of the central goals of the book: we will present a collection of examples illustrating how things can always be seen differently.

Acknowledgments

We would like to thank all the members of the Artificial Intelligence Laboratory of the University of Zurich for continued discussions, excellent research, enthusiasm, and the many ideas that finally found their way into this book. Big thanks go to our friends Yasuo Kuniyoshi, Olaf

Sporns, Akio Ishiguro, Hiroshi Yokoi, Koh Hosoda, Fumio Hara, and Hiroshi Kobayashi, who kept encouraging us to move ahead with the project as quickly as possible. Josh would like to express his warmest thanks to Hod Lipson for selflessly providing time and space within which to work on this project. We would also like to express our thanks to the many funding agencies that have made the research described in this book possible, in particular the Swiss National Science Foundation and the IST Program of the European Union. Moreover, I (Rolf) would like to express my very personal thanks to Yasuo Kuniyoshi, Tomomasa Sato, Hirochika Inoue, Yoshi Nakamura, and all the other members of the Department of Mechano-Informatics, for inviting me to the University of Tokyo to be a twenty-first-century COE (Center of Excellence) professor of Information Science and Technology, where many draft chapters of this manuscript were written. Their perspective on intelligent agents as complex dynamical systems has strongly influenced the contents of the book.

Our great thanks go also to Gabriel Gomez, who has researched many issues concerning the project. Also, we highly appreciate the contributions of Max Lungarella, who, in particular with his PhD thesis but also with many personal discussions, is largely responsible for the quality of chapter 5. Also, the ideas of Fumiya Iida, to whom we owe the title of chapter 5, "From Locomotion to Cognition," have been instrumental and have strongly helped shape the ideas of chapter 5. We are extremely grateful to Shun Iwasawa for his outstanding, inspiring, and instructive illustrations: they further help bridge the gap between science, engineering, and entertainment.

Thanks go also to all the researchers around the world from many different disciplines for their ideas that have provided inspiration for our arguments so that we were able to put together a coherent story. And, of course, to Rodney Brooks, for having started this exciting research field in the first place, and for providing the foreword.

We would also like to express our sincere thanks to the MIT Press, in particular to Bob Prior for supporting this project, to the copy editor, Suzanne Schafer, and to a number of anonymous reviewers who, with their constructive criticisms, have enormously helped improve the quality of the manuscript. Our thanks go also to Britta Glatzeder, who was involved in the initial stages of the project and to whom we owe the title of the book. Rolf would also like to thank Claudia Wirth, who kept everybody off his back when he was trying to finalize the manuscript and who kept the lab running during his long absence.

There are many, many others—faculty, staff, students, friends, and family—who have provided support one way or another to both authors, and without whom this book would never have been finished, let alone begun: we are deeply in debt to all of you. I (Josh) would like to thank my family—Toby, Carol, and Ralph—for understanding and helping me in my long journey to get to this point. I (Rolf) would like to thank in particular my two sons, Serge and Mischa, who have always encouraged me to continue when times were hard.

1 Intelligence, Artificial Intelligence, Embodiment, and What the Book Is About

How does the body shape the way we think? Is this even the right question, or should it perhaps be the other way around: how does our thinking influence the body? It seems obvious that the way we move, walk, talk, write, dance, and sing are all controlled by the brain, i.e., the brain quite obviously controls the body. We decide that we want to drink a cup of tea, go see a movie, or do some push-ups, and then we do it. But the brain controls the body not only at the conscious but also at the unconscious level. The basic digestive and life maintenance functions such as breathing and heartbeat, on the one hand, and automatic movements on the other are only a few examples: we do not explicitly tell our stomach to digest, and when walking we do not consciously control the movement of our legs; the control is largely automatic, unless there are disturbances. If we do try and consciously control our movements, we are likely to trip over: this is a phenomenon that many of us will have experienced when learning to dance or play a new sport. So the brain is in control of everything, it seems. Also, there is a lot of evidence that we can influence our body's functions through various kinds of mental control, such as relaxation and meditation techniques, and they can make us feel much better. Moreover, in the medical domain there is a lot of evidence that diseases can be caused by mental processes, especially stress, depression, and neurotic disorders. So again, the brain appears to be controlling the body.

Now the title of our book suggests the exact opposite. But how could the body influence our thinking? We can think whatever we like, about anything we choose, in whatever way we want. Thoughts are free and immaterial in some sense—or are they? This book tries to address some of these questions, even if we cannot present exact solutions. We will show that thoughts are perhaps not as free and independent as we would like them to be, and that indeed they are highly constrained—shaped—

by our bodies. But we will also demonstrate that the body not only constrains, but also enables thought. The crucial notion needed to explain all of this is that of embodiment. There is a lot of popular science literature about "the wisdom of the body": body language, nonverbal communication, and how to accept your body the way it is in order to feel good. Of course, when we are in pain or when we feel in great physical shape, relaxed, and strong, our thoughts will be influenced by such bodily conditions, and this is certainly important. However, what we have in mind here is more specific: the idea we will pursue is that the kinds of thoughts that we can produce or carry out ultimately have their foundation in our embodiment. Roughly, the rationale is as follows.

One of the most elementary capacities of any creature is categorization: the ability to make distinctions in the real world. If we cannot distinguish food from nonfood, dangerous from safe objects and situations, our parents from other people, or our home from the rest of the world, we are not going to survive for very long. Likewise, robots incapable of making basic distinctions, e.g., a household robot that cannot distinguish garbage from antiques, a vacuum cleaner from a dishwasher, or pets from babies will not be very useful. We will attempt to demonstrate that the formation of such categories is very directly determined by our embodiment, i.e., our morphology and the material properties of our body. Morphology includes the shape of the body, the kinds of limbs and where they are attached, the kinds of sensors (eyes, ears, nose, skin for touch and temperature, mouth for taste) and where on the body they are found. By material properties we mean, for example, the deformability of the fingertips and of the skin, or the elasticity of the muscle-tendon system. When interacting with the real world, the body is stimulated in very particular ways, and this stimulation provides, in a sense, the raw material for the brain to work with. As we will see later, this raw material can be used to create categories—cups, apples, pets, people—that describe the environment in a natural way.

Of course, we can construct very abstract categories in our head, but even they are influenced by the basic categories we can form. The linguist and philosopher George Lakoff of the University of California, Berkeley, argued in a provocative book coauthored with Rafael Núñez of the Cognitive Science Institute at the University of California, San Diego, entitled *Where Mathematics Comes From*, that even abstract mathematical notions such as the concepts of a real number or a set have their origins in our specific embodiment and could not have been construed differently. Mathematical concepts, according to Lakoff and

Núñez, are based on metaphors (e.g., a point "moving" toward infinity) and these metaphors are in turn grounded in, or based on, our embodiment. Empirically they demonstrate some of their insights by discussing the gestures mathematicians typically use to explain their ideas. The hypothesis that we will pursue is that not only categorization is grounded in (shaped by) the body, but so is cognition in general, including spatial and social cognition, problem solving and reasoning, and natural language.

In the first part of this book we provide some general background and briefly describe, in chapter 1, concepts such as thinking, cognition, and of course intelligence, and we briefly discuss the notorious mind-body problem. We look at why people, throughout history, have been fascinated by the topic of intelligence. We introduce the goals of artificial intelligence research, because this is the main methodology we will employ throughout the text. Then we present the notion of embodiment and outline some of its far-reaching, radical, and often surprising implications. They can hardly be overestimated, and they will fundamentally change the ways in which we view ourselves and the world around us.

The introduction of embodiment roughly two decades ago has dramatically changed the research field. Therefore, in chapter 2, we portray the research landscape, i.e., what scientists in the field of artificial intelligence do, how they perceive themselves, and how they work. We will try to provide a (more or less) comprehensive overview of these intriguing developments. We feel that an understanding of the research landscape will greatly facilitate comprehension of the somewhat theory-laden second part of the book.

1 Intelligence, Thinking, and Artificial Intelligence

"I think, therefore I am"! Thus the famous and popular quote by the seventeenth-century French philosopher René Descartes, from his *Discourse on Method*, published in 1637. What is surprising about this quote is that it implies that the reason I exist is not the body, but the mind! In Descartes's view there are two separate systems: the body and the mind. This division raises the problem of how these two systems relate to one another, an issue that is referred to as the mind-body problem (see focus box 1.1). One of the main challenges posed by the mind-body problem is the question of how a thought—something happening in the immaterial mind—can potentially influence the body. For example, I can decide in my mind to pick up a cup to drink a sip of coffee, and subsequently my arm and hand begin to move to perform the action. This is the way we like to think about ourselves: the mind controls our actions, which implies that we are in control of our behavior and therefore our lives—which is, so to speak, the "Cartesian heritage" of Western culture. The importance of the individual—individualism—and being in control are two extremely cherished values in Western societies: We, as individuals, decide about something—a goal that we want to achieve, such as becoming a doctor or catching a Frisbee—and then we make plans and go about doing it. Or when at a party, we decide that we would like to meet someone, so we start talking to that person. It all seems very natural, the way things should be. But is it really? In other words, is this an accurate way of describing how we as intelligent beings function? As you might expect, after what we have said so far, our answer is "no." While there may be some truth to this way of viewing ourselves, it is largely based on wishful thinking; on how we would like to see ourselves rather than on how things actually are (see also focus box 1.1 for more details). It turns out that instead of our ideas—our minds—controlling our actions,

Focus Box 1.1
The Mind-Body Problem

The so-called dualist position, as laid out by René Descartes in the seventeenth century, states that there are two separate systems within a human being: a mental thing, the *res cogitans*, and a physical thing, the *res extensa*. Descartes was concerned about how these two worlds—the mental and physical—talk to one another. His ideas have raised many deep issues, which together are known as the mind-body problem. This problem is probably the most famous in the philosophy of mind, and is concerned with the relation between the mental and the physical, or between mind and matter: more specifically, how can the physical processes of our bodies and brains give rise to abstract mental phenomena such as consciousness? David Chalmers, one of the leading philosophers of consciousness, is very clear about how important this question is: "Consciousness is the biggest mystery. It may be the largest outstanding obstacle in our quest for a scientific understanding of the universe." (Chalmers, 1997, p. ix). There is a vast literature on this issue, but rather than providing a systematic review—the interested reader is referred to David Chalmers's and Thomas Metzinger's popular online bibliographies on the philosophy of mind—we would like to point out just one particularly enticing issue; that of conscious will.

Most people would probably agree that mental phenomena, such as thinking and cognition, originate from brain processes. Assume for a moment that your hand is on the desk in front of you and you are about to move your finger. The neuroscientist Benjamin Libet and his colleagues, in an often-cited landmark experiment (Libet et al., 1983), asked people to move their finger spontaneously, whenever they liked. In addition, the subjects had to look at a clock with a revolving point of light, and report where the dot was on the clock when they experienced "conscious aware-ness of 'wanting' to perform a given self-initiated movement" (quoted in Wegner, 2002, p. 52). Moreover, he recorded brain activity, the so-called readiness potential, from electroencephalography (EEG) sensors attached to the scalp, and he meas-ured actual finger movement using electromyography (EMG), a method for detect-ing muscle movement. The results were stunning: the onset of brain activity starts more than half a second before the actual finger movement and over 300 msec before the subjects become aware that they want to move a finger! In other words, the conscious will of wanting to move the finger occurs a significant interval after the onset of the relevant brain activity. So the experience of conscious will kicks in after the brain has already started preparing for the action. In other words, the mental will to move the finger could not have been the initiating agent of the move-ment. This is quite contrary to what we would expect, and runs counter to the sub-jective experience of the individual: we "feel" that our decision to move our finger is what kicks off the proper brain processes necessary to move the finger. The sur-prising conclusion from this experiment—whether we like it or not—is that the ini-tiation of the voluntary act of moving the finger seems to be caused by unconscious neural activity, not the other way around! Needless to say, this is a serious blow to the notion of free will. Or is it? Libet notes that even if the movement is indeed ini-tiated by unconscious forces, there is still enough time to veto an act—to decide not to move the finger—once one is aware of one's intentions. Perhaps this keeps the door open to the notion of free will. As you can imagine, these findings have created a flurry of discussions in the scientific community. The issue of free will, however, is just one of the many scientific debates that are currently raging about how the mental and physical aspects of a person influence each other. And it is not just a question of how they interact: in the extreme case, many philosophers hold, we may never be able to know how the mental and the physical communicate. To use the words of the legendary German brain physiologist DuBois Reymond: ignoramus ignorabimus (we do not know, we will not know). Or will we? The deep issues raised by Descartes still await final explanation, but the progress in modern neuro-science—and artificial intelligence—provides a scientific way, rather than just a philosophical one, for dealing with them.

to a surprising extent our body determines our thoughts. And this is what we will explore in this book: how the body shapes the way we think. We are convinced that the exploration of this relationship between body and thinking will clarify the conundrum of intelligence in interesting ways; we hope that it will indeed lead to a new view of intelligence, as suggested in the title.

In this chapter we will proceed as follows. First, because it has a prominent position in the title of the book, we will briefly examine the term *thinking* and how it relates to cognition and intelligence. We will talk about why the topic of intelligence has captured the attention of philosophers, scientists, and people at large throughout the history of humankind. Then we will explain how, in this book, we as researchers attempt to tackle these issues, namely by employing the methodology of artificial intelligence. We will end the chapter by introducing the notion of embodiment from which the major contributions to "a new view of intelligence" have originated and which, we believe, holds the most promise for our future understanding of intelligence.

1.1 Thinking, Cognition, and Intelligence

So far, we have used the term *thinking* without much reflection, with the assumption that everyone has a fairly clear notion of what it is all about. But let us look a bit more closely. Intuitively—and this is the way it is defined in psychological dictionaries—thinking is associated with conscious or deliberate thought, with something high-level or abstract. The trouble with this conception is that it relies on the assumption that a process either is or is not conscious. But perhaps matters are not as clear as they might seem at first sight. Here is one possible reason why.

Do newborns think? We cannot be sure, but perhaps they don't. Or maybe it would be better to say that they think less than adults. What about after a few days? Or after a few weeks? Certainly after a few months or years, and clearly as adults, we do think. But if this is true, it raises the question at what age children actually do start thinking. Again, this is difficult to answer, but it is clear that their skills gradually improve as they grow older; perhaps then their ability to think also improves gradually over time. This way of viewing thinking—and more generally, intelligence or cognition—is referred to as a developmental approach, i.e., it posits that the ability to think develops over time. From this perspective, the question shifts from whether an agent—an animal, robot, or human—is thinking or not to how much thinking is actually going on.

In other words, we can escape the limiting view that thinking is a binary property: i.e., an agent either thinks or it does not. (Throughout this book we use the term *agent* whenever we do not want to make a distinction between humans, animals, or robots, i.e., when what we say applies to all three. Much of what we have to say about intelligence in this book is general: it applies not only to humans, but, to a greater or lesser degree, to animals and robots as well. For example, agents have interesting properties related to intelligence that other nonagents, like cups or rocks, do not have: we will discuss this in more detail in chapter 4.)

It seems obvious that the ability to think increases over time as the organism grows and matures. But even as adults, "thinking" remains a vague term that for most people implies conscious thought. However, consciousness is an equally vague concept, and again we can imagine that there is a continuum rather than an all-or-none property. We would suspect that, for example, bacteria, insects, birds, rats, dogs, chimpanzees, and humans are conscious to a greater or lesser extent, rather than being either conscious or not. Moreover, in clinical psychology there is the concept of unconscious thoughts, which are thoughts that, even though we are not consciously aware of them, influence our behavior, often in undesirable ways. Therefore, rather than trying to come up with a definition for thinking or consciousness, it is probably best to agree that we are dealing with a continuum, with a gradual phenomenon. We side with Douglas Hofstadter, who, in his clever and entertaining book *Metamagical Themas*, laments the fact that people seem to have a compulsion for "black-and-white cutoffs when it comes to mysterious phenomena such as life and consciousness." And he adds that "the onward march of science seems to force us ever more clearly into accepting intermediate levels of such properties." (Hofstadter, 1985).

Consciousness is a peculiar, fascinating, but highly elusive sort of thing. Because it is tied to subjective experience, it is hard to investigate scientifically. However, recent advances in brain imaging and neuroscience in general have yielded stunning but also puzzling results (e.g., Crick and Koch, 2003). A particularly enticing issue concerns the role of consciousness in free will, which we briefly describe in focus box 1.1. In this book we will not go into the subject of consciousness. Some people appear to believe that unless we have explained consciousness, we have understood nothing about intelligence. We hope that we can convince the reader that this is not the case and that we can acquire a deep understanding of intelligence by pursuing the idea of embodiment. But we also feel that because we discuss the issue of how cognition can emerge from a physically embodied system—and most people seem to agree that consciousness is related to cognition—we will ultimately contribute to the understanding of consciousness.

Cognition, closely related to intelligence, is another vague and general term that is often used to designate those kinds of processes of an agent that are not directly related to sensor or motor mechanisms. Examples of cognitive processes are abstract problem solving and reasoning, memory, attention, and language. Again, as we will see, if we inspect the underlying mechanisms of these phenomena we find that cognition cannot really be distinguished from other (noncognitive) kinds of sensory-motor processes. As we will argue later, even simple activities such as walking or grasping a cup have cognitive qualities, so to speak. And perception, which is obviously related directly to sensor processes, is an important subfield of cognitive psychology. Lachman et al. (1979), in their well-known book *Cognitive Psychology and Information Processing*, described the field using a computer metaphor: "[cognitive psychology is about] how people take in information, how they recode and remember it, how they make decisions, how they transform their internal knowledge states, and how they translate these states into outputs" (p. 99). Cognition is sometimes employed as a more general term than thinking because it does not necessarily imply consciousness. However, it is important to keep in mind that despite the more abstract connotations of thinking as compared to cognition, thinking is not a disembodied process: as we will see, it seems to be directly tied to sensory-motor and other bodily (i.e., physiological) processes, as is cognition.

The last term to be characterized is that of intelligence, which closely resembles thinking and cognition, but is typically used in an even more general way. There is no good definition for intelligence, but we do not feel this is a bad thing. Throughout the book we will always take care to clarify what we are talking about, but at the same time we will try not to get bogged down in debates about definitions. We will see that some of the concepts that are defined in the literature—e.g., learning, memory, and perception—are not, from the perspective of the underlying mechanisms, clearly separable. For example, learning and memory are always involved in perception; what we perceive—for example, the sight of a friend in a bar—is determined by our memory, and of course, our memory is affected by what we perceive. As we will also see later on, these terms are used by an external observer to characterize certain behaviors, and are therefore largely arbitrary: the definitions depend more on the observer than on the observed phenomena themselves.

But back to intelligence. The entry for "intelligence" in the Penguin Dictionary of Psychology starts by stating that "Few concepts in psychology have received more devoted attention and few have resisted clarification so thoroughly" (Reber, 1995). If Reber's comment is about the definition of the term, we fully agree. However, we disagree with the idea that intelligence itself has resisted clarification. This book, we claim, clarifies many aspects of it. Before we turn toward elucidating the mystery of intelligence, though, we should introduce a bit of additional terminology.

We have been using the term *agent* to indicate that an argument holds whether we are talking about a human, animal, or robot. We do not use it in its everyday sense, referring to an insurance agent who offers us particular services, a secret agent who unearths information for a government, or a chemical agent that reacts with other substances. In this book, an agent is "anything that can be viewed as perceiving its environment through sensors and acting upon that environment through effectors," as defined by Russell and Norvig in their classical textbook on artificial intelligence (1995, p. 33). In other words, an agent differs from other kinds of objects such as a rock or a cup, which are only subject to physical forces: they cannot react on their own. Moreover, we are particularly interested in embodied agents, which are agents that have a physical body with which they can affect, and be affected by their environment. Software agents, which is a term used to designate certain types of computer programs, such as internet agents that search for information, are not embodied and will not be further considered here.

Finally, we use the term *robot* in a relatively broad sense. The original sense of the word—it derives from the Czech *robota*, meaning something like "work" or "forced labor"—implies that robots were initially meant to do work for humans. So, factory robots are the "species" that most closely conform to this idea. However, for the purpose of this book they are not of central interest; they will not be further discussed because their behaviors are essentially preprogrammed and they do not tell us much about the nature of intelligence. We expect these robots to do precisely what we want them to do—they should not all of a sudden come up with some interesting, unexpected ideas or behaviors on their own. The term *robot* as used here refers to machines that have at least some agent characteristics in the sense discussed above, irrespective of whether they do useful work for humans or not. This includes humanoids, pet robots, entertainment robots, service robots, rescue robots, etc. In chapter 11 we will review and analyze different types of robots. Whether or not a particular machine or device deserves to be called a robot is largely arbitrary and cannot be precisely defined.

With all of this in mind, let us now familiarize ourselves intuitively with intelligence and explore its fascination and its mysteries.

1.2 The Mystery of Intelligence

Intelligence is obviously an important issue. Literally hundreds of books have been written about it, and here we add yet another book on the subject. Well, yes and no. Yes, this is another book about intelligence, but we feel that it is very different from its predecessors. The fact that there is an enormous literature on the topic is not really surprising. Throughout human history, philosophers, psychologists, artists, teachers, and more recently neuroscientists and artificial intelligence researchers have been wondering about it, have been fascinated by it, and have devoted much of their lives to its investigation. And many of them have written books about it. Still, there are good reasons why it makes sense to write—yet another!—book about this topic because, we believe, it presents some novel points that previously have not even been considered to be part of the field of intelligence. These novel points all relate, one way or another, to the notion of embodiment, the seemingly simple idea that intelligence requires a body. As we will see in this section, and as we hope to demonstrate throughout the book, this new perspective of embodiment has led to often surprising insights and new research issues for studying intelligence.

Intelligence is a highly sensitive topic because we tend to believe that intelligence is what distinguishes us from animals: we are so much more intelligent than them, we tell ourselves—and in many ways this is certainly the case. In our societies, Western or Eastern, an enormously high value is attached to intelligence. Our schools and universities are almost universally considered our highest cultural resource: indeed many of them look like temples built to honor the gods. Universities are monuments with strongly symbolic character. The goals of these institutions are, in one way or another, to preserve and further increase the level of intelligence in our societies. "You are very intelligent" is one of the highest compliments one can give or receive. We are constantly reminded that intelligence is good, positive, and desirable. Parents always think that their children are highly intelligent. You are allowed to say virtually anything about someone's children—you can call them lazy, cheeky, aggressive, nervous, easily distracted, shy—but never, ever, say they are not intelligent! We continue to place this premium on rational intelligence despite the recent surge of interest in emotional intelligence, which argues that rationality is limited and that we should also take emotions into account when measuring intelligence. In other words, in this view, intuition and the ability to emotionally judge a situation is considered just as important as the "cold" kind of intelligence required to pass high school exams or to achieve high scores on intelligence tests. This perspective is documented by the famous books of the well-known neuroscientist Antonio Damasio (e.g., *Descartes' Error*), and by the tests developed by the American psychologist Daniel Goleman to measure emotional intelligence (Goleman, 1997). Regardless of these developments, rational, logical intelligence is still considered to be one of the most enviable characteristics of human beings.

But there is another reason why intelligence is a sensitive issue. For many decades the question of whether intelligence is inherited or can be acquired during a person's lifetime has been hotly debated: this is the famous (or infamous) nature-nurture debate (see, for example, Ridley, 2003; Ceci and Williams, 2000, for a collection of articles on the topic). We assume that part of the reason this debate is so emotionally charged is because it is about intelligence. Other personality traits besides intelligence cause much less controversy. For example, whether a person has an honest character or high moral standards, and how these traits are acquired, is not discussed as much, although honesty and morality are still considered desirable qualities. Having a high IQ (intelligence quotient), or more generally scoring high on the many standard intelligence tests now on the market (in spite of all the current interest in emotional intelligence), is still considered one of the most desirable personality traits to have. In order to be politically correct we hesitate to attribute value to IQ scores publicly; however, privately, we suspect, most people do value them. When the two Harvard psychologists Richard Herrnstein and Charles Murray published their controversial analysis of the IQ in their famous 1994 book *The Bell Curve: Intelligence and Class Structure in American Life*, they spurred another extremely emotional debate in America and throughout the world. Among other findings, they reported, with a number of qualifications, that Asians have the highest scores on IQ tests, Caucasians are second, and black people have the lowest! It seems easy to conclude from this result that class structure is a result of intelligence, regardless of whether intelligence is inborn or acquired. The interesting scientific question in this seemingly eternal debate is not whether intelligence is inherited or acquired during the lifetime of an individual, but how evolution and development interact such that intelligence arises in an agent. This topic will be broached in chapters 5 and 6, where we discuss the relationship between development, evolution, and intelligence.

Intelligence is highly mysterious, and we all wonder what it is: How was it possible that something so sophisticated could have been produced by evolution? How does it develop as a baby grows to become an adult? How can we walk, talk, or solve a problem? And how can we, without effort, recognize a face in a crowd, or play a piece of music? Just to take one example of a process essential for intelligence, memory is a highly enigmatic phenomenon, and nobody really understands how it works. Memory performance varies greatly depending on the person's mood or physical conditions; sometimes people are really forgetful, and sometimes we are astonished by their accuracy of recall. How do we retrieve something from memory? In a computer, the stored items have addresses that can be used for this purpose. But where are the addresses in the brain? There are events that have long passed of which we have the most vivid memories, whereas others are murky and dark, at least temporarily. Then, suddenly—we have all had the experience—we remember something long forgotten. The tip-of-the-tongue phenomenon, a mostly frustrating experience, is also something that everyone has experienced: we know that we know something, but we just cannot seem to spit it out. For example, just before, I was thinking about the name of the author of *Descartes' Error*, but I just could not seem to mentally call it up. But five minutes later, it was there without effort, even though I hadn't been thinking about it any more in the meantime. How do we know that we know something if we cannot remember it? Why is it so easy to recognize the face of a casual acquaintance when he appears, but so hard to describe in his absence? And how come we firmly believe certain facts to be true which are demonstrably false? That such phenomena exist is easy to verify, but hard to explain.

But memory—and, by extension, intelligence—is not just mysterious, but incredibly valuable and necessary. Having no memory implies the inability to learn, and not being able to learn is incredibly debilitating. Hollywood has a long-standing love affair with amnesia or memory loss, because it challenges those affected in interesting ways. In the Hollywood thriller *Memento*, the protagonist loses the ability to make new memories through a blow to the head. The excitement in the movie comes from watching how he tries, through various adventures, to reconstruct what happened to him. In the comedy *50 First Dates*, the main character one day encounters Lucy, who also has lost the ability to make new memories because of an accident. The comic side of the film is that whenever the lead character talks to her, she has forgotten that she ever met him! Memory is of fundamental importance, not only to intelligence but also to our own well-being, yet many fascinating problems relating to memory remain to be answered. Like intelligence, memory is a very important but still poorly understood phenomenon. For this reason we have devoted an entire chapter (chapter 10) to memory. Moreover, we believe that the perspective of embodiment developed in this book may clarify at least some of the issues surrounding memory and, more generally, intelligence.

1.3 Defining Intelligence

So intelligence is important, sensitive, and mysterious, but what is it really? We start from the assumption that everyone has a good intuition of what intelligence is all about. It has to do with consciousness, thinking, and memory (as already mentioned), along with problem solving, intuition, creativity, language, and learning, but also perception and sensory-motor skills, the ability to predict the environment (including the actions of others), the capacity to deal with a complex world (which may result from a combination of other abilities), and performance in school and on IQ tests and the like. In general, a good definition should capture at least some of the intuitions. But given the length of the list and the vagueness of the concepts, it seems unlikely that we will ever agree on a single one.

Here are some sample definitions from an inquiry by the *Journal of Educational Psychology* in 1921, wherein leading experts of the time were asked for their suggestions. L. Terman: "the ability to carry on abstract thinking"; W. F. Dearborn: "the capacity to learn or profit by experience"; S. S. Colvin: "having learned or ability to learn to adjust oneself to the environment" (this definition is so general that it can hardly be wrong, depending on what we mean by "adjust oneself to the environment"); R. Pintner: "the ability to adapt oneself adequately to relatively new situations in life" (similar to the previous one; the question here is what an expression like "relatively new" means in a definition); V. A. C. Henmon: "the capacity for knowledge, and knowledge possessed," and so on and so forth. We could go on for quite a while, but it is not clear what we would gain by adding more definitions to this list.

One of the reasons for the difficulty in coming up with a good definition is the breadth of the concept, as illustrated by the many intuitions it encompasses. Another is that our definitions will depend on our professional and personal background, subjective expectations, and individual interests and preferences. Gregory (1987), in *The Oxford Companion to the Mind* (p. 378), points out that biologically minded researchers tend to stress concepts such as adaptation and capacity for adjustment to the environment (e.g., Colvin and Pintner), whereas the more philosophically minded intellectual is likely to emphasize the element of abstraction (as in Terman's definition). Such a concept will always have many definitions; there is little hope that there will ever be general agreement on any particular one.

Also, trying to come up with a definition suggests that a property—in this case, intelligence—is either there or not, which is obviously not the case: Are ants intelligent? Perhaps to some degree, but an entire ant colony might be. This idea that not just a single agent, but also a whole group of agents might together be considered intelligent is known as collective intelligence, and we will look into this in some depth in chapter 7. Biologists studying ants are obviously fascinated by the richness of the behaviors they observe, but whether they, or we, would term such behavior "intelligent" is another matter. If we do, though, is the intelligence of an ant colony comparable to the intelligence of a human, or to that of a single ant? One point in our favor is that ant colonies cannot speak, while humans can. So, if we consider language to be an important part of intelligence, we might be tempted to conclude that all humans are more intelligent than ant colonies. Maybe ants, or their colonies as a whole, are not really intelligent, but what about rats or dogs? They are certainly more intelligent than ants, because they can do things that ants cannot, such as learning to navigate in a maze or catching a Frisbee while running. But humans are clearly more intelligent than rats and dogs. Perhaps dogs and rats are more intelligent than us in certain respects: again, dogs and rats cannot speak, write, or build cars, but when it comes to finding survivors at disaster sites or drugs in luggage at airports, dogs are far superior to humans, which is why they are employed for these tasks. It also seems obvious that some humans are more intelligent than others, but when we really think about it, what do we mean by this? Is it because they do some things better than others, for example they perform better at an intelligence test? Or is it because they are more successful in their careers than others? Or is it because they can do math? But then what about those who can sing or survive in the wild? So we see that the issue is very involved and multifaceted, and trying to come up with a clear-cut definition seems doomed to failure from the very start.

So, rather than trying to come up with a definition of intelligence, our suggestion for how to make progress is to look for a topic of interest (such as how dogs can run or catch a Frisbee; how rats learn so quickly to orient in a maze; how ants find their way back to the nest as they return from a trip searching for food; or how humans walk and recognize a face in a crowd) and then try to understand how this particular behavior comes about. Whether one would want to call any of these behaviors intelligent is largely a matter of taste and not really important.

In spite of all the difficulties of coming up with a concise definition, and regardless of the enormous complexities involved in the concept of intelligence, it seems that whatever we intuitively view as intelligent is always vested with two particular characteristics: compliance and diversity. In short, intelligent agents always comply with the physical and social rules of their environment, and exploit those rules to produce diverse behavior. These ideas will be discussed in detail in chapters 3 and 4. Here, just to provide some intuition, we give a brief example to illustrate the idea of diversity-compliance. All animals, humans, and robots have to comply with the fact that there is gravity and friction, and that locomotion requires energy: there is simply no way out of it. But adapting to these constraints and exploiting them in particular ways opens up the possibility of walking, running, drinking from a cup, putting dishes on a table, playing soccer, or riding a bicycle. Diversity means that the agent can perform many different types of behavior so that he—or she or it—can react appropriately to a given situation. An agent that only walks, or only plays chess, or only runs is intuitively considered less intelligent than one that can also build toy cars out of a Lego kit, pour beer into a glass, and give a lecture in front of a critical audience. Learning, which is mentioned in many definitions of intelligence, is a powerful means for increasing behavioral diversity over time. This general characterization of intelligence will be discussed in more detail in chapter 3.

Intelligence can be studied in many different ways, e.g., by performing experiments with humans as in psychology; by studying brain processes as in neuroscience; or by thinking about it in different ways, as in philosophy. In this book we will employ the method of artificial intelligence, which we consider especially productive for this purpose. So, let us briefly get acquainted with it.

1.4   Artificial Intelligence

By artificial intelligence we mean the interdisciplinary research field that has, in essence, three goals: (1) understanding biological systems (i.e., the mechanisms that bring about intelligent behavior in humans or animals); (2) the abstraction of general principles of intelligent behavior; and (3) the application of these principles to the design of useful artifacts. It is important to note that "mechanism" implies not only neural mechanisms or brain processes, but also the body of the agent and its interactions with the real world: the fact that muscles are elastic, and that the weight on one leg increases if the other one is lifted are just as much part of the mechanism of walking as are the reflexes and brain centers involved in this behavior.

In the next chapter we will give a more detailed history of the field, but here we present a very short introduction. Artificial intelligence dates back to 1956 when John McCarthy of MIT invited many leading researchers of the time to a workshop where he introduced the term *artificial intelligence.* Among the participants were Marvin Minsky, Herbert Simon, and Allan Newell, the founding fathers, so to speak, of artificial intelligence. Very roughly, they were convinced at the time that, by using the notion of computation or abstract symbol manipulation, it would soon become possible to reproduce interesting abilities normally ascribed to humans, such as playing chess, solving abstract problems, and proving mathematical theorems. What originated from this meeting, and what came to be the guiding principles until the mid-1980s, was what is now known as the classical, symbol-processing paradigm, also known as the cognitivistic paradigm. We might want to characterize this approach with the slogan "cognition as computation": what matters for intelligence in this approach is the abstract algorithm or the program, whereas the underlying hardware on which this program runs is irrelevant. An implication of this way of thinking is that not only can intelligence arise in biological systems and run on wet, biological brains, but it can also arise in artificial systems and run on computers.

The cognitivistic paradigm is still very popular among scientists. Some choose to view computer programs as *models* of actual thinking, a position called "weak AI," while others claimed and still claim that these programs *are* actually thinking—this is known as the "strong AI" stance. The weak AI position is unproblematic and generally accepted: the nature of the simulation model is clearly different from the thing it simulates. Just as in a simulation of rain the computer does not get wet, the model of thinking is different from the thinking process itself. It is the strong AI stance with which people often take issue. This is not surprising. It is unsettling for many people to believe that a computer is actually thinking, rather than just simulating the process. For more details on the history of AI and on the different positions, see, for example, McCorduck's thoughtful book *Machines Who Think* (1979), with many entertaining anecdotes; or Pfeifer and Scheier (1999); or consult focus box 2.1, which outlines the history of AI. Unlike the cognitivistic view of intelligence, which is algorithm-based, the embodied approach envisions the intelligent artifact as more than just a computer program: it has a body, and it behaves and performs tasks in the real world. It is not only a model of biological intelligence, but a form of intelligence in its own right.

As we will explain in chapter 2, the classical paradigm has had its definite successes, but it has failed to make clear the nature of intelligence, which is the main purpose of this book. Our intention here is not to give a comprehensive overview of the field—for that purpose, the interested reader is referred to the classic by Russell and Norvig (1995)—but rather to investigate recent advances that not only have fundamentally changed the field, but have led to a host of surprising insights. The most significant of these novel insights by far is the importance of embodiment.

1.5   Embodiment and Its Implications

By embodiment, we mean that intelligence always requires a body. Or, more precisely, we ascribe intelligence only to agents that are embodied, i.e., real physical systems whose behavior can be observed as they interact with the environment. Software agents, and computer programs in general, are disembodied, and many of the conclusions drawn in this book do not apply to them. As simple as the statement "intelligence requires a body" may sound, the implications are overwhelming, as we will see. There are some consequences of embodiment that are obvious, and some that are not. For example, if a system is embodied, it is subject to the laws of physics and has to somehow deal with gravity, friction, and energy supply in order to survive. While this is interesting and poses new challenges for our view of intelligence, the real importance of embodiment comes from the interaction between physical processes and what we might want to call information processes. In biological agents, this concerns the relation between physical actions and neural processing— or, to put it somewhat casually, between the body and the brain. The equivalent in a robot would be the relation between the robot's actions and its control program. Since the whole book is about precisely these issues, we will not go into any detail about this here. Instead, we would like to provide a flavor of what is to come, and for now it is all right if the reasons why embodiment is necessary for intelligence are not one hundred percent clear. Also, as a kind of preview, we merely mention the claims without substantiating them; we will do that in later chapters. Here are a few examples.

First, embodiment is an enabler for cognition or thinking: in other words, it is a prerequisite for any kind of intelligence. So, the body is not something troublesome that is simply there to carry the brain around, but it is necessary for cognition. It seems that the body is required even for functions such as mathematical thinking—something we often assume is a purely abstract, mental process—as argued by Lakoff and Núñez. Second, many tasks become much easier if embodiment is taken into account. For example, grasping objects requires much less control if stiffness and deformability of materials are used properly: just consider how the soft, deformable tissue of your fingertips makes the grasping of hard objects easier; imagine if you had to grasp a glass wearing thimbles on all your fingers! The reason the task becomes easier is that part of the neural control that would otherwise be required for grasping is in fact taken over by the morphological and material properties of the hand: if you were to grasp a glass with thimbles, you would have to be much more careful about how and where you placed your fingers. Third, if the sensors of a robot or organism are physically positioned on the body in the right places, some kind of preprocessing of the incoming sensory stimulation is performed by the very arrangement of the sensors, rather than by the neural system. That is, through the proper distribution of the sensors over the body, "good" sensory signals are delivered to the brain; it gets good "raw material" to work on. For example, grasping an object is easy because the anatomy of the human hand is such that the finger-tips will tend to touch an object, rather than the backs of the fingers, and there are many more touch sensors in our fingertips than in the backs of our fingers and hands. Fourth, if the material properties of an agent's muscle-tendon system are exploited, rapid movements such as running can be achieved very easily even though the neural system would be too slow to control all the details of the movement. For example, when your foot hits the ground, the elastic stretching and recoil of the ankle is taken over by the springy material of the muscle-tendon system and need not be controlled by the neural system (this point will be elaborated in detail in chapter 4). Fifth, through an agent's physical interaction with its environment, informative and correlated sensory signals are generated in different sensory channels. This idea sounds complicated—and in fact it *is* complicated—but it lies at the heart of intelligent action, and we will explore it in great detail later on. For example, when you walk, the environment seems to flow past your eyes at the same time that the sensors in your leg muscles register the strains of moving. For example, when an agent moves, objects closer to the agent seem to move by faster than those farther away, which provides the agent with distance information. This kind of "information structuring" will be explored in later chapters. So, there exists a subtle interplay or balance between an agent's neural activity (the brain), its morphology (the body's shape and its material properties), and its interaction with the environment, and that interplay can be exploited to achieve certain tasks. Recall that the elasticity of the muscle-tendon system, or the deformability of the tissue on the fingertips, in a sense takes a load off the brain.

In addition to laying the groundwork for a new theory of intelligence using these ideas, we will attempt to dismantle the widely held assumption that the brain controls the body. This may be disconcerting for some, because it is an idea that runs very deep in our society and has a long history, as we have already pointed out. Rather than postulating that there is a hierarchical structure in which one part—the brain—controls another—the body—the new theory focuses on the interaction between these two systems. We will argue that although clearly of great importance, the brain is not the sole and central seat of intelligence; and that intelligence is instead distributed throughout the organism. We will dig even deeper and show that the notion of control itself needs to be revised. We will also make a case that brain processes cannot be understood by looking at the brain alone: in order to understand the function of the brain, we must consider embodiment; we must deal with the coupling between brain, body, and environment. It may be easier for us to think about hierarchical systems where one person or thing, e.g., the brain, is in control, rather than about distributed, flat systems where components influence each other—but that doesn't mean it's the way things really are. It is one goal of this book to demonstrate how things—especially ourselves—can be viewed differently.

We will argue—convincingly, we hope!—that the notion of intelligence as computation, which underlies the cognitivistic paradigm, is misleading, and that speculations about the future of artificial intelligence by extrapolating from Moore's law—the law that computing power doubles roughly every one to two years—are fundamentally flawed. The futurist, entrepreneur, and computer scientist Ray Kurzweil, author of *The Age of Spiritual Machines*, is a case in point. Because he assumes that intelligence is exclusively a function of computational power, he sketches a scenario where in the near future computers will outperform human brains simply because they will have as much or more number-crunching power. We hope to convince the reader that computational theories of intelligence are doomed to failure from the very outset. Also, we will show that in much of the literature on the subject there is confusion between what exists within the agent itself and what is present within the head of the person observing the agent: this is the frame-of-reference problem that we will encounter many times throughout the book.

We will also demonstrate that in spite of its limitations, artificial evolution (a class of computer algorithms modeled on biological evolution that will be described in chapter 6) is a very powerful design tool, especially for designing intelligent agents. We will in fact show that computers have automatically designed complex artifacts, and that in some cases these artifacts are superior in performance to those designed by human engineers. These results deal a heavy blow to the common belief that computers cannot be creative. But when we want to design an artifact that has to function in the real world, the designs have to be tested either in physically realistic simulations or directly in the real world, and needless to say this means that the artifact cannot be merely abstract, but must have a body.

The last implication of embodiment to be discussed here concerns the synthetic methodology, an approach that we will employ throughout the book and which we describe in detail in the next chapter. It can be characterized by the slogan "understanding by building." When studying embodiment, it is essential to build actual physical systems, which, because we are interested in intelligent systems, will most likely be robots. For example, if we are trying to understand human walking, the synthetic methodology requires that we build an actual walking robot. Of course, simulations can also be employed, but they have to replicate the actual physical processes of walking in order to tell us something about walking in general. And there is always the question of the accuracy of a simulation. Experience has shown that building a real physical system always yields the most new insights. It is easy to "cheat" with simulation: a real-world walking agent, like a human or a physical robot, has to somehow deal with bumps in the ground, while this problem can be ignored in a simulation (where each problem has to be explicitly programmed in). The synthetic methodology contrasts with the more classical analytical ways of proceeding as in biology, psychology, or neuroscience, where an animal or human is analyzed in detail by performing experiments on it. Having said that, it is interesting to note that the sciences in general have become more synthetic lately, as the brisk rise of the computational sciences demonstrates: physicists increasingly prepare experiments in simulation; surgeons prepare operations in simulation; and pharmacologists test the effects of drugs in simulation. If these simulations are to be useful, they of course have to be as accurate as possible. But even if there is a high level of simulation accuracy, it will always be necessary eventually to perform experiments in the real world.

1.6 Summary

Let us briefly summarize the main points we have made so far. We started by inspecting Descartes's famous quote, and the mind-body problem. Then we introduced the terms *thinking*, *cognition*, and *intelligence*, and showed that even though we all have a pretty clear idea of what we mean by these terms, they still are ill defined. Moreover, they are best conceived of as a continuum: intuitively, we view some behaviors as requiring more thinking than others, and some animals as being more intelligent than others. Because these are all descriptive terms, we should not spend too much time on trying to find clear-cut definitions. That being said, in normal usage, *thinking* is often associated with conscious thought, *cognition* is somewhat more general and is used for behaviors not directly coupled with sensory-motor processes, and *intelligence* is even more general and encompasses any kind of behavior—including abstract behaviors such as cognition and thinking—that is beneficial to the agent. We then highlighted a few of the reasons intelligence is so fascinating, e.g., because it is a sensitive issue in that it distinguishes us from other species, and because of the nature-nurture debate, which is about the extent to which intelligence is inherited or acquired during one's lifetime. We pointed out some intelligence-related phenomena that are hard to explain, such as perception and memory. Next, we outlined the difficulties and issues involved in actually defining intelligence, e.g., its subjective nature, the large variety of types of intelligence, and its continuous character. We then very briefly introduced the research field of artificial intelligence, which is about understanding biological systems, abstracting principles of intelligent behavior, and designing and building artificial systems. We then gave a rough idea of what embodiment is, touching on some of its far-reaching implications. We also stressed the importance of actually building physical systems.

Somewhat provocatively, we said that we will challenge the classical notion of the brain controlling the body, and we will try to show that computational theories of intelligence are doomed to failure. We will also, along the way, attempt to dismantle the myth that machines cannot be creative.

In summary, the import of assuming the embodied perspective for understanding and designing intelligent systems can hardly be overestimated. In the next chapter we will outline the conceptual landscape of artificial intelligence as it now stands: we will take a crack at clarifying the structure of this scientific discipline, describing the kinds of research that are being conducted, and explaining how the various subdisciplines relate to one another.

2 Artificial Intelligence: The Landscape

In the winter term of the 2003–2004 academic year, I (Rolf) gave a series of lectures on modern artificial intelligence that was broadcast from the University of Tokyo over the entire globe, to Beijing (China), Jidda (Saudi Arabia), Warsaw (Poland), Munich (Germany), and Zurich (Switzerland). This global virtual lecture hall was connected via video conferencing technology, enabling the full participation of the students from all the sites; they could ask questions, and could also show video clips or presentations from their laptops. The main topic of this series was the impact of embodiment on a theory of intelligence, or in other words how intelligence and body are related to one another. Every week, the last half hour of these global lectures was devoted to the presentation of the latest research in the field of artificial intelligence, mostly from Japanese researchers. Most of these top-notch researchers presented robots that locomote: robots that move like snakes, or two-legged robots that walk like humans, or that can stand up from a lying-down position. This observation raises the question of what this walking and locomotion business has to do with intelligence; with thinking. Why do research on how robots, animals, and people move if you are interested in understanding intelligence? One of the goals of this book is to try and answer this rather puzzling question. We hope that as we go along it will become clear that the question is very sensible, that the relations between moving and thinking are in fact quite straightforward, and that intelligence cannot be understood if we do not understand basic movement—a point that we have already argued in the previous chapter.

But before we embark on this endeavor, in order get a better feel for the research area that we are talking about, we would like to outline the landscape of artificial intelligence: that is, the structure of this scientific discipline, the kind of research performed, and how the various disciplines relate to one another.

The first thing to note is that there is a clear distinction between a traditional or classical approach, also called the symbol-processing approach, and a modern, embodied one, a distinction that will be explained in more detail just below (see figure 2.1). It is interesting to observe that when you type "embodied artificial intelligence" into a search engine such as Google, you do not find many books or articles with this term in their title. And, as closer analysis shows, the results from the search do not reflect in any way what researchers in this field actually investigate these days. Now what does this mean for the field? This is one of the questions this chapter tries to answer.

After outlining the successes and problems of the classical approach we will turn to what we have called "the embodied turn," i.e., the new paradigm for artificial intelligence research. We will discuss how the role played by neuroscience in this endeavor has changed over time, and then look at how the field of classical AI split into many disciplines. This will be followed by an overview of the disciplines most relevant to embodied intelligence, such as biorobotics, developmental robotics (including humanoid robotics), ubiquitous computing and interfacing technology, artificial life and multiagent systems, and evolutionary robotics.

Figure 2.1
Two ways of approaching intelligence. (*a*) The classical approach. The focus is on the brain and central processing. (*b*) The modern approach. The focus is on the interaction with the environment. Cognition is emergent from the system-environment interaction, as we will argue throughout the book.

2.1 Successes of the Classical Approach

The term *embodied intelligence* was introduced in the mid-1980s in the field of artificial intelligence as a reaction against the classical approach, which views intelligence as merely a matter of abstract symbol processing. What matters in the classical approach is the algorithm or the program—the software, if you like—and not the hardware (the body or brain) on which it runs. Abstract functioning that is independent of the specifics of a particular hardware is an extremely powerful idea and constitutes one of the main reasons why computing has conquered the world, so to speak: all that matters are the programs that run on your computer; the hardware is irrelevant. This line of thinking goes back to the famous Dartmouth conference, held in 1956 in the small town of Hanover, New Hampshire, when "artificial intelligence" was officially launched as a new research discipline (for a very short history of artificial intelligence, see focus box 2.1). The American philosopher John Haugeland of the University of Chicago, author of the well-known book *Artificial Intelligence: The Very Idea*, an excellent philosophical treatise on traditional or classical artificial intelligence, coined the term GOFAI—"Good Old-Fashioned Artificial Intelligence"—to designate this approach (Haugeland, 1985).

In the classical perspective of artificial intelligence the human being was placed at center stage, with human intelligence as the main focus. As a consequence, the favorite areas of investigation were natural language, knowledge representation and reasoning, proving mathematical theorems, playing formal games like checkers or chess, and expert problem solving. This last area became extremely popular in the 1980s. Expert systems, as these models were called, were intended to replace human experts, or at least take over parts of their tasks, in areas like medical and technical diagnosis, configuration of complex computer systems, commercial loan assessment, and portfolio management. These systems epitomize the classical approach of viewing humans as symbol processing systems, i.e., as systems that manipulate symbols as computer programs do. This so-called information-processing approach strongly influenced researchers not only in artificial intelligence but also in psychology and the cognitive neurosciences. And now it seems that scientists as well as people in general see human intelligence as information processing: "What else could it be?" is the standard defense of this view. Computer scientists and psychologists teamed up to develop information-processing models of human problem-solving behavior, in particular expert systems.

Focus Box 2.1
The History of AI

Some authors (Brighton, 2004) consider the history of AI to begin around 3000 BC, apparently in Luxor, where a papyrus has been found that reports medical knowledge in expert system form: "IF patient has this symptom, THEN he has this injury with this prognosis IF this treatment is applied." But usually it is agreed that the field really began with the famous Dartmouth conference in 1956 where, among others, the "fathers of AI," Marvin Minsky, John McCarthy, Allen Newell, Herbert Simon, and Claude Shannon convened to proceed on "the conjecture that every aspect of learning or any other feature of intelligence can in principle be so precisely described that a machine can be made to simulate it." (Dartmouth Artificial Intelligence Project Proposal, McCarthy et al., Aug. 31, 1955). The discussions revolved around the question of how or whether human thinking and processes could take place in a computer. Addressing this question required, and still requires, knowledge from many different disciplines. Finally, a common language had been found with which researchers from different disciplines could talk to each other and formulate their theories; this was the language of information processing and abstract symbol manipulation. The field started to take off and spread across the United States. Natural-language programs, programs for proving mathematical theorems, for manipulating formulas, for solving abstract problems, for playing formal games like checkers and chess, for planning, and for solving real-world problems—the expert systems—emerged and multiplied everywhere: the field was booming.

Expert systems were developed specifically for medical diagnosis, analysis and repair of malfunctioning devices, commercial loan assessment in banks, configuration of complex computer systems, and portfolio management, to name but a few. The idea was to model a human expert, such as an experienced physician, using sets of rules such as "IF the patient has red spots on skin, and patient has high fever, and . . . THEN the infection is most likely caused by . . ." (note the similarity to the Egyptian system). Herbert Simon, in 1965, predicted that by 1985 machines would be capable of doing any mental work a man can do. However, toward the end of the 1980s most companies that had started developing expert systems went bankrupt, and the goal of building systems capable of autonomously solving problems—and thereby replacing human expertise—was largely abandoned. It had become clear that conceptualizing human experts as symbol-processing machines was inappropriate and did not lead anywhere. Practitioners changed the focus from autonomous problem solving to supporting human intelligence.

Besides the field of expert systems, there were serious setbacks and disappointments in the areas of computer vision and speech processing. Human-level performance in perception—recognizing objects at various distances, orientations, lighting conditions, and partial occlusions—has not even remotely been achieved in artificial systems. Similarly, in spite of huge investments in speech systems, their capacity, accuracy, and therefore their practical utility has remained below expectations. Vision and speech are particularly challenging because they are natural phenomena that rely heavily on the real world. Trying to model human visual perception and language through (typically computationally intensive) algorithms did not seem to work either.

Luckily for many researchers in these fields, a new discipline arose in the early 1980s, connectionism, which tries to model phenomena in cognitive science with neural networks. Neural networks are computational models that are inspired by biological brains, and therefore many of them inherit the brain's intrinsic ability for adaptation, generalization, and learning. Because they are based on pattern processing rather than symbol manipulation, researchers were hoping that neural networks would be better able to describe natural mental phenomena, after expert systems and related algorithms had failed to do so. In fact connectionism was not exactly a new discipline: neural networks had been around since the 1940s, when they were first suggested as models of biological neural networks (e.g., McCulloch and Pitts, 1943). Their reappearance in the 1980s as computational devices was more like a renaissance. However, although there was definite progress, because most of these models were just algorithms like all the others, they did not end up solving the big problems of mastering the interaction with the real world either. Despite the progress there were no real breakthroughs in the use of neural networks for capturing expert knowledge, for building speech systems, or for perception of the environment. The recognition of this fact was another frustration for artificial intelligence researchers.

After these setbacks, the field was in dire need of a real paradigm shift. In the mid-1980s Rodney Brooks suggested that all of this focus on logic, problem solving, and reasoning was based on our own introspection—how we tend to see ourselves and our own mental processes—and that the way artificial intelligence was proceeding was misguided. Instead, he proposed, essentially, that we should forget about symbol processing, internal representation, and high-level cognition, and focus on the interaction with the real world: "intelligence requires a body" was the slogan of the new paradigm of embodied intelligence. With this change in orientation, the nature of the research questions also started to shift: the community got interested in locomotion, manipulation, and, in general, how an agent can act successfully in a changing world.

As a consequence, many researchers around the world started working with robots. However, even working on robots did not automatically solve the problems: the performance of most robots on real-world tasks—walking, running, perception, and object manipulation—remained unsatisfactory. So, there was still something missing. The reason for this, we strongly suspect, was that the robots were often used in the classical way: researchers programmed the robots directly to do their tasks. This often led to computationally expensive solutions that not only produced unnatural behavior, but were also too slow to achieve, for example, running behavior. Thus, the concept of embodiment not only implies that the agent must have a body—obviously robots do have bodies—it also means that one should follow a particular style of thinking when building robots or generally intelligent agents; one should design with a particular theoretical attitude in mind, as we will elaborate in this book. Although we are convinced of the potential of this approach, only time will tell whether it results in greater success than the previous ones.

In the 1980s there was a lot of hype surrounding expert systems and many companies started to develop them—alas, many soon went bankrupt after this way of conceptualizing human expertise and human intelligence in general turned out to be flawed, as discussed in the next section (see also Clancey, 1997; Pfeifer and Scheier, 1999; and Winograd and Flores, 1986).

By the mid-1980s, the classical approach had grown into a large discipline with many facets and with fuzzy boundaries, but despite some of its flaws, it can now claim many successes. Whenever you switch on your laptop computer you are starting up many algorithms that have their origin in artificial intelligence. If you use a search engine on the internet you are, for example, making use of clever machine-learning algorithms.[1]

If you use a text-processing system, it in turn uses algorithms, which try to infer your intentions from the context of what you have done earlier, and will often volunteer advice. Natural-language interfaces, computer games, and controls for appliances, home electronics, elevators, cars, and trains abound with AI algorithms. More recently, data-mining systems have been developed that heavily rely on machine-learning techniques, and chess programs have been designed that can beat just about any human on Earth, which is a considerable achievement indeed! The development of these kinds of systems, although they have their origin in artificial intelligence, has now become indistinguishable from applied informatics in general: these systems have become an integral part of today's computer technology.

2.2 Problems of the Classical Approach

However, the original intention of artificial intelligence was not only to develop clever algorithms, but also to understand natural forms of intelligence, which requires a direct interaction with the real world. It is now generally agreed that the classical approach has failed to deepen our understanding of many intelligent processes. How do we make sense of an everyday scene or recognize a face in a crowd, for example? How do we manipulate objects, especially flexible and soft objects and materials like clothes, string, and paper? How do we walk, run, ride a bicycle, and dance? What is common sense all about, and how are we able to understand and produce everyday natural language? Needless to say, trying to answer these questions requires us to consider not just the brain, but how the body and brain of an intelligent agent interact with the real world.

Classical approaches to computer vision (which is one form of artificial perception), for example, have been successful in factory environments where the lighting conditions are constant, the geometry of the situation is precisely known (i.e., the camera is always in the same place, the objects always appear on the conveyor belt in the same position, the types of possible objects are known and can therefore be modeled), and there is always ample energy supply. However, when these conditions do not hold, such systems fail miserably, and in the real world, stable and benign conditions are never assured: the distance from an object to your eyes changes constantly, one of the many consequences of moving around; lighting conditions and orientation are always changing; objects are often entirely or partially blocked from view; objects themselves move; and they appear against very different and changing backgrounds.

Vision systems with capacities similar to human vision, which can deal quickly with such conditions, are far from being realized artificially.

Animals and humans—including simple animals like insects—are enormously skilled at manipulating objects. Ants, for example, are known for their great ability to carry large, bulky objects such as leaves, and they do so by cooperating with other ants. Watch a dog chew on a bone by controlling it with its paws, mouth, and tongue: unbelievable! Although there are specialized machines that can outperform humans on virtually any given manipulation task—like driving a screw, picking up objects for packaging in production lines, lifting heavy objects on construction sites, or making very precise movements in minimally invasive surgical operations—the general-purpose manipulation abilities of natural systems are still unparalleled.

Locomotion is another case in point. Animals and humans move with an astonishing flexibility and elegance. Watching insects fly in complex patterns and with enormous precision is simply mind-boggling, especially since we know how small their brains really are: a million times smaller than the human brain. Watching a cheetah running at great speed is an esthetic pleasure. Monkeys move through the rain forest by climbing, swinging, walking, and running with uncanny talent. Humans can walk with a bag in one hand, an arm around a friend, up and down stairs, while looking around and smoking a cigarette, or they can walk in arbitrarily silly ways, as demonstrated by John Cleese in the famous Monty Python sketch "The Ministry of Silly Walks"; no robots can even come close to any of these feats of agility yet. And building a running robot is still considered one of the great challenges in robotics.

Although there has been a considerable amount of work on robots since the early days of classical artificial intelligence, starting in the 1960s, the performance of these robots has not been very impressive in terms of orientation ability, speed, and capacity to manipulate objects. One of the important reasons for this is that in the classical view, the ability to figure out where you are is based on detailed inner models or representations of the outside world—which implies that these representations either have to be programmed into the robots (which is done, for example, in industrial robotics) or the robots have to learn them as they interact with their environment; and they have to be continuously updated in order to remain consistent with the real world. The more complex these models are, the more effort is needed to acquire the relevant data to maintain them. Take a map of a city as an example of a model of part of the real world. The more detail the map contains, the harder it will be to keep it in tune with reality. If construction sites, temporary roadblocks, or current traffic density are taken into account, the entire map has to be updated almost continuously. If the map is intended for car drivers, as are those used in car navigation systems, information about traffic density and diversions is extremely useful, but keeping it up to date requires considerable resources. For other purposes, such as a geography class, a coarse map is more than sufficient and requires very little updating.

An issue which has attracted a lot of attention is that of common sense, because it is fundamental to mastering our everyday lives and is also crucial for understanding natural language. In the classical approach, common sense has been viewed as "propositional": the building blocks of common-sense knowledge are considered to be statements—propositions—such as "cars cannot become pregnant," "objects (normally) do not fly," "people have biological needs (they get hungry and thirsty)," "viruses cause infections," "diseases should be avoided," "if you drop a glass it will normally break," etc. Building systems that incorporate this type of common-sense knowledge has been the goal of many classical natural-language and problem-solving systems like CYC (see Guha and Lenat, 1990, for a report on the first five years of the project). The letters CYC stand for encyclopedia, which indicates what the researchers in this project were after, namely this kind of encyclopedic, or propositional, knowledge. The Stanford computer scientist and artificial intelligence pioneer Doug Lenat started this controversial project in 1984, and in 1991 he predicted that by the mid-1990s his software would be able to obtain new knowledge by simply reading text rather than being programmed by humans (Wood, 2002); this is one of the many predictions in AI that have not materialized. Surprisingly, some researchers continue to believe that a large collection of propositions—logic-based statements—together with a set of rules of inference is, in essence, all that is needed to represent common-sense knowledge: in 2004 DARPA, the Defense Advanced Research Project Agency, the American military's research arm, awarded two American researchers a $400,000 research contract to try and build a machine that could learn only by reading text. One of the problems with the CYC project, and with all succeeding projects with a similar aim was (and still is) that common sense cannot be captured by a set of rules, but requires interaction with the real world.

For example, we all have an intuitive understanding of the word *drinking*. If you now freely associate to *drinking*, what comes to mind might be: thirsty, liquid, beer, hot sunshine, the feeling of liquid in your mouth, on the lips, on your tongue when you are drinking, how it runs down your throat and how it feels in your stomach, and the experience of relief after drinking when you have been really thirsty, the experience of seeing a cold drink being served in a seaside bar on a hot summer day, the frustration at the stain on your new suit as wine is spilled over it, the sensation of wetness as water is poured over your pants, etc. It is this kind of common sense that forms the basis of everyday language communication, and it is firmly grounded in our own specific embodiment; in our experience of interacting with objects in the real world. And to our knowledge, there are currently no artificial systems capable of dealing with this kind of knowledge in a flexible and adaptive way, because it is not propositional and thus hard to formalize in a symbolic system.

Speech systems are another offshoot of classical AI. Natural language—which is different from formal languages like mathematics or computer programs—is one of the most striking abilities of an intelligent being, and the quest to understand and build systems capable of natural language has a long history in artificial intelligence. Initially, efforts were mostly geared toward processing written language. Later on, speech captured the interest of many researchers, but expectations and false predictions about the speed of development of such systems have abounded. Consequently there have been many disappointments, and the reputation of the field of artificial intelligence has suffered as a result. While in restricted applications speech systems are helpful, especially where single-word commands are sufficient as in some mobile phone applications, speech systems that can handle complete sentences or continuous streams of speech, in a robust way and in noisy environments, have not yet appeared on the market.

Speech-to-text systems—also called "phonetic typewriters"—have to be tuned to the speaker's voice, and typically a lot of post-editing needs to be done on the text produced by the software, i.e., the text usually contains many errors and needs to be corrected. This may be one of the reasons why speech systems have not really taken off, even though the idea of not having to type anymore—of producing text rapidly by simply talking into a microphone—is highly appealing. But although some of the systems may function to some degree and have turned out to be quite useful, there are still no general-purpose natural-language systems whose performance even remotely resembles that of humans in everyday conversation. (It is also interesting to note that major companies dealing in speech systems have gone bankrupt in recent years. The most famous example is L&H, Lernout and Houspie Speech Products in Belgium, which marketed speech-to-text systems as one of the three major players in the field worldwide, the others being Dragon Systems and IBM. The bankruptcy is officially due to illicit financial transactions and incorrect sales figures, but we would speculate that while there certainly have been financial and legal problems, the current immaturity of the underlying speech technology probably made matters worse.)

Another way of looking at the successes and failures of classical artificial intelligence is that it has been successful at those tasks that humans normally consider difficult—playing chess, applying rules of logic, proving mathematical theorems, or solving abstract problems—whereas actions we experience as very natural and effortless, such as seeing, hearing, speaking, riding a bicycle, walking, drinking from a glass, assembling a car from a Lego kit, talking, getting dressed, putting on makeup, or brushing our teeth—all skills requiring common sense—have proved notoriously hard. The successes in achieving these latter skills in artificial systems have been very limited, to say the least; the algorithmic approach has simply not helped much in understanding intelligence (see also Pfeifer and Scheier, 1999).

2.3   The Embodied Turn

These failures, largely due to the lack of rich interaction between system and environment, have led some researchers to pursue a different avenue; that of embodiment. With this change of orientation, the nature of the research questions also began to change. Rodney Brooks, director of the MIT Computer Science and Artificial Intelligence Laboratory, a laboratory of about a thousand researchers, was one of the first promoters of embodied intelligence. Brooks argued in a series of provocative papers entitled "Intelligence Without Representation" and "Intelligence Without Reason" that intelligence always requires a body and that we should forget about complex internal representations and models of the outside world; that we should not focus on sophisticated reasoning processes but rather capitalize on the system-environment interaction (Brooks, 1991a). "The world is its own best model" was one of his slogans at the time. Why build sophisticated models of the world when you can simply look at it? In the second half of the 1980s he started studying insect-like locomotion, and building, for example, the famous six-legged walking robot "Ghengis."

Why did he choose insects as his object of investigation? Brooks made a case that because it took evolution so much longer to move from inorganic matter to insects than it took to get from insects to humans, we should start by studying insects. Once we understand insect-level intelligence—thus Brooks's argument—it will be much easier and faster to understand and build human-level intelligence because achieving insect-level intelligence from scratch should be a much harder problem than moving from insect-level intelligence to human-level intelligence. To gain some perspective on this claim, consider this greatly abridged history of evolution on Earth. Single-cell entities arose out of the primordial soup roughly 3.5 billion years ago. A billion years passed before photosynthetic plants appeared. After almost another billion and a half years—around 550 million years ago—the first fish and vertebrates came into being, and 100 million years later insects emerged. Let us quote directly from Brooks's argument:

Then things started moving fast. Reptiles arrived 370 million years ago, followed by dinosaurs at 330 and mammals at 250 million years ago. The first primates appeared 120 million years ago and the immediate predecessors to the great apes a mere 18 million years ago. Man arrived in roughly his present form 2.5 million years ago. He invented agriculture a mere 19,000 years ago, writing less than 5,000 years ago and "expert" knowledge only over the last few hundred years. (Brooks, 1990, p. 5)

Because of this interest in insects, walking and locomotion in general became important research topics. This, of course, represents a fundamental change from studying chess, theorem proving, and abstract problem solving, and it is not so obvious what the two areas have to do with one another (an issue we will elaborate on later). Other topics that people started investigating include orientation behavior: finding one's way in only partially known and changing environments, which includes searching for "food" (symbolized by certain kinds of objects such as small cylinders); bringing the food back to the "nest," a behavior also called homing; or generally exploring an environment. A lot of effort has also been invested in the study of very elementary behaviors such as wall following, moving toward a light source, and obstacle avoidance. It is interesting to note that researchers in the field started using vocabulary like "search for food," "homing," "going back to the nest," etc., suggesting that the robots developed in fact have animal-like properties. Attributing lifelike properties to inanimate objects has a long history in artificial intelligence, where researchers since the very beginnings have ascribed humanlike properties to their computers or computer programs, calling them intelligent or clever, claiming that they understand when replying to questions, and so on. Attribution of lifelike properties to artifacts seems to be a characteristic intrinsic to humans, or, as David

McFarland, Oxford University behavior scientist and inventor of the field of "animal robotics," put it: "Anthropomorphization, the incurable disease." But then, anthropomorphization has been around for centuries: think how many talking animals or objects there are in fairy tales or Disney movies. McFarland's point was that we have to be careful with the attributes we ascribe to animals, computers, or robots when we observe their behavior, for instance when we say that the animal "wants" to eat or that the robot "sees" a person. How do we know the animal "wants" something, and what do we really mean by this? But more about that later.

Now, the perspective of embodiment requires working with real-world physical systems, such as robots. Although computers and robots are often mentioned in one phrase, suggesting that they are roughly the same, they are in fact quite different: the input to computers consists of keystrokes or mouse clicks, and because keystrokes are discrete, the user has to prepare whatever he or she wants to enter into the computer for further processing in terms of the limited number of keys on the keyboard. By contrast, biological agents—animals and humans—have complex sensors that provide a lot of continuously changing stimulation and thus, potentially rich information about the real world. But the real world does not come with labels: we have to try to make sense of this sensory stimulation on our own, whereas in the case of the computer this job has to be taken over by the user. Thus, truly autonomous robots, those that are largely independent of human control, have to be situated, i.e., they have to be able to learn about the environment through their own sensory systems, something computers simply cannot do. Also, computers are neat and clean, and almost anybody can understand, use, and program them, and they lend themselves well to performing simulations. But building robots requires engineering expertise which is typically not present in computer science laboratories; it is messy, you have to get your hands dirty, which is something that, in the age of information technology, many people strongly dislike.

Generally speaking, the interaction of an embodied system with the real world is always "messy" and ill defined, and there are many issues one has to deal with, such as deciding on the kinds of environments in which the robot has to function (e.g., office environments, factories, outdoors in the city streets, in rough terrain, in homes, under water, in the air, in outer space), the kinds of sensors to use (cameras, microphones, infrared, ultrasound, touch), the actuators (hands, arms, legs, wings, fins, wheels, or perhaps hooks or magnets), the energy supply (a notoriously hard problem), and the materials from which the robot should be constructed. To make matters worse, the physics of the agent-environment interaction must also be considered. This includes accounting for the forces, torques, and friction that the robot will experience: the environment changes rapidly and is predictable only to a very limited extent, and the information about the world is always very limited. Most of these considerations are normally not associated with the notion of intelligence. The design principles for intelligent systems that will be introduced in part II of this book try to capture all of the design considerations that must be taken into account for embodied systems in the real world.

So, the nature of the field of artificial intelligence changed dramatically when embodiment entered the picture. While in the traditional approach the relation to psychology—in particular, cognitive psychology—had been very prominent, the interest, at least in the early days of the embodied intelligence approach, shifted more toward nonhuman biological systems such as insects, snakes, or rats. Also, at this point, the meaning of the term *artificial intelligence* started to change, or rather started to adopt two meanings: the first implies GOFAI, the traditional algorithmic approach, while the other more generally designates a paradigm in which the goals are to understand biological systems while at the same time exploiting that knowledge to build artificial systems. As a result the modern, embodied approach started to move out of computer science laboratories and into robotics, engineering, and biology labs.

2.4 The Role of Neuroscience

It is also of interest to look at the role of neuroscience in the context of the shift to an embodied approach. In the 1970s and early 1980s, as researchers in artificial intelligence started to recognize the problems of the traditional symbol-processing approach, they began to search for alternatives. Artificial neural networks seemed to provide the solution. Although they had been around since the 1950s, neural networks only started to really take off in the 1980s, just when artificial intelligence was in a deep crisis and desperately looking for a way out. Loosely speaking, artificial neural networks, or simply neural networks, are models that implement "brain-style computation," as some researchers call it. Neural networks are collections of abstract models of neurons that are connected to many other neurons to form large networks that function in a massively parallel fashion. Although inspiration was drawn from the brain, neural networks relate to brain activity only at a very abstract level and neglect many essential properties of biological neurons and brains. Despite these abstractions, the algorithms based on these simple networks demonstrate impressive performance and can achieve, for example, difficult classification and pattern-recognition tasks like deciding from an X-ray image whether some tissue contains a cancerous tumor or not, or distinguishing bags containing plastic explosives from innocuous ones at airports. In chapter 5 we will provide a more detailed account of neural networks (see also focus box 5.1).

In the field of cognitive psychology, artificial neural networks became very popular for modeling a variety of phenomena such as categorization (making distinctions between different types of objects) and perception in general, but also language acquisition (how children learn to master language) and memory. An exciting new discipline called connectionist psychology emerged as a result (e.g., Ellis and Humphreys, 1999). Using neural network models of this kind was definitely a step in the right direction, as they have highly desirable properties. For example, like natural brains, they are massively parallel; they can learn, i.e., they improve their behavior over time; they are noise and fault tolerant, i.e., they still function if the inputs are distorted and if some of the artificial neurons cease to operate; and they can generalize, meaning they continue to work in situations that have never been encountered by the network before, as long as those situations are similar to what they have already learned. The main problem with the approach, however, was that the networks were mostly disembodied, which means that they were trained on data prepared by the designer; the networks did not collect their own data in the environment using a body. With some exceptions, real-time response was not required, because the models were not connected to the outside world. In particular, they were not used in robots.

In the embodied approach, by contrast, the connection to the outside world is crucial. As artificial intelligence researchers realized that because natural neural systems are so skillful at controlling their host body's interaction with the real world, they might benefit by paying more attention to biological detail, and interest in neuroscience was renewed and strengthened.[2] The kinds of networks suitable for these sorts of interactions are different from the connectionist ones used in psychology because they have to deal with real physical bodies and have to act in real time. As a result, the artificial neural networks developed for these purposes paid closer attention to biological properties, and researchers in artificial intelligence started cooperating much more closely with neurobiologists. Around the same time, a new breed of neuroscientist started to appear, the so-called computational neuroscientists, and university departments with names such as Computational Neuroscience or Neuro-Informatics emerged almost overnight. Rather than performing experiments with real brains, however, they developed detailed models either of individual neurons or of specialized collections of neurons in the brain such as the cerebellum, which plays a key role in motor control, or the hippocampus, an area thought to be involved in memory functions, as well as a host of models about aspects of the visual system. These are but a few examples; the literature in the field is awesomely vast. And some researchers in computational neuroscience became interested in issues similar to the ones artificial intelligence researchers had started tackling, e.g., locomotion, categorization, and sensory-motor coordination. Most would not consider themselves to be doing research in artificial intelligence, even though their research topics strongly overlap; for the most part computational neuroscience has not (yet!) taken a strong interest in embodiment. Finally, along a different but related line of development, engineers have started cooperating with neuroscientists to connect electronic and electromechanical devices directly to neural tissue (as we will see when we discuss cyborgs in chapter 8).

2.5 Diversification

So, in terms of research disciplines participating in the AI adventure, in the classical approach it was computer science (of course), psychology to a greater degree, and neuroscience to a lesser degree. A very close cooperation with linguistics and computational linguistics became popular due to the seminal—but somewhat misleading—work on grammatical structures pioneered by the outspoken linguist and political activist Noam Chomsky of MIT; and finally there was a very close connection with philosophy. This last connection specifically involved the field of philosophy of mind, which is an attempt to unravel the mysteries of the human psyche, of thinking, intelligence, emotion, and consciousness. At least in some areas of philosophy, there was a lot of optimism about the potential contributions of the computer metaphor toward a scientific understanding of the mind, as shown in the enthusiastic book by the British philosopher and AI researcher Aaron Sloman, *The Computer Revolution in Philosophy* (Sloman, 1978). Alas, this hope has not yet been fulfilled.

In the embodied approach, the picture altered considerably. Computer science and philosophy are still part of the game as before, but now also engineering, robotics, biology, biomechanics (the discipline studying how humans and animals move), material science, and neuroscience have come into play, whereas psychology and linguistics have—at least temporarily—if not disappeared, at least lost their status as core disciplines. So we see somewhat of a shift of interest from high-level processes (as studied in psychology and linguistics) to more low-level sensory-motor processes. Recently psychology, especially developmental psychology, has reentered the game in the context of developmental robotics, where the grand goal is to mimic in robots the processes by which babies develop into capable adults.

Although, as mentioned above, a certain amount of robotics work was done in the initial years of artificial intelligence, as exemplified by the research on the world-famous robot "Shakey" at Stanford Research Institute in Palo Alto, California, robotics at the time played only a marginal role (Shakey earned its name by its hesitant, jerky way of moving). Moreover, even though Shakey was indeed a physical robot acting in the real world, the focus was very much on its internal processing; on the kinds of computations it would have to do to navigate and orient in the real world. In this sense, although Shakey had a body, it was very much computational, and therefore in line with the classical paradigm. Because of this, it could only operate in simple and judiciously designed static environments. But, as always, it is easy to criticize with hindsight, and this in no way diminishes the value of Shakey's contribution to the development of artificial intelligence. Just recently it was elected to the Robot Hall of Fame of the Carnegie-Mellon Foundation, where historically significant robots are on display. Other "laureates" include HAL 9000 from Stanley Kubrick's movie *2001: A Space Odyssey*, the Mars Sojourner, Honda's Asimo, C3PO from *Star Wars*, and Astroboy. (Astroboy—called Tetsuwan or "Iron Arm" Atom in Japan—the hero from an extremely successful comic strip of the 1950s in Japan, has inspired many researchers and visionaries in Japan who, today, build robots in the most highly respected institutions. Astroboy is very much the spiritual father of the contemporary intelligent robotics movement in Japan.)

As the participating disciplines have changed, the terms for describing the research area have also shifted: researchers using the embodied approach no longer refer to themselves as doing artificial intelligence but rather robotics, engineering of adaptive systems, artificial life, adaptive locomotion, or bio-inspired systems. But more than that, not only have researchers in artificial intelligence moved into neighboring disciplines, scientists who have their origins in these other fields have started to play an important role in the study of intelligence. Computational neuro-science is a case in point, although researchers in that field typically do not perceive themselves as part of artificial intelligence. Thus, on the one hand the field of artificial intelligence has significantly expanded, while on the other hand its boundaries have become even fuzzier than they were before.

So we now have a partial answer to the question of why we do not get a representative sample of the research being done in modern artificial intelligence when we type "embodied artificial intelligence" into a search engine. Because the communities started to split, researchers in embod-ied intelligence started going to other kinds of conferences that were not purely artificial intelligence–based, as the names of these conferences indicate: "Intelligent Autonomous Systems," "Simulation of Adaptive Behavior—From Animals to Animats," "International Conference on Intelligent Robotics and Systems," "Adaptive Motion in Animals and Machines," "Artificial Life Conference," "Evolutionary Robotics," the "International Joint Conference on Neural Networks" (among many other neural network conferences), the "Genetic and Evolutionary Com-putation Conference" (there are several other conferences dedicated to artificial evolution, a topic we will explore in chapter 6), or the various IEEE conferences (Institute of Electrical and Electronics Engineers), and so on. In the early 1990s, when I (Rolf) tried to convince people at AI conferences that embodiment is not only interesting but essential for intelligence, and that unless we understand embodiment we will never crack the conundrum of high-level intelligence, I mostly got negative reactions, and no real discussion took place. So, I and many colleagues turned to these other conferences, where people were more receptive to the ideas of embodiment. More recently, perhaps because of the stagna-tion in the field of classical AI in terms of tackling the big problems about the nature of intelligence, there has been a growing interest in the issue of embodiment. Most AI conferences have started hosting workshops and special tracks on issues related to embodiment. But by and large the communities of classical artificial intelligence and of the embodied approach to intelligence are still separate, and will probably remain so for a while.

2.6 Biorobotics

This diversification has resulted in a number of interesting developments. One, as already mentioned, is the move away from human toward more animal-like intelligence, which was originally triggered because the efforts to achieve human-level intelligence had not met with success. Others include the appearance of the fields of biorobotics, developmental robotics, ubiquitous computing, artificial life, interface technology, and multiagent systems. We will look into all these different areas briefly throughout the course of this book.

Let us start with biorobotics. Biorobotics is a branch of robotics dedicated to building robots that mimic the behaviors of specific biological organisms. A good illustration is the work done by the mathematician and engineer Dimitri Lambrinos while he was working at the Artificial Intelligence Laboratory at the University of Zurich. He started to cooperate with the world leader of ant navigation research, Ruediger Wehner, also of the University of Zurich. Jointly, the two laboratories built a series of robots, the Sahabot series (the name stands for Sahara robot). The Sahabots mimic the long- and short-term navigation behaviors of the desert ant *Cataglyphis*, an extraordinary animal that lives in a salt pan, a very flat sandy ecological niche, in southern Tunisia. One of the challenges was to provide a proof of existence for the navigational mechanisms that biologists proposed to explain how this animal gets around. In other words, the goal was to demonstrate that these mechanisms could, in principle, on a robot, reproduce the orientation behavior of the desert ants. Note that this does not imply that the processes underlying the ant's behavior are indeed the same or similar to the one used on the robot.

One such mechanism, and a very simple one at that, is the so-called snapshot model, which was originally postulated by the British insect biologist Tom Collett of Sussex University (Cartright and Collett, 1983), who has worked with Wehner for many years. According to Collett, the snapshot model is used by the ant (and other insects) for precise short-range navigation to find the nest as it returns from a food-searching trip (also known as foraging in biology). This model posits that as the ant leaves the nest, which is essentially just a hole in the ground, it takes a snapshot, a photographic picture of the horizon as seen from the position of the nest, which is then stored in the ant's brain (ants, unlike humans, have almost omnidirectional vision, i.e., they see not only in the front, but all around them). The ant then goes out on a foraging trip, traveling sometimes up to 200 meters away from the nest, and returns to the vicinity of the nest using a second navigation system, which is based on an estimate of the distance from the nest and on polarized sunlight. The polarized sunlight provides the ant with direction information and can be used as a kind of compass. This system is especially suited for long-term navigation, but because long-term navigation systems always accumulate error, the ant has to use the short-term navigation system—the snapshot method—to find the exact location of the nest. From the long-term navigation system the ant gets a signal that it is near the nest and that another system must take over. The snapshot method then guides it to the nest entrance. This model, which has been verified in literally hundreds of experiments with real ants (e.g., Wehner et al., 1996), has also been tested on robots in the very environment in which the ants live, in the Sahara desert, with impressive success. While this does not imply that the model used on the robot is the one actually employed by the ants, it does show that such a mechanism could work in principle. Lambrinos, together with his colleague Ralf Möller, developed another navigation model, the so-called average landmark vector model (Lambrinos et al., 2000), which is even simpler than the snapshot model. Both of these navigation models can be used to make predictions of the animals' behavior in certain situations that can be tested on the robots and with real ants.

Note that in this navigation system the agents—the ant and the robot—do not need a map of the environment in order to navigate successfully. In other words, it does not need a model of the real world in order to behave successfully, even though the ant cannot see the nest from a distance! This is in contrast to the standard assumption that detailed environmental information, like a map, is necessary for this kind of navigation. The only "model" of the world consists of the estimate of distance and direction to the nest for the long-term system, and the snapshot for the short-term system.

Just to illustrate the richness of the field, here is a selection of other successful biorobotics projects: the insect-like flying robots (Miki and Shimoyama, 1999) and the silkworm moth robots with pheromone sensors (Kuwana et al., 1999) developed by the futurist engineer Isao Shimoyama of the University of Tokyo; the fantastically realistic snake robots developed by the renowned roboticist Shigeo Hirose of the Tokyo Institute of Technology (Hirose, 1993); Barbara Webb's work at the University of Edinburgh in Scotland on the phonotactic behavior of crickets, i.e., how males are attracted by and move toward the sound of females undeterred by the complexity, ruggedness, and noisiness of their environment (Webb, 1996); the Robot Tuna developed at the MIT Ocean Engineering Lab by Michael Triantafyllou (e.g., Triantafyllou and Triantafyllou, 1995); Joseph Ayer's projects on lobster and lamprey robots (Ayers 2004) at Northeastern University in Boston; Auke Ijspeert's work on the simulated robot salamander at the Swiss Federal Institute of Technology in Lausanne, Switzerland (Ijspeert, 2001); the "artificial mouse" developed at the University of Zurich to investigate the role of whiskers in rodent behavior (e.g., Fend et al., 2003); and Frank Kirchner's research on robotic scorpions (Klaassen et al., 2002). There are many additional examples of biorobots which have all been very productive and have significantly contributed to our understanding of locomotion and orientation behavior (for a collection of pertinent papers see, for example, Webb and Consi, 2001, or the proceedings of the Adaptive Motion in Animals and Machines Conference, e.g., Kimura et al., 2006). The list could be continued almost indefinitely. In the meantime, locomotion and orientation have become important research topics in artificial intelligence.

2.7   Developmental Robotics

The research in biorobotics is still gaining momentum and multiplying throughout research laboratories worldwide. Toward the mid-1990s, however, Brooks, who had been one of the initiators of the biorobotics movement, argued that we had now achieved "insect-level intelligence" with robots and we should move ahead toward new frontiers. But what does it mean to say that we have achieved insect-level intelligence? Ghengis, Attila, and Hannibal, three of Brooks's six-legged robots, have achieved impressive walking performance in terms of obstacle avoidance and walking over uneven ground. However, insects can do many more things. For example they can manipulate objects with their legs and mouth, they can orient in sophisticated ways in different kinds of environments (even in the desert!), they can build complex housing, they have highly organized social structures, and they reproduce and care for their offspring. Many of these abilities, for example reproduction or complex social organizations, are far from being realized in robotic systems. So, before we have achieved true insect-level intelligence, there is still much research to be done.

But it is true that even though insects are fascinating, human-level intelligence is even much more exciting; so it is understandable that after a number of years of research on insect-level intelligence, Brooks and many others wanted to do more interesting things. This seemed a good time to tackle something more challenging: the human. Thus we are back to the goals of traditional artificial intelligence, but now we can tackle them with the experience of biorobotics. Throughout the book we will

give many examples of how the insights gained have changed our thinking about intelligence. While in Japan humanoid robots had been a
research topic for many years already, these activities were not directly
related to artificial intelligence. This seems to be the reason why Brooks's
move into humanoids had a strong impact on the research community,
although it was initially, and still is, met with considerable skepticism:
many researchers believe human intelligence is still way out of reach.
Nevertheless, in the early 1990s Brooks started the "Cog" project for the
development of a humanoid robot with the goal of eventually reaching
high-level cognition (Brooks and Stein, 1994).

The term *humanoid robot* is used for robots that typically have two
arms and legs, a torso and a movable head with a vision system, and
sometimes additional sensory modalities such as audio and touch. They
are called humanoid because there is a superficial visual resemblance to
humans. Because of their anthropomorphic shape, people have a strong
tendency to project humanlike properties onto these robots. But, careful:
remember David McFarland's reference to anthropomorphization as an
incurable disease. Some science-fiction movies can also be misleading by
suggesting humanlike properties in their robots: Hollywood robots typically have a very high level of intelligence. Some are mean and want to
enslave mankind, reflecting a fear that, given the current state of the art
in robotics, is entirely unjustified. (Of course, we don't have to wait for
superintelligent killer robots to be enslaved by machines—we are
already almost entirely dependent on our cars, computers, and mobile
phones, and we do many things just to please the machines, not because
we want to. A case in point was the Y2K problem, the year 2000 problem,
where companies and governments all over the world invested billions
of dollars in order to cope with the issue. We were forced to do so by our
computers: it was definitely not an act of free will. The only question is
whether we attribute evil intentions to the computers; but this is a philosophical question—a matter of argument—not an empirical one. An
empirical question is one for which experiments can be devised to
support or falsify a hypothesis, and for this question—Are machines
evil?—that is not possible.)

But back to the Cog project. "Cog" is a pun, alluding both to its cognitive abilities and to the cogs of a cogwheel, insinuating that cognition
or intelligence is really based on many simple cogs—processes—that
function together. Inspired by this project, many researchers were
attracted by the idea of moving toward human-level intelligence, which
had been the target of artificial intelligence all along, both classical and

embodied. Around this time the field of developmental robotics emerged. Its pertinent conferences come under many labels: "Emergence and Development of Embodied Cognition," "Epigenetic Robotics," "Developmental Robotics," "Development of Embodied Cognition," "Humanoids," etc. This was, of course, a happy change of direction for those who might have been disappointed by the turn the field had taken—insects simply are not as sexy as humans! And human intelligence happens to be the most fascinating type of intelligence that we know of. But once again, this strand of conferences is separate from the traditional ones in artificial intelligence, and although the terms *embodiment* and *emergence* might appear in the pertinent publications, "embodied artificial intelligence" most often does not.

In the meantime, developmental robotics has grown into a considerable research and engineering community in its own right. Many people in the field started developing humanoid robots, and in Japan, for example, the research in this area is really exploding. In 1998 the powerful Ministry of Economy, Trade, and Industry (METI) in Japan launched a large five-year program for building humanoid robots: the HRP, or Humanoid Robotics Program. The program was directed by the grand old man of Japanese robotics, Hirochika Inoue, at the time professor of engineering at the University of Tokyo, who has been a pioneer in robotics since 1965. The HRP had the long-term goal of developing a partner for humans, especially for the elderly, that could take over many of their household chores, thus providing independence and autonomy for as long as possible. This endeavor unites researchers from mechanical and electronics engineering, robotics, artificial intelligence, developmental psychology, and developmental neuroscience, and most of them would probably not object to being classified as working in artificial intelligence. But not only in Japan has the field gained momentum: Europeans have also warmed to the topic, and the EU is sponsoring a number of large projects in the field, such as the RobotCub (Robotic Open-architecture Technology for Cognition, Understanding, and Behavior) (not to be confused with the better-known Robocup competitions, in which robot teams play soccer), and Cogniron, the Cognitive Robot Companion. We will discuss in more detail the research issues being tackled in this exciting field when we embark on the challenge of building high-level intelligence from the bottom up (chapter 5), and when we look at robotic technology in everyday life (chapter 11).

It is perhaps worth mentioning that—fortunately—not everybody has moved into humanoid or developmental robotics because there are a vast number of fascinating research issues to be tackled in animal behavior, and biorobotics seems to be a highly productive way of doing so.

2.8 Ubiquitous Computing and Interfacing Technology

Another line of development that must not be overlooked is that of ubiquitous computing and interfacing technology. We will discuss ubiquitous computing in detail in chapter 8. Here we only discuss what is needed to map out the research landscape of artificial intelligence.

Like artificial intelligence, computer science in general has undergone dramatic change: the "core" areas of computer science—software engineering, algorithm development, operating systems, and the virtual machine—are topics that we by now understand relatively well, so people have begun switching their focus to other, more challenging areas, such as the largely unexplored territory of how computers can interact with the real world beyond the typical keyboard-and-mouse setup. The very primitive interaction of computers with humans and, by extension, with the outside world in general, has for many years been one of the greatly bemoaned facts of computer technology. There is a great deal of activity in the human-computer interaction research community, aimed at improving this situation. One way toward more sophistication in the interaction with the environment is, of course, to put sensors and more interesting input-output devices into the computer such as microphones, cameras, and touch sensors. But the interaction of computers with humans is not the only focus of interest. Rather than having computers as "boxes" or devices separate from the rest of the world, it would be nice if the computing technology were integrated with the world around us so that humans could smoothly interact with it and no longer have to push keys on a keyboard as in the old days. Computers should disappear; they should become "invisible."

The original idea was, as a first step, simply to put sensors everywhere: into rooms, cars, furniture, clothes and so on and so forth. We are already surrounded by systems working around the clock, doing work for us without our being aware of it: this would just be a further step in that direction.

More recently, ubiquitous computing researchers have also begun exploring actuation: ways in which systems can not only sense, but also influence and act upon their environments. The simplest example, the thermostat, has been around for a very long time: based on a temperature measurement, the furnace is turned on or off. Another very well-known example is the garage door that opens automatically when it senses the right car entering the driveway. It is one of the fundamental discoveries in (embodied) artificial intelligence that the close coupling between sensory and motor systems is essential for intelligent behavior (see chapter 4). This insight is starting to make its way into the ubiquitous computing community.

Even though user interfaces have always been an important topic in computer science, the main problem has been the low bandwidth of communication, so to speak: normally only a mouse and keyboard are used to get information into a computer. As we have already pointed out, a lot of effort has been directed toward making speech an easy input method for computers, but these efforts, for various reasons, have not been extremely successful (yet). Just recently more interesting and rich interfaces have been developed, such as the use of pressure sensors to provide information about the user's level of aggression, and to some extent vision, using cameras that watch the user and try to collect information about gaze direction (where is the user looking?) and emotional state. There is also work on smell, but that, although very promising, has not yet advanced significantly. Whether we actually want a computer that can smell us, especially after a 14-hour nonstop programming session, is another issue altogether. The study of wearables—computers that are actually a part of our clothing—is related to ubiquitous computing, and also raises fascinating ideas about the future of human-computer interaction. What is interesting about all of these "movements"—human-machine interfaces, wearables and ubiquitous computing—is that now virtually all computer science departments are venturing into the real world. They are not doing robotics per se, but many have started hiring engineers and are establishing workshops where they can build hardware, because now real-world devices need to be constructed. So far as we can tell, there has been little theoretical development yet, but there is a lot of creative experimentation going on. We feel that the set of design principles that we have worked out for embodied systems, and which we will describe in detail through chapters 4, 5, 6, and 7, will be extremely useful in designing such systems. We will return to the topic of ubiquitous computing in chapter 8.

In conclusion, it seems that a highly innovative and dynamic part of computer science has moved from disembodied algorithms to embodied real-world computing, or rather real-world interaction, just as artificial intelligence has. Researchers in ubiquitous computing and interfacing technology are—directly or indirectly—making important contributions

to artificial intelligence. Conversely, advances in artificial intelligence—
from a perspective of embodiment—and robotics, specifically in sensing
and actuation technology, will contribute significantly to ubiquitous
computing and thus to modern computer science in general.

2.9 Artificial Life and Multiagent Systems

Another interesting development has its origins in the field of artificial
life, also called ALife for short. The classical perspective of artificial intelligence had a strong focus on the individual, just like psychology does,
and as we have seen, psychology was the major discipline with which artificial intelligence researchers cooperated at the time. ALife has strong
roots in biology rather than psychology, and focuses on the emergence
of behavior in large populations of agents. In other words artificial life
research is interested in multiagent systems. We have to be a bit careful
with the term multiagent systems: in ALife research, the term *complex
dynamical systems* is usually preferred, because it also includes physical
inorganic systems, where the individual agents or components, such as
molecules or sand grains, only have limited agent characteristics. An
agent is assumed to have certain elementary sensory-motor abilities, so
that it can perceive aspects of the environment and, depending on this
information and its own state, perform certain behaviors. Molecules,
rocks, or other "dead" physical objects do not have this ability.

One early success of this field of study was the realization that complex
global behavior can emerge from simple rules and local interactions (e.g.,
Langton, 1995). Cellular automata are the typical representatives of this
approach, where the "agents" are individual cells of a grid. The next state
of each cell is determined by the cell's own state and the state of its
neighbors. John Conway's "game of life" (Gardner, 1970) is probably the
best-known example of cellular automata behavior: the cells on a two-
dimensional grid have two states, "on" or "off" ("alive" or "dead"), and
are controlled by four rules: If a live cell has less than two neighbors,
then it dies (loneliness); if a live cell has more than three neighbors, then
it dies (overcrowding); if a dead cell has three live neighbors, then it
comes to life (reproduction); otherwise, a cell stays as it is. The fascination of the game of life is the enormous variety of fun and sophisticated
spatiotemporal[3] patterns that emerge from these very simple rules.
People have given many of them names, such as oscillators, blinkers, flip-
flops, gliders, glider cannons, and so on; dozens of live demonstrations of
this game can be found on the Internet.

What counts in typical artificial life systems is the entire population of agents, not the individual. In the case of cellular automata, the individual "agents" are the cells on the grid, but these individuals are only of interest in the context of many cells. Work on self-organization in insect societies, for example by Jean-Louis Deneubourg of the Université Libre de Bruxelles (at the Center for Nonlinear Phenomena and Complex Systems), who studies social insects, also capitalizes on a population perspective and has attracted many researchers: "ant algorithms" (Dorigo et al., 2002) and "swarm intelligence" (Bonabeau et al., 1999) are among their coinages (see also Dorigo and Stützle, 2004). Deneubourg and Dorigo were both inspired by the intellectual atmosphere created by the physicist Ilya Prigogine, who was awarded the Nobel Prize in 1977 for his work on dissipative structures. His thinking on self-organization and complex systems has influenced many researchers in artificial life. Prigogine, who had been living in Brussels for many years as the director of the famous Solvay Institutes for Physics and Chemistry, had become known outside the physics community for, among others, the book with the provocative title *Order out of Chaos* (Prigogine and Stenger, 1984).

Self-organization is indeed one of the concepts that continually pops up in modern artificial intelligence (see for example Camazine et al., 2001), and we will encounter it throughout this book. By self-organization we mean that some structure or pattern—for example, patterns on butterfly wings, stripes on the fur of a zebra, or a particular social organization in insect societies—comes about as a result of the local interaction of many components, rather than by external direction, manipulation, or global, centralized control. Self-organization is an extremely powerful concept but hard to grasp intuitively because we always try to understand the phenomena around us in terms of control. However, once we grasp the idea, it becomes very natural and then it seems hard to understand how we could have done without it before, as we will see in chapters 6 and 7.

A beautiful example of how self-organization can lead to highly sophisticated behavior is the formation of ant trails. Certain species of ants are able to find the nearest food source among several sources present in the vicinity of their nest, so the ants are somehow solving a complex optimization problem. Deneubourg and Goss (1989) asked the question of whether this ability is due to the intelligence of the individual ants or due to their social interaction. Attributing this capacity to the individual ants would imply that the ants compare the distances to the various food sources and based on this knowledge choose the nearest source. This in turn would require ample calculations and considerable exploration and knowledge of the environment on the part of the individual ants. But there is a much simpler solution. Ants mark their paths with pheromones—chemicals with a strong scent—as they leave the nest to search for food and when they come back from this journey. The ants follow the pheromones, and at the crossings where several paths intersect they choose the most heavily marked one with a certain probability. Ants return sooner from nearer food sources and as a consequence shorter paths are marked more intensively than those leading to sources farther away. Because shorter paths are more heavily marked, they will attract more ants which will accelerate the speed at which the shorter paths are marked. This kind of process is an example of a positive feedback loop, and is often called an autocatalytic or self-reinforcing process. Thus, we have a very simple explanation of how ants find their way to the nearest food source in terms of self-organization rather than the cognitive power of the individual.

Modular robotics, a research area that has drawn a lot of inspiration from ALife research, also relates to multiagent systems. In this case the individual agents are robotic modules capable of assembling into robots with different morphologies (see, for example, the volume by Hara and Pfeifer, 2003, for illustrations of modular robotic systems). One of the goals of this research is to design systems capable of self-repair, a property that all living systems have to some extent: a minor bruise or a cut will automatically heal without any external intervention. Self-assembly and self-reconfiguration are fascinating topics that will become increasingly important as systems have to operate over extended periods of time in remote, hostile environments, like the deep sea or other planets. The seminal work by the futurist engineer Satoshi Murata of the Tokyo Institute of Technology and his coworkers (Murata et al., 2004) demonstrates how self-reconfiguration can be achieved not only in simulation but with real robotic systems (see figure 7.1 in chapter 7). It should be mentioned, however, that to date self-repair and self-reconfiguration is tightly controlled by a centralized algorithm, rather than emerging from local interactions. But more about this in chapter 7.

Evolutionary systems are another example of so-called population thinking, where the adaptivity of entire populations is studied rather than the adaptivity of individuals. We will discuss the impact of evolutionary thinking in chapter 6. Because of its close relation to biology, economics has also taken inspiration from evolutionary thinking and created the discipline of agent-based economics (e.g., Epstein and Axtell, 1996).

Often, evolutionary algorithms and ant algorithms are used not as biological models, but rather as powerful optimization techniques: several large industrial companies now make use of evolutionary and ant-based algorithms for design and optimization (for an overview of the use of ant algorithms in industry, see Dorigo and Stützle, 2004).

Interestingly, the term *multiagent systems* has quickly been adopted by researchers in classical artificial intelligence, but their use of multiagent systems is somewhat different. Rather than looking for emergence, as is common in the field of ALife, they usually employ multiagent systems to achieve particular tasks, for example search tasks on the Internet (e.g., Ferber, 1999). Often in this line of research the individual agents are endowed with centralized control similar to that employed in the classical approach. So in many cases the multiagent approach in artificial intelligence does not in fact study emergence.

In robotics there has also been a growing interest in multiagent systems. The recent surge of interest in robot soccer clearly demonstrates this point. This movement, known as RoboCup, is passionately promoted by the Japanese researcher and robot enthusiast Hiroaki Kitano and his colleagues (Kitano et al., 1997), and interest in the project is not limited to the scientific community but has spread to the population at large. During the RoboCup world championship in 2002 in the Fukuoka Dome, a stadium in the southwestern city of Fukuoka on the island of Kyushu in Japan, there were more than 100,000 passionate, emotional spectators, just like at a real soccer championship! One of the problems in multi-agent robotics has been that often only a few robots are available for study—making copies of real-world robots is so much harder than making copies of software—so that no truly interesting emergent phenomena have been observed. In robot soccer, winning the game, rather than emergence, is the goal. Recently, RoboCup teams have achieved impressive performance: the games are beginning to look like real soccer where the individual players are not only extremely fast but cooperate with each other to score a goal.

One of the important research problems so far has been the achievement of higher levels of intelligence in the simulations created by the multi-agent community. Typically, as in the work of the ethologist turned ALife researcher Charlotte Hemelrijk, who studies groups of virtual primate-like agents, hierarchies among the agents and separate subgroups emerge on their own, or migration patterns materialize based only on agent-agent interaction, without the need for preprogrammed "desires" to form social hierarchies or to migrate. Thinking, reasoning, and language have typically not been topics of interest in the ALife field. An exception is perhaps the work by the artificial intelligence researcher and linguist Luc Steels, who, in his "Talking Heads" experiment (not to be confused with the rock band of the same name), attempts to investigate high-level cognition—natural language—from a population perspective (Steels, 2001, 2003). In an ingenious set of experiments he and his students demonstrated how, for example, a common vocabulary emerges through the interaction of the agents with their environment and with each other. There is also some preliminary work on the emergence of syntax. In this research, much insight has been gained into how communication systems establish themselves—how they self-organize—and how something like grammar could emerge without being predefined in the individual agents. Although this approach is fascinating and highly promising, the jury is still out on whether it will indeed lead to something resembling natural language.

Because of the fundamental differences in goals, the distributed agents community that has its origin in the artificial life community, and the one that developed out of artificial intelligence and robotics, have so far remained largely separate. Generally speaking, the artificial life community has more of a focus on populations, distributed systems with local interactions, self-organization, and complex dynamics and somewhat less on embodied systems, but researchers in this field are definitely contributing to (embodied) artificial intelligence—again, whether they realize it or not.

2.10 Evolutionary Robotics

One of the principal research topics within ALife is trying to understand how life originated on Earth, and for all we know, evolution played the key role in this process. Thus it comes as no surprise that much of the research within ALife is devoted to evolution: this includes trying to understand natural evolution and designing creatures using artificial evolution. Since the 1960s when artificial evolution was invented, so to speak (see chapter 6), there have been many intriguing developments that have led to insights into the general nature of evolution and have yielded fascinating technological results. For example, using automated evolutionary design methods, devices have been produced that at times surpass the performance of those designed by humans, such as electronic circuits (e.g., Koza et al., 2004) or antennas (e.g., Lohn et al., 2004). For our purposes, because of our interest in embodiment, the area known as evolutionary robotics is especially relevant. Methods from artificial evolution can be used to design various aspects of robots. Traditionally, in evolutionary robotics only the controller—the brain—of the robot was evolved. But more recently, with the advent of more sophisticated concepts such as models of genetic regulatory networks, entire robots—including their body and neural systems—have been evolved. The Japanese-Canadian evolutionary robotics enthusiast and entrepreneur Takashi Gomi was one of the first to recognize the importance of this field beyond its scientific interest, and he attempted to incorporate evolutionary methods not only into robotics but into business. He organized a highly successful conference series on evolutionary robotics at the Canadian embassy in Tokyo. Since then, the field has become very popular not only in Japan but throughout the world and a considerable research community has been established. Understanding how embodied systems emerge from an evolutionary process is an important contribution to artificial intelligence. But once again, few evolutionary roboticists consider what they are doing to be artificial intelligence. We will explore evolutionary robotics more deeply in chapter 6.

2.11 Summary

In summary, we can see that the landscape of artificial intelligence has changed significantly in recent years: while originally the field was clearly a computational discipline dominated by computer science, cognitive psychology, linguistics, and philosophy, it has now turned into a more multidisciplinary field requiring the cooperation and talents of researchers in many other fields such as biology, neuroscience, engineering (electronic and mechanical), robotics, biomechanics, material sciences, and dynamical systems. And this exciting new transdisciplinary community, which is very different from the traditional AI community, has been called "embodied artificial intelligence" or "embodied cognitive science." But since this is the modern view in artificial intelligence, we will no longer employ the term *embodied* artificial intelligence: what we have described in this chapter *is* what the discipline has become; it is not merely a subset of the "real" or overarching field of artificial intelligence: embodied artificial intelligence is now artificial intelligence.

Although for some time psychology and linguistics have not been at center stage, with the rise of developmental robotics there has been renewed interest in these disciplines. The ultimate quest to understand and build systems capable of high-level thinking and natural language, and ultimately consciousness, has remained unchanged. What has changed is the path—the methodology—to get there. Although the emergence of ideas of embodiment can be found throughout the history of philosophy, the recent developments in artificial intelligence that enable not only the analysis but also the construction of embodied systems are supplying ample new intellectual material for philosophers.

In spite of the multifaceted nature of artificial intelligence, there is a unifying principle: the synthetic methodology that we will describe in detail in the next chapter. Briefly, the synthetic methodology states that by actually building physical agents—real robots—we can learn a lot about the nature of intelligence. Moreover, and this is crucial for such a diverse field, physical agents, by bringing together results from all the different areas described in this chapter, have a highly integrative function. In addition, they allow for concrete testing of ideas in an objective way: a robot either works or it does not; there is no glossing over details. Moreover, robots serve as excellent platforms for transdisciplinary research and communication. By building systems using the synthetic methodology, we not only produce fun and—at least sometimes—useful artifacts, but we can acquire a deeper understanding of natural forms of intelligence. Again, the impact of applying an embodied perspective is astonishing: the insights are surprising and change the way we view ourselves and the world around us in very fundamental ways. This is what our book is all about.

II Toward a Theory of Intelligence

Part II is an attempt to formulate the first steps toward a theory of intelligence. Developing a theory of intelligence is definitely a massive endeavor, and many great minds have tried their luck at it. Starting in the nineteenth century, we find the American psychologist and philosopher William James (1842–1910) (author of *Principles of Psychology*); the great Austrian psychologist and physician Sigmund Freud (1856–1939) (father of psychoanalysis); the Swiss biologist and psychologist Jean Piaget (1896–1980) (champion of the development of intelligence in children); the Russian psychologist Lev Vigotsky (1896–1934) (theorist of the constructivist perspective on psychology); and the British psychologist Charles Spearman (1863–1945) (inventor of the general intelligence factor *g*, which became the basis of IQ testing), to name but a few. All have contributed in important ways to our understanding of intelligence and can be said to have developed, in some broad sense, theories of intelligence. More recently, Robert Sternberg with his *Triarchic Theory of Intelligence* (1985), Howard Gardner with his *Theory of Multiple Intelligences* (1982), Marvin Minsky (*Society of Mind*, 1987), Allen Newell (*Unified Theories of Cognition* 1990), John Anderson with his ACT theory (*The Architecture of Cognition*, 1983), and Steven Pinker, in *How the Mind Works* (1997), have all presented research efforts that can also be seen as theories of intelligence.

The reason we think that, despite all of these distinguished efforts, we can make a valuable contribution is that our own ideas have grown from a perspective of embodiment and through applying a synthetic methodology, which is mostly absent in previous theorizing. So, this part of the book represents an attempt to take some steps toward a theory of intelligence that is based on recent developments in our understanding of embodiment. It is the core piece, and it is, conceptually speaking, the heaviest one. To make it more accessible we have included many examples to support our arguments.

Given the relatively chaotic landscape of the field outlined in the previous chapter, the question arises as to what form a theory might have in such an interdisciplinary environment. Because our science, artificial intelligence, not only analyzes existing biological systems but also builds artificial systems, we are in fact dealing with a new kind of science, a synthetic rather than a purely analytic one like biology, neuroscience, physics, or chemistry, where existing systems in nature are investigated. Moreover, the analytic disciplines have been around for much longer than artificial intelligence and there are widely accepted standards for what constitutes good science in them, whereas for the synthetic approaches, the criteria against which experiments and theories are judged first need to be developed.

So, chapter 3 outlines what type of theory we are looking for and introduces a general framework provided by a number of important notions such as diversity-compliance, frame of reference, the synthetic methodology, time perspectives, and emergence. This chapter contains a bit of philosophy of science, which we use to outline the nature of the theory, and describes what it means to make progress and to do actual research in the field. We only scratch the surface, but it is interesting to see that the kind of theory we are aiming for has not been covered in the literature.

To illustrate our general framework let us just take one example, the notion of the three time frames or time scales at which we can study behavior. Chapters 4, 5, and 6 are organized around these three time frames: "here and now" (pushing the brakes when you see a red traffic light); learning and development (how the behavior of applying the brakes at a traffic light is learned); and evolution (how the brain evolved so that this learning could happen).

Chapter 4 first describes properties of real-world agents and then sketches a set of design heuristics, the "design principles for intelligent systems," that can be used to guide us in engineering synthetic agents, but also to help us understand biological ones. These design principles mostly concern the "here-and-now" time frame. This is the longest chapter in the book and will require some stamina on the part of the reader. However, there are many surprising insights in there that have not previously been covered in the literature, for example, the fact that through the interaction with their environment, not only *that* agents structure their own sensory information but *how* they do this—a point we will elaborate and illustrate in detail.

Chapter 5 explores design and analysis issues from a developmental perspective, and asks how high-level cognition can emerge during a process of ontogenetic development; how cognition emerges as the agent matures into an "adult." For example, how is it possible that something discrete such as abstract symbol processing or cognition can arise in a completely continuous system—and we are all continuous dynamical systems—over time? A specific, somewhat provocative instance of this question is what walking—or, more generally, locomotion—has to do with thinking, which we will explore in detail in that chapter. Another way of looking at this issue is in terms of the notorious symbol grounding problem, i.e., how symbols get their meaning, or how the connection between symbols and the environment can be established. The chapter concludes with a set of design principles focused at the developmental time perspective. Many of the ideas are taken from the booming field of developmental robotics, where the goal is to mimic processes of psychological and biological development on robots, typically of the humanoid kind.

Chapter 6 looks at how we can harness ideas from biological evolution in order to design agents—complete with bodies, sensors, motors and brains—from scratch. Of course, "from scratch" is not to be taken literally, but it means that the designer's decisions are made at a different level than in a "here and now" or a developmental approach. Here, we as designers step back and let simulated evolution do the work for us. The point is to let evolution design virtual agents that perform increasingly complex tasks, so that at some point, we might be inclined to use the term "cognitive" to characterize their behavior. One of the goals of this chapter is to demonstrate the power of artificial evolution. Specifically, we will give some impressive examples of where it has outperformed humans on sophisticated engineering tasks. While chapter 5 focuses on the lifetime of an individual, in chapter 6, we extend the time frame to encompass many generations of agents, and widen our view to consider not just single agents but populations of them. Again, we summarize the main results as a set of design principles, this time for evolutionary systems.

The implications of considering populations rather than individuals are discussed in chapter 7. There, we look at emergent phenomena that arise in populations of agents—that is, phenomena, or behavioral patterns, in the group that come about as the agents interact with each other without knowing about the global pattern. These kinds of emergent behaviors are often referred to as "collective intelligence." Such phenomena are mostly investigated in so-called agent-based simulations, rather than on real robots: we speculate a bit about the reasons why this might be the case. We will also introduce another kind of collective intelligence, namely modular robots: robots that are composed of many modules, which, as they interact with each other, can achieve interesting collective behaviors. In modular robotics, the modules themselves can be viewed as agents, in addition to the robot itself. Because modular robots can change their morphology, they are much more adaptable than those that can change only their controllers. The field of modular robots today is fascinating, but the modules currently used are on the order of 5 to 10 cm in size, and only relatively few—typically less than 100—are used. With the recent developments especially in the area of nanotechnology, it may become possible to make the modules much smaller and more numerous, which might boost the application potential of such robots. Science fiction–like scenarios involving swarms of microscopic robots might become reality in the not-too-distant future. The main points in this chapter are captured in a set of design principles for collective intelligence.

3   Prerequisites for a Theory of Intelligence

In 1935 the Austrian-born British philosopher and champion of the philosophy of science, Karl Popper, wrote the influential book *The Logic of Scientific Discovery*, originally published in German as *Logik der Forschung* (Popper, 1935, 1969). He argued that scientific theories cannot be verified, but that they can only be refuted or falsified. In his view, theories merely have temporary status, i.e., they can only be taken to hold as long as their predictions have not been shown to be incorrect by experimental evidence. This was his way of coming to grips with the problem of how to distinguish scientific theories from pseudotheories, those that claim to be scientific but in fact are not. To Popper, Einstein's theory of general relativity has the status of a scientific theory whereas Marx's theory of economics or Freud's theory of psychoanalysis are pseudotheories because they lack this property of falsifiability. According to Popper, whenever new evidence arises—such as, in Freud's case, a new clinical observation or a new patient whose symptoms and behavior do not seem to fit into the theory—it can somehow be accommodated, and may even be taken to confirm the theory rather than refute it. It should be noted, however, that despite this lack of falsifiability, psychoanalysis has had and continues to have an enormous impact on modern thinking (even much broader than Popper's ideas).

Popper's position has had a significant effect on what is considered good scientific methodology, but it has not remained undisputed. Paul Feyerabend, also born in Austria and considered the enfant terrible of the philosophy of science, sharply criticized Popper's stance. Although he had been deeply influenced by Popper's work—he was one of his students—he later became one of Popper's strongest opponents. In his highly controversial book with the contentious title *Against Method*, Feyerabend argued that Popper's view was much too restrictive, that science could not make progress by following strict rules. He pointed out that often when real scientific progress had been made, the scientists involved were not following precise rules. "Anything goes" was his somewhat anarchistic motto. Because this book is about artificial intelligence and not philosophy of science, we will not dig deeper into the Popperian or Feyerabendian view of science here. Rather we propose that, as always, the truth presumably lies somewhere in the middle: some rules and generally accepted methodologies are definitely required, but very stiff adherence to them will stifle progress. It is in this middle ground that we will, over the course of this book, attempt to sketch out a theory of intelligence.

Unlike physics, psychology, or biology, artificial intelligence is a young and immature discipline; up to this point it lacks a firm foundation. Given the relatively short history of the field, and taking into account its intellectual landscape and its interdisciplinary nature, we cannot expect there to be a generally accepted methodology. Moreover, artificial intelligence differs in essential respects from the other sciences: it is not only about understanding nature, as are the analytical sciences of physics, biology, psychology, and neuroscience, but also about designing and building things: it is synthetic. The theory that we are looking for will have to incorporate this essential aspect. Most of the theories of intelligence that we mentioned in the introduction to part II, are purely analytic and therefore better suited for Popper's stringent criteria. However, Minsky and Newell, for example, coming from an artificial intelligence background, do include this design aspect in their theories. Finally, the artifacts built in a synthetic context (programs or robots) are interesting in their own right, not only as models of biological systems. So we can see that a narrow view like the one advocated by Popper will not work in artificial intelligence.

In this chapter, we will proceed as follows. First we will talk about the sort of theory we are aiming for, which will take the form of a set of design principles. Then we will browse through some important considerations and some "metaprinciples" that constitute the general framework for our theory.

3.1   Level of Generality and Form of Theory

This section presents the various potential forms a theory of intelligence might take and argues for the scheme of so-called design principles. The discussion is fairly theoretical and abstract, and can safely be skipped without losing the thread of the argument. So, the reader may want to continue directly with section 3.2, "Diversity-compliance."

Many books have been written about what theories are, what form they take in different disciplines, and how specific models relate to the theory. These discussions tend to become very lengthy and intellectual, and we don't feel a detailed discussion is necessary. Moreover, because of the different nature of a synthetic discipline, many of the points in such a discussion might not apply. Here, we include only the conceptual groundwork that will allow us to begin exploring intelligence in all its forms, acknowledging that philosophers of science may find this method of presentation superficial.

So, let us turn our attention briefly to the level of abstraction the theory should have. One way or another, a theory should capture our understanding of the field in a compact way, so that the insights can be applied to many different problems in the area and can be widely communicated. We want our theory to characterize not only ants and rats, but also humans, robots, and perhaps other kinds of artifacts such as mobile phones, intelligent cars, and wired T-shirts.

Because our theory should cover such a broad spectrum of phenomena we cannot expect to be able to derive—in a very direct sense—specific models or designs from it. For example, we cannot expect to derive something as detailed as the snapshot model for ant navigation, or the design for the quadruped Puppy directly from the theory. For the purpose of developing concrete models, specific biological or engineering knowledge will be required. What the theory should be able to do is provide general guidelines on how to proceed: these guidelines, as we will argue, take the form of design principles. One aspect of these guidelines is their use of dynamical systems as a metaphor. This contrasts with the methods previously used in artificial intelligence.

For example, Herbert Simon (whom we introduced in the previous chapter), one of the founding fathers of artificial intelligence, was convinced that the theory of intelligence would be cast in information-processing or algorithmic terms, a legacy that lives on in the cognitivistic paradigm. Although, for reasons that we outlined previously, we do not think this is a proper way to model intelligence, the approach does incorporate the two aspects that we said would be important for a theory of intelligence: explaining behavior (the analytic aspect) and designing behavior (the synthetic aspect). Artificial intelligence since its beginnings has had this goal of understanding by building. The idea of couching a theory of intelligence in information-processing terms goes back to Alan

Turing's notion of computation as the essential characteristic of intelligence (Turing, 1950). Interestingly, Turing produced groundbreaking results not only in computation, but also in a completely different field, dynamical systems (in particular, pattern formation in biological systems; see Turing, 1952), which brings us to the metaphor that we will make use of throughout the text.

Dynamical systems theory has generated a lot of hype in the artificial intelligence, cognitive science, and neurobiology communities as a potential solution for escaping the impasse of the cognitivistic approach. At scientific conferences around the world, it has been loudly declaimed from lecterns (if not quite shouted from the rooftops) that the theory of intelligence (or cognition) will have to be couched in terms of dynamical systems (see, e.g., the volume edited by Port and van Gelder, 1995). An important class of behavior in nonlinear dynamical systems is chaos, and often "chaos theory" is used in place of "dynamical systems theory" (depending on the area, the terms nonlinear dynamics, complex dynamics, and chaos theory are used for essentially the same idea). In the 1980s and 1990s chaos achieved cult status, so to speak. Professionals from all disciplines—managers, teachers, journalists, and even politicians—started using terms from chaos theory. The title of Prigogine's famous book, *Order out of Chaos*, has become a slogan for the emerging field. The popular interpretation of Prigogine's book is that chaos is a necessary ingredient of any system from which interesting behavior is to be expected. The well-written and highly entertaining book *Chaos* by James Gleick became a national bestseller immediately upon its release in 1987. The euphoria was, at least for some time, enormous. Managers started to "organize" chaos workshops: everyone "realized" that nothing appealing could emerge from boring, well-ordered structures. "Chaos theory" came to be used to explain virtually everything, from tornadoes to climate change to slum growth in cities to group dynamics in families to deforestation in Africa to the development of schizophrenia to . . . cognition! "What might cognition be if not computation?" asked the philosopher Tim van Gelder in an influential paper (van Gelder, 1995). He proposed dynamics as the missing ingredient, and in the paper van Gelder discusses how dynamics might be able to explain cognition.

In brain science—and in cognitive science—chaos and dynamical systems have been important topics since the 1980s when Agnessa Babloyantz and her colleagues published an article about chaotic brain dynamics during sleep (Babloyantz et al., 1985). Christine Skarda and

Walter Freeman, in their seminal paper "How the brain makes chaos to make sense of the world," argued that chaos might in fact be highly beneficial to the brain (Skarda and Freeman, 1987)—and thus to intelligence, we might add. For example, it has been argued that chaotic activity, as the neural dynamics of the brain, makes animals and humans extremely adaptive: they can almost immediately react to changes in their environment (for further references on the topic of brain dynamics and dynamical systems, see, for example, Basar, 1990; Kaneko and Tsuda, 2001; and Kelso, 1995, to mention but a few). We discuss an example of chaotic activity in the brain, the olfactory bulb (the brain region responsible for smelling) of rabbits, in chapter 10.

Although the hype surrounding dynamical systems in the 1980s and 1990s has largely faded away, the basic idea is decidedly compelling. One reason for the relatively slow progress of the field of complex dynamics might be that the mathematical formalisms are highly sophisticated and require specialized skills. One point that we should perhaps mention is that the way the theory of dynamical systems is mostly used at the moment is as an analytical tool, to understand phenomena in natural systems, and not so much to actually design artifacts; in other words, the synthetic aspect is largely absent. However, because we find the metaphor of dynamical systems extremely appealing and intuitive—it helps us think and build intuitions and research questions about intelligent agents—we will make intensive use of it throughout the book.

In conclusion, there is no framework that we can simply pull off the shelf and use for a theory of intelligence. So, we are looking for a scaffold or structure that will get us somehow the best of all these worlds: the analytic component for understanding natural and artificial agents, the synthetic one for designing and building systems, and the dynamical systems metaphor for developing ideas and getting inspiration about intelligent behavior in general. We feel that we can combine them all if we formulate the theory as a set of design principles.

The core of our approach to intelligence, then, is a set of design principles that on the one hand represent fundamental ingredients for a general theory of intelligence and on the other provide powerful engineering heuristics for the design of intelligent artifacts. There are a number of reasons for couching a theory of intelligence in terms of design principles. First, they instantiate the synthetic methodology, i.e., the idea of understanding by building, and therefore they implement the engineering flavor of the field. They capture heuristics for actually building systems and at the same time they characterize natural or artificial systems. Second, a lot of ideas can be gained from studying natural evolution: evolution can also be seen as a powerful designer, albeit a blind one, as referred to by the famous evolutionary biologist Richard Dawkins in his book *The Blind Watchmaker* (1986); artificial evolution has now been incorporated (along with development and collective intelligence) into a broader set of design principles than those we outlined in *Understanding Intelligence* (1999). We hope to convince the reader that having principles for designing and understanding intelligent systems is a good idea, and that young, talented researchers will take it up, modify the principles, add new ones, and try to make the entire set more comprehensive and coherent. And third (and perhaps less important) design principles communicate the flavor that in its current state of development the theory is still rather informal. The set is not complete and final, but it can be extended or modified if new insights emerge. We are convinced of the strength of the design principles as a guiding force. Moreover, they support the synthetic nature of the science of intelligence: they enable us to do good science through engineering, so to speak. However, we cannot know at this point whether our design principles will ultimately survive or be overtaken by some other theory.

We have organized the design principles according to the three time perspectives because of the fundamentally different nature of the processes involved at each level. Moreover, we have added the collective intelligence perspective—in contrast to the individual one—as a separate set of principles because these two perspectives represent a different way of carving up the field. Thus the following chapters discuss the general design principles as they pertain to the "here-and-now" perspective (chapter 4), developmental systems (chapter 5), evolutionary systems (chapter 6), and collective intelligence (chapter 7).

In addition, in order to properly apply the design principles, the theory includes a set of more general or metatheoretical principles and considerations that provide the framework or context within which design and analysis takes place; they are the focus of this chapter. First, we have to characterize the general class of phenomena to be covered by the theory, which we sum up using the complementary ideas of diversity and compliance. Second, it is important to be clear about what we are referring to when we use the term *intelligence*: are we talking about something that is going on in the animal or the robot; is it something that we, as observers or designers, attribute to the animal or robot but that actually resides only in our heads; or is it some combination of the two? This is the notorious frame-of-reference issue. Third, we have to specify how to proceed and what we accept as a valid research methodology. We believe there are a number of necessary components for this way of working: There is the synthetic methodology, which states that we can learn by building intelligent agents, not just studying existing ones. Then there are the three time frames at which we study, design, and build systems: the here-and-now time scale (what the agent does in a particular situation), the ontogenetic time scale (the lifetime of an individual agent), or the evolutionary time scale (generations of agents). And finally, we can generate powerful explanations by referring to the concept of emergence, as we will elaborate. Once we have addressed these questions we are ready to roll up our sleeves and get to work on the design principles.

3.2 Diversity-Compliance

As you might have guessed by now, we are not much into definitions; therefore we will not try to define intelligence. What we will do, however, is to describe what it is that we intuitively view as intelligent. Very briefly, as already outlined in chapter 1, intelligent agents are characterized on the one hand by the fact that they comply with and exploit their ecological niche, and on the other that they exhibit diverse behavior.

"Soft" Rules: Language and Esthetics

Here is an illustration of diversity-compliance. In order to take part in a conversation I have—at least to some extent—to master the rules of English grammar: I comply with the rules of the language. If I master the rules of grammar I can then exploit them to communicate my thoughts in diverse ways. In principle, I could utter an infinite number of sentences and communicate any content I like. However, if I always repeat the same utterances, such as "we must take embodiment into account," irrespective of what my partner in the conversation says, my behavior would not be very diverse and you would intuitively consider me not very intelligent (alas, the author—Rolf—has been accused of doing exactly that on more than one occasion). The other extreme would be to utter grammatically correct but contentless random sentences. Although random thrashing about can be viewed as diverse action—it is always different—it is intuitively not considered intelligent behavior. Natural language is a nice illustration of the fact that intelligent agents tend to exhibit both diversity and compliance. It demonstrates that enormous diversity can be generated once an agent complies with and exploits the given rules: imagine all that can potentially be expressed in natural language!

Another set of "rules" that humans can comply with and exploit in order to generate new forms of expression is art. You can make scribbles on a piece of paper that presumably no one else on Earth has ever produced or will ever produce again, but people will not find it very interesting unless there is at least some compliance with the—admittedly vague—rules of esthetics. But if you master these rules, you can exploit them to produce pieces that people may possibly like and consider as works of art. The rules of esthetics and the rules of language are social conventions, and we can choose to abandon them. Whether that is a wise thing to do is another issue, but at least we have the option to follow these rules or not, which is why they are called "soft."

"Hard" Rules: The Laws of Physics

The examples so far have been drawn from domains where the rules are not rock-solid but changeable. However, there is at least one set of rules that cannot be modified: the laws of physics. In other words, there is no choice between complying with them and not; there is only a choice as to which laws to exploit in order to achieve a particular purpose. In walking, for example, we exploit gravity and friction, but we do not exploit electromagnetic waves, whereas for seeing we do. In domains such as language and art we can ignore the rules altogether, for example, we can babble incoherently or scribble at random if we so decide; but we cannot stop gravity from exerting a downward force on our body.

So, diversity-compliance implies that systems we intuitively consider to be intelligent tend to comply with a set of laws such as grammar, esthetics, or physics, and to exploit them for a particular purpose. To get a better handle on this abstract concept, let us consider a few more examples. Take a rock in a river: it lies on the ground and is occasionally pushed forward by the water. Its behavior complies with the laws of physics, but it does not exploit these laws for any purpose; it just passively sits there. Also, its behavior is not highly diverse: there are only occasional small, random movements, as a result of the water flow. And, intuitively, none of us would consider a rock to be very intelligent. The same view holds for an atom in a gas: it complies with the laws of physics, and even though its trajectory is much more complicated than the one of the rock in the river, it is still not interesting, because in the same circumstances it will always do the same thing. Once the system we are viewing starts behaving in ways that are not always identical, but also are not random, things get interesting.

Intuitively we are more likely to apply the label "intelligent" to a system if it is equipped with sensory and motor abilities, i.e., if it has agent characteristics, because then it can use its sensors, its body, and its arms, legs, or fins to exploit the environment for different purposes. For example, a swimming robot equipped with light sensors might swim toward a light source, even if that entails swimming against the prevailing current: it does not have to be merely dragged along with the flow of water. Consequently, agents can exploit physical laws in many different ways: friction and gravity for walking, drinking, and writing; fluid dynamics for swimming; electromagnetic forces for seeing; sound propagation and vibration for talking and listening; and so on. The ability of computers, on the other hand, to exploit the environment is very limited, if they can be considered to do so at all. Despite their awesome computational capacities, computers' abilities in this regard are crippled because of their virtually nonexistent sensory and motor systems.

Let us look at another concrete example, one from robotics. This morning, to take a break from writing, the authors visited the "Future Creation Fair" in downtown Tokyo's architectural marvel, the Tokyo International Forum. Our purpose—aside from resting our weary brains—was to watch a demonstration of the currently most technologically advanced humanoid robot in the world, Asimo, developed by the motorbike and car manufacturing giant Honda Corporation. The name of this robot is a tribute to Isaac Asimov, the prolific science fiction writer who explored in great depth the ramifications of future societies in which humans and robots coexist: the recent movie *I, Robot* was inspired by his work. Now how does Asimo "score" in terms of diversity-compliance? It can exhibit several behaviors such as walking over flat ground or up and down stairs, it can wave its hands and dance a bit, it can grasp and carry a package, and it can connect to the Internet. It also exploits physics to some degree, specifically friction and gravity—without these two forces, walking would not be possible. Because Asimo, in contrast to many other robots, has a relatively high behavioral diversity, it is the favorite of the media (and of course, because it looks cool). While behavioral diversity can easily be grasped intuitively, exploitation of the givens is a less well known idea. As we will see in chapter 4, humans not only have much higher behavioral diversity, but they exploit their environments in clever ways, much more so than current robots.

Note that in order to exploit the givens of a particular environment, you need not know that you are doing so. It is we, as observers or scientists, who say that fish exploit fluid dynamics; the fish know nothing about it—at least we think they don't. Similarly, Asimo does not know that it exploits gravity and friction, but still does so. Even we humans may or may not realize that we are exploiting some aspect of a physical (or linguistic or esthetic) law. For example, when writing a poem you may realize that you have just exploited a particularly delicate phrasing to emphasize a subtle point, but have you ever noticed that when you walk, you do not use your muscles to extend your lower leg before placing your foot on the ground, but that gravity does the job for you? Thus, you are exploiting the laws of physics for locomotion, whether you are aware of it or not.

One interesting implication of diversity-compliance is that it forces us to adopt a continuous notion of intelligence rather than viewing it as a binary property (an agent either is intelligent or it is not). First, the exploitation can be more or less sophisticated: e.g., an agent can just be passive like the rock in the river or it can exploit gravity and friction for walking; it can exploit electromagnetic fields for vision and pressure waves for sound processing; and all of these phenomena can be exploited to a greater or lesser degree.

Stability-Flexibility

Diversity-compliance pops up, in various guises, in different areas of science, for example, stability-flexibility in learning theory, Piaget's theory of accommodation-assimilation, and the evolutionary concept of exploration-exploitation.

The preeminent neuroscientist Steven Grossberg, among others, pointed out that in learning, there is a trade-off between stability and flexibility. Both are aspects of his powerful theory of category learning, known as the adaptive resonance theory (ART) (see, e.g., Carpenter and Grossberg, 2002). Through category learning an agent is able to make new distinctions in the real world, for example distinctions between food and nonfood, or in the case of a robot, perhaps making distinctions between the different types of parts to be assembled in a manufacturing plant. Categorization is one of the most fundamental cognitive abilities: if you can't make any distinctions in the real world, you are not going to survive for very long, and a robot unable to categorize things is not going to be very useful.

Let us look at an example of category learning. A child may form certain categories for apples such as Macintosh, Golden Delicious, and Idared, and then encounter a new kind of apple for the first time: Granny

Smith. The question is whether he should extend one of the existing categories, or form a new one. What if the child encounters a very small sour apple? What if he encounters a pear for the first time? Categories, in order to be useful, must a have certain stability, but then they should also be flexible so that the agent can remain adaptive and learn new things.

When we learn, we want the categories that we already know to guide us in interpreting the world; in other words, we want to comply with what we are already familiar with. However we also want to be able to deal with novel kinds of sensory stimulation that we have not experienced before, possibly by creating new categories, thus potentially increasing our behavioral diversity. We can then react differently to different situations.

A closely related idea is the distinction proposed by the famous Swiss psychologist Jean Piaget, who used the terms *accommodation* and *assimilation* for very similar phenomena as the ones described by Grossberg to characterize perception (e.g., Piaget, 1963).

Exploration-Exploitation
Diversity-compliance is not limited to individual agents but applies to entire populations as well. In evolutionary theory, we talk about the exploration-exploitation trade-off: on the one hand we want to benefit from what evolution has already discovered and build on top of it, but on the other we want to keep open the options of developing novel traits. Exploitation implies the improvement of a particular trait, such as the resolution of the eye or the ability to hunt fast-running deer. By contrast, through exploration, novel characteristics can occur. For example, when organisms that had been living in the water, primarily fish, began to colonize the land, gills had to be "abandoned" and lungs "invented." (We use the quotation marks to indicate that evolution is not knowingly doing any abandoning or inventing). We will further explore this trade-off in chapter 6.

In summary, diversity-compliance seems to be a nice way to characterize systems in terms of what we intuitively consider to be intelligent. Also, it provides a continuous, rather than an all-or-none notion of intelligence, and it shows that often no direct comparison of "levels of intelligence" is possible or sensible. For example, if two agents exploit different aspects of their environment for different purposes—pressure waves for talking, electromagnetic waves for reading—a direct comparison of their intelligence level no longer makes sense.

3.3 Frame of Reference

As we have mentioned, agents can exploit physical laws even if they are not aware of them. Intelligence, in this sense, is not so much a property of an agent or of the brain or of evolution, but rather resides in the eye of the beholder, so to speak, who observes the exploitation. This leads us to the next general problem that the study of intelligence raises: the so-called frame-of-reference problem.

The frame-of-reference issue, which is concerned with the perspectives that we can adopt when observing or designing agents, implies that we must be very clear about what we are observing and how we interpret what we observe. The initial inspiration for this line of thought comes from Herb Simon's seminal book *The Sciences of the Artificial*, in which he introduced the anecdote of an ant walking along a beach (Simon, 1976). He argued that from an observer's point of view, the ant describes a complex path because it walks around puddles, rocks, twigs, and pebbles. However, from the point of view of the ant, the mechanisms that bring about this behavior might in fact be quite simple, such as "if obstacle on right then turn left" or "if obstacle on left then turn right," and "go straight." The final path of the ant emerges from its interaction with the environment; in this case, a beach. The ant knows nothing about puddles, pebbles, and twigs but still manages to find its way around quite well (see also Pfeifer and Scheier, 1999).

An Illustration: The "Swiss Robots"

Let us consider the now classic example of the "Swiss robots" in some detail. The Swiss robots are a set of simple robots that were built in the Artificial Intelligence Laboratory at Zurich University in the 1990s by the ethologist Rene te Boekhorst and the engineer Marinus Maris (Maris and te Boekhorst, 1996). Each robot was equipped with two motors, one on the left and one on the right, and two infrared sensors, one front left and one front right (see figure 3.1). Infrared (IR) sensors provide a rough measure of distance to an object by sending out a signal and measuring the intensity of its reflection: the closer the object, the stronger the intensity of the reflection (see figure 3.1c, d). If you now set three or four Swiss robots loose into an arena with randomly distributed Styrofoam cubes, they will eventually shuffle most of the cubes into two or three clusters, with a few pushed against the walls. To an observer it may seem that they are forming clusters, cleaning up, or making free space. But let us look at the world through the "eyes" of a Swiss robot. The robots were

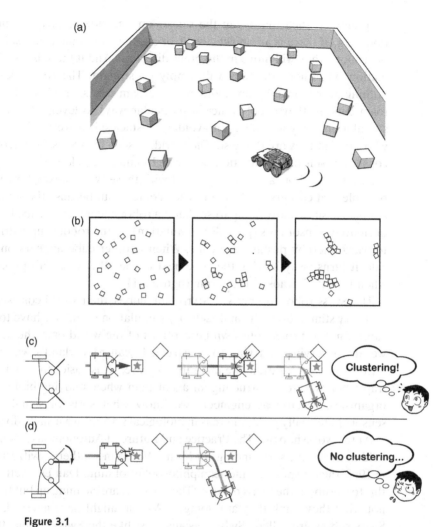

Figure 3.1
Frame of reference: the "Swiss Robots." (*a*) Arena with randomly distributed Styrofoam cubes. (*b*) Sequence of images showing the clustering procedure. (*c*) Schematic explanation of why clustering takes place. The drawing illustrates how two cubes come together. (*d*) Changing the morphology: the front left sensor is moved toward the front of the robot. When encountering a block head-on, instead of pushing the block, the robot will turn away and no clustering takes place. Although the robot's control program has not changed ("turn away if sensor stimulated"), and the environment is also the same, its behavior is different.

programmed such that when the sensor on one side receives stimulation—e.g., if there is an object, a wall, or another robot near that side of the robot—they will move in the other direction. And if there is no stimulation on either side, they will simply go straight. The robots know nothing about cleaning up, avoiding Styrofoam cubes, or what a Styrofoam cube is; they simply react in particular ways to levels of sensory stimulation. They are not even avoiding obstacles: it is we as observers who say that they are doing so. The world, as seen by a Swiss robot, only consists of sensory stimulation on the right and on the left.

But if the robots are only equipped with these two reflexes, how is it possible that clusters are formed? They come about because the sensors are placed sufficiently far apart so that if a robot encounters a cube head-on, neither sensor fires (provides stimulation), so the robot simply drives forward, thereby pushing the cube. When another cube appears on its side, it turns away, leaving the cube next to the other one. This process, when repeated, leads to clustering (figure 3.1).

The Swiss robots do not see Styrofoam cubes; their world consists of "sensory stimulation left" and "sensory stimulation right." We have to be careful not to project our own perceptions of the world onto the agent we are observing or trying to construct. Recall McFarland's warning: "Anthropomorphization, the incurable disease." It is easier to avoid this trap when we are constructing an agent than when studying biological organisms, because as engineers we know what sorts of signals the sensors potentially yield, whereas in biological systems we usually do not.

At the workshop on "The Practice and Future of Autonomous Agents," held in the idyllic surroundings of Monte Verita in southern Switzerland in 1995, the outspoken American philosopher of mind Dan Dennett had this to say about the Swiss robots: "These robots are cleaning up but that's not what they think they are doing!" (As you might have guessed, the Swiss robots are called "Swiss" because just like the Swiss people, they "like" to clean up.) In a sense the roboticists are in the same boat as the Swiss robots. Dennett, in his paper for that workshop (entitled "Cog as a Thought Experiment"), had this to say about the roboticists: "These people are doing philosophy but that's not what they think they are doing!" Dennett, among others, believes that by building these kinds of robots we are, perhaps unintentionally, tackling some of the deep issues in philosophy, such as the notorious mind-body problem.

What can we conclude from the example of the Swiss robots? First, we have to make a clear distinction between the perspective of the designer or observer and the perspective of the robot. From our point of view, the robots are cleaning up; from their point of view they are reacting to sensory stimulation. This is the so-called perspectives issue of the frame-of-reference problem.

Second, behavior in animals and robots cannot be reduced to internal mechanism alone. Behavior is the result of an agent interacting with the real world, which includes not only the agent's neural system but also its entire body: how the sensors are distributed, the material properties of the muscle-tendon system and the joints, and so on. This collection of interdependent mechanisms is referred to as the agent's embodiment. Therefore, behavior cannot be reduced to the control program. To do so would constitute what philosophers call a category error, because two different conceptual categories—internal mechanism (the control program) and observed behavior (requiring the interaction of a physical system with its environment)—are mistakenly considered to be directly comparable. In other words, we cannot predict the robot's behavior based solely on our knowledge of its control program: we also have to take into account its embodiment and the environment. The frame of reference also has strong implications when we turn to building, not merely analyzing, robots. It is no longer sufficient to just program the robot in order to achieve some behavior: both its physical makeup and its control program must be engineered, and the environment must be kept in mind as well. For example, the sensors of the Swiss robots had to be placed farther apart than the length of a Styrofoam cube for the clustering to come about. This is the "behavior versus mechanism" issue.

The third message we can take away from this example is that seemingly complex behavior can result from very simple neural mechanisms or simple control programs. This is called the complexity issue. We do not want to overstate the sophistication of the behavior of the Swiss robots: moving blocks into clusters does not, after all, require university-level education. Still, the behavior is, from an observer's perspective, nontrivial and leads to interesting results. Simon's ant on the beach is another case in point.

The Quadruped Puppy

Although the case of the Swiss robots is fascinating and instructive, they are wheeled robots with only a very few degrees of freedom, i.e., they can only move in a very limited number of ways. So, let us look at a more recent robot with more degrees of freedom, the quadruped Puppy developed by the young and gifted engineer Fumiya Iida, working in the same Zurich laboratory (see figure 3.2). Developing a running robot is still considered a very hard problem in robotics. As we will explain in

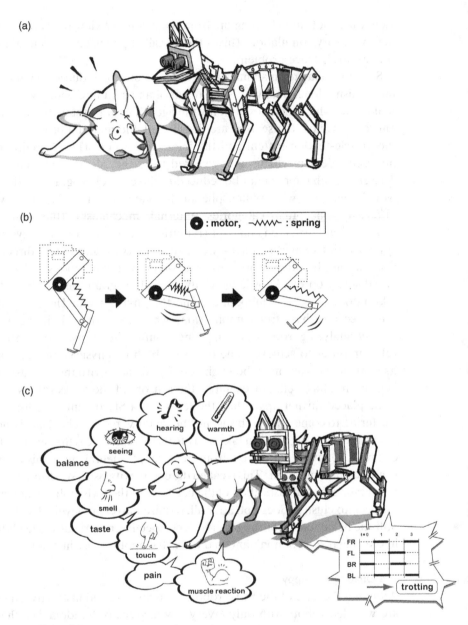

Figure 3.2
The four-legged robot Puppy. (a) Picture of the robot with the animal that inspired its construction. (b) A dog relies on the elastic properties of its muscle-tendon system for rapid locomotion; Puppy relies on springs in its legs. (c) Sensor modalities of the real dog and the robot. Although Puppy generates only very little sensory stimulation compared to the real dog, this is a starting point for showing how a robot can create grounded symbols. There is also a frame-of-reference issue here: to an observer, the outside world is rich in detail; to the robot, the world consists only of patterns gleaned from the pressure sensors in its feet.

more detail later, Puppy, like the Swiss Robots, has a very simple design (see, e.g., Iida and Pfeifer, 2004). However, in spite of this simple design, or rather *because* of this simple design, its behavior is amazingly lifelike and stable. Puppy has a total of 12 joints, four at the shoulder and hips, four at each knee, and four at each ankle. In addition there are a number of springs connecting the lower and upper parts of each leg (for more detail, see chapters 4 and 5). There are also pressure sensors on the bottom of the feet that indicate when a foot is touching the ground. The control is very simple: the "shoulder" and "hip" joints are moved back and forth in a periodic movement. When the robot is placed on the ground and begins moving, it scrabbles at the floor, but after a few oscillations it settles in to a rather smooth running gait. This is the result of the interaction between its oscillatory movements, the robot's morphology (i.e., its shape and the springs attached), the friction on the feet, and gravity. The running behavior is entirely in the head of the observer: Puppy only knows about the pressure patterns on its feet, which are its sole means of connecting to the outside world (see figure 3.2c).

Like the action of the Swiss robots, the running behavior of Puppy cannot be reduced to or explained by its control mechanisms alone. The simple oscillatory movements programmed into the robot lead to running behavior only if its embodiment is right, i.e., if the controller is embedded into a physical system with exactly the right kind of morphology. Also, Puppy's behavior from the point of view of an external observer is relatively sophisticated and complex compared to the simple underlying mechanisms that generate it.

Having said all that, it should be noted that the opposite can also occur in certain situations: behavior that looks very simple to an outside observer might in fact require complex underlying processes. For example, moving your hand in a straight line necessitates much more neural control than swinging it around your body. Also, aspects of human visual perception, such as recognizing an object, seem to occur without effort, but in fact perception is a sophisticated system requiring the co-ordination of many sensory and motor mechanisms.

Clearly, the frame-of-reference issue raises a lot of questions about intelligence. We will encounter many examples throughout the book.

3.4 The Synthetic Methodology

As we have already mentioned, artificial intelligence does not yet have a well-established methodology. And, unlike the classical scientific disciplines, artificial intelligence has a definite engineering flavor: we are concerned not only with analyzing natural phenomena, but also with building artificial systems. Recall the three research goals we outlined earlier: (1) understanding natural forms of intelligence, i.e., biological systems such as animals and humans; (2) abstracting general principles of intelligent behavior that hold not only for biological systems but for behaving systems in general; and (3) building intelligent artifacts. These three goals are united by the synthetic methodology. The synthetic methodology that we briefly introduced in chapter 1 can be characterized by the slogan "understanding by building." If we are interested in how desert ants find their way back to their nest, or how humans walk or recognize a face in a crowd, we build a system—an artifact—that mimics certain aspects of the behavior we wish to study (figure 3.3). This way of proceeding has proved enormously powerful: because you have to build something that actually works in the real world, there is no way of glossing over details, which is possible when you formulate a theory abstractly.

An early example illustration of the synthetic methodology is computer vision. Forty years ago, the approach to building a machine that can "see" was, roughly speaking, to hook a camera up to pattern recognition software. The software was given the images taken from the camera in order to perform classification tasks or to build internal representations of what could be detected in the image. It soon became clear that this could not possibly be how perception works: it turned out to be difficult to deal with the problem that in the real world objects appear at varying distances, lighting conditions, and orientations, and that they are often partially hidden from view, a problem that humans deal with easily. Obviously, for perception in the real world, something else was required: mapping a camera image onto an internal representation by a process of pattern matching could not be easily achieved. Active vision, the paradigm that emerged in the 1980s where the cameras can be moved depending on the sensory stimulation (i.e., depending on the camera image itself), represented a major advance and a significant step toward more realistic perceptual systems. (It should be noted that the traditional approach to computer vision, even though it turned out not to resemble natural perception, has led to a host of useful applications.) Throughout the book we will provide many examples of the synthetic methodology.

The synthetic methodology lies at the heart of artificial intelligence. Many researchers have been inspired by the neuroscientist Valentino Braitenberg's delightful, slim book *Vehicles* (1984), which carries the telling subtitle "Experiments in Synthetic Psychology." Braitenberg

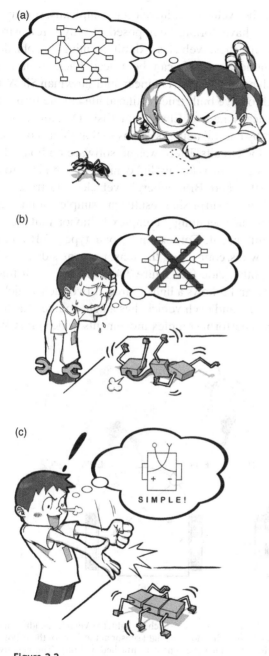

Figure 3.3
The synthetic methodology: scientist trying to understand ant behavior. (*a*) Directly mapping observed behavior onto an internal representation. (*b*) Using this representation to control walking in a robot fails. (*c*) Applying a much simpler model—resembling a Braitenberg architecture (figure 3.4)—to control walking in a robot. This latter, simpler model seems more plausible as an explanation of the originally observed behavior.

presents a series of robot vehicles of increasing complexity, starting with very simple ones that have "brains" composed of only a few wires. In spite of their simplicity, these vehicles exhibit seemingly sophisticated behavior. The synthetic approach can be traced back even farther, though, to the British neuroscientist, engineer, and showman Sir W. Grey Walter, who claimed to have built true "artificial life" in the form of two turtle robots, whimsically named Elmer and Elsie (Walter, 1950). His robots were inspired by natural neural systems so that their "controllers" were realized as analog circuits. There was no software on board Elmer or Elsie: the view of cognition as (symbolic) computation had yet to arise.

Grey Walter's turtles and Braitenberg's vehicles illustrate a very important and at first quite surprising result: very simple "brains," in the right context, can produce seemingly complex behavior that we might even want to call intelligent. For example, one type of Braitenberg vehicle contains two wires, connecting the sensor on one side of its body to the motor on the other side (see figure 3.4), with the result that the vehicle moves toward and follows a light source. If two such vehicles are placed near each other—and each vehicle has a light source attached on top of it—the vehicles perform complex movements, which Grey Walter

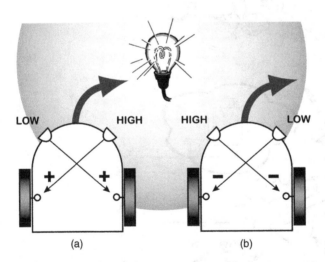

Figure 3.4
Simple Braitenberg vehicles. (a) Vehicle approaching light. (b) Vehicle avoiding light. The positive connections indicate that the more the light sensor at the front of the robot is stimulated, the faster the wheel to which the sensor is attached will turn. The negative connections indicate that the more the sensor is stimulated, the slower the wheel will turn. So, depending on the sign of its connections a robot will either turn toward or away from the light.

himself rather provocatively described as reminiscent of mating dances or territorial aggression (Walter, 1950).

Since then, a long legacy of robots with simple controllers that nonetheless exhibit complex behaviors have been created: the Swiss robots have already been described; Craig Reynolds's "boids" (1987), a group of simulated birds endowed with only three simple rules that allowed them to fly in a "flock" (this algorithm has since been used in movies such as *Jurassic Park*, *The Lion King*, and the *Lord of the Rings* trilogy; see chapter 7); the tag-playing cubic-inch-sized swarmbots built by the young innovator James McLurkin (see chapter 7); Kismet, a humanoid robot that engages users in simple social interactions using a set of reflexes (see chapter 4); and many others, some of which will be described in later chapters.

Because seemingly complex and sophisticated behaviors can emerge from simple rules we suspect that there might be correspondingly simple neural circuits involved in producing behavior in natural organisms. Perhaps we will find that intelligence emerges in any agent, be it natural or artificial, in which a host of relatively simple neural circuits, mediated by the agent's morphology, give rise to increasingly complex behaviors. The results of such explorations could tell us a lot about ourselves, but the idea that we as human beings may be nothing more than a collection of reflexes is a frightening prospect for many. But more on that in the final chapter of the book.

Often, when using the synthetic methodology, we start with a behavior of interest—such as the way that people recognize a face in a crowd, or an ant gets back to the nest after finding food, or a human infant learns to make distinctions in the real world, or a dog catches a Frisbee at a full run—and then derive a model of it by building a computer simulation or a real physical robot. Our experience has been that in doing this we learn an awful lot about the natural system of interest. While biologists might be satisfied with such a model, as researchers in artificial intelligence we want to go one step further: we aim to find general principles of behavior because we are interested not only in natural forms of intelligence, but in intelligence in general. This goal is based on our belief, which is shared by many in the field, that intelligence is not only a characteristic of biological agents, but could arise in artificial ones like robots as well. With our theory and the many examples that we develop in this book, we hope to persuade the reader that this is indeed a reasonable and productive assumption. Still, many individuals—laypeople and researchers alike—are convinced that only systems built from biological, carbon-based stuff can ever be truly intelligent, whatever that may mean.

Let us take this idea of general, nonbiological intelligence a little further. When we try to understand intelligence, or other lifelike processes like reproduction or self-organization, as something not limited to biological systems, we have more freedom as investigators. This idea was summed up by the founder of the field of artificial life, Chris Langton, one researcher among many who hope to understand life as a general, not just a carbon-based, phenomenon. According to Langton, "life as it is," as we know it from biology, is only a specific instance of the much broader class of possible life forms, and we should study "life as it could be." This puts the engineers in a far better position than biologists, because all biologists can do is study existing systems, whereas engineers have the opportunity to create entirely new ones. At the same time, genetic technology is empowering biologists to actually design and build biological systems previously unknown to nature—but the materials they use are still the familiar ones: DNA, proteins, organic molecules, and so on.

Although building artificial yet lifelike agents is certainly very challenging, we can gain interesting insights by making simple and concrete experiments. For example, building artificial muscles with characteristics different from natural muscles, rather than just trying to build precise replicas of natural muscles, may help us to learn more about the dynamics of walking in general. Furthermore, perhaps we can eventually produce artificial muscles superior to natural muscles. Biological muscle tires easily, it is relatively weak when it is almost fully stretched or contracted, and has other limitations. Finally, because we can potentially build virtually anything we like, we can systematically explore the larger space of intelligent (and not so intelligent) agents, which will help us to nail down just those characteristics that contribute to intelligence and those that do not.

3.5   Time Perspectives

The next component in our theoretical framework for a good research methodology concerns the time scales. A comprehensive explanation of the behavior of any system must incorporate three perspectives, which span increasingly longer periods of time: (a) state-oriented, the "here and now," which relates to the actual mechanism, i.e., how something works, (b) learning and development, the ontogenetic view, and (c) evolutionary, the phylogenetic perspective (see figure 3.5). The "here-and-now"

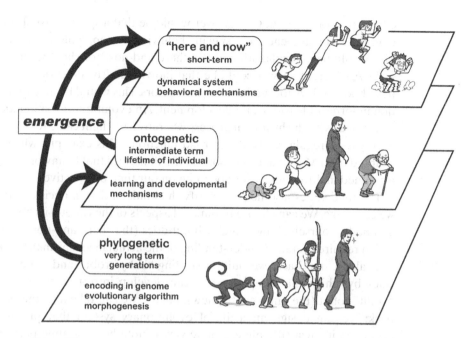

Figure 3.5
Time scales and emergence. Three time scales must be taken into account when designing or analyzing an intelligent agent: "here and now," ontogenetic, and phylogenetic. If it can be shown that a mechanism observed in one time scale, e.g., "here and now", emerges from another, e.g., the ontogenetic one, this allows us to better understand the observed mechanism.

perspective is about what is currently happening; the ontogenetic perspective spans the lifetime of an individual; and the evolutionary perspective extends over several generations of a population of agents. Note that adopting these perspectives by no means implies that they are separate. On the contrary, processes that occur at one level often affect the other two. For example, hitting your thumb with a hammer teaches you how to better handle it in the future, i.e., "here and now" affects development. Learning affects what you will do in future situations, i.e., development affects the "here and now." And the evolution of hand morphology changes what an organism can do with its hand, i.e., evolution affects the "here and now." However, teasing apart these three perspectives for the purpose of scientific investigation is useful, as we will see later. This distinction, which serves as a guide for understanding and designing intelligence, has its origin in biology (e.g., Huxley, 1942; Tinbergen, 1963).

Often there is more than one way to answer the question, "Why is an agent doing what it is doing?" For example, we ask why drivers stop their cars at red traffic lights. One answer would be that a specific visual stimulus, the red light, leads to a specific behavior like applying the brakes. This would be an explanation at the "here-and-now" or short-term time scale. A different answer could be that individual drivers learn this rule from books, television, and driving instructors. This would be an explanation in terms of learning and development. An evolutionary explanation would deal with the historical process whereby a red light came to be used as a way of regulating traffic at road junctions. This example, which is adapted from Martin and Bateson (1993), illustrates that behavior can be explained in different ways, depending on our time perspective.

The time scales also help us clarify the kinds of design decisions that we can make. We can choose to build all aspects of the robot—its "brain" and body—ourselves and watch what it does (the "here-and-now" view, which requires detailed understanding of the actual mechanisms). Or, we can take a step back: we build a starting "baby" robot and define the rules by which that simpler agent can develop into a more complex "adult" robot (the ontogenetic view). Finally, we can take a further step back: we can design an artificial evolutionary system that produces agents on its own (the phylogenetic view). Note how the time perspectives help us, as designers, to influence the design either very directly, as in the "here-and-now" position; or by letting emergence play an increasing role as in the ontogenetic and phylogenetic stance, an idea that will be elaborated in the chapters on development (chapter 5) and evolution (chapter 6). "Here-and-now" behaviors emerge from development (learning), and both learning and "here-and-now" behaviors emerge from evolution. Another important reason for separating the three time scales is that the mechanisms and principles that hold for each of them are different. Evolutionary processes that are based on mutation and selection are different from ontogenetic ones that deal with growth and learning. In the "here-and-now" perspective, the mechanisms and principles concern very directly how a particular behavior comes about: how, for example, are the visual stimuli encountered at an intersection transformed such that I apply the brakes?

Assume that we want to understand how the desert ant *Cataglyphis* finds its way back to the nest. We can build a robot that implements the snapshot model, in which the ant takes a photographic image of its environment as it leaves the nest, stores it, and uses it to orient itself when it returns to the area near the nest. This approach models the mechanism of navigation itself, and thus adopts the "here-and-now" perspective. The biorobotics researcher Verena Hafner and colleagues have asked whether the snapshot model might actually be learned as an agent interacts with its environment, or whether it is a behavior that is "hard-wired" into the agent at birth. Indeed, what the antlike robots in her experiments seem to learn is something very similar to the snapshot model. In this sense, the "here-and-now" process is emergent from the particular learning mechanism as the robots interact with the environment (Hafner and Möller, 2001). These experiments—like most learning experiments at the ontogenetic time scale—assume a fixed morphology and allow only the control architecture to change. For example, it is assumed that the shape of the eye is fixed by the designer (e.g., *Cataglyphis* and the robots used by Hafner and Möller can see in all directions). This path of exploration could be extended by evolving agents in which the properties of the eyes or, even better, other aspects of the brain and body change over phylogenetic time during evolution: would agents with eyes different from *Cataglyphis* still learn the snapshot model? Although this issue has not been studied yet, it has already been shown that it is possible to evolve eye morphologies on a real robot (Lichtensteiger and Salomon 2000), as we will see in the next chapter.

3.6 Emergence

As we have just seen, the time perspectives are directly related to the concept of emergence. For example, if we can say that a phenomenon at one time scale emerges from another, longer time scale, we have made progress in understanding the phenomenon: in other words, we can describe not just how the process works but how it was formed, and why. Thanks to Hafner and Möller's experiments, which have demonstrated that the snapshot model ("here and now") can be learned, we now have a better understanding of the conditions under which the snapshot model will arise. In a similar way, showing how a particular learning mechanism emerges from an evolutionary process implies a scientific advance in understanding learning.

Types of Emergence

Generally speaking, *emergence* designates behavior that has not been explicitly programmed into a system or agent. We distinguish between three types of emergence: (1) global phenomena arising from collective behavior, (2) individual behavior resulting from an agent's interaction with the environment, and (3) emergence of behavior from one time scale to another. The formation of ant trails is an example of the first type. The ants themselves know nothing about the fact that they are forming a trail that will develop into the shortest connection to a food source (see chapter 2). This is emergence from collective behavior and will be further discussed and illustrated in chapter 7. In Braitenberg's vehicles, light-following behavior emerges because the robot has two wires connecting its sensors to its motors in a particular way, and there is a light source in its environment. This is emergence of behavior resulting from an interaction with the environment. Finally, there is emergence with respect to the time scales, as discussed above.

The term *emergence* has both very positive and very negative connotations depending on who you talk to. For the researchers working in the field of artificial intelligence or artificial life, emergence is not only a good thing, but the very thing to strive for. The critics—and this includes cognitivists, i.e., those still adhering to the classical symbol-processing paradigm, but also more conservative scientists in other fields as well as journalists—tend to poke fun at the idea of emergence: whenever a phenomenon is surprising, and you do not understand it, call it emergent! Obviously, merely labeling a phenomenon as emergent has no explanatory value whatsoever. However, if a phenomenon can be explained as emergent from simpler processes, this constitutes an explanation and a deeper level of understanding. For example, we can understand the mating dance of Grey Walter's robot turtles much better once we know how they react to light, and showing that the snapshot model for navigation emerges from a learning process in different environments corroborates its generality. By watching how one process or characteristic of an agent emerges from processes acting over a longer time scale, we can learn not only about the process itself but about how and in what situations it arises. For example, when using evolutionary algorithms to automatically design agents for locomotion, we can study what morphologies and neural systems develop depending on the environment (e.g., land or water). Or if it can be shown that robots evolved for light-seeking behavior will have a Braitenberg-like architecture, we will say that a Braitenberg-like architecture is emergent from an evolutionary process, because the light-seeking mechanism is not explicitly programmed into the system (see chapter 6). Finally, if we can show that the evolved agents follow the design principles to be discussed in the next chapter, this adds validity to the principles themselves.

Design for Emergence

Before we conclude this chapter let us briefly raise the point of how emergence and design go together. Once we have the behavioral rules of a system, e.g., how ants drop chemical signals and have a tendency to move in the direction of high pheromone concentration, or how the infrared sensors on the Swiss robots are positioned and how they react to sensory stimulation, it is straightforward to find out about the emergent behaviors of a system by simply running it. There is no mystery about emergence and we can give a perfectly rational explanation of how the Swiss robots form the clusters. But we are often asked how we came up with the design of the Swiss robots in the first place. It is by no means obvious that if you want to have robots that form clusters you should design them for obstacle avoidance! So, given a certain desired behavior, devising the rules that will lead to the desired behavior is more difficult than explaining the behavior if the system is run—i.e., if the agent interacts with its environment. This is called *design for emergence* (e.g., Steels, 1991), and it is still an open question how this can be done systematically. At the moment, design for emergence is an art rather than a hard-core engineering discipline. Because of the fact that behavior itself cannot be preprogrammed but is always the result of an agent-environment interaction, we must design for emergence rather than directly for a specific behavior. In some cases this is simpler than in others, but it is still a difficult process. We will try, throughout the course of this book, to provide evidence that the design principles for intelligent systems can help.

To conclude, let us raise an additional point of interest. One area in which design for emergence has turned out to be astonishingly simple is artificial evolution. In some experiments, fantastically complex behaviors and structures have emerged from relatively simple evolutionary systems. Using the concept of emergence, in particular using artificial evolution, we may be able to automatically design systems that are more complex than what we could design by hand. In fact, our examples will suggest that this is indeed the case. Perhaps the evolutionary roboticist Inman Harvey of the University of Sussex is right when he proclaims, "Design is out, evolution is in!" Maybe if we want to create really complex systems, human design is on the way out and we will have to use tools such as artificial evolution. We have to keep in mind, however, that using evolution for design often makes it difficult for us to understand the results: as an extreme example, the human brain is a complex structure produced by evolution, and we have an extremely hard time trying to understand it! It may turn out that even evolving robots will not be sufficient for producing a comprehensive understanding of intelligence, because we will end up with complex intelligent artifacts whose behavior we cannot figure out.

3.7 Summary

In this chapter we have tried to come to grips with the challenging problem of what a theory of intelligence might look like, and we proposed that a set of design principles, complemented by a general framework in the form of a number of meta-principles, would be suitable. As we pointed out, these principles can be used in an analytic way for understanding, and in a synthetic way for building. We then outlined the general framework for our theory. Diversity-compliance characterizes the class of phenomena that the theory is about: agents have to comply with and exploit their ecological niches while exhibiting diverse behavior. The notorious frame-of-reference issue reminds us about what we are referring to: processes going on in our head as observers or designers, in the "head" of the agent, or in the agent's interaction with the environment. The synthetic methodology, "understanding by building," tries to understand natural phenomena by modeling aspects of the natural system in simulation or on a robot. Designing artificial agents and analyzing biological ones can be done at three time scales: the "here and now," the developmental, and the evolutionary scale. A comprehensive explanation of intelligent behavior always requires all three. We identified three types of emergence: arising in the individual, in groups of agents, and from the time scales. Powerful explanations often refer to emergence, where a process at one time scale can be shown to emerge from a process at a longer time scale, e.g., a "here-and-now" action that emerges from a developmental or learning process. Because behavior is always emergent, we always must design for emergence. While it is easy to understand emergence once we have the basic rules that determine a behavior, it is not easy to come up with the rules that will lead to a particular desired behavior. But in the case of artificial evolution it seems to be the other way around: it is easy to design the underlying rules of the evolutionary algorithms, but it is hard to understand how complex structures and behaviors emerge from them. Before we get to evolution and development, we will explore the properties and principles of intelligent agents themselves, in the next chapter.

4   Intelligent Systems: Properties and Principles

In the 1960s, the Japanese psychologist Masanao Toda proposed to study hypothetical creatures he called "Fungus Eaters" as a fun way to think about intelligence, an alternative to the traditional methods of academic psychology. Fungus Eaters are artificial creatures that are sent to a distant planet to collect uranium ore. Because they have to collect ore, they must be physical systems, i.e., they must be embodied—a computer simulation simply wouldn't do. Also, since there are no people on this planet, the Fungus Eaters have to be autonomous—i.e., independent of human control; they should be self-sufficient, which means that they should be able to take care of themselves over extended periods of time, and they must to be situated, i.e., they have to be able to learn about the environment through their own sensory systems. These hypothetical creatures are called Fungus Eaters because they feed on a particular type of fungus that grows on the planet. The planet is so far away that they cannot be remote controlled because the signals take too long to travel between Earth and the planet. By comparison, NASA's engineers wanted to maintain as much control as possible over the Mars Sojourner, because apparently they did not fully trust its autonomous operating abilities. As a compromise, the robot was extremely slow; it traveled only a few meters per day, adding up to a little over 100 meters in three months. Sojourner's replacements, the twin Mars exploration rovers Spirit and Opportunity, can travel more than 100 meters per day (very speedy compared to Sojourner), but the target locations to which they have to move are still commanded from Earth. Toda's Fungus Eaters illustrate the many challenges facing a complete agent: it must fend for itself, deal with unforeseen situations, create its own objectives, and forage for energy, among other things. In traditional artificial intelligence, on the other hand, agents were much more limited and did not have to deal with all of the difficulties of the real world.

Toda further argued—and many psychologists would probably agree with him—that in laboratory studies people are often tested on tasks that are not only somewhat artificial but also unusually difficult for humans: subjects are asked, for example, to remember long lists of numbers or to read text upside down. Toda stressed that if we are to learn something relevant about intelligence—something that holds true in real-world behavior—we need to study *complete* systems, i.e., systems that have to act and perform tasks autonomously in the real world (Toda, 1982). While Toda's Fungus Eaters provide a rough intuition about the sorts of systems we are interested in, we will make the notion of complete agents more precise in this chapter.

In the previous chapter we outlined what a theory of intelligence should look like, and we discussed some of the general theoretical considerations in the study of intelligent systems: diversity-compliance, frame of reference, the synthetic methodology, time scales, and emergence. But we have not yet said much about how to actually design real agents when applying the synthetic methodology; we will do so in this chapter. The agents we are interested in designing are complete creatures—Fungus Eaters, so to speak—endowed with everything needed to behave in the real world, which obviously implies that they have to be embodied and situated, autonomous, and self-sufficient. All of the robots that we discuss in this book are autonomous in the simple sense that they are not directly controlled by a human. Of course, their level of autonomy is still very limited because they depend on humans for their energy supply, for maintenance, and to be placed in their proper task environment. Clearly, like intelligence, autonomy is not an all-or-none property; an agent may be controllable to a greater or lesser extent by another agent. There is a long-running philosophical debate about the concept of autonomy and how it relates to intelligence, but we will not go into that debate here; the interested reader is referred to Pfeifer and Scheier, 1999.

In this chapter we will briefly describe what we mean by the "real world," and contrast it to virtual ones. Then we will discuss the properties of embodied agents and describe what happens when they interact with the real world. Finally, we will introduce the basic set of design principles.

4.1 Real Worlds and Virtual Worlds

This book is about embodied agents that have to function in the real world. The real world has properties very different from those that characterize virtual or formal worlds, and intelligent agents have to be able to deal with the physical world if they are to survive or function in it for an extended period of time. Moreover, unlike virtual worlds, the real world challenges an agent in various ways. First, because real-world agents are embodied, acquisition of information always takes time: if I want to know who is in the room next door, I have to go there and look, call them, or ask someone.

Second, the information that an agent can acquire about the real world is always very limited: we can only see what is in the range of our visual field or hear the sounds that reach our ears. Thus we can never have complete information. This situation is different from a formal game like chess, where knowledge of the board position constitutes all the information about the state of the game, assuming that the strategies of the players are not part of the game proper. Moreover, it is not clear what "complete information" in the real world would mean in the first place: would it imply that an agent must have knowledge about the state of all the atoms in the universe? This is clearly an absurd idea. One way of summarizing information about a part of the real world is to make an abstract model of it. For example, we can characterize a lecture hall by specifying the number of students in it, the temperature, the light settings, and whether the projector is on or off, which for many purposes will be entirely sufficient. But such a model abstracts away most of the potential information available: it does not contain anything about the students' blood flow or their thoughts about the quality of the lecture.

Third, physical devices are always subject to disturbances and malfunctions, and since sensors are physical devices, the information acquired through them will always contain errors. From these considerations it follows that since knowledge about the real world is always very limited, it is therefore intrinsically uncertain and only predictable to a limited extent: For example, if it's noisy you may not hear the car that is approaching you from behind because of the physical limitations of your ears: they only deliver the summed noise, so that you may not pick out the sound of the car. Note that this point holds irrespective of the speed and accuracy of the agent's sensors: even if we have an ultra-high-resolution camera, if it suddenly gets dark, the images it delivers will be blurred and noisy. The uncertainty and limited predictably of information collected from the real world is a principle that holds for any agent.

Fourth, the real world is not characterized by clearly defined, discrete states: the weather is never simply good or bad, but rather sunny, cloudy, misty, rainy, windy, or dull, all to greater or lesser extents. Because there are no discrete states, there are therefore no clearly defined actions that can be executed when the world is in a particular state: it is a good idea to take your umbrella with you when it is raining outside, but what if it is only cloudy, or raining a little bit, or perhaps likely to rain later? This lack of definable states is different from formal worlds like chess, where there are uniquely prescribed board positions—a piece either is or is not occupying a square—and for every board position there is a finite set of possible moves from which a player has to choose.

Fifth, agents in the real world always have several things to do simultaneously: animals have to eat and drink, but they also have to take care that they are not eaten by predators, they have to build nests, clean themselves, breathe, fight off infection, reproduce, and care for their offspring. Similarly, robots which have to function in the real world always have many tasks to perform in parallel. For example, a robot designed to serve coffee to employees in an office has to keep itself functioning, recharge its batteries, avoid breaking or bumping into things, and not harm humans, all while it is serving coffee. In contrast, in the formal world of chess there is only one thing to do: make one move at a time in order to win the game.

Sixth, because the real world has its own dynamics—things out in the world happen even if we do not do anything—there is always time pressure due to ongoing change. Thus agents are always forced to act, whether they want to or not. In many formal settings an agent can take as long as needed to decide which action to take. And finally, related to this point, the real world is a highly complex dynamical system, making it intrinsically unpredictable because of its nonlinear nature and its sensitivity to initial conditions (see focus box 4.1). (Herbert Simon has coined the term *bounded rationality* to designate, in essence, decisions that have to be taken under such circumstances [Simon, 1976, 1969]).

To summarize before continuing, the real world requires time to extract information from it, and extraction is always partial and error-prone; it is not neatly divisible into discrete states; it requires agents operating in it to do several things at once; and finally the real world changes of its own accord, not only in response to agent action. So, the real world is challenging and "messy." Clearly, there are several constraints that a physical agent faces as a result of being in the real world: there are certain things it simply cannot do, such as extract noise-free information instantaneously from the environment. In the next section we will describe how these constraints place certain hard limitations on real-world agents, but also provide them with opportunities. These

Focus Box 4.1
Dynamical Systems

There is a vast literature on dynamical systems, and although at a high level there is general agreement on the basic concepts, a closer look reveals that there is still a considerable diversity of ideas. We will use the terms *dynamical systems*, *chaos*, *nonlinear dynamics*, and *complex systems* synonymously to designate this broad research field, although there are appreciable differences implied by each of these terms. Our purpose here is to provide a very short, informal overview of the basic notions that we need for the book. Although we do not employ the actual mathematical theory, we will make use of the concepts from dynamical systems theory because they provide a highly intuitive set of metaphors for thinking about physically embodied agents and groups of agents.

A dynamical system in the real world is one that changes according to certain laws: examples include the quadruped robot Puppy, human beings, economical systems, the weather, a swinging pendulum, or a society of monkeys. Dynamical systems can be modeled using differential equations (or their discrete analogs, difference equations). The mathematical theory of dynamical systems investigates how the variables in these equations change over time: for example the angles of Puppy's joints can be used as variables in a set of differential equations that describe, mathematically, how the robot moves. However, to keep matters simple, we will not use differential equations in this book.

The dynamical systems we look at here are nonlinear because interesting systems in the real world are typically nonlinear. One of the implications of nonlinearity is that we can no longer, as we can with linear systems, decompose the systems into subsystems, solve each subsystem individually, and then reassemble them to give the complete solution. In real life, this principle fails miserably: if you listen to two of your favorite songs at the same time, you don't double your pleasure! (We owe this example to Strogatz, 1994.) Similarly, we cannot understand the motion of one of Puppy's legs without considering how it is affected by the other three. In other words, the system must always be treated as a whole (see the complete-agent principle). Another important property of nonlinear systems is their *sensitivity to initial conditions*: if the same system is run twice using very similar initial states, after a short period of time, they may be in completely different states. This is also in contrast to linear systems, in which two systems started similarly will behave similarly. The weather is a famous example of a nonlinear system—small changes may have enormous effects—which is what makes weather forecasting so hard.

The *phase space* of a system is the space of all possible values of its important variables. For Puppy we could, for example, choose the joint angles as important variables and characterize its movement by the way the angles change over time. If there are two joints per leg, this yields an eight-dimensional phase space: each point in phase space represents a set of values for all eight joints. (Alternatively, we could use the contact sensors on the feet only, a different and simpler way of defining the phase space, which would then be only four-dimensional). Neighboring points in phase space represent similar values of the joint angles. As Puppy runs, the joint angles change continuously. Thus we can say that these changes are analogous to the way the point in phase space (the values of all joint angles at a particular moment) moves over time. The path of this point in phase space, i.e., the values of all these joint angles over time, is called the *trajectory* of the system.

An *attractor state* is a preferred state in phase space toward which the system will spontaneously move if it is within its *basin of attraction*. There are four types of attractors: point, periodic, quasi-periodic, and chaotic. Physical systems, such as Puppy, by their very nature as physical systems, have attractor states. It is important to realize that the attractors will always depend on the way the actuators are driven and on the environmental conditions.

Focus Box 4.1
(continued)

If Puppy runs and settles into a particular gait, the joint angles, after a short period of time (less than 1 sec), will more or less repeat, which means that the trajectory will return to roughly the same location as before: the values of the joint angles will be very similar to what they were in the previous cycle. This cyclic behavior is known as a *periodic attractor*, or, because the angles in the real world never exactly repeat, a *quasi-periodic attractor*. Puppy's different gaits correspond to different (quasi-) periodic attractors: this is illustrated by figure 4.2. If Puppy falls over and stops moving, then its joint angles no longer change over time, and the trajectory in the phase space remains at a single point: such points are called—not surprisingly—*point attractors*. Finally, if the trajectory moves within a bounded region in the phase space but is unpredictable, this region is called a *chaotic attractor*. Systems tend to fall into one of their attractors over time: the sum of all of the trajectories that lead into an attractor is known as the *basin of attraction*. Attractors—and this is relevant for our ideas on emergence of cognition (see chapter 5)—are discretely identifiable entities within a continuous system: Puppy's joint angles change smoothly over time, but we can reliably tell whether Puppy is walking, running, or standing still.

Again, there is a frame-of-reference problem here. How do you know the system is in an attractor state? And how does the agent itself know it? So, you need to provide some way of measuring the system's change over time: for example, if you are interested in locomotion, you can measure joint angles using sensors (as in the example given), or you can put pressure sensors on the feet. On the basis of these measurements, the robot (or the researcher) can then detect its attractor states and may change its actuation pattern: changing the frequency of actuation and the phase difference between front and hind legs (e.g., when the front legs start stretching, the hind legs may start bending), alters the dynamics and thus the system might transition into another attractor state, such as from walking to running. While the notion of an attractor is powerful and has intuitive appeal, it is clear that transitions between attractor states are equally important, e.g., for generating sequences of behavior.

Attractors, together with the transitions between them, reflect in some sense the natural dynamics of the system, in our case the agent. If the agent is driven by an oscillator (to generate periodic motion), the complete system will, depending on the frequency, settle into a (quasi-periodic) attractor state whose period is emergent from the coupling of the neural and the physical system yet different from the period dictated by the oscillator. This phenomenon is known as *mutual entrainment*: the resulting frequency will represent a "compromise" between the systems involved (see also our discussion of Sten Grillner's experiments on the Lamprey in chapter 5).

For those who would like to know more about the mathematical foundations of dynamical systems we recommend Strogatz (1994), and for those interested in its application to cognition, Port and van Gelder (1995) and Beer (2003).

limitations and opportunities can be described as a set of properties that all complete agents share.

4.2 Properties of Complete Agents

Here are the most important properties of complete agents that follow from their embodied nature:

1. *They are subject to the laws of physics* (energy dissipation, friction, gravity).

2. *They generate sensory stimulation* through motion and generally through interaction with the real world.

3. *They affect the environment* through behavior.

4. *They are complex dynamical systems* which, when they interact with the environment, have *attractor states*.

5. *They perform morphological computation.*

The interesting point here is that these properties are simply unavoidable consequences of embodiment. These are also the properties that can be exploited for generating behavior, and how this can be done is specified in the design principles. Before we go on to the design principles, let us briefly clarify each of these properties.

1. *A complete agent is subject to the laws of physics.* Walking requires energy, friction, and gravity in order to work. Because the agent is embodied, it is a physical system (biological or not) and thus subject to the laws of physics from which it cannot possibly escape; it must comply with them (see also our discussion of compliance in chapter 3). If an agent jumps up in the air, gravity will inevitably pull it back to the ground.

2. *A complete agent generates sensory stimulation.* When we walk, we generate sensory stimulation, whether we like it or not: when we move, objects seem to flow past us (this is known as optic flow); by moving we induce wind that we then sense with our skin and our hair; walking also produces pressure patterns on our feet; and we can feel the regular flexing and relaxing of our muscles as our legs move.

3. *A complete agent affects its environment.* When we walk across a lawn, the grass is crushed underfoot; when we breathe, we blow air into the environment; when we walk and burn energy, we heat the environment; when we drink from a cup, we reduce the amount of liquid in the glass; when we drop a cup it breaks; when we talk we put pressure waves

out into the air; when we sit down in a chair it squeaks and the cushion is squashed.

4. *Agents tend to settle into attractor states.* Agents are dynamical systems, and as such they have a tendency to settle into so-called attractor states. Horses, for example, can walk, trot, canter, and gallop, and we—or at least experts—can clearly identify when the horse is in one of these walking modes, or gaits, the more technical word for these behaviors. These gaits can be viewed as attractor states. The horse is always in one of these states, except for short periods of time when it transitions between two of them, for example from canter to gallop. We should point out here that the attractor states into which an agent settles are always the result of the interaction of three systems: the agent's body, its brain (or control system), and its environment. Because the concept of dynamical systems and attractor states is important for our arguments, we will elaborate it a bit more by returning to the case study of Puppy, the four-legged running robot that we introduced in chapter 3 (see also focus box 4.1 and chapter 5).

5. *Complete agents perform morphological computation.* By "morphological computation" we mean[1] that certain processes are performed by the body that otherwise would have to be performed by the brain (see figure 4.1). An example is the fact that the human leg's muscles and tendons are elastic so that the knee, when the leg impacts the ground while running, performs small adaptive movements without neural control. The control is supplied by the muscle-tendon system itself, which is part of the morphology of the agent.

It is interesting to note that systems that are not complete, in the sense of the word used here, hardly ever possess all of these properties. For example, a vision system consisting of a fixed camera and a desktop computer does not generate sensory stimulation because it cannot produce behavior, and it influences the environment only by emitting heat and light from the computer screen. Moreover, it does not perform morphological computation and does not have physical attractor states that could be useful to the system.

The Quadruped Robot Puppy as a Dynamical System

In what follows we will use the robot Puppy to illustrate how cognition might emerge from the simple, basic actions of walking or running. We have tried to capture this idea of going from locomotion to cognition with the phrase "bootstrapping cognition from the bottom up," in order

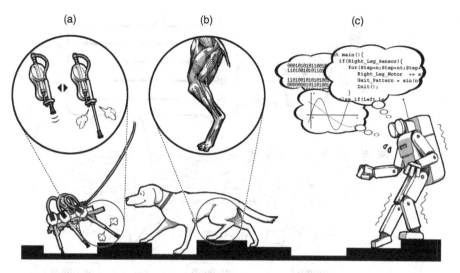

Figure 4.1
Morphological computation. (*a*) Sprawl robot exploiting the material properties of its legs for rapid locomotion. The elasticity in the linear joint provided by the air pressure system allows for automatic adaptivity of locomotion over uneven ground, thus reducing the need for computation. (*b*) An animal exploiting the material properties of its legs (the elasticity of its muscle-tendon system) thus also reducing computation. (*c*) A robot built from stiff materials must apply complex control to adjust to uneven ground and will therefore be very slow.

to distinguish it from the goal of traditional AI, which was to somehow program "thinking" directly into a computer.

We mentioned that running is considered a hard problem in robotics. Running by definition includes a certain time when all legs are off the ground, which is known as the flight phase; the stance phase refers to the rest of the time, when one or more feet are on the ground. Figure 3.2 shows some of the details of Puppy's morphology. Continuing our description from chapter 3, there are two springs attached to each leg, inspired by the muscle-tendon systems in four-legged animals. Also, there is a strong elastic metal blade that can bend up and down, providing the robot with a spine that is flexible, although somewhat different in design from the segmental spines of animals or the humanoid robot Kenta (Japanese for "tendon boy"; we will come back to Kenta in chapter 5). The springs and blade give Puppy a more dynamic and organic feel compared to most other robots, which are tightly engineered and move rigidly using complex control programs and strong motors: this aspect of traditional robotics is parodied by a dance called the Robot that was popular in the 1970s and the 1980s, which required the dancer to hold

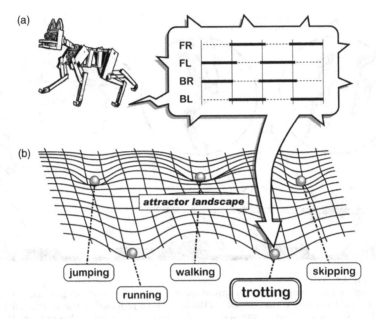

Figure 4.2
Attractor states. (*a*) Different gait patterns for Puppy as recorded from pressure sensors on the feet: the dark lines in the graph indicate when a foot is touching the ground; the dotted lines indicate when it is not. These gait patterns correspond to attractor states of the joint physical/neural system. (*b*) The same gait patterns shown in the "attractor landscape." The gait patterns correspond to minimum energy basins in the attractor landscape.

his body rigid and produce a disconnected series of localized, discrete movements.

The body, the legs and the feet are built from aluminum, which implies that on most surfaces the feet will slip a little. This slippage turns out to be an important factor in stabilizing the robot when it is running: if we increase the friction by putting rubber pads on the feet, the robot has a strong tendency to fall over. All Puppy's controller does is move the legs back and forth in a periodic manner. When the robot is put on the ground it will, after a few steps, settle into a natural running rhythm: the robot's interaction with the environment causes a particular gait pattern to emerge (see figure 4.2). For example, all four feet occasionally leave the ground together for a short period of time, causing the robot to exhibit alternating flight phases and stance phases.

In the Puppy experiment, the speed at which the robot runs cannot be varied arbitrarily, even though the speed of the motors can: within certain ranges, the robot moves erratically or even falls over, but within others, stable gaits emerge. A few observations about Puppy's behavior are in order here. First, the number of stable gaits for any given system is limited: a legged robot (or animal, for that matter) has certain preferred speeds corresponding to those gaits. Second, because the gaits are attractor states that the robot "falls into" based on its motor speeds, morphology, and environment, the robot will resettle into an attractor after it has been perturbed slightly. For example when the robot moves from smooth to rough terrain it may struggle a bit, but when it re-enters an environment with smooth terrain it will settle back into its original gait. However if the perturbation is too big, the robot will change behavior and settle into a new attractor: it may fall over and come to rest, or fall on its side and kick itself around in a circle (Mimicking the infamous stage antics of Angus Young, lead guitarist for the rock band AC/DC), or switch from running to walking. If the perturbation is not too large, the system will move back into the original attractor state, as we mentioned before. This region of states is called a *basin of attraction*. The important point here is that this falling back into a natural gait—or falling into a new one, for that matter—does not have to be controlled by a program running on the robot's microprocessor but arises naturally as a result of the usual suspects: the robot's morphology and environment. And third, related to this point, some gaits are more stable than others, i.e., they have a larger basin of attraction.

One of the big differences between a legged and a wheeled robot is that wheeled robots can typically move at any speed, and they can speed up and slow down continuously. In other words, there are no preferred patterns of motion or speeds that are clearly distinct from others, except perhaps for stopping. Legged robots and animals, by contrast, do have preferred speeds, corresponding to the different types of gaits: walking very quickly or jogging very slowly often feels uncomfortable for us, and we tend to want to slow down or speed up. Wheeled robots, like legged robots, can also have attractor states, but because of their simpler dynamics, the attractor states are less interesting and their number is much smaller. For example, a light-seeking Braitenberg-style vehicle moves toward a light source by performing a kind of "wiggling" behavior: the robot always turns in the direction of its most stimulated light sensor, which then causes the opposing sensor to face the light and become more stimulated, causing the robot to turn back, and so forth. This behavior might be called an attractor state of the robot. In any case, it will not have many of them. The point here is that all physical systems, because they are physical, will have attractor states, but those with complex morphologies have more (Kauffman, 1993). Therefore, although so far we have restricted ourselves to simple robots, in the future we want to work with more complex ones that have a large number of attractor states. It is important to have many, because attractor states may ultimately become the building blocks for cognition, as we will see in detail later on. For now, it is sufficient to think of the connection between attractor states and cognition by adapting an ancient metaphor: the wider you build the base (the more attractor states there are), the higher you can build your tower (the richer are the possibilities for combining attractor states). In the next chapter we will explore how attractor states can be used to form the basis of a kind of symbol-processing system.

To summarize the discussion so far, complete agents must comply with the laws of physics; they generate sensory stimulation when they act; they perform morphological computation—bodies can perform functions that would otherwise have to be performed by brains—and finally, complete agents are dynamical systems and their behaviors can be viewed as attractors. Also, because unlike formal systems, the real world is messy, so to speak, we cannot expect a clean, axiomatic theory or a set of principles that logically follow from one another. So the set of design principles that we will present is not a formal system, but a tightly inter-dependent set of design heuristics that on the one hand provide guidance on how to go about building agents, and on the other characterize the nature of intelligent systems. There is partial overlap and a certain level of redundancy among the principles, but this is not undesirable: they support one another because of this overlap. Moreover, all the design principles apply to all agents, to a greater or lesser degree. Finally, the individual principles should always be viewed in the context of the other principles: they form an interdependent set and should not be considered in isolation.

Let us now go through the agent design principles one by one.

4.3 Agent Design Principle 1: The Three-Constituents Principle

Designing an intelligent agent involves the following constituents: (1) definition of the ecological niche, (2) definition of the desired behaviors and tasks, and (3) design of the agent.

Intelligence, as we have said, is not a property of an agent, nor is it a "thing" that resides in a box inside an agent's brain, but rather it arises from the interactions of an agent with its physical and social environment. Thus, when designing an agent it is not sufficient to focus on the agent itself, but we also have to think about the ecological niche in which it is to function, as well as what the agent is supposed to do.

The three-constituents principle can be summarized as follows. Designing an intelligent agent involves the following constituents: (1) definition of the ecological niche, (2) definition of the desired behaviors and tasks, and (3) design of the agent itself. The first two constituents are often collectively referred to as the task environment. The ecological niche, in the case of robots, is always a physical and social environment: for entertainment robots the niche encompasses children's homes, including other people, the siblings, the parents, friends, and pets. In this chapter we focus on the physical aspects of the task environment, and in the next we consider the social aspect.

Design Stances

If we design a robot to entertain children, it will have to function in people's homes and should behave so that it achieves the desired goal: keeping kids amused over extended periods of time. Finding the kinds of properties and behaviors that the robot should have in order to achieve this goal has turned out to be a formidable challenge. Cute robots like Sony's AIBO (the Artificial Intelligence roBOt, which in Japanese also means something like "buddy"), Omron's NeCoRo (a cat robot covered with fur), or NEC's PaPeRo (Partner-type Personal Robot) that, to some extent, can respond to sentences uttered by a human partner are popular examples of this particular species of robot. More straightforward examples are robots for mowing lawns or assembling motorbikes on an assembly line in a factory: in these cases the ecological niche and the desired behaviors can be more clearly defined.

In the design of such robots, the ecological niche—people's homes, backyards, factory environments—and the desired behaviors and tasks are taken as given, and the agent is designed such that in its interaction with the environment, the desired behaviors emerge and the robot achieves its tasks. But there are two additional versions of the design task. The second alternative is to take a given robot, put it into an ecological niche, and observe what sorts of behaviors appear. And the third, given the robot and the desired behaviors, is to look for the niches in which it will in fact function properly. We will give examples of some "design stances" in this chapter and in chapter 9 when discussing business applications of the design principles.

Recall from our discussion about frame of reference and about Puppy's gaits that behavior always emerges from the agent-environment interaction and cannot be directly programmed into the robot. Therefore robot behaviors can only be indirectly designed: to use the term introduced in the last chapter, we have to design for emergence. If we want to make a robot walk, we have to account for adaptivity: it has to be able to deal with uneven ground, slopes, walking over loose material, walking while carrying something, and so on. It becomes impossible to preprogram all the different varieties of walking needed for the near-infinite variety of agent-environment interactions that the robot will encounter in the real world. More simply, if the walking movements are entirely preprogrammed, the robot will fall over whenever something unanticipated—something not programmed into the robot—arises. Indeed, many walking robots do fall over when they encounter uneven ground.

The relationship between an agent and its ecological niche is complex; so, let us briefly discuss some of the implications. First, the ecological niche of a robot is not simply the environments in which it can operate successfully: as in biology, there is always competition for resources. Entertainment robots have to compete not only with other entertainment robots, but also with toys, pets, and humans. Ultimately, the market will decide which (if any) entertainment robots get to share this niche with the occupants (toys, pets, and humans). If on the other hand we are interested in explaining the behavior of natural systems we can start from a particular set of behaviors that we observe, try to identify the ecological niche, and then ask how the behaviors come about. The orientation behavior of desert ants that we already discussed is a case in point. Their highly specialized sensors enable them to navigate over large areas in relatively featureless terrain. Recognizing the characteristics of their unique ecological niche—the desert—has helped biologists to better investigate and understand their behavior.

We can also turn the design problem around. If we already have an agent designed for a particular ecological niche, such as the AIBO robot designed for entertainment, we can drop it into a different ecological niche and ask what kinds of behavior will emerge. A company with a robot already on the market might look for additional ecological niches in which the robot will display its desirable behaviors and achieve its tasks, and thus widen its consumer base. For example, in addition to homes, AIBO might in fact also be useful in schools, thereby serving as an educational tool.

There is yet another way in which we can look at the design problem. Often engineers—the clever ones—design the agent and its ecological niche at the same time because in this way much better solutions can be achieved. The global positioning system or GPS is a great example of this idea. Putting satellites into the sky largely solves the navigation problem on Earth once and for all, at least outdoors; robots that need to orient can be made much simpler because they don't require sophisticated navigation strategies, but only a sensory system for tuning into the GPS signals!

Scaffolding

Scaffolding describes the way in which we, and other agents, structure our environments to simplify our tasks. In the GPS example, having many satellites in orbit makes the lives of robots—and of many car drivers—much easier. Another example is the use of road signs: if signage is done properly, the driver needs absolutely no geographical knowledge and can easily arrive at the target location by simply following the signs. Thus with adequate scaffolding, the mechanisms required for successful navigation will be very cheap, so to speak: there is no need to plan the route or consult a map. This exemplifies the principle of cheap design, which we will shortly discuss. Information and communication technology provides powerful scaffolding, leveraging our intellectual abilities far beyond those of our ancestors two thousand years ago, even though our brains have not grown in the meantime. Bioinformatics, which is the combination of new scientific instruments, database and networking technology, and pattern detection and modeling algorithms, has provided the "scaffold" which enabled the research community to sequence the human genome.

Aside from technology, language is another extremely potent means of scaffolding: because our knowledge can be written up in books, and thus communicated, we are now able to perform tasks that before the existence of written language would simply not have been possible. Now we can build on top of what has already been established and written down: the ideas in one text rely (directly or indirectly) on those in other texts, and so on. The World Wide Web, stuffed as it is with text, images, sound and video, has simply made this web of ideas more explicit and much more easily accessible. Natural language and information technology are among the most powerful scaffolding tools around, a point that is elaborated in the engaging book by the British philosopher Andy Clark, *Natural-Born Cyborgs*.

Recall how embodied agents always affect their environment when they act: as the "Swiss robots" make their clusters, they also make free space to move around in. But manipulating the environment to serve one's purposes can be found everywhere: we take notes, we write documents and books, we type things into computers, we use sticky-note pads, we store phone numbers in our mobile phones, we put information on bulletin boards, we take pictures and videos, and we put up Web pages. Given the obvious usefulness of changing the environment to simplify our lives—that is, of scaffolding our environment—it is truly surprising that most robots do not significantly change their environments to make their tasks easier! Thus, scaffolding is an important part of the three-constituents principle, because it requires consideration of the agent's niche, what tasks it is to perform, and how it should be designed.

4.4   Agent Design Principle 2: The Complete-Agent Principle

The complete agent principle states that when designing agents we must think about the complete agent behaving in the real world.

This principle contrasts with the paradigm of "divide and conquer" that pervades virtually all scientific disciplines: decompose a problem or system into simple subsystems which can then be developed separately. Once the subsystems have been designed, they can then be put together again. But it often turns out that in practice, subsystems create unnecessary problems, known as artifacts, which would not exist if the system were taken into account in its entirety. A good example of this comes from the field of computer vision, where it seemed obvious at the outset that vision could be understood as a separate process from the rest of the agent's behaviors. Computer vision thus focused almost exclusively on the analysis of static photographic pictures, such as desks cluttered with objects. Highly sophisticated and computationally intensive algorithms were developed to "understand" the images by identifying and categorizing the object in the image. However, vision turns out to be much easier when the agent interacts with the environment. In other words, we should treat vision as an interactive process, not just a set of operations performed on a set of static images. If you move your head back and forth, objects that move more quickly over your visual field are closer to you than objects that move less; if one object blocks your view of another object, you can simply walk to another location and look again. Simple. Having a body and being able to act in the world simplifies vision—and many other things as well, as we will see. This insight helps us when building agents, but it is also useful in trying to understand existing agents, like ourselves.

Here is another example drawn from the related research area of perception, in which researchers in the cognitive sciences, psychology, and neuroscience try to figure out how individuals can interpret sensory stimulation in the real world. It has been demonstrated in many experiments that the function of a particular part of the brain can be very different depending on whether the agent—typically an animal—is studied as it behaves in the real world, or the particular subsystem, in this case the vision system, is studied in isolation. In what would eventually lead to a Nobel Prize in 1981, the neuroscientists David Hubel and Torsten Wiesel conducted a famous experiment in the late 1950s in which they inserted a microelectrode into individual cells in the visual cortex of an anesthetized cat. They then presented the immobilized animal with different kinds of visual stimuli while recording the signals from these cells. One of their fascinating results was that some cells did not respond to light intensity but rather to orientation of edges. In other words, some of these cells would respond only if the left of the visual scene was light and the right was dark (or vice versa), while others would respond only if the top was light and the bottom dark, and so on. It seemed natural to conclude from this that some neurons in the cat's visual cortex act as edge detectors. Later, when experiments with moving cats became technologically possible, it was found that these cells were in fact involved in many other activities as well (Haenny et al., 1988). Although it is correct to say that there is a correlation of the activity of these so-called edge-detection cells and the presentation of the visual stimuli containing the edges, it cannot be said that they are edge-detection modules, because they are involved in other behaviors as well. We are not criticizing Hubel and Wiesel's groundbreaking experiments but merely pointing out that these neurons cannot be considered basic modules from which the complete system could be assembled. The results still hold: they only need to be reinterpreted.

Often, it turns out that viewing only part of an agent when explaining its behavior causes us to attribute more "brainpower" to it than may actually be there. In other words, by considering the entire agent we can often find other, simpler mechanisms for achieving the behavior. So the complete agent principle is related to the principle of cheap design that we will discuss next: given the right body for the job, and keeping the agent's behavior and environment in mind, agents can get away with less computational hardware. Remember the navigation behavior of the desert ant *Cataglyphis*? It has been shown in many experiments that the ant can use landmarks to find the precise location of the nest when it returns from a foraging trip. In these experiments, the landmarks are typically large black cylinders that are placed around the nest. In order for the landmarks to be useful, the ant has to recognize them first, then make a decision in which direction to move; at least that is what we would think should happen. Recognizing landmarks is a difficult task that would require a perceptual system potentially entailing a lot of computation, as we explained in the computer vision example. However, as described in chapter 2, the ants take a kind of "snapshot" of the surroundings as they leave the nest. When they come back near the nest, they simply compare the stored snapshot with what they currently see—the current sensory stimulation—and they move in the direction that will further reduce the difference between the two. When the two fully match, the ant is precisely at the location of the nest. At this point, we can say that the ant has recognized the landmarks, but the "recognition" is fully integrated into the behavior of the ant, and we cannot separate "finding the nest" from "recognizing the landmarks." This implies on the one hand that there are not two separate modules for these tasks, and on the other that by looking at the behavior of the complete agent, rather than at the perceptual subtask only, we can see that the solution is much "cheaper," from the perspective of the agent's design (for more details see Lambrinos et al., 2000).

Furthermore, when observing complete agents behaving in the real world, we are less prone to modularize our systems inappropriately: in the previous example, two incorrect modules that we could have proposed to explain the ants' behavior are "find the nest" and "recognize landmarks." Psychology has as its research topic the most complex known system in the universe, the human. In order to come to grips with the awesome complexities involved, researchers in this field carve up the human psyche in particular ways for the purpose of investigation, for example into cognition, perception, categorization, memory, attention, social interaction, learning, development, motivation and emotion, motor action, problem solving and reasoning, planning, creativity, communication, language, awareness, and consciousness, to mention but a few. Separate fields within psychology are devoted to the study of many of these areas. If we look at the complete agent and ask what processes underlie behaviors such as walking, talking, or recognizing a face in a crowd, we see immediately that these subdisciplines do not so much correspond to actual "modules" but are in fact different perspectives on the same (or at least largely overlapping) set of processes. For example, learning makes no sense without perception, and memory makes no sense without learning. Planning can only be performed on the basis of perception and memory, and so on.

Moreover, when studying complete agents, we always have to deal with complete sensory-motor loops. If we follow this principle we will never be in danger of decoupling certain aspects—such as the planning of movements—from the sensory system, as is usually done in classical robotics. In 1999, I (Rolf) was a guest in a research laboratory of a large car manufacturer in Germany, where, for the first time in my life, I was served coffee by a robot. It was a great experience: the robot went over to a table, grabbed a cup, moved over to the coffee machine, deposited the cup, pushed the button, waited for the cup to be filled, moved over to my chair, and handed me the cup. I was impressed. But in fact it was not actually as smooth as all that: motion planning had been developed separately from the rest of the agent, which led to a few problems. For example, while performing the planned movement, at the time (I am sure this has changed meanwhile) the robot received no sensory feedback from the environment. As a result, the robot grasped the cup in a slightly different way from how it was supposed to, causing the cup to bend and almost break the tube where the coffee came out of the machine. In a complete-agent approach, one is forced to always take the complete sensory-motor loops into account: if the robot had been able to sense the way it grasped the cup or the strain the cup was placing on the coffee dispenser, this particular problem would have been avoided. This also illustrates the principle of sensory-motor coordination, described below.

In summary, the complete agent principle has important implications both for how we study agents, as in psychology and neuroscience, and for how we design and build them, as in robotics. This principle also emphasizes that in a complete agent, everything is tightly interconnected.

4.5 Agent Design Principle 3: Cheap Design

The principle of cheap design states that if agents are built to exploit the properties of the ecological niche and the characteristics of the interaction with the environment, their design and construction will be much easier, or "cheaper."

Recall for a moment our discussion of what we intuitively mean by intelligence. We suggested that the concept is related to compliance and diversity. Agents that comply with and exploit their ecological niche in order to generate diverse behavior are intuitively considered more intelligent. We have to comply with the givens: there is no way in which we can ignore the fact that there is gravity on Earth; or rather, to ignore it will generally not be very beneficial to the organism. If I step off a roof-terrace, I will fall, whether I like it or not. But this is not always a negative thing: the laws of physics can also be exploited in smart ways. It is worth distinguishing here between two closely related aspects of exploiting the ecological niche: the properties of the niche, which includes the laws of physics, gravity, friction, electromagnetic forces; and the properties of the interaction with the environment, such as the sensory stimulation generated as an agent moves. The principle of cheap design simply states that if agents are built to exploit these kinds of properties, their design and construction will be much easier. So cheap design is about exploitation of the properties of a niche, and the term *cheap* should not be taken too literally. However, it is indeed often the case that if the principle is applied properly, the resulting agents will be cheap in the literal sense of the word: if they are simple, they will be inexpensive to design, manufacture, and maintain. The related design principle of ecological balance (described below) helps us to figure out *how* this exploitation should be done; cheap design simply illustrates *that* the more and better the exploitation, the simpler agent it will be.

We are now going to illustrate these points with a few examples: the Swiss robots that we have already introduced; the "passive dynamic walker," a "brainless" and nonmotorized robot capable of walking down a slope without control, and its successor, "Denise," which has a little bit of brain mass and some actuation; and finally we will look at how insects can coordinate their legs when they are walking even though there is no center in their brain that actually manages the synchronization of the movements. We introduce these examples in the context of the cheap design principle, but it should be kept in mind that all of the design principles apply to all agents to a greater or lesser extent.

The Swiss Robots

Recall the case study of the Swiss robots that we introduced in the previous chapter where the task was to design robots that together tidy up an arena cluttered with Styrofoam cubes. (This is admittedly not the most glamorous of tasks, but it is definitely related to one of the reasons we want robots in the first place!) Intuitively we would think that the following steps have to be taken. First, the robot has to find a cube. Once it has found one it has to look for the nearest heap or cluster. Then it has to move and deposit the cube there, and the procedure is repeated until all the cubes are clustered. These steps all require sophisticated visual processing and planning, and would thus be computationally expensive, so to speak. Remember that just because visual perception is natural and effortless for us humans by no means implies that it is a simple process.

The Swiss robots take an alternative approach: they master the job by exploiting their own morphology and the properties of the ecological niche. Remember that in fact they achieve the task by being programmed only with simple reflexes for obstacle avoidance. In order for the clustering to come about, the following aspects of the ecological niche had to be exploited: the size of the cubes (if they are too big or too small it does not work), their weight (if cubes were too heavy for pushing, it would no longer work), the fact that the environment is enclosed by surrounding walls (otherwise, the robots would drive away, rather than cleaning up), the fact that the ground is flat and provides, together with the tires of the wheels, the right kind of friction (if you put soap on the ground, it will no longer work). If any of these constraints do not hold, the Swiss robots will miserably fail to achieve their task. But if they are fulfilled, this solution works very well, and it is cheap: the Swiss robots exploit the properties of their niche, the laws of physics, and their own morphology in clever ways, so that computationally expensive vision is not required. The Swiss robots do not need to know what they are doing; they merely react to sensory stimulation.

The Passive Dynamic Walker and "Denise"

The passive dynamic walker, illustrated in figure 4.3b, is a type of robot (or, more accurately, a mechanical device, since it has no sensors or motors and no control program) that was first proposed by McGeer (1990). It is capable of walking down a ramp without any sensing, actuation, or control: in other words, it is literally brainless, if you like. In this sense, it is not really an agent. Nonetheless, in order for this task to be achieved, the dynamics of the robot—how gravity, friction, and the forces generated by the swinging of the legs and arms act on it—must be exploited. The result of this exploitation is that the walking behavior is very energy efficient and looks surprisingly natural.

However, its ecological niche, i.e., the environment in which the robot is capable of operating, is extremely narrow: it consists only of slopes of certain angles. Just as in the case of the Swiss robots, if you change anything whatsoever in the ecological niche, such as the angle of inclination or the surface properties (e.g., by putting a soft rug on it), the device will no longer work. The fact that an agent will cease to function if some aspect of its niche (specifically some aspect that the agent exploits) is

(a)

(b)

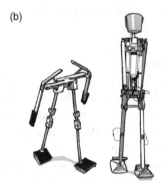

Figure 4.3
Passive dynamic walkers. (*a*) The patron saints of the city of Zurich in Switzerland: Felix, Regula, and Exuperantius. They were beheaded in the third century because of their religious beliefs. The legend says that they carried their heads under their arms to a spot where later the Grossmünster church, the symbol of Zurich, was built. Legend? No, passive dynamic walkers! (*b*) The "classical" passive dynamic walker by Steve Collins that walks down a declined ramp with no actuation (left), together with the 3D biped robot "Denise" by Martijn Wisse (right). Denise is a hybrid passive dynamic walker: its ankle and knee joints swing passively, while a motor drives the hips to induce walking over flat ground.

changed is an unavoidable trade-off of the principle of cheap design. Energy efficiency is achieved because the leg movements are entirely passive, driven only by gravity in a pendulum-like manner. To make this work, a lot of attention was devoted to morphology and materials. For example, the robot is equipped with wide feet of a particular shape, elastic heels, and counterswinging arms that all help it to walk in this way (Collins et al., 2001).

Loosely speaking, we can also say that the neural processing normally required for controlling walking is taken over by the proper morphology and the right materials, and thus is another instance of morphological computation. In fact, the neural control for this robot reduces to zero. But, if anything is changed, e.g., the angle of the incline, the agent ceases to function—the price of cheap design.

Because the fully passive dynamic walker exploits many properties of its ecological niche, it is entirely dependent on that niche. But the ecological niche can be widened if we augment the agent's capabilities: by adding motors, adding some control, and modifying the morphology of a passive dynamic walker we enable the robot to walk over flat terrain. This has been achieved by the team led by Martijn Wisse, a highly creative young engineer at the Technical University of Delft, in Holland, who was also involved in the development of the passive dynamic walker at Cornell University. He recently created "Denise" (figure 4.3b), an almost completely passive dynamic walker, by augmenting the earlier model with some actuation, adding two electrical motors to move the legs. Its walking behavior (or should we say "her" walking behavior?) is actually quite natural, presumably because it exploits the passive forward swing of the leg.

One might be inclined to say that cheap design only works for very simple systems, and admittedly the examples we have given so far are all indeed very simple. But look at humans for a moment. When we walk, the forward swing of our legs is—like "Denise's"—mostly passive, i.e., the muscles are passive and the leg swings forward like a pendulum, thereby exploiting gravity. Our legs are complex indeed, with their bones, joints, tendons, ligaments, muscles, nerve cells, and skin, but complexity does not preclude exploitation. In this sense we can say that we ourselves as humans, even though we are incredibly complex, are "cheaply" designed. It will certainly be interesting to see whether Wisse's approach to robot walking will scale up to even more complex systems, in particular complex humanoid robots, or whether alternative approaches will have to be employed.

Even though the passive dynamic walker is an artificial system (and a very simple one at that), it has a very natural feel. The term "natural" applies not only to biological systems but to artificial ones as well: perhaps the natural feel comes from the exploitation of the dynamics, e.g., the passive swing of the leg (for an elaboration on this point see Pfeifer and Glatzeder, 2004).

Leg Coordination in Insect Walking

The first two examples were drawn from robotics, so let us now look at one from biology: leg coordination in insect walking. It has been known for a long time that leg movements in insects are controlled by largely independent controllers (von Holst, 1943), in other words, there seems to be no center in the brain that coordinates the legs in walking. But if there is no such coordination center, how then can insects walk in the first place, and how does leg coordination come about? And the legs do need to be coordinated, otherwise walking is not possible. A couple of years ago the radical thinker and trendsetting German biologist Holk Cruse, who has been studying insect walking for many years, cracked the conundrum. It turns out that the trick these insects use is to exploit their interaction with the environment (Cruse, 1990). Assume that the insect stands on the ground and then, in order to move forward, pushes backward with one of its legs. As a result, the joint angles of all the legs standing on the ground will instantaneously be changed. The body is pushed forward, and consequently the other legs are also pulled forward and the joints will be bent or stretched. This is one of those unavoidable repercussions of being an embodied agent, and the insect can do nothing about it. However, and this is Cruse's fascinating finding, this fact can be exploited to the animal's advantage. All that is needed is angle sensors in the joints—and they do exist—for measuring the change, and there is global communication between the legs! But the communication is through the interaction with the environment, not through neural connections.

So, the local neural leg controllers need only exploit this global communication. There is an additional benefit of all this. Because the insect is moving forward, the angles of the other legs are all moving in the right direction—information that, in addition to being free, i.e., available without computation—is extremely useful and can be directly exploited for controlling the individual legs. This is not trivial, but Cruse and his colleagues have worked out a neural network architecture that does the job (Dürr et al., 2003). And this architecture, the WalkNet, can also be used to control six-legged robots.

This is another beautiful instance of cheap design: if the insect had to do everything through computation, it would be more costly and much slower. This is also an instance of morphological computation: part of the task that would have to be done by the brain—the communication between the legs and the calculation of the angles on all the joints—is performed by the interaction with the real world.

The principle of cheap design is very general because it only states that the ecological niche can be exploited to simplify the agent, but does not tell us *how* the exploitation should be accomplished or what dynamics should be exploited. Other design principles such as ecological balance, redundancy, and sensory-motor coordination are more specific and more about the *how*. But cheap design can be applied to more specific issues, such as the design of the visual system—a field that is becoming known as "cheap vision." The literature on vision is full of examples of how an ecological niche and specific interactions with the environment can be exploited. An instructive and entertaining example, the "Eyebot" robot, is discussed later in this chapter.

To conclude the discussion of cheap design let us briefly mention some examples that do not conform to this principle, in order to clarify it a bit. A laptop computer, as explained before, does not exploit the environment in interesting ways, and neither does a humanoid robot in which the movements required for walking are largely "programmed into" the robot. Famous humanoids like Asimo, Qrio, or HRP (from the Japanese Humanoid Robotics Program) are largely preprogrammed, and there is no substantial exploitation of their system-environment interaction (yet).

4.6 Agent Design Principle 4: Redundancy

The redundancy principle states that intelligent agents must be designed in such a way that (a) their different subsystems function on the basis of different physical processes, and (b) there is partial overlap of functionality between the different subsystems.

The redundancy principle is geared toward designing robust systems, i.e., systems that continue to function even if there are significant changes in the environment. The term *redundancy* has a long history and is used in many different ways, and so, once again, rather than trying to come up with a definition we introduce the term intuitively using a number of examples.

Visual and Haptic Systems in Humans

The term *modality* is often used in the literature to designate different sensory channels: we talk about the visual, the haptic, or the auditory modality. The visual system, or visual modality, provides us with precise spatial information that enables us to move around very quickly because we can see where to go and where obstacles and desired objects are. Because this visual information is so extremely valuable, many species have evolved, one way or another, visual systems. But what if it suddenly gets dark? Vision, alas, only works in the presence of light. But all is not lost: we can resort to other sensory modalities; we can still hear and feel. Although we can extract some spatial information from our auditory system—we can roughly hear where a sound is coming from—it is much less precise than what we get from the visual system. But from our sense of touch—also called the haptic system—we can get very precise spatial information: we can feel with our hands and fingers, and it is relatively easy to identify an object. Moreover, we often consider touch to be more reliable than what we observe with our eyes: sometimes we have to touch things because we do not fully trust what we see. One of the authors of this book (Josh) learned this lesson the hard way: when a guest at a party, it is best to reach out with your hand when crossing from the house into the backyard so as not to blunder headfirst through a hard-to-see screen door and thereby turn yourself into the focus of the party.

While touch is good at short distances, it is not very efficient in the long range. For walking around, it can be used as long as we go slowly, because unlike the visual system it requires physical contact. All this is common sense, of course, but the essential point is that even if we have to slow down, we can still function because we can rely on a different set of sensors appropriate to the new situation. The reason this works is that the two systems are based on different physical processes: the visual one on stimulation by electromagnetic waves, and the haptic one on mechanical pressure. Nevertheless, the two modalities yield partially overlapping information: the information extracted from one can be used to—at least partially—predict the information that can be extracted from the other. If you see a glass of beer on the table with condensation on the outside you already know more or less what it will feel like when you touch it. The information contained in both sensory channels is technically referred to as mutual information and plays an important role in building concepts: the concept of a glass of beer e.g., includes not only information extracted from the visual system but information from the haptic and the taste systems as well.

The Meaning of Redundancy

Because the information extracted from one sensory system includes some information that can also be extracted from another, this phenomenon is called redundancy. The term *redundancy* is actually a tricky one because it depends very much on the point of view we are adopting and it has many different interpretations. Sometimes redundancy is taken to mean duplication of components, or the part of a message that can be deleted without essential loss of information.

Natural language is a good example of this latter interpretation of the word. We can understand others even if there is a lot of noise in the environment and we physically hear only part of the message, or when the sentences are grammatically wrong and some words are missing. If we ask someone how they are and they reply with either "I'm feeling better, thanks," or simply a mumbled "better," the same message is conveyed. Granted, we often repeat what we say if we think the listener did not understand us, but more often than not we tend to say the same thing in different ways—or support our ideas with a bunch of examples—in order to make sure we get our message across. In fact this entire book is filled with different versions of the same message: intelligence requires a body.

In general, biological systems are extremely redundant because redundancy makes them more adaptive: if one part or process fails, another, similar part or process can take over. Brains also contain a lot of redundancy; they continue to function even if parts are destroyed—which should come as comfort to many of us since we know that alcohol has a tendency to destroy brain tissue. So, it sounds like redundancy is a good thing. Note, however, that redundancy also has its price. Additional parts have to be genetically represented (one way or other), they consume energy, they have weight, they take up space on the organism, etc. In short, adaptivity has to be paid for: there is no free lunch.

In engineering, redundancy often means duplication of components. In an airplane, instead of having one navigation system, there are two. But duplication on its own is not very interesting. If you have, say, two eyes instead of one, or even if you have a thousand, this is not very helpful if it gets dark. However, if you then have a touch system and an acoustic system, which are independent of whether there is light or not, you can still function. Interesting redundancy is also found in aircraft engineering. The braking system consists of two or three parts: the wheels, the jets, and sometimes, in high-speed aircraft, the parachutes. If there is ice on the runway, wheels are not very efficient, but then the jets can be used because their functioning does not depend on the condition of the runway. If the electrical system of the airplane ceases to function, the parachutes, which are purely mechanical, will still work. Wheels are used not only for braking but for maneuvering on the ground in general, jets are also—in fact, mostly—used for propulsion, whereas the parachutes are used only in emergency situations for braking; they usually do not cost much in terms of weight and manufacturing expense, but might come in handy.

What we can learn from these examples is that we should design agents that must function reliably under many different conditions with redundancy in such a way that there is partial overlap of functionality. If the overlap were complete, the two systems would be doing the same thing, which is not very economical and—normally—not terribly interesting in terms of adaptivity.[2] Another way of viewing partial overlap of functionality is that the same task can be achieved in different ways: braking can be done by using the wheels or the jets; recognizing an object can be achieved by looking at it or by touching it.

Robot Whisker Systems: The Artificial Mouse

Let us now look at an example from robotics: the "Artificial Mouse" developed at the Artificial Intelligence Laboratory at the University of Zurich by the engineer Hiroshi Yokoi, the neuroscientist Miriam Fend, and the theoretical physicist Simon Bovet (Fend et al., 2002). Rats and mice have sophisticated whisker systems that they can employ to acquire all kinds of information about the world. They can be used to detect the distance to an object (if the object is within reach of the whiskers), surface texture, and vibrations. Often water in the jungle is too muddy to see through: cats can solve the problem of hunting fish by dipping their whiskers into the water so that, through the vibrations produced by the movement of the fish, they can with uncanny precision locate and catch them. Rats and mice perform active whisking, i.e., they not only passively sense the environment with their whiskers as they move past objects, they also have muscles that enable them to move their whiskers back and forth. This ability has been built into the Artificial Mouse as well.

If a whisker from a real rat is attached to a microphone which in turn is connected to an amplifier, and the whisker is moved over different surfaces such as plastic, glass, wood, fabric, or sandpaper, one can, by merely listening to the sound produced, easily discriminate the different textures. The goal of the Artificial Mouse project is to study the use of the whisker system, in particular how the information from two morphologically very different sensor modalities, such as the visual and the whisker system, can be exploited by an animal or a robot to solve a problem, such as finding its way through a maze in which the walls have different textures. If there is a partial overlap in the kind of information that can be

ments, for example only on flat surfaces with particular frictional properties.

As we explained earlier, Puppy's legs are moved back and forth by servo motors at the "shoulder" and "hip" joints only; all the other joints are passive: they are not driven by any motors. The two springs that are attached to each of the legs (see figure 3.2b) can be seen as very simple artificial muscles or muscle-tendon combinations, and because of their intrinsic material properties less electronics are required: the springs take over the task that would otherwise have to be explicitly controlled. Springs are, of course, extremely simple, but they do capture some of the key properties of natural muscle-tendon systems, such as the elastic movement of the knee joint when the foot hits the ground. One of the problems with springs, though, is that their spring constant (that is, how stiff they are) does not change, whereas an important property of natural muscles is that their spring constants, so to speak, can be changed on the fly to meet the demands of the current situation. For example, on impact it is important that the muscles controlling the knee joint have the right stiffness. The higher an animal jumps, the more stiffness is required to support the body on landing, but there still must be some elasticity to soften the impact. But what exactly is the right stiffness for running or for jumping? Note how our thinking has moved from controlling trajectories of joints to controlling morphological properties; now we are asking what the right material properties of Puppy's springs should be. It is just this focus on morphology that we want to stress in artificial intelligence, because such considerations will benefit our design of robots and, ultimately, our understanding of intelligence. This also relates back to the idea of designing for emergence: if we get the material properties right, the desired trajectories will emerge from the interaction with the environment. Finding the proper stiffness for each situation, however, is a hard problem and will require a lot of research.

Artificial muscles are an emerging robot technology that now exist in many variations, but the most popular kind so far has been the pneumatic actuator—a kind of rubber tube surrounded by a braided fabric—that contracts when air pressure is applied. Because of the rubbery material, there is intrinsic elasticity and passive compliance, meaning that the muscle will yield elastically if the agent in which it is embedded encounters an object. And if we have robots interacting with humans, we want them to yield elastically so they will not hurt anyone: this general idea of yielding to external objects is known in robotics as *compliance*. A number of other technologies for artificial muscles are beginning to be used by roboticists: polymers that work on the basis of charge displacement; gels that contract depending on the chemical properties of the solution they are immersed in; metals whose lengths vary depending on the current that flows through them; and several others that are still just being developed in research laboratories. Like any kind of technology, each variety of artificial muscle has its pros and cons. Some cannot be bought off the shelf, some can extend quickly but only retract slowly; another type may wear out quickly or be too slow, etc. Pneumatic actuators are fast and robust and can be bought off the shelf in many variations. Their main disadvantage is that pressurized air is required for their operation and that they have to be controlled by valves.

One desirable property that we get free from artificial muscles—in contrast to servomotors—is that because of their springlike properties, they act as energy stores: on impact, part of the kinetic energy from the flight phase is transformed into potential energy in the muscle (or rather the muscle-tendon system), and some of it can be reused for the next step. A hopping kangaroo, for instance, regains about 40% of the energy absorbed in landing when it bounces up again (Vogel, 1998).

But back to Puppy. The right combination of material and morphological properties, i.e., the particular shape of the body and the limbs, is what allows Puppy to run. The servo motors that move the legs back and forth provide the energy supply and the basic rhythmic activation. The springs, the elastic spine, and the specific morphology take care of the harmonious distribution of the forces throughout Puppy's body when it interacts with the environment and make it adaptive to variations in its environment. The slightly slippery materials of the feet provide the additional degrees of freedom required for self-stabilization, the robot's ability to stabilize its gait without explicit control. Note that because Puppy is only a very simplified version of a dog, its dynamics is very different from that of an actual dog, but its movement is natural with respect to its own construction. As a consequence, there is a definite sense of aesthetics in Puppy's movements. You can verify the naturalness of Puppy's movements by watching the video clip at the book's Web page.

The Brain Controlling the Body, or Vice Versa?

While for a robot there is a clear distinction between the controller—which resides in the microprocessor—and the controlled—the actual physical robot, this distinction is far less clear in natural systems. Ultimately, the neural system of an animal or human is just as physically embodied as the rest of the body: it is not hidden away in a micro-processor that operates more or less independently from the body. One criterion that distinguishes the controller from the controlled in robots is energy consumption: typically the energy consumption of the con-troller is much less than that of the motors that are controlled by it. However, as is well known, the energy consumption of the human brain is very high, making up about 20% of the body's total energy usage. But the distinction gets even more fuzzy if we take into account that the body itself—the morphology and the materials—and the system-environment interaction also take over control tasks, i.e., perform morphological computation.

To illustrate: Imagine that you are running along a level jogging path and then the path goes downhill a bit. You will start running a bit faster, not because the brain "tells" the body to run faster, but because gravity accelerates the body, which in turn makes the limbs move faster, which in turn speeds up the brain's oscillatory circuits! So, the body "controls" the brain just as much as the brain controls the body. In other words, no one system is dominant over the other; the body and brain mutually determine each other's behavior. We will see more examples of this mutual coupling throughout the book.

"Computation" by Sensor Morphology: The "Eyebot"

In about 1995 the theoretical physicist and AI researcher Lukas Lichtensteiger, together with his colleague Peter Eggenberger, came up with a brilliant idea inspired by insects. In insects, at least in some species, the specific arrangement of the facets in their compound eye can be seen to perform an important function, i.e., to compensate for motion paral-lax. Facets are the small units that together make up an insect's com-pound eye. Motion parallax is just a fancy name for a phenomenon that is very familiar to all of us. Assume that you are sitting on a train looking out the window in the direction in which the train is moving and, still far away, you see a tree. As long as you are far away, this tree will move slowly across your visual field. When you pass close by the tree it will move much more quickly across your visual field, even though the train is moving at constant speed. This is purely a geometric phenomenon and holds for the human eye just as for the insect eye: objects nearby move faster across the visual field than objects farther away. Even though the insect eye is much more primitive than the human eye, it is nevertheless extremely effective and suited for its task, i.e., for guiding the insect during rapid flight.

The prominent neuroscientist and robot enthusiast Nicolas Franceschini, working at the Centre National de Recherche Scientifique (CNRS) in Marseille, France, found that in the housefly, the spacing of the facets is not homogeneous: the density toward the front is higher than on the side. What could be the advantage of this arrangement? First of all, it makes sense to have high resolution in the direction where you are going, which is usually forward. But second, with this arrangement of facets, a slow-moving point of light—from a distant object—will pass from one facet to the next at the front of the eye roughly at the same rate as a fast-moving point of light—from a close object—at the side of the eye. So the eye, because of its morphology, effectively compensates for motion parallax (see figure 4.5).

Let us assume that an insect "wants" to fly past an obstacle at a certain safe distance. One way of doing this is to maintain a fixed lateral distance from the object during flight, as do the railway lines going past the tree. Because of the facet distribution, all the insect needs to do is maintain a constant optic flow; that is, it has to move such that the time interval needed for a point of light to travel from one facet to the next remains constant: this is cheap design indeed! If there were a homogeneous arrangement of facets, because of motion parallax, computation would be more complicated (differently tuned neural circuits would have to be used for different pairs of facets). This is another illustration of morphological computation, or trading morphology for computation: the computation is, so to speak, performed by the morphology of the insect eye.

Inspired by these discoveries about the morphology of insect eyes, Lichtensteiger and Eggenberger developed the "Eyebot," a robot with a linear array of "facets," which are simply plastic tubes with a light sensor inside each one (see figure 4.5). These "facets" can be moved individually by electrical motors, and the motors in turn can be controlled by a program. Now, the ability to adapt one's behavior is normally attributed to plasticity of the brain. Lichtensteiger and Eggenberger were interested in the adaptive potential of morphology and asked the following question. Assume that an agent has the task of moving in such a way that its lateral distance to an obstacle remains constant: if we keep the brain fixed for the duration of the experiment, but we allow the agent to change its own morphology, will it be able to solve the task by adjusting its morphology (in this case the arrangement of the facets)? They ran an evolutionary algorithm (see chapter 6) on the "Eyebot" to optimize the angular position of the facets so that light would move past each facet

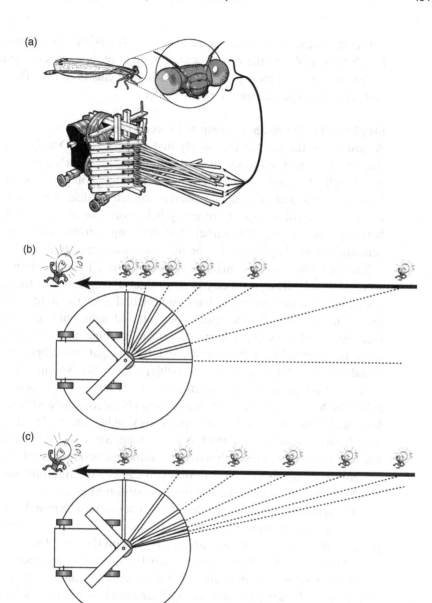

Figure 4.5
Ecological balance: morphological computation through sensor morphology. (*a*) The
"Eyebot" has adjustable hollow tubes with light-sensitive cells at the base, thereby mimicking the facets of an insect eye. (*b*) If the facets are evenly spaced, a point of light,
depicted by the running lightbulb, moves slowly across the visual field if the lightbulb is in
front and far away, but moves fast as it passes by the side of the robot. This is the phenomenon of motion parallax. (*c*) If, however, the facets are more dense toward the front
of the robot, a point of light will move at the same speed across all of the tubes, no matter
whether it is in front or to the side of the robot; the motion parallax is therefore compen-
sated away by this particular morphology.

pair at the same rate. Indeed, after about five hours, the robot managed to solve the problem: the resulting arrangement of the facets was similar to the one found in biological insects, with most clustered near the front and fewer arranged along the robot's side.

Morphological Computation, Cheap and Diverse Locomotion: Stumpy

At just about the start of the twenty-first century, Raja Dravid, a physicist, engineer, and self-made man who runs an "inventor's cooperative" in Zurich—together with the engineers and computer scientists Chandana Paul and Fumiya Iida—had an ingenious idea: they developed a very simple robot capable of many behaviors like walking, dancing, hopping, and turning. But rather than building a robot with legs and actuating them, they decided to actuate only the upper body.

Stumpy's lower body is made up of an inverted T mounted on wide, springy "feet." The upper body is an upright T connected to the lower body by a joint that can move back and forth, the "waist" joint: with this joint, Stumpy can move the upper body left and right, but cannot turn it (see figure 4.6). This upper horizontal beam is connected to the vertical beam by a second joint that can rotate left and right, providing an additional degree of freedom, the "shoulder" joint. So, Stumpy has two degrees of freedom: it can move its upper body left and right, and it can rotate its shoulder left and right, but it cannot bend forward and back. The horizontal beam at the top of the robot has weights attached to the ends in order to increase the effect of its movements. Since the first Stumpy, a whole series of Stumpies with somewhat different designs, morphologies, and materials have been built in order to explore the different ways in which simple bodies can give rise to lots of different behaviors.

Although Stumpy has no real legs or feet, it can move around in many ways: it can move forward in a straight or curved line, it has different gait patterns, it can move sideways, and it can turn on the spot. Interestingly, all this can be achieved by actuating only the two joints. In other words, control is extremely simple—the robot is virtually "brainless." The reason this works is because the dynamics, determined by its morphology, its materials (elastic, springlike materials, the surface properties of the feet), and the way it is actuated, are exploited in clever ways. Stumpy's many appealing and entertaining ways of moving arise not just from actuation of the two joints in particular ways, but because Stumpy is built in a specific manner (for more detail, see Iida et al., 2002 and Paul et al., 2002); if its morphology were different, it would exhibit less behavioral diversity, as illustrated in figures 4.6a and b.

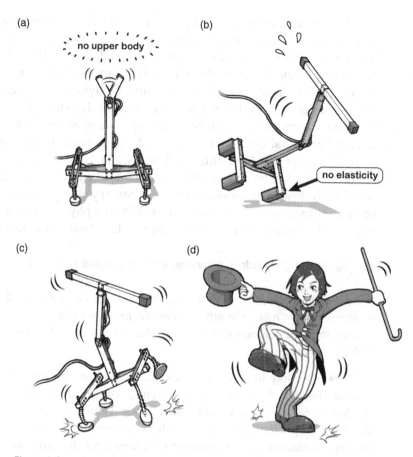

Figure 4.6
Ecological balance: morphological computation through shape and materials. Three morphologies are shown, two that do not work properly and one that achieves the desired dancing behavior. (*a*) A robot without a heavy enough upper body cannot generate enough momentum to get its feet off the ground. (*b*) A robot with no elasticity in its feet will not move properly or will fall over because the forces are not adequately propagated through the robot to the ground for locomotion. (*c*) Stumpy has the right morphology (an upper body) and the right materials (elastic feet) so that it can perform a large variety of interesting behaviors. (*d*) The biological system that is modeled by Stumpy: we use our upper body and the elasticity in our legs to move in interesting ways.

Before moving on to the next principle, let us briefly summarize the ideas concerning ecological balance, i.e., the interplay of morphology, materials, interaction with the environment, and control. First, given a particular task environment, the (physical) dynamics of the agent can be exploited which leads not only to a natural behavior of the agent, but also to greater energy efficiency. Second, when the dynamics of the agent is exploited, control can often be significantly simplified while a certain level of behavioral diversity is maintained. Third, materials have intrinsic control properties (e.g., stiffness, elasticity, and damping). And fourth, because ecological balance is exploited, agents like Stumpy can display surprisingly diverse behavior. In this sense, Stumpy also illustrates diversity-compliance: on the one hand, it exploits the physical dynamics in interesting ways and on the other it displays high behavioral diversity.

4.9   Agent Design Principle 7: Parallel, Loosely Coupled Processes

The principle of parallel, loosely coupled processes states that intelligence is emergent from a large number of parallel processes that are often coordinated through embodiment, in particular via the embodied interaction with the environment.

The way we like to view ourselves, and the way we usually conceptualize intelligence, is in terms of hierarchical organizations: there is the "I" that perceives an event in the outside world and maps the event onto an internal representation (e.g., a coffee cup standing on my desk), uses this representation to plan an action (drinking from the cup), and finally executes the action (reaching for the cup, grasping it, and drinking from it). This way of viewing behavior, also called the sense-think-act model, has proved inappropriate in the real world because (1) it is a one-way model, assuming that sensory stimulation comes first and leads to internal representation, and (2) because of real-time constraints, this way of functioning would simply not be fast enough. Recall our discussions of sensory-motor coordination and running (for additional arguments, see for example Pfeifer and Scheier, 1999). In reaction to this kind of thinking, in the mid-1980s Rodney Brooks of MIT suggested an alternative way of viewing intelligence, namely as a collection of parallel, asynchronous processes that are only loosely coupled. In this view intelligent behavior is, in essence, emergent from a large number of such processes. As discussed earlier, it was really Brooks who finally triggered the embodied turn in artificial intelligence. In a paper with the innocuous title "A Robust Layered Control System for a Mobile Robot," published in 1986, Brooks presented a radical alternative to designing control systems, the famous subsumption architecture (Brooks, 1986). The principle of parallel, loosely coupled processes is, in essence, a general way of interpreting the subsumption architecture. As outlined in chapter 2, the original publication was complemented later by the more provocatively titled papers "Intelligence Without Reason" and "Intelligence Without Representation." The debate on whether such architectures are suitable to achieve high-level intelligence is still open. We will return to this point later.

The term *loosely coupled* is used in contrast to hierarchically coupled processes. In the latter there is a control program (the "I") that calls the subroutines (e.g., for perception), and the calling program then has to wait for the subroutine (the perceptual act) to complete its task before it can continue (and go on to the action planning phase and then the action phase). This hierarchical control corresponds to very strong coupling; there is a very tight control regime between the calling and the called routines. But of course, in a complete agent there is strong coupling between processes simply because the system is embodied: for instance two joints such as the shoulder and the elbow, connected by a physical link (the upper arm), are very strongly coupled.

"Loosely coupled" also refers to the coupling of subsystems of an agent through its interaction with the environment, as we have seen in our discussion of leg coordination in insect walking, where the individual leg controllers were coupled through the interaction with the environment via the angle sensors in the joints of the legs. The coupling is called "loose" because the global coordination is achieved indirectly—through the environment—and not directly through the neural system. In grasping a coffee cup, the movement of the head, the eyes, the arms, and the fingers are also coupled through the interaction with the environment, so sensory-motor coordination always implies this kind of organization. Put another way, there is loose coupling between parallel processes, which in this case are the different sensory and motor processes involved in the grasping task: foveation—looking at the object—reaching, touching, and finally grasping. Note that in order to coordinate these processes, little internal neural processing is required: the coordination comes about through the environment.

Parallel, loosely coupled processes also play a role in social interaction. The social interaction robot Kismet, with gremlin-like features, which the robotics researcher Cynthia Breazeal developed while at the

Artificial Intelligence Laboratory at MIT, is another beautiful illustration of this design principle. Kismet is in fact simply a head, but by actuating various parts of its head—turning its head, focusing its eyes, or uttering sounds—it can engage an observer in seemingly complex social interactions. Rather than getting into the details of how Kismet functions, here we ask what we can learn from Breazeal's experiments, and provide our take on the question.

When watching Kismet interact with a person, one cannot help but attribute high social competence to this robot. It is essentially controlled by a collection of relatively simple reflexes that work in parallel. One reflex focuses on salient objects, i.e., objects that attract the robot's attention. A salient object might be one that has just appeared in the visual field, is moving rapidly, or is very bright. The object-tracking reflex causes the robot to follow slowly moving objects with its head and eyes, and a third reflex performs sound localization, turning the head in the direction of loud noises. There is also a habituation reflex, meaning that if the robot has been engaged in the same activity for some time it will get "bored," and look for something else to do. Note the anthropomorphic vocabulary that we are using, and remember to keep the frame of reference in mind: Kismet does not actually get bored (or does it?), but an observer may attribute boredom to Kismet based on its interactions with the environment. Despite the sophistication of Kismet, what matters for our discussion is that there are processes that work more or less independently of each other but are loosely coupled, i.e., they are coordinated through the interaction with the environment. Also, our simple description does not do justice to Kismet; for example, there is in fact a sophisticated model of emotion underlying Kismet's facial expressions that we will not discuss here (for more detail, see Breazeal, 2002).

Imagine now that I am talking to the robot so that it focuses on my face. If a door to the side opens with a noise and a person enters the room, the robot will turn its head toward the door (sound localization), it will track the human who has entered the room for a bit (following slowly moving objects), then it will get bored (habituation), and if I talk to Kismet again it will turn its head back toward me (sound localization) and continue our interaction. This kind of behavior is precisely what you would expect from a socially competent individual: someone new enters the room; you turn your head, perhaps briefly follow the person, and then turn back to your previous activity. One of the amazing things about Kismet is that it demonstrates that sophisticated algorithms or complex reasoning are not necessary to achieve this behavior. This leaves us with a deep philosophical question about human nature: perhaps we are much more driven by low-level reflexes rather than by our high-level rational thoughts. For some people, this idea is decidedly disconcerting, especially those with a Cartesian attitude: that is, people who believe there is a clear distinction between body and abstract thought, and that we can rationally decide what we want to do. Others might be relieved, because if our social abilities are indeed to a high degree controlled by reflexes and these reflexes are automatic, we do not have to think or worry about them: they take care of themselves. The latter is more related to the "Zen" attitude to being in the world. We surmise that this is why Rodney Brooks's term "the Zen of robot programming" has become a catchphrase among artificial intelligence researchers interested in embodiment.

4.10 Agent Design Principle 8: Value

The value principle states that intelligent agents are equipped with a value system which constitutes a basic set of assumptions about what is good for the agent.

The value principle is on the one hand very important because it deals with the fundamental issue of what is good for the agent, which then leads to the question of what the agent will or should do in a particular situation. On the other, the value principle is also extremely vague, and there is no consensus in the vast literature about how to approach it, neither in biology and psychology, nor in robotics and artificial intelligence. So, we cannot provide a satisfactory answer. All we can do, in contrast to the other design principles, is raise a number of issues for discussion. The question of value is certainly one of the open questions in intelligence research. We will start in this chapter and follow some of the points up in chapters 5 and 6.

Let us first talk about value in the context of designing and building artificial systems. The value principle states that intelligent agents are to be equipped with a value system which constitutes a basic set of assumptions about what is good for the agent. And once these assumptions have been made, they are no longer questioned—at least for a certain period of time, typically the lifetime of the agent. When designing, for instance, a companion robot (see chapter 11), the assumption is that anything that enables and helps the robot to perform its tasks—entertaining humans, serving coffee, mowing the lawn, performing household chores, looking after the kids, shopping—constitutes value. Thus, the set of design decisions make up the value system: cameras, microphones, wireless LAN, legs, arms and hands, mechanisms for walking, for manipulating objects, and for deciding what to do in a particular situation, etc. The more fully the agent conforms to the design principles outlined earlier, the more value it will be able to get from its setup (for example, it may be able to run more quickly if it exploits the elasticity in the artificial muscles). But we have to mind the frame-of-reference problem here: To the designer, these decisions are explicit, but once they are implemented on the robot, its behavior is emergent from a combination of all the components and mechanisms. So, the value is in the head of the designer rather than the head of the robot.

Let us now turn to a more specific question: given a particular agent, how does it decide what to do in a particular situation? This is especially important if the agents are to be autonomous and self-sufficient like the Fungus Eaters, which always have to achieve a number of tasks in order to keep functioning. Often, so-called action selection schemes are used: given a particular situation—e.g., the children have come home from school, there is no ice cream in the fridge, and the vacuum cleaner is broken—there are a number of actions the robot can take: buy cookies, take the vacuum cleaner to the repair shop, play with the children, etc. From these alternatives one is chosen based on an analysis of the current circumstances and an evaluation of the alternatives. This kind of approach is often employed in real-world applications where the objective is to build a working robot. But how much can we learn about intelligent behavior from this approach, which essentially implements how we as designers feel decision making is best done? We can learn about how well robots programmed in this way can function in dynamic complex environments such as people's homes, but this may in fact bear little relation to how "decisions" are taken in biological systems such as humans.

Let us briefly illustrate this point here with an example from psychology, the famous "A not B error," originally studied by Piaget. Imagine an experimenter at a table across from a baby sitting on his mother's lap. There are two holes in the table, A and B, each covered with a lid. The experimenter takes a toy, shakes it in front of the baby to attract his attention and puts the toy into hole A, and repeats this procedure a few times. It turns out that in most cases the baby will reach for hole A and take off that lid. Then, again in front of the eyes of the baby after shaking the toy back and forth, the experimenter puts it into hole B. Surprisingly, the baby will reach for lid A. This effect, called the "A not B error" has been shown to occur in babies aged seven to twelve months. Most of the literature tries to explain this phenomenon in terms of the cognitive processes of the babies. By contrast, Thelen and colleagues (2001) hypothesized that, rather than being the result of cognitive processes, this behavior might be emergent from a dynamical system. And indeed, if the physical dynamics of the system (the reaching system of the baby) is changed, the baby no longer makes the error. For example, when, after the training phase, the position of the baby is changed from sitting to upright, or when weights are attached to the baby's arms—both measures that change the physical dynamics of the reaching system—the baby no longer makes the error. The explanation is that through the various trials in the experiment, the babies, viewed as dynamical systems, get "stuck" in a particular attractor state from which they cannot escape unless the dynamics of the system is changed. At a later age, the external stimulus of the experimenter who puts the toy into hole B is sufficient to change attractors, and the babies do not make the error any more. Thus, something that looks very much like action selection, or a cognitive decision process, might in fact be emergent from a dynamical system.

This relates to the general issue of how to conceptualize the behavior of biological agents in complex situations when trying to explain their motivation, which is, in essence, the question of value. Without going into the details—there is a substantial literature on this issue—we have a strong tendency to attribute goals and decision processes to other humans (and even to animals and robots), which is in line with a Cartesian mindset: we have a goal, and then we plan and execute our actions to achieve the goal. Alas, it seems that goals are more like post hoc rationalizations, attributed to give the behavior the flavor of coherence, than the actual causes of behavior (for a review of these issues, see McFarland and Bösser, 1993; Pfeifer and Scheier, 1999; or the collection of articles in Montefiore and Noble, 1989). One of the key insights from the embodied approach has been that often much simpler explanations can be given and that there is no need to attribute sophisticated goal hierarchies or decision processes to the agent. An instructive example is Kismet, whose behavior, in essence, is emergent from a number of reflexes. And in the "A not B" experiment, the apparent decision behavior is emergent from a dynamical system, the baby's reaching system. These insights might provide valuable intuitions for the design of artificial agents.

To conclude our (admittedly somewhat superficial) discussion of the value principle, let us briefly discuss the time frames. What we have been saying so far applies mostly to the "here-and-now" perspective, where the designer decides what will be of value for the robot to achieve its tasks. In chapter 5, we will provide the details on value from a developmental perspective. One of the deep and largely unresolved questions there is why an agent should learn anything in the first place. In other words, how is learning related to value? Why continue to acquire more and more sophisticated skills and not be happy with what you have? Chapter 6 will discuss the evolutionary perspective on value, which raises the conundrum of why organisms become more complex during the process of evolution—that is, of how increased complexity is linked to value.

4.11 Summary and Conclusions

In this chapter we have outlined a set of principles that, on the one hand, characterize biological systems and on the other can be employed as heuristics for designing and building artificial ones. Although we are convinced that these principles are essential and capture the major insights into the intricacies of how intelligent behavior comes about, they constitute a preliminary set that will eventually need to be extended and revised. The basic set outlined in this chapter will be complemented in the subsequent three chapters by a number of additional principles for development, evolution, and collective intelligence. We have tried our best to boil down the principles to the bare minimum while maintaining comprehensibility: for a more detailed, but perhaps somewhat less up-to-date elaboration, see Pfeifer and Scheier (1999). A summary of all the design principles from chapters 4, 5, 6, and 7 will be given in the concluding chapter of the book.

5   Development: From Locomotion to Cognition

More than half a century ago, in 1950, the great mathematician Alan Turing, whom we have already encountered in chapter 3 as the "creator" of the notion of computation, published a seminal article in the philosophy journal *Mind* entitled "Computing machinery and intelligence" (Turing, 1950). This paper, in a sense, marks the beginning of artificial intelligence, as indicated by its first sentence: "I propose to consider the question, 'Can machines think?'" Rather than coming up with definitions—and as you know by now, we do not particularly relish definitions either—he suggested a test for intelligence or thinking that he called the imitation game. In essence, the idea was to see whether a human could distinguish another human from a computer: just by typing questions into a communications terminal, could you find out whether a human or a computer program was answering your questions? In other words, if the computer has the capacity to imitate a human, we can safely assume that it can think. This test, which later entered the literature under the name of the "Turing test," has raised a lot of controversy and there is an extensive and highly stimulating debate on whether it is a good test for intelligence. But the reason for mentioning this article here is not so much to introduce the Turing test itself (the interested reader is referred to Searle, 1980; Crockett, 1994; or Moor, 2003) but to get us thinking about how to create a machine capable of passing the test. Turing predicted that within 50 years one would have computers that would in fact pass his test. This claim became the first of many false predictions in artificial intelligence. Even though he underestimated the extent of the complexities involved, Turing did realize that the endeavor would be a tough one. This is why he suggested that rather than "hand designing the system," we should use a developmental approach:

Instead of trying to produce a programme to simulate the adult mind, why not rather try to produce one which simulates the child's? If this were then subjected to an appropriate course of education one would obtain the adult brain. Presumably the child brain is something like a notebook as one buys it from the stationer's. Rather little mechanism, and lots of blank sheets. (Mechanism and writing are from our point of view almost synonymous.) Our hope is that there is so little mechanism in the child brain that something like it can be easily programmed. The amount of work in the education we can assume, as a first approximation, to be much the same as for the human child. (Turing, 1950/1963, p. 31).

So what Turing suggests is to start with an initial system which—he hopes—would be relatively simple to design, and then train the system by means of an educational process, which is exactly what developmental robotics is all about. One of the major differences is that a computer is an entirely disembodied system with only trivial interaction with the real world, whereas developmental roboticists work with embodied systems—with robots.

Following up on this idea of Turing's, this chapter raises some fundamental issues in the study of cognition, and, alas, we cannot claim to have any ready-made solutions to offer. So rather than pretending to provide answers to currently unresolved problems, we will present, to the best of our knowledge, an overview of the main issues involved in the emergence of cognition, and describe some experiments that attempt to tackle them. So far, we in the research community have only scratched the surface, so this chapter is in many ways speculative. Nevertheless, there has been a lot of progress.

In this chapter we first introduce the motivating factors for a developmental approach, and then outline the basic idea. Then, in the following sections, using the case study of the dog robot Puppy, we will sketch out a path by which one might be able to move from the most basic physical dynamics all the way up to cognition. As we will see, development provides a framework for actually doing so. Development also provides an approach that might allow us to resolve the symbol grounding problem, which will be discussed next. In the subsequent section we will bring together ideas from robot locomotion, biology, and complex dynamics with the design principles to understand how to match brain and body dynamics. We will then broaden our discussion to include some ideas that are related to development, such as social interaction, development over long time periods, and natural language, to mention but a few. Then we will summarize the features of this field and compile a set of design principles that apply specifically to development.

5.1 Motivation

The motivation for a developmental approach to cognition comes from several sources. First, and this is essentially Turing's point, it comes from the simple fact that at the moment we obviously do not have truly intelligent robots that can parallel the mental or physical capabilities of humans. We still seem to lack the skills to build the hardware, nor do we know how to program robots to achieve anything like human-level intelligence. Perhaps we simply do not have sufficient understanding of the mechanisms underlying intelligent behavior. It has turned out that using only the "here-and-now" time scale to hand-design behaviors for robots is much more difficult than expected. For example, we still do not have artificial perceptual systems that even remotely resemble those of humans, monkeys, or rats. Neither do we have robots that can walk or run at different speeds and over rough terrain, while carrying a bag and holding a child by the hand. Maybe, however, such systems could be designed using a developmental approach, starting with an initial system that would—hopefully—be much simpler, so that a robot would learn to perceive or to run on its own, rather than having to be explicitly programmed to do so. Before we go any further it should perhaps be mentioned that there is a distinction between learning and development, although the two concepts partially overlap. During development the organism grows and matures, whereas in learning, morphology is normally not taken into account: in other words during development the agent's body and brain both change, while in learning only the brain does.

Second, as outlined in chapter 3, there are always three time scales at which we have to consider intelligent behavior. In the last chapter we explored the "here-and-now" perspective. In this and the following chapter we will investigate the ontogenetic (lifetime of the individual) and the phylogenetic (evolutionary) scales respectively. A developmental approach to cognition capitalizes on the ontogenetic time scale. The hope is that some of the properties of intelligent agents or some of the design principles outlined in the last chapter will emerge from a developmental process. For example, a robot may, as it develops, come up with several useful parallel, loosely coupled sensory-motor processes, thereby reinforcing design principle 7. More exciting still, by allowing agents to develop on their own, rather than having to be programmed directly with behaviors, additional properties and design principles may emerge that we have not yet thought about.

The third motivation comes from the fact that learning ability is considered one of the important ingredients of intelligence, and learning in turn is an important aspect of development, and thus should be investigated in embodied systems. Learning has a long history in artificial intelligence, and the field of machine learning—a computational offshoot of artificial intelligence research—has developed into a large discipline in its own right. However, one of the problems with this field is that it is highly algorithmic and almost entirely disembodied. That approach has been very successful in some areas, for example internet browsers that pick up on the habits of the user, or data-mining systems in which the learning algorithm discovers interesting relations in very large data sets. However, because these systems are entirely disembodied, they work only in formal, virtual environments like the internet, which has clearly defined states, as discussed earlier. Thus, mapping these ideas to the real world—to robots—has been very hard. Even though ingenious roboticists like Minoru Asada of Osaka University's Adaptive Machine Systems Laboratory have programmed their soccer-playing robots such that they learn how to shoot a goal using machine-learning techniques, adapting these methods to deal with real robots continues to be a problem. Biological neural networks are excellent at enabling biological agents like animals and humans to interact with the real world, but artificial neural networks are mostly studied in a disembodied context in machine learning. Even researchers in computational neuroscience usually consider the brain in isolation, as illustrated, for example, by the highly lauded book by a group of connectionist researchers entitled *Rethinking Innateness*, which presents only disembodied models of development (Elman et al., 1996).

Fourth, development turns out to offer a potential solution to the symbol-grounding problem: how can what goes on inside an agent's head be connected to the real world; in short, how do agents acquire meaning? This is a hard question that we will discuss in detail below.

A fifth motivating factor comes from the synthetic methodology, in which robots are used as models of development and thereby may shed light on natural development and its underlying mechanisms. It is generally agreed that cognition, or higher-level intelligence, includes abilities that are acquired one way or another during ontogenetic development, i.e., as the human grows from a baby into an adult. Thus, we could make a valuable contribution to the field of development by showing how intelligence in robots can be achieved not by programming them, but rather by initiating a developmental process during which the robot interacts not only with its physical environment but also with people and other robots in order to become a being to which (or to whom?) we would be inclined to attribute cognitive abilities. Although modeling growth processes on real hardware is still in its infancy, techniques are now emerging for mimicking, at least at a rudimentary level, physical growth.

And last but not least, we suspect that there is a kind of romantic motivating factor behind the developmental approach: the desire to create a robot that can grow into a functioning system with little outside help, just like a human baby. This is reflected in the names researchers give to their robots, such as Giorgio Metta's "Babybot" or Hideki Kozima's "Infanoid." Although building an autonomously developing robot remains far out of reach, it is certainly a fascinating vision. Just imagine if we could watch a robot acquire more and more skills over time, eventually starting to walk and talk by interacting with the world, and with us, on its own! This is the ultimate, grand goal of the field of developmental robotics.

So, to summarize, there are a number of reasons why we might want to build robots that learn: we cannot yet program them directly to perform complex tasks; the design principles outlined in the last chapter—as well as some we may not have thought of—may emerge from a developing robot; developmental robotics may shed new light on the nature of learning, how agents acquire meaning, and development in general; and finally, robots that grow and learn would be immensely gratifying to researchers as creators. The question now becomes not why to study developing robots, but how.

5.2 Toward Developmental Robot Design

When talking about intelligence, we tend to focus on high-level functions such as problem solving, designing a computer program, writing a report, finding a mathematical proof, preparing a lecture, or running a scientific experiment, which are all activities that can be described as abstract symbol processing. In the traditional approach, researchers tackle these skills directly, so to speak, by actually programming symbol-processing systems into their computers. Because in our own laboratory (Rolf's AI laboratory in Zurich) we are pursuing the embodied route to intelligence, we have been doing a lot of work on sensory-motor processing, and focusing on so-called low-level dynamics like locomotion in four-legged and two-legged robots. This has also drawn a lot of criticism from the community: "Your work on locomotion is interesting in itself, if you want to study walking or running, but you are not working on cognition!" Thus, in essence, we have been identified as defectors, as researchers who have left the path of virtue, fallen away from the goal of studying intelligence, and drifted down toward the low-level engineering goal of creating robots that only move about.

But we were in for a big surprise. Remember our discussion of the properties of embodied agents in the last chapter, where we pointed out that agents, by the mere fact that they are physical systems, have attractor states? As we started working on the running dog robot Puppy with Fumiya Iida we suddenly realized that the complex body dynamics that seemed to make locomotion so hard—controlling a system with many joints is a complicated control task—turned out to open the way toward symbolic systems! Because the complex dynamics of Puppy's body has many attractor states, and since attractor states are, within a completely continuous system, discretely identifiable entities (see focus box 4.1), the attractor states themselves provide a potential basis for low-level symbols. So, metaphorically speaking, "going down" to lower levels turned out to be a prerequisite for "going up" toward symbol processing, in a principled and grounded way. In other words, we do not arbitrarily define symbols to which the robot then has to try and attach meaning. We will use Puppy as a vehicle to show how we can move from studying sensory-motor issues to studying cognition using this insight. As we will see, this discussion will also lead to a solution—or at least a promising approach—to the widely debated symbol grounding problem.

Of course, ideas never appear out of the blue. For a number of years we have been communicating and working with the champion of robot imitation, Yasuo Kuniyoshi of the University of Tokyo, who has been exploring a dynamical systems–oriented approach to the problem of finding symbols in continuous dynamical systems. Because we have been increasingly engaged in studying robot locomotion (such as walking, running, dancing, flying, and swimming), it was natural to incorporate ideas from the theory of dynamical systems into our work. The search for discrete symbols in dynamical systems is being pursued by a number of researchers, whose work has been a great source of inspiration for us (e.g., Inamura et al., 2004; Ito and Tani, 2004; Hertzberg et al., 2002; Jaeger, 1998; Kuniyoshi et al., 2004; Okada and Nakamura, 2004).

It is interesting that in developmental robotics, humanoid robots are usually used. We suspect that this has to do with the fact that we would ultimately like to achieve something like human-level intelligence in our robots. The real question, however—and we will ask this throughout the book—is what can we learn from humanoid robotics? First, because of the enormous engineering challenge of building humanoid robots, a number of new technologies had to be developed. Miniaturization is a big area of research, as are actuator technologies, new types of sensors (such as sophisticated touch and pressure sensors), battery technology (or in general technology for energy supply), and conceptual issues in control theory such as how to control systems with very many degrees of freedom. So, technologically speaking, there is much to be learned.

Second, by actually building robots we quickly come to appreciate what the real difficulties are. For example, when we build humanoid walking robots and observe their behavior, we immediately realize that the walking style of these robots is very different from the way humans walk. This sharpens our eye and focuses our attention on the underlying drawbacks of the design approach. These insights provide us with new conceptual directions in which we might want to look. For example, we might want to think about exploiting the material properties of a robot's body by using artificial muscles instead of electric motors, or exploit the passive dynamics of a swinging leg rather than programming the motion of the leg explicitly.

One of the great potentials of humanoid robots is that because they have roughly the same shape and size as we do, we would not need to change anything in the environment in order for them to function. They could use the same utensils for cooking; they could use the same tools for repairing cars, appliances, and themselves(!); they could play cards, golf, ping-pong, and chess; they could use the subway system to transport themselves; they could type on the keyboard of a computer or use the keys of a piano; or they could even drive our cars or lawnmowers. At the final presentation of the Japanese Humanoid Robotics Program in 2002, a robot was presented that could in fact operate a backhoe just like a human by sitting in it and manipulating the controls (see figure 5.1). The Wabot, an ingenious humanoid robot developed in the 1980s at Tokyo's Waseda University, could not only play the organ by pushing the keys at 15 strokes per second, it could also read normal music scores. And the recent anthropomorphic robot WF-4 can even play the flute! (For a full description of WF-4, see chapter 11.) Of course, one can construct a control system for a backhoe, or electronic circuits for producing the sound of an organ, but the point of the demonstration was to show the general utility of humanoid robots in our society.

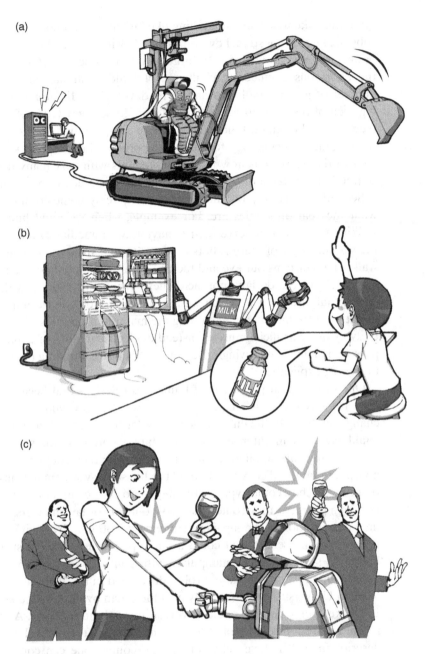

Figure 5.1
Humanoid robots interacting with environments built for humans. Because humanoid robots have a similar morphology to that of humans, they can interact naturally with our world. (*a*) Humanoid driving a backhoe. (*b*) Humanoid getting food from refrigerator. (*c*) Humanoid receiving guests for a party.

There is a danger, however, in the use of humanoid robots. Because of their superficial similarity to humans, we as humans have a strong tendency to attribute humanlike properties to them which they simply do not have, such as language abilities, experience of pain and pleasure or emotions in general, or a sense of responsibility and commitment. Remember David McFarland's warning, "anthropomorphization, the incurable disease": humanoid appearance further encourages human observers to anthropomorphize. Surely this is intended by some researchers (but certainly not all of them) and attracts the media to their work, but it also triggers inappropriate associations concerning the robot's actual abilities.

Humanoids in their present state are impressive and represent highly sophisticated technological achievements. However, they are far from approaching human-level intelligence. Just take the example of walking: as we mentioned in chapter 2, people can walk in very many different ways. This incredible behavioral diversity has not yet even been approached by any robot, including the most advanced ones like H-7 of the University of Tokyo, Asimo of Honda Motor Corporation, QRIO of Sony Corporation, or DB, an 80-kilogram humanoid robot with 30 degrees of freedom, from the Utah-based robotics company Sarcos.

Despite the fact that humanoids play a large role in developmental robotics, they may not be the only tool. In the following case study we used the four-legged robot Puppy to demonstrate how we might achieve a developmental process in a robot. We feel that this example nicely illustrates how an animal, robot, or human might be able to learn about its interactions with the real world and might eventually build up something like a body image, which, as is generally agreed, plays an important role in the development of cognition. We will show an approach that builds up everything incrementally: starting with the agent's basic movements—its low-level dynamics, so to speak—identifying attractor states (gait patterns) in this dynamics, creating a body image, and resulting in the first traces of symbol processing. It turns out that in practice, as is so often the case, the story is much more complicated than what we present here, but the basic idea is simple and compelling.

5.3 From Locomotion to Cognition: A Case Study

Let us recall Puppy, the four-legged robot that, among other things, is capable of running. One striking observation is that all four-legged animals have a small number—typically six (McMahan, 1984, p. 171)—of distinct and clearly identifiable gaits, for example walking, trotting, racking (also called pacing or ambling), cantering, and (two kinds of) galloping and variations thereof, and when they move they will usually use one of these gaits. Because the gaits correspond to some of the attractor states of the animal's particular physical system, the movement is natural with respect to the animal's body and it requires minimal energy and little control. In other words, the muscles and neural system have to perform less work. To be more precise we can think about the gaits of an agent as corresponding to the attractor states of its combined physical and neural system, not just the physical system alone, because the neural system has its own intrinsic dynamics—its operating speed—and this system must be in tune with the physical one. The more complex the body of an animal, the more ways there are to move, and therefore the more potential attractor states for that body. The same holds for the neural system and thus for the combined body-brain system. It is important to realize that the specific attractor states always come about in the interaction with the environment. If the ground is slippery, goes uphill or down, or is uneven, the corresponding gaits—and thus the attractors—will be different: moving uphill will lead to shorter steps than going downhill. When we talk about the attractors of the body-brain system it is implied that the agent is always interacting with a particular environment. There are a number of interesting points to note about gait patterns as attractors.

First, because the gaits correspond to attractor states when viewed as a dynamical system, they are clearly and discretely identifiable, even though the animal itself is a completely continuous dynamical system. The different gaits are noticeably distinct from each other: an animal is either walking or trotting but not both at the same time. When changing speed, an animal will typically transition quickly from one gait to another, and then maintain that gait for some time.

Second, depending on the particular phase in the locomotion cycle that the animal is involved in it either can change its behavior or it cannot. During the flight phase (all feet off the ground), the system is tightly coupled to the environment, or, metaphorically speaking, it is firmly in the grip of the physical dynamics. Like the path of a rock thrown up in the air, the trajectory of the animal's body cannot easily be changed, and it is very difficult (or impossible) to exert control at this point. It is best to leave the system to its own dynamics, so to speak; gravity will—one way or another—bring it back to the ground. In contrast, it is obviously much easier to control the system during the stance phase (one or more feet on the ground).

Third, because the stance phase is a kind of control point in the agent's running behavior, it provides a good basis for the segmentation of behavior, an idea that we owe to Yasuo Kuniyoshi. When we watch, analyze, and communicate about the behavior of an agent, we always perform some kind of segmentation, often without realizing it. We say that the agent is running, walking, on the ground, eating, grasping a bottle, involved in a conversation, drinking from a cup, watching TV, eating peanuts, reading the newspaper, etc. It is clear that there is a lot of arbitrariness in segmentation because it is observer-based. If, by contrast, the criterion for segmentation is based on control points, behavior segmentation is the result of the agent's behavior itself, rather than the observer's (arbitrary) perspective, and is therefore more objective. However, in this case, because the stance phase is clearly recognizable by an observer, the observer-based segmentation and the one which is grounded in the agent's movement match.

Assume for a moment that you are walking out of a room, but there are a group of people between you and the door and you have to go considerably out of your way to actually get there. Are you then "leaving the room," "going to the door," or "going out of your way"? Whichever you choose is fine, but note that the choice of which explanation to use is entirely arbitrary, and depends more on your perspective of the behavior than on the behavior itself. However, there is at least one natural way of segmenting the behavior, namely in terms of individual steps. Thus, sometimes, it is possible to come up with a natural segmentation at one level, while at a different level segmentation might be arbitrary. Segmentation of continuous behavior into discretely identifiable, nonarbitrary chunks represents an important step toward forming symbolic behavioral categories such as jumping or stepping. More important, we can see how symbol manipulation—the combining of symbols—might follow. For example, by extending the observation time, we can aggregate several steps to produce a new concept, "walking," which is viewed as a set of sequential steps.

Fourth, the dynamics of the neural system and the dynamics of the body have to be in tune. In animals we can safely assume this to be the case because neural and morphological structures have evolved together: selection pressure, leading to survival of the fittest, works on the whole organism, not just one part of it. Let us look at an example.

The famous neuroethologist Sten Grillner at the Karolinska Institute in Stockholm, Sweden, found that the locomotion of the lamprey, an eel-like jawless fish that drinks the blood of other fish, is controlled by

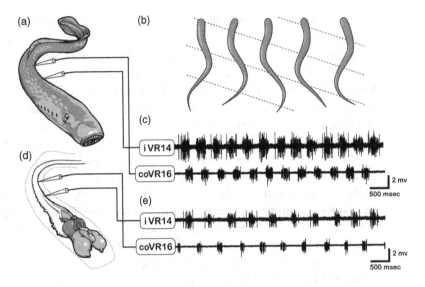

Figure 5.2
Mutual coupling between neural and body system during locomotion. The lamprey. (*a*)
Lamprey swimming in water. (*b*) Oscillatory movements while swimming. (*c*) Recordings
from the central pattern generators (CPGs) while swimming. (*d*) Isolated spine of the
Lamprey. (*e*) Recordings from the CPGs in the isolated spine.

so-called central pattern generators, i.e., neural structures that periodi-
cally activate the muscles of the lamprey at a particular frequency in
order to produce rhythmic movement (for an excellent and easy-to-read
review, see Grillner, 1996). The body of the lamprey is divided into 100
segments that each contain a bundle of neurons (the central pattern generators), a spinal bone segment, muscles, and sensors, among other things
(see figure 5.2). The segments are activated by the neural system one
after the other, in sequence, in such a way that a kind of wave travels
along the body. The delay between the activation of subsequent segments
is called the phase difference. When the spinal cord of the lamprey is isolated from its body through a surgical operation and put into a nutritious
solution, both the phase difference and the frequency of the neural
signals change, which can be detected by neurophysiological recording
methods (e.g., Guan et al., 2001). But unlike what we might expect, the
frequency of oscillation is actually faster in the intact animal. It turns out
that the body does not simply slow down the system; rather, through the
muscle movements and the resulting interaction with the environment,
sensory feedback is generated which in turn influences the neural activity of the lamprey. This demonstrates that we cannot understand the

natural behavior of the animal by only studying either the brain or the body in isolation. So—once again—we have an instance where the body shapes the brain activity just as much as the brain activity shapes body movement: it is not the brain controlling the body, but there is mutual coupling between brain and body. The brain-body coupling changes the preferred oscillation frequencies of the animal, which means that when identifying attractor states, we should always look at the joint neural-body system.

The important point is that there are these preferred frequencies and they correspond to the attractor states that allow the animal to move efficiently, as is seen during swimming, walking, or running. Similarly, the frequency of the isolated control signals for the servomotors in the robot Puppy differs from the resulting frequency of its leg movements when it is on the ground and actually running. In the next section we will look at how we can use Puppy's gait patterns to create something like a body image.

5.4   From Gait Patterns to Body Image to Cognition

Before we engage in a discussion on body image let us briefly comment on terminology. When we talk about body image here, we mean (artificial) neural structures that can be used by the agent to guide its movements and to make predictions about the sensory stimulation that might result from a particular movement such as making a step, grasping a cup, or turning the head. We feel that this characterization captures at least some of the essence of how the term is used in the literature.[1]

But back to Puppy and to the case study. So far we have talked about running, exploitation of material properties, dynamical systems, attractor states, and control. But we still have not shown how this all might eventually lead to cognition. So let's have a go at it. Gait patterns can be easily visualized by plotting time versus ground contact for all four legs as illustrated in figure 4.2a. Line segments in the graph indicate which foot was on the ground and when. These diagrams can be used to recognize gait patterns. If the pattern is periodic or quasi-periodic corresponding to a particular gait, it would be possible not only for an external observer but also for the robot itself to recognize its own gait patterns. In some experiments with Puppy, the robot had no sensors, which implies that the robot "knew" nothing about its own movements. Whether it was up in the air or not could only be seen by an outside observer; the robot itself "had no idea," so to speak. The quotation marks are used here to indicate that we are not talking about conscious knowledge or actual ideas, but rather saying that there is simply no data available to the robot concerning the particular phase in locomotion it is currently in. If we now add some sensors, for example by putting pressure sensors on the robot's feet, and collect signals from them (at a frequency of, say, 500 times per second), the robot can "know" about its gait patterns. These signals can then be fed into an artificial neural network as shown in figure 5.3.

Let us now briefly see how such a network might be constructed to detect periodic patterns. There are many ways in which this could be done, and there is no generally accepted approach to this problem; we discuss one possibility here. We have already seen some very simple neural networks for controlling Braitenberg vehicles to achieve light-following and light-avoidance behaviors in chapter 3, but now we are going to consider networks that are more complex. For an overview of artificial neural networks, see focus box 5.1. In artificial neural networks there is always an input layer that makes the signals from the sensors available to the network itself. In the Braitenberg vehicle the input layer was the light sensors or the proximity sensors; in Puppy, we have four pressure sensors on the feet, so the input layer consists of four nodes, each representing whether the foot at this point in time is touching the ground (value = 1) or not (value = 0).[2] This input data can be processed by a recurrent neural network, which in addition to input from the sensors, also receives input from itself. This is accomplished by including loops that can be used to maintain activation in the network for a certain period of time, thus acting as a kind of short-term or working memory. This memory is necessary in order to detect the regular periodic patterns in the sensor data over time. Put differently, the system has to "remember" the previous signals in order to tell whether there has been a repetition or not. Detecting periodic patterns is a tricky business because, in the real world, no two sequences will ever be identical.

Biological neural networks are champions at dealing with these variations because they evolved in the real world. They can also, if need be, adapt to changes in the environment. Artificial neural networks, simple as they may be, also have these abilities to some degree, which is why they are very popular in robotics. If the sensor data indeed contains regular, repetitive patterns, because the network is itself a dynamical system, it will settle into an attractor state. If the agent then starts to transition into another gait, the network may settle into a different stable attractor state (see figure 5.3). However, before we can talk about a body

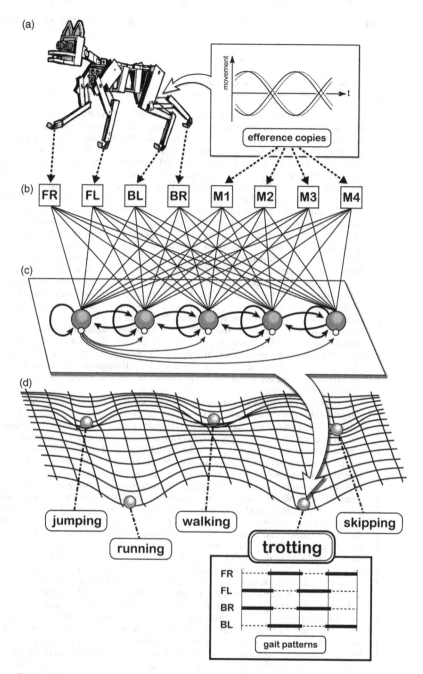

Figure 5.3
Symbol grounding: Attractor states and embedded neural networks. The illustration shows a neural network embedded in the robot Puppy (*a*) Puppy with pressure sensors on the feet. (*b*) The input layer of the network receives signals from the pressure sensors on the feet (FR, FL, BR, BL) and copies of the control signals for the motors, the "efference copies" (M1–M4). (*c*) Recurrent connections (curved arrows) provide a kind of short-term memory, which is necessary to recognize spatiotemporal patterns. (*d*) Attractor states corresponding to gait patterns (see also figure 4.2 on attractor states). They are discretely identifiable states within the continuous robotic system, and they can be designated by symbols such as "walking," "running," and "trotting."

Focus Box 5.1
Neural Networks for Adaptive Behavior

Neural networks are abstract computational models of the brain; they implement what some like to call brain-style computation. Natural brains have a number of highly desirable properties that are especially useful for agents that have to interact with the real world—properties that we would like to achieve at least to some extent with artificial brains, known as neural networks. First, brains are fault and noise tolerant, i.e., they continue to function even if some parts are damaged or if there is noise in the data. In the real world, this is always the case: just think of the famous "cocktail party effect"—when you are at a cocktail party talking to someone, you can still understand what he or she is saying, even though it's really noisy. Second, biological brains can generalize: they continue to function in situations they have never encountered before. The value of this can hardly be overestimated since in the real world no two situations are ever alike (you can recognize the face of your mother even though she never looks exactly the same twice; the sensory stimulation on your retina depends on distance, lighting conditions, whether you see her face from the front or the side, with or without makeup, with different hairstyles, etc.). Third, neural networks have a high degree of plasticity; they can adapt to changes in the organism as it grows from a baby into an adult. Fourth, they are intrinsically learning systems; they always learn and thus improve their own performance (this is a property that we expect from any intelligent system). Finally, neural networks are massively parallel; they process distributed patterns (like incoming stimulation from different sensor modalities) rather than discrete symbols. This implies that they can react very quickly even though the individual neurons are relatively slow; for moving quickly around in the real world, this property in particular is mandatory.

There is an enormous literature on different kinds of neural networks, but they can all be characterized by a small set of properties. They consist of nodes (the artificial neurons) which are connected to (typically, many) other nodes by means of weighted connections, or simply weights (the artificial synapses). The nodes have an activation level represented by a number which can be taken to model the average firing rate of the neuron, i.e., the number of spikes it produces per second. In biological neural networks, the more rapidly a neuron emits spikes, the more active it is. Nodes can influence each other's level of activation by passing signals along the connections. Typically, a node becomes active when the summed input received from other nodes exceeds a certain threshold. The weights, corresponding to the strengths of the synaptic connections, are also represented by numbers, indicating how strongly a neuron can influence the ones to which it is connected. The knowledge or the "personal history" of these networks is contained in the particular connection strengths. They acquire knowledge by applying some kind of learning rule that specifies how the connections change, given the current state and input to the network. A famous example is the Hebbian learning rule, which states that the connections between neurons that are simultaneously active are strengthened.

For neural networks used in robots, there is an input layer to which the sensors of a robot—the camera, the pressure sensors on the feet, the infrared sensors—are connected, one or several internal layers of neurons (often referred to as hidden layers), and an output layer which is linked to the motor system. The hidden layers frequently contain so-called recurrent connections or loops, so that their activation can be maintained, for example, to implement some kind of short-term memory. In other words, the activation of the nodes of the output layer are not just determined by the input to the network, but are also influenced by the previous values of the hidden layers, i.e., by the network's recent history. The activation of the output layer is then used to control the motors and thus the actual movement of the robot.

What is truly surprising is that despite the enormous abstractions made from real brains, artificial neural networks are extremely powerful; and therefore they have become very popular in the robotics community, especially where adaptive robots are concerned. Although biological brains are superior to artificial neural networks in many respects, impressive results have been achieved, for example, in the areas of pattern recognition, generation of locomotion patterns, and sensory-motor coordination.

There are literally thousands of publications suggesting variations of neural networks, but they can be classified into roughly four classes (this is for the more technically interested reader). First, there are the classical feedforward networks, where the connections go only from input to output; this type is well suited for large classes of categorization and pattern-recognition problems (e.g., recognizing a tumor in an image from a brain scan). The second class, the dynamical networks, include recurrent connections; this type is closer to biological reality and is required for controlling periodic locomotion (walking, or running) and for recognizing cyclic patterns. It is also this type of network that, although continuous, will have attractor states that can potentially be related to some basic kind of symbol processing, as we illustrate in this chapter (see also figure 5.3). The third category, the spiking neural networks, are even more biologically realistic because the neurons no longer simply have an activation level that represents average spike frequency, but instead the neurons emit individual spikes at particular times. This strongly increases their power because the information contained in the time intervals between the spikes can also be exploited. This is important, for example, in speech processing, where time is crucial. The last class of networks—also biologically realistic—is neuromodulator based, where the activity at the synapses is controlled by artificial molecules known as neuromodulators. These molecules control when the synapses should learn, i.e., when they should change the synaptic weights. For example, we may want a robot to learn only when it has successfully grasped a bottle, but not when it fails to do so. Generally, neuromodulators significantly increase the adaptivity of a neural network.

While brains, with their more than a hundred billion neurons, are truly parallel, most of the parallelism in artificial neural networks is still simulated on a serial microprocessor, which requires a lot of computation because the activation of each neuron has to be updated, one after the other. This implies that the benefit of parallelism for real-time processing falls flat: it is only conceptual, so to speak, not real. Thus, in spite of today's enormously powerful microprocessors, computational speed is still a true bottleneck, especially for robots that have to behave in the real world. This is an important reason why for most robot applications, simple neural network models are preferred. For example, models of spiking neurons are not often employed because they are computationally expensive. With the development of more parallel hardware this may change in the future; however, for the time being we are stuck simulating parallel networks with serial processors. (The historical development of neural networks was briefly covered in chapter 2 and will not be elaborated here.)

But even if we had much more powerful parallel processors, this alone would not solve the issue of designing neural networks for robots, because the networks must always be developed together with the robot's morphology. Focusing only on the design of networks themselves will, for example, not solve the problem of recognizing an object in the real world, whereas a developmental, embodied approach, as outlined in this chapter, might eventually do so because it allows for active interaction with the environment, thereby generating the necessary sensory stimulation (see chapter 4).

image, there is still something essential missing. These patterns represent only the sensory inputs, and there is no indication to the agent about how these patterns actually come about. Thus, in addition to the pressure-sensor data, the motor commands—i.e., the signals that generated the joint movements—must also form part of the input to the network. These signals, called efference copies, provide the basis for the agent to learn something about the causal structure of its interaction with its environment: the motor commands *cause* the robot to move in such a way that sensor data are generated which in turn are fed into the input layer of the network. And it is precisely these causal structures that are the foundation of body image.

This is all very simple and basic. So, let us now speculate a bit about how we might want to continue from here, i.e., how a behavior could be achieved that we might want to call symbol processing. Given that we have the different attractors in the network, what can we do with them? Better yet, what can the agent do with them? Imagine that instead of a human observer, there could be other dynamical neural networks (or other parts of the same network) "watching" the activity of the first one. (This idea is very similar to Minsky's A and B brains; Minsky, 1985.) The attractor states of these other networks are influenced on the one hand by the activity of the network they are "watching," and on the other by their own intrinsic dynamics. Thus, the activity of these "watcher" networks, in particular the transitions between attractor states, can be interpreted as a very simple kind of "symbol processing": transitions between attractor states in the first network may trigger state transitions in the "watcher" networks. This activity can, in turn, influence the dynamics of the network they are "watching," and because these networks directly influence the motors, this "symbol processing" can directly influence the robot's behavior: it is not merely internal to the agent. In this way, the "symbol processing" is completely grounded in the robot's brain-body system. We use quotation marks here to indicate that this "symbol processing" differs from that of the classical perspective where explicit symbol structures are programmed into the systems.

What we have said here is still preliminary and admittedly speculative, but we feel that this way of proceeding is promising and opens new perspectives on the symbol grounding problem and on the nature of development in general. Elaborating the connection between symbol processing and attractors in networks is currently an active area of research in robotics (e.g., Inamura et al., 2004; Okada and Nakamura, 2004; Kuniyoshi et al., 2004). An interesting future possibility would be to reduce designer bias in regards to what these "watcher" networks should do and what form they should take by using something like an evolutionary algorithm to produce them.

Before showing how these ideas can be used to tackle the symbol grounding problem, perhaps some final remarks on body image are in order. While we do believe that this approach holds a lot of promise, we have to remain aware that, compared to the complexity of biological systems, we have only scratched the surface. The basic notion of body image presented so far will have to be extended to include additional factors such as implicit or explicit information about the geometry of the body, the shape of limbs, sensor positions, actuator locations, and perhaps knowledge about its physiology.[3] In spite of the simplicity of the "Puppy" case study, we feel that it carries enormous potential both in terms of understanding how (real) cognition might come about, and in terms of clarifying the notion of a body image. The crucial advantage of the synthetic methodology is that we can always precisely pin down what we are talking about. Because of its central importance, how to build a body image has attracted the attention of researchers in developmental robotics (e.g., Yoshikawa et al., 2004b; Kuniyoshi et al., 2004).

Let us now turn to the symbol grounding problem.

5.5 The Symbol Grounding Problem

Since the mid-1980s the symbol grounding problem has been a widely debated issue in artificial intelligence and in the cognitive sciences, but it has remained largely unresolved. According to the psychologist Stevan Harnad, the symbol grounding problem addresses the question of how "the semantic interpretation of a formal symbol system [can] be made intrinsic to the system, rather than just parasitic on the meanings in our heads" (Harnad, 1990). This idea can be rephrased as follows: how can the individual symbols and the symbol structures acquire meaning for the agent itself (or him or herself), rather than for an outside observer? Examples of symbol structures are logical rules of inference like "all humans are mortal, Aristotle is human, thus Aristotle is mortal," and grammatical structures like "Harnad has written an important article about the symbol grounding problem." These examples contain symbols such as "mortal," "Aristotle," "Harnad," and "article."

There is an enormous amount of literature in philosophy and linguistics about "meaning." The way we use the word here is very pragmatic: if an agent is capable of exploiting its sensory stimulation in a way that serves its purposes, e.g., running or getting food, it has understood the meaning of the sensory stimulation. For example, as discussed above, Puppy could use the patterns from its pressure sensors, together with the control signals from the actuators, to identify but also to generate its gait. Or if a frog is capable of catching an insect with its tongue, based on the neural signals it receives from its visual motion detectors in the retina, it has, in some sense, "understood" the meaning of "catching a fly." The fact that it may not be aware of this knowledge does not imply that there is no meaning in this action: it helps the frog survive. So, we might want to associate these patterns of neural stimulation with symbols, and because they arise naturally and in nonarbitrary ways from the agent's dynamics, they are fully grounded.

In traditional AI systems, the meaning of symbols arises from how they relate to other symbols. It is highly questionable whether this can be considered as meaning in the first place, because there is no relation to the outside world whatsoever: the relation is only between symbols. Also, in traditional systems, including expert systems, the meaning of the symbols is entirely attributed to them by an external observer, the user. The systems themselves have no "knowledge" of this connection. Let us elaborate this point a little further.

Expert systems typically contain logical (symbolic) rules of inference such as "If the patient is over 16 years of age, the white blood cell count is less than 2000, and the patient has high fever, then the organism that is causing the infection is likely to be org-12 (with probability 0.7)." Now consider the following thought experiment, which is inspired by the cognitive scientist Bill Clancey's insightful book entitled *Situated Cognition*. If you replace all the variable names in these rules with names such as $x1, x2, x3$, and so on, then, formally speaking, where the functionality of the algorithm is concerned (i.e., what conclusions can be drawn) this new system is equivalent to the one with the meaningful terms. But the new rule will read, "If $x1$ and $x2$ and $x3$ then $x4$ 0.7." Recognizing a collection of such rules as human-level expertise seems far-fetched. In fact, the system itself has absolutely no medical knowledge whatsoever; it simply applies a set of logical rules. Meaning can only be attributed to the variables by the user: it is he or she who makes the connection to the outside world (in other words, provides the grounding for the symbols), not the expert system itself. Thus, in order to achieve real grounding, it is not sufficient to have a system of logical rules of inference that perform some internal processing. If we want a system to generate its own meanings, we need to take the human out of the loop so that the system is forced to interact with the real world on its own. This is one of the important reasons why researchers in artificial intelligence started working on autonomous systems in the first place. With the Puppy case study we have tried to sketch how this connection to the outside world might be achieved.

The entire line of reasoning that we have just laid out rests on one important insight, i.e., that the robot itself must have rich, natural dynamics when it interacts with its environment. We will look into this issue in the next section.

5.6 Matching Brain and Body Dynamics

In the early phases of embodied artificial intelligence, many people worked on navigation and orientation out of a conviction that locomotion and orientation are somehow the underlying driving forces in the development of cognition and in the evolution of the brain. This is corroborated by the question asked by the neuroscientist Daniel Wolpert, Why don't plants have brains? He suggested that the answer might actually be quite simple: Plants don't have to move! After the "embodied turn," researchers started working with robots, and because they were readily available and easy to use, wheeled robots were the tools of choice. While there was a lot of progress (researchers were forced to deal with the real-world problems such as noise, imprecision, change, and unpredictability), there were also some fundamental problems inherent in the approach. Remember that one of the aspects of the principle of ecological balance is that the complexity levels of sensory, motor, and neural systems should match.

Wheeled robots typically have only a few degrees of freedom in their motor system: they often have two motors, one for each wheel, thus enabling the robot to move around on a flat surface. Because it is easy to put a high-resolution camera on a robot, and because wheeled robots are very simple, many experimental designs were unbalanced: complex sensory systems, very simple motor systems. As a result of these unbalanced designs, the systems had relatively uninteresting physical dynamics: no matter how the camera data was used, or what control algorithm was implemented, the robot still just drove around on flat ground. Although some of the algorithms were biologically inspired, they were arbitrary with respect to the robot's own dynamics, which implies that one algorithm could be exchanged for another while achieving essentially the same behavior. Something essential was missing, and there is strong evidence that it was a complex sensory-motor system with rich dynamics. By rich dynamics we mean that the system has many degrees of freedom that enable it to move in a large variety of different ways. Robots with only two wheels and no arms typically do not have rich dynamics, whereas complex humanoids with arms, legs, and hands do. An example of a robot with rich dynamics is Kenta (the Japanese word for "tendon boy"), developed by one of the leading researchers in humanoid robotics, Masayuki Inaba of the University of Tokyo (e.g., Yoshikai et al., 2003). In contrast to other humanoids, it has a flexible, segmented spine and a host of tendons that allow it to move in many different ways. Thus Kenta can achieve truly rich dynamics.

To further elaborate the seemingly contradictory conclusion of this chapter about complex sensory-motor dynamics as a prerequisite for high-level cognition, let us look at another case study. Rats are fascinating animals: they are cute, funny, clever, and curious; they can swim, climb, jump, and manipulate objects; and they can learn and behave in ways that are obviously intelligent. They also have extraordinary orientation abilities. Learning to navigate in a maze is just one of the many tasks they are good at. This fascinating ability—in addition to the fact that they can be grown and handled easily in the laboratory—is one of the reasons why rats are the subject of such a vast amount of research in psychology and behavioral neuroscience. The discovery of place and head-direction cells (O'Keefe and Dostrovsky, 1971) was a landmark event on the road to explaining their navigational skills. When rats are placed in a particular location in an arena, certain groups of cells in the hippocampus (a region in the temporal lobe of the brain that is believed to play an important role in the formation of long-term memory) are activated. When the rat is moved to another location, another group of cells—another set of "place cells"—fire. This phenomenon tells us that different groups of cells are associated with different places in the rat's environment. Together with the so-called head-direction cells, i.e., cells that fire only when the rat's head is pointing in a particular direction, they provide an excellent representation, or map, for the rat. These groups of cells seem to account at least partly for the uncanny navigational skills of rats (e.g., Best et al., 2001).

In robot experiments that mimic rat behavior based on place and head-direction cells, it is common to use wheeled robots like the Khepera, which has an omnidirectional camera (a camera with a 360° visual field). Omnidirectional cameras are often used to account for the fact that rodents have almost omnidirectional vision. The advantage of using robots is that because they function in the same environment as rats, they have to deal with roughly the same sensory stimulation. The disadvantage of using wheeled robots is that because they are wheeled, their dynamics is much simpler and completely different from that of rats, and, as we have discussed earlier, there are no constraints on the robot's control architecture. In this sense, the robot is basically a computer, and it can be programmed arbitrarily. For example, it could be programmed with a detailed model of thousands of place and head-direction cells. In this respect robots with complex computational components but simple bodies have a definite cognitivistic flavor. This may sound paradoxical: on the one hand the robot control system is biologically inspired, but on the other it is still ungrounded because the controller does not match the robot's body dynamics. In order to add validity to the robot models, it would be necessary to take into account the complex sensory-motor skills of the animal being modeled, and for this purpose a more complex dynamics—resulting from a more complex body—would be required. For example, the rat can move its head (and therefore its vision system) independently of its body (a Khepera normally cannot), a morphological condition which might in fact play a role in the evolution of place and head-direction cells.

But rats can do a lot more than just move around. So, obviously, other behaviors will be necessary to build up their body image and cognition. For example, they will need to be able to make distinctions in the real world, i.e., they must have the ability to perform categorization. There is a lot of experimental evidence that categorization is based on sensory-motor-coordinated actions such as looking at an object (foveating), grasping, pointing, touching, moving the fingers (or whiskers!) over a surface or along an edge, etc. The body image contains (typically implicit) knowledge about the interplay between motor systems and the different sensor systems. For example, when you grasp and lift an object, the simultaneous activation of the pressure sensors in your hand and the light sensors in your retina, together with proprioceptive sensors such as the force sensors in your muscles, gives you information not just about the object but also about how your hand and arm work. Needless to say, proprioceptive sensors are important for a body image.

Again, the body image need neither be symbolic nor conscious, and it will typically be continuous, not discrete. But within this dynamical system, which includes the motor, sensory, and neural systems and the environment, there will be many attractor states that also form part of the body image. Imagine that a robot grasps an object and lifts it up. As in the case of a human, this behavior will cause the touch sensors in the hand, the force sensors on the actuators, and the camera to fire together, and this sensory stimulation is caused by the way the motors are actuated. This will create an attractor state that could allow the robot to "understand," in a sense, the causal relationship between the motor signals, the muscle activity (proprioception), and the sensor stimulation.

5.7   Broadening the Scope: Other Aspects of Development

As mentioned at the beginning of the chapter, the ultimate motivating goal of developmental robotics is to grow an intelligent adult robot from scratch. And as we have just seen in our discussion of Puppy, sensory-motor processes will play a fundamental role in this pursuit. However, developmental roboticists have identified several other essential issues that form part of a developmental process. As we will see, these issues, together with our case study of Puppy, lead to a number of design principles that apply specifically to developmental systems. In the remainder of this chapter we will explore these issues and discuss what role they play when moving from locomotion to cognition—or, more generally, from sensory-motor behaviors to intelligence. The research landscape in this area is still very rugged, and there are many exciting research directions waiting to be explored. A developmental approach raises a large number of puzzling problems to which there are currently no real solutions. There are, however, many interesting and promising ideas.

A biological organism grows from a baby into an adult, and during this development it significantly changes its shape and learns many things. So far, with our current technology we cannot grow artificial systems, so growth cannot yet be modeled well on robots. However, some interesting ways to get around this obstacle have been proposed by developmental roboticists. Max Lungarella, for example, whom we mentioned earlier, started out with a robot equipped with high-precision motor systems and high-resolution sensory systems, but at the beginning of this particular experiment, low precision and low resolution are simulated using software. Low-precision movements can be achieved by simply locking some of the degrees of freedom, such as the knees, or by adding random numbers—noise—to the control signals for the joints. Low-resolution sensing can be achieved in a high-resolution camera in software by simply averaging over neighboring pixels of the camera. Over time, both precision and resolution are increased, thus mimicking a kind of embodied development: in a sense the body changes or matures into a more adult organism.

Lungarella's experiment is one of a number of recent attempts to answer what is known as Bernstein's problem, which is about how an agent with many degrees of freedom learns to control its own body (e.g., Bernstein, 1967). Of course, to allow this process to occur, the experiment will require extended periods of time.

Development over Time

Development is a long process that, in humans at least, takes many years. In order to study long-term development we would need robots capable of interacting with the real world over extended periods of time. Currently available robots are not robust and self-sufficient enough to do so. The development of a biological organism requires that the different time scales of the components be integrated, from the operation time of the neurons (about 10 to 100 ms) to short-term memory (seconds to minutes), long-term memory (minutes to years) and the learning of motor skills such as grasping, walking, or complex tool manipulation, which could take weeks, months, or even years (see figure 5.4). Just think of how long it takes to master a musical instrument.

Researchers are often frustrated that learning takes so long in their experiments. But learning in children can also take a very long time. When babies learn to walk, they fall over literally thousands of times before they manage to walk coherently. This is another reason why long-term learning experiments in robots are very rare; robot technology is simply not yet ready for that kind of wear and tear. Today's learning experiments on robots are performed almost exclusively over very short periods; a robot typically acquires one type of skill, such as reaching for and grasping a cup, or learning to kick a ball into a goal, and then the experiment stops. Very little research exists in which the robot uses previously acquired skills to learn new ones. But what is the point of learning to grasp an object if you do not then learn to do something useful with it? One exception is perhaps Luc Steels's Talking Heads experiment, which took place over several months and which we will briefly discuss below. Because much of biological learning requires a long time, short-term experiments will not help elucidate its mysteries. And natural forms of learning although far from perfect, have of course proved enormously useful in the real world.

There is another challenge to long-term experiments: motivation. If we want to apply a developmental approach to the flute-playing robot WF-4, for instance, the robot must not only have many degrees of freedom in the hand and the mouth, but it should also somehow have the motivation to actually use them.

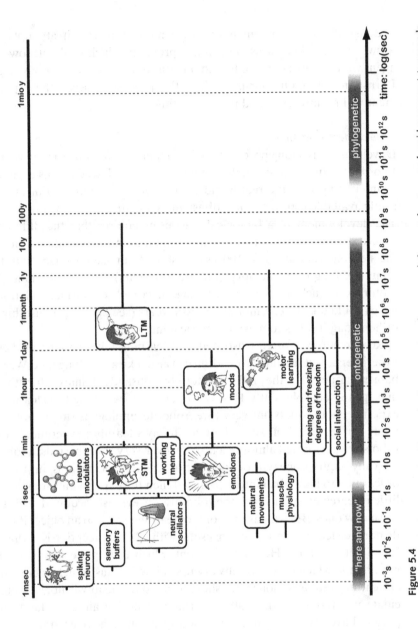

Figure 5.4
Time scales in human behavior. Time scales from very short (msec range), for neural systems and rapid movement, to seconds for short-term memory (STM), to minutes and hours for moods and for moving from one place to another, to days, months, and years for ontogenetic development and long-term memory (LTM), to decades, centuries, and millions of years for phylogenetic processes. Many of these time scales need to be integrated in a human being living in the real world.

Now, what mechanisms account for motivation? Let us look at two of them: Hebbian learning and neuromodulators. It is not uncommon to design neural systems that work on the basis of Hebbian learning, a biologically inspired neural mechanism in which connections between neurons that fire simultaneously—those whose activation is correlated—are strengthened (Hebb, 1949). A catchy and popular summary of Hebbian learning is "neurons that fire together wire together." In other words, Hebbian learning forms explicit associations between correlated neural activity. Keep in mind, though, that researchers who put Hebbian learning into their systems implicitly assume that association is of value for the agent. If the robot is equipped with Hebbian learning, it does not *want* to associate; it is just doing so. Picking up correlations turns out to be especially useful because through sensory-motor-coordinated behavior, correlations are induced, as summarized in the principle of sensory-motor coordination (see, for example, Lungarella et al., 2005, which provides a quantative analysis building on the foundational ideas of Tononi et al. [1994, 1996]). In other words, these correlations most likely indicate underlying causal structure: e.g. the simultaneous sensory activity in both the force sensors in the muscles and the pressure sensors in the hand is caused by the act of grasping.

The second mechanism is based on neuromodulators, which are molecules in the brain that influence its plasticity, i.e., how easily neural structures change—or how little they change—in response to incoming signals. So from this perspective neuromodulators provide a kind of value system because they signal to the organism that now is, or is not, a good time to learn. Neuromodulators can be viewed as relevance indicators, telling the organism when an event of interest has occurred. This helps the organism learn important events and ignore irrelevant ones.

Another important question that we want to tackle is why an organism is motivated to accomplish ever more complex tasks. Luc Steels and his group at Sony Computer Science Laboratory in Paris suggested that it might be sufficient to provide an agent with a single motivational principle, a principle they have dubbed the *autotelic* principle (Steels, 2004). Steels drew inspiration from the psychologist Mihalyi Csikszentmihalyi, author of the self-help book *Flow: The Psychology of Optimal Experience*, which has reached cult status since its publication in 1990. Flow is the kind of feeling experienced by any kind of experts, be they surgeons, rock-climbers, authors, athletes, or mechanics, whenever they are performing their expert activity well. Or, to use the words of the Taoist scholar Chuang Tzu: "Perception and understanding have come to a stop and the spirit moves where it wants. You stop 'thinking' and just do." Interestingly, this idea, despite its slightly esoteric feel, was also very popular with the classical AI expert systems community in the mid-1980s, where Csikszentmihalyi's ideas were used to characterize the nature of human expertise.

When the idea of flow is applied to motivation, it means, by analogy, to maintain a constant flow of information through the system. If the organism masters one skill, its processing demands will decrease and it is then free to use exploration strategies to increase its inflow of information. For example, imagine a robot learning to drink from a cup. First, it has to be able to reach, which initially will require its entire learning capacity. After some time, this movement will become automatic, thus freeing the learning resources, at which point it can begin to explore the environment using the additional degrees of freedom in the hand that it had not used earlier for grasping. Had it used all the degrees of freedom from the start, there would have been an information overflow and it would not have learned to reach or grasp, or to do so would have taken much longer. This idea of flow is another instance of diversity-compliance: the agent can exploit previously learned behaviors to explore—and eventually learn—new ones. In other words, the more skills the organism has mastered, the more readily it can indulge in exploratory activities. Flow is intuitively plausible but hard to measure in a complex embodied system; how to quantify such effects is an important research question.

5.8 Learning in Embodied Systems

Let us now look at an example that links these ideas about building up complexity to our earlier discussion about how sensory-motor behaviors can lead to cognition. More specifically, the following example illustrates how embodiment guides exploration such that learning becomes easier. Assume for a moment, just for the sake of argument, that as an exploration strategy a baby's brain randomly stimulates the muscles of his arms. Although the neural signals may be more or less random, the resulting arm movements will be far from random because the arm is highly constrained by its morphology—its anatomy—and the material properties of the muscle-tendon system. For example, the arm will most likely move forward with the hand swinging toward the front of the torso, the palm of the right hand will face left as the arm moves, and so on. In this way, while the arm is moving forward there is a better chance that the palm of the hand will hit an object near the baby than that the back of the hand will. (If the baby is below a certain age, it will simply hit the object and not much will happen except that the object might tip over). Again for the sake of argument, assume that the hand is equipped with a grasp reflex that causes the baby to grab an object when its palm is stimulated. If the baby does grasp an object, his fingertips will come into contact with the object. Rich sensory stimulation is then generated because our fingertips have a high density of sensors, much more dense than on the back of the hand. Note that this is a morphological property—a physical property of the organism—but it significantly influences what kind of sensory stimulation will be generated.

Let's continue the story. Because the arm tends to swing forward, the baby's hand—and therefore the object—will enter into the visual field of the baby, so that he will see the object in addition to feeling it. Very likely the object will end up on (or in) the baby's mouth, because the forward swing of the arm tends to cause the baby's hand to come close to his mouth. So there will be additional sensory stimulation generated by the object touching his lips or tongue. And all of this sensory stimulation is correlated so that it will be easy for the child to make the proper associations between the signals produced by the different sensory channels involved: the correlated stimulation of the force sensors in the arm, the touch sensors in the palm, fingertips, and lips, the eyes, and the taste buds on the tongue provide information not just about the baby's own body but also about the object's shape, color, texture, weight, and taste. And all that essentially from random neural signals and a bunch of simple reflexes!

The resulting correlations in the different sensory channels caused by these exploration processes then become the raw material for learning. Recall our previous discussion where we pointed out that Hebbian learning, in essence, forms associations by picking up on correlations. From such processes, complex sensory-motor coordination—and thus complex concepts—can be generated. While in young babies categorization involves sensor and motor processes, over time there is a certain decoupling of the motor system so that the baby need not always act on the environment: he can start categorizing objects just by looking at them. In other words, he can perform categorization without sticking everything into his mouth (Thelen and Smith, 1994). While it is not known how these decoupling processes actually work, there is some experimental evidence to support this idea. It has been found that the same parts of the human brain are involved when performing an action, watching an action, or just thinking about an action (the "mirror neurons" described in the next section). Although this description may not reflect exactly how babies form high-level concepts, the guiding influence of the body is clearly a prerequisite.

5.9 Social Interaction

Now we come to the final—and what many people consider the most important—aspect of development, social interaction. However, a full treatment of this topic is beyond the scope of this book. Instead we will look at a number of aspects of social interaction, all of which are directly related to the agents' sensory-motor processes: imitation, joint attention, scaffolding, and natural language. Jacqueline Nadel of the Centre National de la Recherche Scientifique in Paris very clearly pointed out that sensory-motor coordination and social interaction constitute two different types of causalities (Nadel, 2002). For example, knowing that a child's scream will cause the mother to quickly appear, or that smiling will elicit a smile from the partner in an interaction, is entirely different from knowing that when I tilt a cup the liquid will spill out. Both screaming and tilting a cup have consequences, but they are different: in social interactions another person responds; in sensory-motor coordination it is the environment.

Imitation, Joint Attention, and Scaffolding

Imitation is a core topic in developmental robotics. Here we only touch on some of the issues; the interested reader is referred to Dautenhahn and Nehaniv (2002), Kuniyoshi et al. (2003), and Yoshikawa et al. (2004a) for more details. As is well known from psychology textbooks, imitation is an extremely powerful learning strategy for human infants. For example imitating sounds helps children eventually learn to master natural language. Getting robots to learn by imitating humans or other robots is certainly, in the long run, a much better strategy than programming the robots for specific tasks; we could simply show the robots what to do (or have them watch another robot), and they could acquire the skill! There is a catch, though: the problem is to find the underlying mechanisms that allow an agent to imitate another individual's behavior.

From the substantial literature on imitating robots we can infer that one of the great difficulties is the situated nature of the agents, which implies that they have to interpret their environment, i.e., the movements and intentions of other agents, through their own sensory-motor system. In other words, imitation requires sophisticated perceptual abilities, a factor that is often neglected in discussions of the topic. Experimenters often make life easy for the robots by presenting them with obvious movements or movements selected from a limited repertoire, by making sure the to-be-imitated behavior is the only thing moving in the robot's visual field, by performing actions against a homogenous background to simplify the problem of separating the image of the teacher from the background, and so on. We must be careful not to fall into the trap that computer vision researchers experienced: perhaps a robot's embodiment can allow it to move beyond image analysis only and help simplify the task of perceiving and recognizing behavior in other embodied agents. However this remains yet another open research topic.

One of the fascinating recent events in neuroscience was the discovery that there is an identifiable neural basis for this sophisticated imitation ability. "Mirror neurons" (e.g., Gallese et al., 1996) caused quite a stir upon their discovery because they fire when the animal either performs a movement or else observes the same movement in another animal. They demonstrate how closely cognitive concepts and sensory-motor activity are coupled in the brain: when executing a motor action or simply perceiving it in another agent, the same brain areas are activated.

The discovery of mirror neurons has triggered an intense debate in the neuroscience literature about the extent to which perceptual abilities require motor skills. Is the ability to grasp a cup a prerequisite for being able to perceive this action in others? There is a tricky issue here. If the agent is to learn by imitation, it has to have the pertinent perceptual abilities: it has to be able to recognize the desired action in others. But if these perceptual abilities require that the agent can perform the action already, there is a Catch-22 sort of problem: in order to imitate, the agent first has to see the action, but in order to see the action the agent must first be able to perform the action.

But the problem can be resolved if we look at development as an incremental process, where one ability builds on top of abilities already present. For example a child may only be able to reach in a loose and inexact way, but this inexact control over arm movements may lead to more precise control. So there is a lot of similarity between movements in a developmental perspective; it is not an all-or-none matter: particular behaviors, like reaching, are not only either possible or not possible, but can be performed with greater or lesser degrees of control.

Another prerequisite for imitation seems to be shared or joint attention: the instructor and the imitator have to focus on the same body part or movement, otherwise the learner does not know what to imitate. Again, joint attention comes in many variations and can be achieved in a number of ways. For example, the instructor can bring an object into the visual field of the robot and move it back and forth. If the robot is equipped with motion detectors, it will start to focus on this object, as in the Cog example we discussed in the last chapter. Another possibility is that the baby or the robot infers where the other person is looking by extrapolating from their gaze direction, also a nontrivial task, especially in a dynamically changing environment. While mechanisms for joint attention are usually preprogrammed by the designer of a system, there have been attempts to achieve joint attention from more basic assumptions, such as learning them during development. What follows is a simplified version of the process described by Nagai and his colleagues. First, the robot learns to focus an object within its field of view, using only visual information about the object. Then, it slowly learns how to look at the same object by looking at the face of someone who is looking at it. In other words, the robot learns how to change from visual attention to joint attention—both the robot and another person come to jointly look at the same object. The interested reader is referred to the literature for more information (e.g., Nagai et al. 2003).

In chapter 4 we discussed scaffolding, which is a particular way of structuring the environment to help an agent perform its task, or to learn how to perform it. Scaffolding also has a specific social meaning. Caregivers typically provide the learner with "scaffolds" in order to facilitate learning and development. For example, a parent will initially hold the child by the hand when walking. As the child improves its walking skills the support is gradually released, making the task more taxing for the child. Although there are some preliminary experiments that demonstrate that this kind of scaffolding is indeed beneficial in terms of speed and quality of development, there have only been very few studies measuring exactly how much scaffolding enhances learning.

To conclude our discussion of social interaction let us now move to the last and perhaps biggest challenge in the development of cognition, natural language.

Natural Language
Communication lies at the heart of social interaction. As is well known, natural language communication is essential for human development:

most of what we know we heard from other people or read from written documents. When studying development in other species like rats, natural language can be discounted, but in human development, this ability must be taken into account.

Alas, only very few concrete experiments in the language domain have capitalized on how language might emerge from embodied systems. One of them, as mentioned above, is the seminal Internet-based experiment by Luc Steels's group on the acquisition of vocabulary in semi-embodied agents, i.e., agents consisting of movable cameras that face a whiteboard. On this whiteboard there are different kinds of patterns, such as triangles, squares, and circles in different colors, sizes, and arrangements. The Talking Heads experiment is a kind of language game, in which agents consisting of these cameras, located either in the same room or in a completely different location in the world, try to guess what the other agent is looking at. At the same time, the agents either create a new word, e.g., *blatesh*, or they use one that they already have for a particular arrangement, such as a yellow triangle above a red circle. The language game is considered successful if the agents agree on a word and a configuration; otherwise it is considered a failure. Astonishingly, after a few thousand interactions, there is a convergence in vocabulary. The details are highly involved, but the experiment exemplifies how something like language might emerge, rather than being programmed in. The fascinating result is that the vocabulary in the community of agents is completely emergent, a result of a self-organizing process. So far, the experiments have dealt only with vocabulary, but Steels and his team are working on the next step, acquisition of syntax. It is fascinating to think about how this could play out in the future: could the Talking Heads discover a common vocabulary, syntax, and grammar, thereby creating their own language? What would that language be like?

5.10   Development: Where Are We and Where Do We Go from Here?

As we have already mentioned, for the better part, in developmental robotics, humanoid robots are the platforms of choice. Humanoid robots are ideal tools for studying complex systems with many degrees of freedom, which, as we have seen in this chapter, are important for studying development. Another advantage is that they can serve as models of human development. A third advantage is that, if we are interested in applications, such robots will eventually be able to function in human environments, a topic we will take up again in chapter 11. And last but not least, the construction of humanoid robots is advancing the state of the art in robotic technology—including new sensors, actuator technologies, and systems engineering tools—at an incredible rate.

However, it is important to maintain a realistic perspective. We have to be aware that in spite of their superficial resemblance to humans, humanoids typically have entirely different morphologies in terms of sensors and actuators. We also should keep in mind that because we are actually building robots and using technologies that are different from those of natural systems—e.g., using a servomotor instead of a muscle—we are introducing an entirely different kind of dynamics that no longer reflects that of the biological system. Because of the humanoid appearance of these robots, they often cause even the researchers themselves to fall into the trap of anthropomorphization. It is not uncommon to hear statements like "the robot has the intelligence of a two-year-old child." But just think of all the things that are different: the haptic system, the mouth region, the tongue with all its sensors, the articulatory system (for producing speech), the complicated muscle-tendon systems, as well as the entire physiology. As a consequence, the concepts the robot can potentially acquire will be very different from our own. In spite of these limitations, we can learn a lot about how, in principle, concepts are learned.

A good question that we can always ask is what we have learned so far from this field. First, it is clear and obvious that developmental robotics is an exciting and thriving research field with ambitious goals—such as growing an "adult" robot from an "infant" robot, understanding human development, and creating self-learning robots with humanlike motor, perceptual, and cognitive abilities. Only the future will tell whether or when these goals will be realized. But many highly interesting first results have been achieved that hold great promise: robots have learned aspects of motor control and sensory-motor coordination skills; others can learn by imitating humans or other robots; some have made inroads into solving Bernstein's problem, etc. Another exciting future possibility of this field is its potential to explore new and different kinds of cognition that may or may not resemble human cognition. This is in the spirit of studying not just "life (or intelligence) as it is," but "life (or intelligence) as it could be." As we said before, nonhuman morphologies may eventually lead to nonhuman kinds of cognition.

We feel that, at the moment, most urgently needed in the field are advances in robotic technology: for example, for building artificial skin, artificial muscles, and artificial neural systems, to mention but a few. Such technologies would almost certainly create breakthroughs in robotics and move the field much closer to its ambitious goals.

5.11 Summary: Design Principles for Developmental Systems

In our short review of developmental robotics, we have implicitly or explicitly referred to a number of design principles, in particular for intelligent systems. To pull together some of the many ideas we have considered in this chapter, we have compiled a number of additional design principles, especially for developmental systems. Many of the ideas have been touched upon in chapter 4, but here we look at them specifically from the perspective of development.

Time scale integration principle The first observation, or principle, if you like, is that there are many time scales that must be integrated when designing robots, a problem encountered only in embodied agents. In disembodied agents there is no real time and thus, from the perspective of the agent (the program), there are just steps, one operation after another. In the real world, however, there is real continuous time during which things happen more or less slowly. We have discussed the different time scales in chapter 3. The developmental perspective introduces a number of additional time scales in order to account for the fact that development extends over the lifetime of an individual. But because sensory-motor processes, which take place in the short term, form the basis of development—which occurs over ontogenetic time—these different time scales must all be integrated in one and the same agent. We call this the *time scale integration* principle.

Development as an incremental process principle The second observation or principle is that development is an incremental or historical process. In order for the organism to learn control of its own complex brain-body system, it is necessary to start simple so that the organism—natural or artificial—can successively build on top of what it has already learned. If, on the other hand, the organism were to begin by using its full complexity, (e.g., high-resolution sensory channels, high-precision flexible motor control), it would never be able to learn anything. Most of the concrete experiments in the field focus, one way or another, on this process. This is called the *development as an incremental process* principle.

Discovery principle The third observation or principle that results from our discussion revolves around the idea of discovery. By moving in lots of different ways, or, more generally, by exploring your body in your environment, you can discover and ultimately learn the attractor states and the transitions between them, i.e., you develop a body image. Because attractor states are a natural result of the agent's dynamics, this process is largely self-organized. We call this the *discovery* principle. It provides heuristics for how to find the kinds of exploratory activities that are best for building a body image, which is currently an open research issue.

Social interaction principle   The fourth observation or principle is that sensory-motor coordination, which we have considered in detail in chapter 4, needs to be complemented by social interaction. It seems that sensory-motor processing combined with social interaction provides the most powerful engine for development. Although some studies have combined the two, especially in the area of imitation and joint attention, much work remains to be done at this interface. This has been called the *social interaction* principle (Lungarella, 2004). Although this principle in itself is somewhat general, there have been many suggestions in the literature on how an agent could exploit the different kinds of social interactions for its own development. Again, there is much more work to be done here.

Motivated complexity principle   The fifth and final observation or principle is that there must be a basic motivation for an agent to augment its own complexity during development: otherwise, why should it not be happy with what it has? This is an important aspect of the value principle described in chapter 4. Recall, as we said before, we do not want to directly program motivations into the agent. Rather, motivation should emerge from the developmental or evolutionary process. This is called the *motivated complexity* principle.

This chapter has explored many facets of development, but of course there are more—a host of literature on developmental neuroscience, for example, could potentially be included here. But we hope we have been able to communicate a bit of the flavor of this exciting research area, which is still in its infancy. Because many young people work in the discipline, there is a lot of energy and optimism. Let us now switch from the ontogenetic to the phylogenetic time scale and have a look at how we can put evolution to work for artificial intelligence.

In the 1960s, Ingo Rechenberg of the Technical University of Berlin started thinking about how the power of evolution might be exploited to solve hard engineering problems.[1] One of these problems was how to optimally design pipes so that the flow through them would be maximized. Figure 6.1 shows the basic idea. Fluid enters the system through the vertical pipe on the left, and it has to be redirected into the horizontal tube drawn at the top. Rechenberg asked himself what the optimal shape of the connecting tube should be, where "optimal" means maximum amount of flow through the pipe, which is essentially the same as minimizing turbulence. Generations of engineers did not even bother asking this question because a quarter circle seemed to be the obvious answer. Rechenberg was in for a huge surprise. It turned out that the optimal shape of the pipe produced by his experiment has a strange looking hump (or hunch, if you like) in it, as shown in the illustration (figure 6.1a). (This shape was automatically produced by an evolutionary algorithm; an overview of these algorithms is given in focus box 6.1.) When you actually do the proper physics on this problem, you can verify that this solution with the hump is indeed the best one. It is interesting to note that the quarter circle fits into the confines of a square that we, without being aware of it, mentally draw around the problem: the vertical and horizontal pipe form the two sides of this imaginary square. (Remember the puzzle from your childhood where you have to connect the four corners of a square such that you end up in the same point you started using only three straight lines? The solution is hard to find because without being aware of it, we confine ourselves to the inside of the square.) The reason why the evolved humped pipe, in spite of its superior flow property, is not used today is because flow is not the only requirement: pipes that contain a

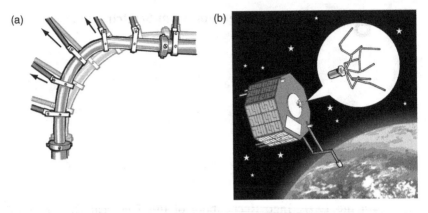

Figure 6.1
Artificial evolution's creative products. Two "inventions" of artificial evolution. (*a*)
Rechenberg's "hunched" fuel pipe problem: What is the optimal shape of the connecting
piece between the vertical tube where the fluid comes in and the horizontal one where the
fluid goes out? Rechenberg devised a mechanism by which the shape of the connecting
piece can be arbitrarily changed under program control. It can be shown that the strange-
looking "hunch" that artificial evolution comes up with in fact reduces turbulence, compared to a quarter circle. (*b*) The antenna used on the NASA ST-5 satellite. The antenna's
shape was evolved using a genetic algorithm by Jason Lohn and his colleagues at NASA's
Ames research center in California.

quarter circle without a hump are cheaper to manufacture and take up
less space.

Since the time of Rechenberg's revolutionary experiments, this idea of
exploiting artificial evolution has infected engineering and computer
science departments all over the world, where the use of evolutionary
algorithms for designing everything from airplane wings to computer
programs to poetry is spreading like wildfire. In addition to designing
mechanical devices, software, and art, in the past few years researchers
have begun to use such algorithms to design virtual and robotic agents,
some of which exhibit sophisticated behavior.

In this chapter we will first look at a few reasons why we might want
to use artificial evolution for studying intelligence. Then we will give a
bit of historical background about the field, briefly describe how evolutionary algorithms work, and look at a few real-world applications. Then
we will get into evolutionary robotics, where we discuss how best to
evolve embodied systems. More specifically, we will discuss why it is
important to evolve all aspects—morphology, materials, neural control—
of the embodied system, and how to evolve them. We will look at models
of genetic regulatory networks, which are a powerful set of tools for
increasing the creative power of artificial evolution by exploiting

Focus Box 6.1
Artificial Evolution

Artificial evolution draws inspiration from biological evolution. However, just as in the case of artificial neural networks (focus box 5.1), we have to make significant abstractions if we want to exploit the power of evolution for design. There is a vast literature and an enormous diversity of evolutionary algorithms, but they can all be mapped onto the simple cycle shown in figure 6.2. The research community uses a lot of biological terminology such as genotype, phenotype, selection, mutation, etc. Although from a biological perspective this may not always be justified (because the biological world is much more complicated), in the context of the algorithms themselves these terms have precisely defined meanings.

First you have to encode your design problem into an artificial genome. In Rechenberg's pipe problem, the positions of all of the rods that control the curvature of the pipe were encoded; in a neural network for controlling a robot the set of all connection weights are included. This collection of values is called the genotype. The algorithm then cycles through the following steps:

1. *Generate initial population* You start with an initial randomly chosen population of genotypes (e.g., a population of individuals that all consist of a list of all the connection weights in the neural network).

2. *Development* You turn the genotype into a phenotype through a process of development (e.g., the values in the genome are assigned as weights to the synapses in a neural network and the network is embedded into a robot).

3. *Selection* You select those phenotypes that perform best on the task to create a new population (e.g., those robots with a neural network that move the farthest without hitting any obstacles); the rest you throw away. "Performs best" is defined through a fitness function such as the distance traveled by the robot minus the number of times it collides with an obstacle.

4. *Reproduction* You copy, and then modify the genotypes of the selected individuals to create a new population, mostly through mutation and crossover (e.g., one of the synaptic weights encoded in the genome is changed a bit [mutation], or two "parents" are chosen and two new individuals are created, inheriting part of their genetic information from one parent and the rest from the other [crossover]). Most of the genotypes thus produced will turn into phenotypes that perform worse, but some will perform better than both of their parents.

5. Repeat the cycle beginning with step 2.

Surprisingly, if you wait long enough, a good solution will often be found.

Most evolutionary algorithms follow this scheme. There are a number of dimensions that can be used to classify the different variations: how information is encoded in the genome; how the developmental process, selection, and reproduction are carried out; and so on. Let us briefly make a pass through the loop.

Where the encoding in the genome is concerned, classical genetic algorithms (Holland, 1992) normally have a discrete encoding (i.e., a string of binary or integer values, or discrete letters) in the genotype, whereas in the case of evolution strategies (Rechenberg, 1994), it is real numbers. In genetic programming (Banzhaf et al., 1998), the genotype is a tree structure which represents a computer program (a string cannot be used for the representation because if one bit is not correct, the program does not run and has a fitness of zero, and will thus not contribute to the evolutionary process).

The developmental process is often omitted so that phenotype equals genotype, and selection can be made directly on the genotype. For example, in the "methinks it is like a weasel" problem, we can use as a fitness function the closeness of a given sentence to the target one, which can be calculated by counting the number of letters in the correct positions. In the case of a neural network for a robot, there is a kind of trivial process of development: the neural network with the genetically encoded weights is embedded in a robot. In this case, the phenotype is clearly distinct from the genotype: the neural network itself cannot be tested for fitness; it must be embedded in a robot. But in almost all evolutionary algorithms, there is no interaction with the environment during development: the weights as encoded in the genome are directly used on the robot. It is only recently that the research community has started taking into account the interaction of a growing organism with its environment before conducting the fitness testing.

As for selection, many schemes have been proposed, and their effect on the evolutionary process has been well studied. A popular one is known as "roulette wheel," in which individuals have a certain probability, proportional to their fitness, of being selected for reproduction. It is important not only to select the best individuals but also to include less fit ones in order to keep the diversity in the population.

Reproduction is typically implemented as mutation and crossover. These processes come in many variations, and their effect on the evolutionary process have been well investigated. In classical genetic algorithms the length of the genome does not change during reproduction, but if we are interested in an increase of complexity during evolution, the genome should have the potential to grow (and perhaps shrink) in length. This idea has always been a focus in genetic programming, but it has also begun to be investigated in evolutionary computation in general (e.g., Poli, 2001; Bongard, 2003).

Artificial evolution can be used for almost any kind of engineering problem. In evolutionary robotics, where evolution is used to design certain parts of the robot, the robot itself is usually given and evolution is employed to find the weights of its neural network. But we are specifically interested in embodied agents; i.e., we want to evolve complete agents, not only their neural controllers. One approach for this is to encode the morphology of the robot into the genome as a set of parameters (e.g., the shapes of body parts, and the types of joints that attach them together), which are then used as the variables evolution can modify. The problem with this approach is that the genome becomes very long for a complex creature made up of many parts. The other approach is to embed developmental processes in the evolutionary cycle, as shown in figure 6.2.

Two main variants have been proposed for development-based artificial evolution. The first is parametric, as just explained, where you define the segments or modules that can then be repeatedly used to construct the entire organism (e.g., Sims, 1994a; Lipson and Pollack, 2000). The second involves modeling the developmental processes via genetic regulatory networks (Eggenberger, 1999; Bongard, 2002). In the latter case, it is no longer the parameters of the structure of the robot that are encoded in the genome, but rather the parameters of the genetic regulatory network. The goal of evolution is to find the optimal values for these parameters to guide the growth of the agent.

In short, an artificial genetic regulatory network is a collection of virtual genes, contained in the artificial genome, that influence each other's behavior. Essential components in genetic regulatory networks are *transcription factors*. These are chemicals that can have two effects: they can turn on and off other genes, which, when turned on, start producing their own transcription factors; or they can influence the growth of the creature, such as by causing one body part to split into two, a sensor to grow somewhere on the creature's body, or a neuron to create a new synaptic connection. A genome consists of a number of genes, e.g., 100 in a standard application, and each gene is made up of a few numbers that indicate which transcription factor it is regulated by, which transcription factor it produces when turned on, and which

Focus Box 6.1
(continued)

concentrations of transcription factors are necessary to turn it on. Examples of virtual creatures evolved using genetic regulatory networks are Bongard's block pushers and Eggenberger's morphological structures. Genetic regulatory networks have the advantage over other models of development in that the interaction with the environment during development can easily be modeled, simply by including a mechanism that translates physical forces—such as bumping into an object—into transcription factors. In other words, a transcription factor is produced at the location in the body where the object is touched, and it is diffused into the agent. In this way the environment can influence gene activity, which in turn affects growth.

self-organization for evolutionary design. Then, as in the previous chapter, we will survey the state of the art and see where the field is going. We will conclude by summarizing the major insights from this chapter as a set of design principles.

6.1 Motivation

In the previous chapter we pointed out why we might want to adopt a developmental approach to cognition. In a similar way, there are several motivating factors for taking an evolutionary route. It is worth noting here that developmental and evolutionary approaches to cognition are by no means mutually exclusive. At the moment, they tend to be studied separately, but we will argue later that combining them—and thus integrating all three time scales—seems to be one of the most promising and exciting future avenues of artificial intelligence research. Of course, the main reason for adopting an evolutionary approach is that biological evolution produced biological intelligence: evolution produced us, and we consider ourselves intelligent, so maybe artificial evolution can produce artificially intelligent creatures. But let us look at some other reasons.

First, when it comes to producing intelligent agents, we are most interested in truly creative and original solutions. But in order to come up with them, we will have to get rid of designer bias. By *designer bias* we mean the following. Because we, as human beings, with our particular embodiment (including morphology—shape, materials, sensory and motor systems—and physiology—hunger, thirst, and sex drives), have grown up in this world with its particular physical, environmental, and climatic conditions (gravity, light and dark, rain, sunshine, temperature), its cities, buildings, homes, objects, and social settings (family, school, work, relationships, leisure), our thinking has been shaped in particular ways—this in fact is the very topic of this book. These biases, of which we are usually unaware, limit us in terms of the kind of intelligent systems and robots that we can design and build; they are always there whether we like it or not—we cannot simply get rid of them. But artificial evolution, which is less restricted by designer bias, may help us explore "life as it could be." As we said in chapter 3, "life as it could be" or rather "intelligence as it could be" may give us powerful insights into intelligence in general, not only in its biological forms. In other words, by studying many different forms of intelligence, we can get a better grip on it.

One of the implications of designer bias—and this was also argued by Lakoff and Núñez in *Where Mathematics Comes From*—is that the ways in which we can conceptualize the world—even something as abstract as mathematics—are tightly constrained by the way we are made. Recall the puzzle with the square and the three straight lines. Despite the simplicity of the problem statement, it is difficult to solve. It turns out that the solution is in fact embarrassingly simple: you have to draw the lines beyond the confines of the square! However, unlike design by humans, evolution is a "blind" process. It creates new designs at random. Some of these designs may be useful even though they may be very different from designs we are accustomed to. Rechenberg's hunched pipe is just one example.

Before continuing we should point out that there is a strong danger of anthropomorphizing evolution itself because it is hard to imagine how something as sophisticated as a human could emerge from a non-goal-directed process. The anti-intuitive idea that a blind process can produce complex forms is described beautifully by Richard Dawkins in *The Blind Watchmaker*.

A second reason for using evolution for design is that, often, engineering problems simply become too hard for human intelligence to solve and so we need the support of machines. Take, for example, the design of a radio antenna, a notoriously difficult problem if designed by hand. (We will later elaborate upon this example.) The hope is that by using artificial evolutionary methods we can explore completely new artifacts that have, until now, been beyond the design capabilities of human engineers simply because they are too complex for humans to comprehend. The buzzword sometimes used for this idea is *breaking the complexity barrier*.

A third reason for using artificial evolution is that, on the more theoretical side, it allows us to explore the design principles for intelligent systems. For example, if we can show that the principle of cheap design or the principle of ecological balance emerge from an evolutionary process, we have added validity to those design principles. Later we will describe in more detail the "block pushers," artificial creatures capable of pushing a large block in their simulated environment. It turns out that the morphologies and neural systems of these creatures conform to the cheap design principle. As we have already seen, biological organisms exploit their environments in interesting ways. Amazingly, artificially evolved creatures also do this, sometimes in unexpected ways: we will see how an evolutionary algorithm "invents" a new sensor for picking up radio signals from a nearby computer in order to exploit that other computer's clock signal.

Fourth, artificial evolution can be used not only for engineering purposes but also to learn more about natural evolution. It is not necessary to model every aspect of it in great detail, but, as we have seen in a number of cases—orientation of the desert ant *Cataglyphis*, running of four-legged animals, or dancing in the contraption-like "Stumpy"—by doing things somewhat differently we can learn a lot about the original animal or process under study. Take the example of the running robot Puppy: by simplifying the mechanisms through which fast locomotion emerges, we can more fully explore the general principles underlying running behavior. Making abstractions is always essential for revealing general principles. And computer models of evolution have several significant advantages over natural evolution. First, artificial evolution runs much faster than its natural counterpart because it takes place in a powerful computer. Second, because we are working in a digital world, we can record everything that happens so that we can look back over the digital fossil record, so to speak, and see a progression from "stupid" agents up to "smarter" agents, and also see why it happened, something that has never been possible in natural evolution. However, as always, there is a trade-off: because the virtual environments used in artificial evolution have to be programmed, they are not as rich as nature, and because of the abstractions we have to make when creating them, we may fail to include important details. For example, one could speculate that apes may have evolved to walk on two legs (bipedalism) in order to see over the tall grasses of the African savanna in order to spot approaching predators. So if our virtual environments do not contain tall objects (or predators, for that matter) bipedal agents may not evolve. (Why and how bipedalism actually evolved is indeed still an open question, and a number of competing hypotheses are being discussed, e.g., Hunt, 1996; Lovejoy and Owen, 1981; Wheeler, 1991).

A fifth attraction of artificial evolution is the romantic idea of evolving intelligence from scratch, which is related to the idea (see the previous chapter) of allowing a robot to develop on its own from "baby" to "adult." The question here is how far back we want to go. While some people, especially in the artificial life community, are interested in how life evolved from the primordial soup, in this book we mean the evolution of intelligent agents from nonintelligent ones. Preliminary examples that illustrate this idea are the block pusher virtual robots that we will discuss below.

Finally, and closely related to the previous point, artificial evolution may be the means by which artificial intelligence researchers eventually realize the dream of having a fully automated design system. Maybe it will someday be possible to design components, circuits, entire devices—even intelligent robots—not by hand but simply by specifying what they should do. Imagine "designing" a new radio by merely telling your computer that the device should somehow pick up radio waves and turn them into sound. Although such a process is currently out of reach, there are a few automated design algorithms that can already compete with human engineers. This area of endeavor is commonly referred to as human-competitive engineering. But even in cases in which the evolved artifacts are not very complex, it is interesting to watch evolution at work, as we will illustrate in this chapter.

So, to summarize, there are several motivating factors for using artificial evolution in artificial intelligence research: biological evolution successfully produced biological intelligence; we are interested in generating agents with as little designer bias as possible; designing complex agents is currently beyond the scope of traditional engineering techniques; we can explore the conditions under which the design principles at the here-and-now and developmental time scales emerge; artificial evolution can help us learn about biological evolution; and it allows for the possibility of creating intelligent agents "from scratch" and perhaps, eventually, of automated design in general. Before we get into the details of the evolution of intelligence, let us first look at how artificial evolution works. (Figure 6.2 provides an overview.)

6.2   The Basics of Evolutionary Computation

The three basic driving forces behind evolution are cumulative selection, variation, and self-organization. Dawkins impressively illustrated the workings of cumulative selection with an entertaining example. Assume

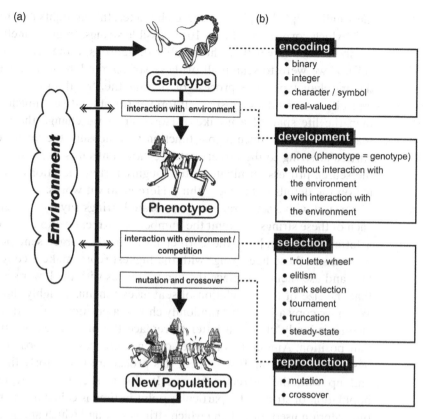

Figure 6.2
Overview of artificial evolution. The vast literature in the field of artificial evolution can be mapped onto this basic scheme. (*a*) The main components. The genotype is translated into a phenotype through a process of development. The phenotypes compete with one another in their ecological niche, and the winners are selected to reproduce, leading to new genotypes. (*b*) Dimensions for classifying evolutionary algorithms.

that a monkey is sitting in front of a keyboard, randomly typing letters. There is a certain—admittedly very low—probability that at some point in time, the sequence of letters typed by the monkey will correspond to the text of Shakespeare's *Hamlet*. To make matters a little easier, Dawkins selected one single sentence from *Hamlet*, namely: "Methinks it is like a weasel," a sentence in somewhat old-fashioned English taken from the passage in which Hamlet talks with Polonius about the shapes of particular clouds, and Polonius essentially repeats (somewhat idiotically) what Hamlet says. (Why this was funny to Elizabethan-era English theatergoers is beyond us, but that's beside the point.) The sentence, including spaces and punctuation, has 29 letters. Assuming 26 letters in the English alphabet plus the space character, this amounts to a total of 27^{29} (which corresponds to 3×10^{41}) possible strings, an awesomely large number, much larger than the number of neurons in the brain (around 10^{11}). If we were to search all of these strings randomly—i.e., if we let the monkey type—the process of finding the "Methinks it is like a weasel" one would take just about forever (or at least very much longer than the life span of a monkey). However, if we change the way we search—if we introduce a goal function and measure the distance of a particular string to the target sentence "Methinks it is like a weasel"—the search process terminates after roughly forty generations (depending on the details of the algorithm). Here is how it works.

We start with a set of randomly generated strings, say ten of them. For each of these strings we count the number of correct positions, i.e., where a letter corresponds to the correct letter in the target sentence. We choose, say, those five strings with the highest score, make a copy of all five, and use them to replace the five sentences with the lower scores so that the size of the population of sentences remains roughly the same. When we copy a string, we randomly choose a position in the string and, again randomly, choose a letter to replace the one currently sitting in that position. Among this new set of ten sentences we choose the five best ones, and so on. If we repeat this procedure about forty times, we end up with the correct sentence. It almost seems like magic! The population of strings at a particular point in time is called a generation, the criterion used for judging which strings stay and which are discarded is usually termed the fitness function, and the process of randomly altering the new strings is known as mutation. The reason that artificial evolution finds the target string so quickly is because the process builds on top of what has already been achieved, a principle that is named cumulative selection.

In nature there are, of course, no target strings: there are no predefined goals that the process works toward; i.e., evolution does not "know" where it is going—it is "blind." The only criteria are survival and reproduction: having fur is not there because evolution has the goal to produce some furry species; rather, having fur is advantageous only if it helps the organism to survive long enough to reproduce. So, even though natural evolution is not goal-directed, the "good" individuals will proliferate because they manage to reproduce. Looking back over the history of a species, it may be that increasingly hairier organisms produced offspring such that a bald species evolved into a hairy species. In such a situation we may be tempted to say that evolution was working toward a hairy species, but this is simply another example of a mistake caused by the frame-of-reference problem: the observer attributes a goal to evolution (which has no goals). In spite of the significant differences between artificial and biological evolution (such as explicit goals or fitness functions), it has nevertheless proved enormously powerful as a design tool, and some of the results are truly stunning. We will soon describe some more of them.

Evolutionary computation has grown into a large and diverse research field, and much work is concerned with developing specific algorithms. However, virtually all approaches can be shown to be instances and variations of a general scheme that we briefly describe in focus box 6.1, "Artificial Evolution." So, all we need to do is to keep this scheme in mind, and we will have a good understanding of what, in principle, artificial evolution is all about. What is of particular interest for our book, of course, is the role of embodiment in artificial evolution. The evolutionary computation community (which is, as the term expresses, a *computational* community) is just starting to pick up on the relationship between embodiment and evolution. But before exploring that idea we will briefly review the history of this field.

6.3 The Origins of Evolutionary Computation

Around the same time that Rechenberg was inventing evolutionary computation in Europe, other scientists were beginning to explore the possibility of simulating evolutionary processes in a computer. One of the first to make this connection was the Australian biologist Alex Fraser, who published a paper in 1957 describing computer experiments in which genomes were represented as strings of binary numbers (Fraser, 1957), just as a string of characters—a sentence—represents a possible solution in the "Methinks" example. Similarly, and around the same time, the German biomathematician Hans Bremermann introduced a computer program in which virtual genomes produced offspring (Bremermann, 1958; for a more complete history of evolutionary computation, see Fogel, 1998).

These tools for viewing evolution—strings of symbols or numbers representing solutions to problems, and each string being assigned a fitness based on how well it "solves" the problem—later became known as genetic algorithms, thanks to the work of the American computer scientist John Holland, who was trying to mimic natural evolution using computer simulation in the 1970s. The term *genetic algorithms* is often used synonymously for the entire field of evolutionary computation. Holland's focus, and that of his former student and successor David Goldberg, has been on the evolution of abstract entities such as computer programs, strategies for formal games such as chess or checkers, and optimization problems in general. Examples of such problems include finding the shortest path in a network, maximizing the number of packages that can be fit into a suitcase of a given size, and so on.

An interesting variation on evolutionary computation is that of John Koza. Koza, a computer scientist at Stanford University, proposed genetic programming as an extension of genetic algorithms. In his scheme genomes are not simply strings of values that specify some problem, like the characters in the "Methinks" example, but are more elaborate and allow for the encoding of more complex things, like computer programs. Using larger populations makes it possible to increase the probability of finding a relatively good solution to a given problem, but evaluating large numbers of candidate solutions takes time—and computing power. Koza used some of the massive capital earned from his former business, which produced the first scratch-off lottery tickets, to put together powerful computing clusters for his own private use, and he used those clusters to demonstrate the power of genetic programming. Recently, Koza introduced the idea of human-competitive design as a benchmark for how well a particular evolutionary algorithm is doing: if it can produce solutions that are as good as or better than the best that humans have produced so far, then the algorithm is considered to be a good one. Genetic programming has been successful for designing computer programs and electronic circuits (see Koza's series of books on genetic programming: Koza et al., 1992, 1994, 1999, 2003), but it has proved particularly useful in areas in which humans have little expertise or intuition, such as developing programs for quantum computers (Spector, 2004). Evolving computer programs is tricky: if a single bit is not correct, the program will not run. Thus, randomly mutating a string of zeros and ones will almost certainly lead to a program that does nothing, i.e., has fitness zero. Fitness zero is entirely useless for artificial evolution, because if every individual in the population has zero fitness there is no way to tell which individuals are better and should produce offspring, and which are poor and should be deleted. So, Koza modified the mutation process in his algorithms so that mutation would always yield a running program (the details are not important here).

One essential characteristic of genetic programming is that the size of the genome is not fixed (i.e., the genome can encode more or less information), a property which is of particular importance if we want to evolve agents of increasing levels of complexity. But, as we will see shortly, the size of the genome is by no means the only way of achieving agent complexity: what matters most is how genes within the genome interact to grow the agent, rather than the total size of the genome or the number of genes.

Evolution strategies, genetic algorithms, and genetic programming are three of the major branches of evolutionary computation.

6.4 Artificial Evolution in the Real World: On Pipes, Antennas, and Electronic Circuits

Now that we have a basic understanding of how artificial evolution works, we can return to our engineering problem of the curved pipe. The specific evolutionary algorithm that Rechenberg used is called evolution strategy. Like the others, it mimics some aspects of natural evolution, but it is particularly suited for engineering problems (because it is designed to work on real numbers). For the pipe optimization problem, Rechenberg devised an ingenious setup. Rather than evolving simulated pipes in a computer program, he attached his evolution strategy to a physical system in the real world. As shown in figure 6.1a, the genome encodes the positions of the various rods attached to a flexible pipe, thus resulting in a particular shape. The genomes that produced pipes with higher flow were subjected to recombination and mutation. (Recombination is often used in evolutionary algorithms in addition to mutation to mimic sexual reproduction, where the genomes of two individuals are combined to produce offspring. In the literature this process is often referred to as *crossover*.) The ingenious feat of this arrangement was that the fitness testing, i.e., testing how the individuals performed on their task, was done in the real world, and was automated, so that someone did not have to manually configure the pipe each time. "Individuals" in this case means solutions to the problem, which are shapes of the pipe determined by the position of the rods.

Rechenberg had the foresight to realize that evolved solutions must eventually be tested in the real world. These days, no matter what the problem, most solutions are evolved using computer simulation. More than thirty years later, Rechenberg's idea is reemerging in human-competitive engineering design and in evolutionary robotics (see section 6.5), where researchers have begun testing phenotypes, i.e., the real devices, in the real world.

A modern example of this idea is antenna design. Even for experts, finding the proper shape of an antenna in order to maximize its efficiency for sending and receiving signals, especially over long distances, is a very difficult and nonintuitive problem. NASA, the National Aeronautics and Space Administration, has recently begun to use evolutionary algorithms to automate antenna design, and figure 6.1b illustrates one of the designs evolution came up with. In fact the antenna shown in the figure was launched as a functional part of the ST-5 satellite in 2006. From the various odd shapes that the evolutionary process generates, it can be seen that designing optimal shapes of antennas merely by thinking about it would be virtually impossible. In fact, evolutionary methods have found creative solutions that have turned out to be superior to the solutions found by human designers. For testing the fitness of an antenna design, sophisticated software systems were used that took years to develop. As a last step, the antennas that had evolved in simulation were built and tested in the real world. In general, if the simulator is accurate enough, simulations can and should be used, because they are much faster than actually building a physical system for repeated testing; however, real-world testing can never be skipped altogether.

But real-world testing need not always be slow and costly. For example, in the field of electronic circuit design there is a way of very rapidly configuring circuits, using so-called field-programmable gate arrays, or FPGAs for short. FPGAs are, in essence, microprocessors that enable users to configure their own circuits, specialized and optimized for particular applications. The circuits are physically configured rather than simulated on a microprocessor. The configuration process is controlled by a computer that defines the contents of a so-called circuit definition memory on the FPGA. The same computer can be used to run the evolutionary algorithm.

The evolutionary computer scientist Adrian Thompson, of Sussex University in England, used FPGAs to configure and test evolved circuits for distinguishing between a high- and a low-pitched tone. Because he was doing evolution in the real world, so to speak, i.e., by using real electronic circuits, the evolved circuits started to exploit the material properties of the FPGA itself! After evolving a circuit that could discriminate a high from a low tone, Thompson used another computer program to figure out which components on the FPGA were actually connected to each other in the circuit. The program did this by removing all components that were not connected by wires; these components could safely be assumed to be nonfunctional. But, to his and everyone else's great surprise, the circuit no longer worked when these components were removed. Thompson concluded that there must be weak electromagnetic interactions between the disconnected components and the circuit. The fact that evolution "found" this solution astounded both scientists and the public when it was first announced at a conference at Stanford University in 1996 (Thompson, 1996).

This evolved circuit violates the fundamental engineering principle of modularity because although some of the units are not explicitly connected to the circuit, they still influence its behavior. The way evolution bypassed this modularity was by exploiting the specific physical properties of the circuit itself.

Artificial evolution, though artificial, does produce artifacts that sometimes exhibit characteristics of biological organisms. For example, biological systems are never completely modular, as we have argued in our discussion of the redundancy principle, but, typically, modules in natural systems perform several functions to some extent. Eyes, as an example of biological "modules," are used for orientation, for recognizing danger, for reading, for measuring speed, for identifying objects, for recognizing faces, and so forth. But eyes also provide additional information for speech understanding when the hearer watches the speaker's lip movements. So, eyes have multiple functionalities that partially overlap with those of other functional modules, like ears, smell organs, or skin (you can judge the roughness of an object by looking at it or by touching it). This contrasts strongly with standard engineering practice in which each component of the system performs an independent function (Suh, 1990). This is usually done so that components can be developed separately, and so that the systems can easily be repaired by simply identifying and replacing the malfunctioning module.

In another landmark experiment conducted by Jon Bird and Paul Layzell (Bird and Layzell, 2002), also of Sussex University, a circuit was evolved to produce an oscillatory signal without using any internal clock. Once again, the results were astonishing. The circuit evolved a radio receiver from scratch, which captured the clock signal from a nearby desktop computer. Computers emit electromagnetic waves, which apparently in this case contained information about their clock signal, and evolution exploited it. This is the first example of artificial evolution evolving a new sensor modality (in this case, for sensing radio signals) on its own. For example, if the circuits had been evolved in a simulation that did not include a model of electromagnetic waves, then this particular way of exploiting the environment would not have been possible.

These examples illustrate how evolution not only designs things we probably would not have thought of, but exploits the environment in innovative ways in order to get the job done. Recall from chapter 3 that one hallmark of intelligent agents is their ability to exploit their environment (compliance) in order to produce different types of behaviors (diversity). Artificial evolution tends to produce devices with this property, thus adding validity to the idea of diversity-compliance: "Stealing" signals from another machine seems like a pretty intelligent trick. Many in the field hope that as we learn to evolve more sophisticated devices, these tricks will increase in number and sophistication, until perhaps one day we will achieve the automated design of a truly intelligent agent. And maybe we will be able to learn a lot about intelligence in general—not just biological intelligence—along the way.

6.5 Evolutionary Robotics

If evolutionary computation is so useful as a design tool, why not use it to evolve not only pipes, electronic circuits, and computer programs, but entire agents and robots? After all, nature has produced complete and intelligent agents, so perhaps we can reproduce this feat in an artificial system. The standard approach, however, has been to evolve not complete agents, but only part of them. The usual formula, which most people still follow (even though the idea of evolutionary robotics has been around since the early 1990s), is to take a robot with a fixed morphology, such as a Khepera or a Sony AIBO, and to evolve its control architecture, which is typically a neural network (Nolfi and Floreano, 2004). The role of evolution in the design process is even more limited in most cases, because the structure of the neural network is fixed and only connection strengths are evolved. In short, the procedure is usually as follows: each genome is used to assign weights to the synapses in the robot's neural network; the robot is allowed to behave for some time, e.g., to walk; the quality of the behavior is then automatically evaluated using a fitness function, e.g., how far it walks; the best ones are selected for reproduction and their genomes are mutated, and crossed over; and the rest are deleted. The genomes are evaluated, and the cycle is repeated.

Despite the limited role of evolution in this case, the approach has proved very successful, and, typically, neural networks evolve that can be directly used to control the robot. The roots of evolutionary robotics can be traced back to the British group including Phil Husbands and Inman Harvey at Sussex University; the Italian group including Stefano Nolfi at the National Research Council in Rome; and Dario Floreano and Francesco Mondada, both now at the École Polytechnique Fédérale de

Lausanne (EPFL) in Switzerland. Since then, Sussex University and EPFL have become centers of evolutionary robotics, and many other research labs have joined in. Recall the slogan "Design is out—evolution is in," which emphasizes the fact that artificial evolution is a powerful design tool in its own right—an engineering tool—and not just a computer-based version of biological evolution.

So, initially, because of the focus on control architectures—on neural networks—evolutionary robotics was a bit like classical artificial intelligence, which had a strong focus on the brain. One of the basic problems of classical artificial intelligence was that the researchers in the field did not consider embodiment simply because they did not know about it. After all, they argued, intelligence is computation, so intelligence must be localized in the control architecture. Of course, this is not how natural evolution works. Evolution does not start with a fixed body and then evolve brains for it; rather, the two, the body and the brain, evolve together over time. For artificial systems, the ability to evolve morphology and neural control together is also crucial if we want to exploit the full power of evolution. Only evolving control imposes strong and unnecessary restrictions on what kind of agents will result because the morphology is determined by the designer, and thus the evolutionary process will be biased. Generally speaking, if we want to study the way the interaction of morphology, materials, control, and system-environment interaction contributes to the agent's behavior, evolving entire bodies is, of course, necessary.

We suspect that one of the reasons researchers shied away from evolving body and brain together for so long was the awesomely large design space. In order to get a feel for this problem, let us briefly look at how information about an agent's "brain" and body is encoded in an artificial genome. In a program for optimizing the shape of a pipe, as we have seen, the genome consists of the positions of the rods resulting in a particular shape of the pipe. If the controller for a four-legged walker is to be evolved, the properties coded in the genome may be the weights of the connections in the neural network. Now let us look at some numbers. If you have a fully connected neural network with only 100 nodes—a very small brain indeed—you have 10,000 connections, or 10,000 parameters in your optimization problem that have to be adjusted simultaneously. So, even if you only evolve these weights, finding a good solution in this massive search space is already a considerable problem. By a good solution we mean a neural network that allows its host robot to achieve a particular task, such as finding a target location (e.g., where the charging station is located), running over uneven ground, swimming in water, or winning control over a piece of "food" (e.g., a ball or a cube) in competition with other robots. If you now want to evolve the robot's body and the neural network at the same time, the search space will be indefinitely large. It turns out that in spite of this, it is possible to evolve interesting agents if we do evolution right. An initial demonstration came from an unexpected direction: computer animation.

6.6 Evolving Morphology and Control

Karl Sims, who studied both computer graphics and life sciences at MIT, was the first to set artificial evolution to work on agent bodies and brains simultaneously (Sims, 1994a, b). Thus, he not only had to encode the brain in the genome somehow, but also the agent's morphology. Sims (and most researchers since) evolved rigid virtual creatures made up of a number of solid objects or segments, like cylinders or rectangular solids, connected by joints. Examples of some morphological parameters of such a system include the length, width, and height of the segments, the types of joints by which they are connected (e.g., like a knee or shoulder joint), the types of actuators (e.g., how much force they can apply at various angles), the types of sensors (e.g., touch, light, eyes, and ears) and their positions on the body, and so on. Sims included in his system parameters very similar to the ones just mentioned. Moreover, inside the body, evolution could build up neural networks that connect sensors to actuators. The way Sims encoded this information allowed for body parts to be repeated: for example, a leg with three segments could be repeated at other locations on the agent's body. When Sims ran his program on the Connection Machine (in the early 1990s a very powerful computer with 64,000 processors), most of the initial creatures could not move at all, or could only twitch a bit. But over time, incredible creatures appeared.

In this case the phenotype, i.e., the functioning agent, was then tested in a physically realistic simulation, a program that determines how the agent's movements affect the environment and vice versa. In some experiments the fitness function was how fast an agent could move on land, swim in water, or compete with another agent. The bad individuals were deleted, and the better individuals were selected, mutated, and crossed over to create genomes for their offspring. This cycle of evaluation, selection, mutation, and crossover was repeated until an interesting, funny, or efficient agent appeared in the population.

Now, what can we learn from Sims's creatures? First they demonstrate that it is possible to evolve morphology and control together in virtual agents. Second, they are fun to watch and they frequently exhibit creative ways of locomotion that we might not readily have thought of ourselves. For example, one very fast creature moved by continuously flipping over itself to move forward: there was no penalty for dizziness! Third, the amount of computation required is enormous, because not only neural control, but also the morphology has to be evolved: thousands and thousands of agents have to be tested before an interesting one finally emerges. Furthermore, because agents were simulated in a physically realistic way, the evaluation of a single agent took a long time.

Although an evolutionary process was used for agent design, and much of the agent's body and brain could be changed by evolution, there was still a lot of designer bias involved: all the creatures consist of segments connected by different types of joints, to which certain sensors and actuators could be attached; these components can be repeated and connected in different ways and their size varied; and so on. But the segments themselves are basically all similar, so Sims's creatures all tended to have the same blocky appearance, simply because Sims chose to work with rectangular solids as his basic building blocks. What evolution can achieve will always be restricted by such designer decisions. Another limitation of Sims's approach is that the environment has no influence whatsoever on how the agent grows: the same genome will always result in exactly the same agent, no matter what environment it is grown in. But as we argued earlier, the environment should definitely be taken into account when evolving agents. Otherwise, evolution does not work well. We will discuss the relationship between growth and evolution in more detail later in this chapter.

It is interesting to note that Sims, with his experiments in artificial evolution, defined a new direction in computer animation. As the underlying physical processes are modeled in the simulation, the agents can react to their environments, rather than executing prespecified motion patterns. Note that this automatically makes them adaptive: when the agent lowers its foot during walking, the foot will stop when it touches the ground, no matter the height of the ground. If the movement of the foot is preprogrammed, then the programmer has to determine where the foot should stop for every ground type over which the agent should walk.

About six years later, the engineer Hod Lipson and the computer scientist Jordan Pollack, both at Brandeis University near Boston, launched the Golem project, which in effect reproduced Sims's experiments, but with an additional twist. While in the Sims approach everything was done in simulation, Lipson and Pollack automatically produced physical copies of the creatures evolved in simulation (Lipson and Pollack, 2000). However, the whole process was not completely automatic because the motors, electronic components, and batteries had to be put in manually. Still, the work attracted huge media attention because many journalists interpreted the project as the first instance of one "robot," the 3D printer (which is not really a robot), creating another robot without human intervention, thereby giving the (incorrect) impression that the first self-reproducing robot had been born. Needless to say, this media hype captured the public imagination and propelled the project onto the front page of the *New York Times* on August 31, 2000. Despite the engineering advance of this work, the question of how evolution can best be used to automatically generate robots remains open, because the entire evolutionary process—including the agent evaluation—was still done in simulation, and there was no feedback from the actual physical robot to the evolutionary process.

6.7 Genetic Regulatory Networks and Developmental Plasticity

How can we lessen the designer bias introduced by the prespecification of the kinds of structures—rigid segments with height, depth, and width—of the to-be-evolved organism? Once again, we can glean inspiration from nature. There are an estimated 5 to 15 million different species, and there exist an unbelievable variety of shapes. This variety is possible because on the one hand cells are very small compared to the organism itself, and on the other there are different types of cells. The smaller the entities (the cells) from which an organism is built, the less constraining they are: just take enough cells and you can build virtually any kind of shape. But many cells are not enough: there also must be different kinds to allow for diverse functionality. In a human body there are many functional structures: each of our organs (e.g., liver, kidney, eyes, nose, brain, and so on) is composed of many different tissue types, and each tissue type is in turn made up of many different cell types.

As we know, organisms develop from one single cell, the zygote, into an adult organism. This is achieved in natural systems by a process of cell division—which leads to an increase in cell number—and cell differentiation—resulting in an increase in the number of different types of cells—both of which are controlled in biological organisms by their genetic regulatory networks. The term *genetic regulatory network* emphasizes that genes do not act in isolation but they interact with each other using chemical signaling to guide growth. In contrast to neural networks, in which neurons influence each other's behavior through direct connections, i.e., synapses, in genetic regulatory networks the connections are indirect, through proteins, which are produced by genes and which can influence the activity of other genes.

These ideas have inspired the medical doctor and theoretical physicist Peter Eggenberger Hotz, a highly creative thinker in the AI Lab in Zurich, who combines his understanding of cell biology and medical training with expertise in formal mathematical modeling. One of his early ideas was to "grow" artificial organisms in simulation by mimicking the function of biological genetic regulatory networks. He demonstrated that with his model he could, in fact, grow almost any arbitrary shape (Eggenberger, 1997, 1999). Picking up on the insights of Eggenberger, Josh Bongard (one of the authors) used similar mechanisms but extended them such that he could grow virtual creatures. Bongard's agents were not simply shapes, but shapes that could move and interact with their virtual environments. The Eggenberger-Bongard approach bears some similarity to that of Sims in that both consist of basic building blocks, and the phenotypes are tested in a physically realistic simulation, but the design of the artificial evolutionary system and the way the organisms grow are fundamentally different.

The basic idea is the following (for details, see Bongard and Pfeifer, 2001, or Bongard, 2002, 2003). Assume that we would like to grow agents for a particular task, such as pushing a large block—thus the nickname "block pushers." The basic scheme is always the same. For each run of the algorithm, a population of virtual creatures evolves to become better at pushing a large block in their environment. The fitness of an agent is determined as follows. First, a virtual zygote—a single small sphere with a genome—is injected with a little bit of virtual chemical. The chemical reacts with some of the genes in the genome, turning them on or off. When genes are on, they produce different chemicals that then turn other genes on or off, and so on. Some of these chemicals, however, not only affect other genes but also affect the growth of the agent: the chemicals may cause the initial sphere to grow in size and to split, or a chemical may change the joint by which two spheres are attached, or it may grow neurons and synapses inside the spheres, and so on. Basically, the genetic regulatory network directs the development of the agent while it is behaving in its virtual environment. Importantly, this allows the environment to influence the growth of the agent, unlike Sims's approach. Once an agent grows and behaves for a while, its fitness—i.e., the distance it pushed the block—is recorded. Selection, mutation, and crossover are then basically the same as we have already explained. Figure 6.3a shows a typical evolved block pusher.

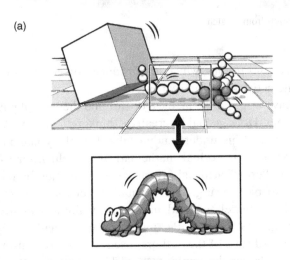

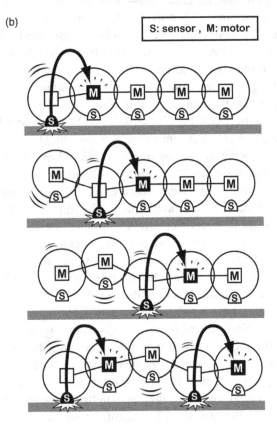

Figure 6.3
Emergence of locomotion: The block pusher. (*a*) the actual block pusher. (*b*) The inchworm-like locomotion of the block pusher. A sensor, S, in one cell is connected to a motor, M, in a neighboring cell. Whenever S touches the ground, it will actuate the motor M, which subsequently will lift up the cell containing S. This reflex propagates through the entire creature and causes the locomotion behavior. (*c*) The pattern of motion is reminiscent of how an inchworm moves: waves travel along the animal's body in order to move it forward.

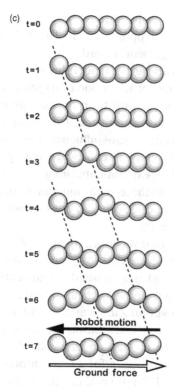

Figure 6.3
(continued)

In Sims's work, there is a much more direct link between the geno-type, in which information about the agent is stored, and the phenotype, which is the agent itself. In Sims's genomes there is explicit information about the structure of the agent, such as how many body parts it has and how big they should be. But in Bongard's block pushers this is not the case. Genes simply influence the growth of the agent, and its final form is emergent from this process. This is much more in tune with biological development, in which organisms grow in response to dynamic processes taking place within their cells, as directed by their genes. Another bio-logical similarity is that all of the block pushers' "cells" contain a copy of the genome: in fact, the spheres that make up a block pusher's body are meant to be rough analogs of biological cells.

As we have mentioned, if development is simulated in this way, the environment will influence the growth of the organism. In biological systems this effect is well known. For example, the visual system does not develop if there is no light, and bones do not grow properly in zero gravity. Similarly, if the evolved block pushers are regrown in a simulated environment with no gravity, they develop differently. This tells us that gravity always plays a role in their growth. In order to take this environmental influence into account, Bongard extended his model so that whenever an agent touches something, or when one of its joints turns, a simulated chemical begins to diffuse outward from the turning joint or the point on its body where the agent was touched. This chemical, like the other gene products in the system, can influence gene activity. Whether or not genes evolve to respond to this chemical is emergent and left to artificial evolution. In most of his experiments, Bongard found that agents became increasingly sensitive to these environmental signals over evolutionary time, indicating that artificial evolution does in fact exploit the environment it given the opportunity.

In the summer of 2000, when Bongard was working at the Zurich laboratory, it was a beautiful day and he decided to go for drinks with a few friends in the afternoon. He had just finished implementing his system, was tired, and, just to see what would happen, started a few simulations before leaving the lab. A beautiful Zurich afternoon turned into a beautiful Zurich evening, and for one reason or another, the researchers did not make it back to the lab on the same day. When Bongard returned the next morning he was in for a huge surprise: creatures with strange bodies had evolved to push and grasp objects in their environment; artificial evolution had worked! I (Rolf) remember that he called me over to his office to watch: I found this hard to believe and suggested we call our colleagues from the neighboring biology department, the developmental biologist Ernst Hafen and his colleague Michael Levine, who was visiting from the University of California–Berkeley at the time. Both researchers are world experts on the development of the fruit fly *Drosophila*, and how genes guide the growth of biological organisms in general. We showed them the results from our simulations, and they were impressed that anything like that could be possible. So, Bongard, with his developmental system, had hit on something that showed how models of genetic regulatory networks can be used to evolve artificial creatures. Bongard has since conducted different kinds of experiments with his system, but in all cases, the interaction with the environment somehow shapes the development of the agent. The potential seems highly promising. Maybe Husbands and Harvey were right after all: "Design is out, and evolution is in."

Although simple in their basic form—much, much simpler than biological evolution or development—the mechanisms implemented by

Bongard have produced a host of interesting agents, and some exciting results. Here are a few observations:

1. Organisms early on in evolution are typically smaller than those of later generations: evolution "discovers" that in order to push a large block, it is necessary to have a large body in order to exert enough force. In other words, evolution had to produce the right morphology for the task. Small organisms were simply not sufficiently fit for the job and lost the competition against their larger brothers and sisters.

2. Evolution results in not only agents that can push, but also those that can move. Small creatures tend to contain simple neural components that, together with the body, give rise to local reflexes that move the entire body. They represent, in fact, an instance of cheap design: there is no central neural control; the individual "cells" communicate locally with their neighbors through the environment. This reminds us of the walking behavior of insects, where the leg coordination is also achieved through interaction with the environment as we described in chapter 4. For more details about this evolved mechanism, see figure 6.3. The distributed control architecture leads to an inchworm-like locomotion pattern that, again, corresponds to an attractor state of the combined neural-body system: the agent's body and brain were evolved such that, in the interaction with the environment, a stable pattern emerged over time that produces some useful behavior, which in this case is locomotion. This is also an example of morphological computation, of how the interaction with the environment can be exploited for locomotion. So, artificial evolution does in fact "discover" cheap design, which adds validity to this design principle and shows that exploitation of system-environment interaction is something very natural not only to biological, but also to artificial evolution. And of course, this is a clear example of the principle of parallel, loosely coupled processes.

3. Later, these moving agents produced offspring that were large and moved less. Instead, they were good at pushing their long appendages against the block from where they sat, and thus had higher fitness. However, they had body parts similar to those of their ancestors: the limbs of the descendants contained neural structures very similar to those of their ancestors. This is an instance of what is termed *exaptation* in biology, i.e., the exploitation of existing structures for a new function. In this case the long limbs were the existing structure, the original function was locomotion (as determined by evolution), and the new function was pushing (also determined by evolution). Because these agents were

created by artificial evolution and ontogenetic development, they are, in some sense, ecologically balanced for this task environment, i.e., for pushing large blocks. This is, admittedly, not a highly complex and taxing ecological niche, but there is no excess brain mass or parts on the agent that are entirely unused. Also, all of the agents exploit gravity and friction for exerting force against the block.

4. There is no direct relation between the size of the genome—or the number of genes—and the size and complexity of the adult agent. For example, in one run a very small agent that moves to the block and pushes it is replaced by much larger offspring that simply push against the block with a longer limb. We might expect that more genes are required to grow this larger and more complex agent, but much to our surprise, the number of genes in the larger one was about equal to that in the smaller agent. A similar surprise was in store for the world when the Human Genome Project—a worldwide effort to crack the conundrum of the human genome—announced in 2003 that there are in fact many fewer genes than anticipated. Around 100,000 had been the best guess up until then, but the current estimate is that there are between 20,000 and 25,000 genes in the human genome. It now seems that the complexity of an organism comes from the interactions between genes, and not merely from the number of them. Because development is guided by genetic regulatory networks that have a very complex and rich behavior that depends on the interaction of the genes, even a relatively small number can generate an enormous complexity. Also, because of this dynamics, there is no one-to-one correspondence between a gene and a part of the agent.

For example, the puffer fish *Fugu rubripes* has about the same number of genes as humans, but it is a much simpler animal. Obviously, puffer fish are not as smart as we are because we eat them and not the other way around. (The puffer fish is the Japanese delicacy known as fugu, which when not properly prepared can lead to instant death because the toxic parts of the fish are more than a thousand times more deadly than an equal amount of cyanide!) As another example, the flatworm *Caenorhabditis elegans*, or *C. elegans*, contains roughly the same number of genes as humans, but while we have about 100 billion (10^{11}) neurons, poor *C. elegans* has only 302. Since the recent findings that very different organisms share very similar gene sets, but that gene interaction differs greatly between species, biologists have begun to focus not only on single genes but on gene networks. In other words, much research now deals with figuring out which genes regulate which other genes, instead of only trying to explain how an individual gene affects the growth of the organism on its own.

Let us return to the human brain with its 100 billion neurons, the most complex known structure in the universe. The neuroscientist and Nobel laureate Gerald Edelman pointed out the amazing fact that the human genome is much too small to encode the entire structure of our brain. In other words, the information content of the genome is not sufficient to encode all the neurons and their connections to other neurons. How then, is it possible that the brain could have evolved in the first place? The answer is that what is encoded is not so much the structure of the brain, but rather the growth processes which, again, can be modeled by the genetic regulatory networks (Edelman, 1987).

5. As we have already mentioned, some block pushers exhibit functional specialization, i.e., their "cells" differentiate into different types, which contain the same kind of structures (e.g., only sensors; only sensors and actuators; sensors, neurons, and actuators; or it is completely empty, etc.) (see figure 6.3 for some examples). Typically, a block pusher will contain anywhere from two to eight different "cell" types. While compared to the thousands of human cell types, eight different ones is not very impressive, nevertheless the block pushers do show the first traces of cell differentiation.

6. Some of the block pushers are hierarchically organized: Just like humans who have two hands and five similar fingers on each, some block pushers have several "limbs" that are similar: e.g., cells with only sensors, followed by a cell with sensors and actuators at their tips, etc. In the human hand, as well as in the block pushers, repeated structures are not identical: fingers differ from each other, and in the block pushers limbs rarely contain identical patterns of "cells." The next step, of course, is to ask how this happens. In the block pushers, at least, it looks like there are a few genes that regulate many other genes. When these genes are switched on, they set off large changes that give rise to large structures, like limbs. So wherever in the body these "master regulatory genes" are switched on, similar limbs begin to grow. Master regulatory genes, otherwise known as *Hox* genes, were first seen in biological organisms in 1994 (Krumlauf 1994). How they operate and evolved is a topic of increasing research, presaging that this approach to artificial evolution may in the future help us understand how biological genetic networks evolved.

7. Finally, it is important to note that not only the growth of the block pushers' bodies is influenced by the environment, but their brains are as well. This is something that we also see in biological organisms, as

illustrated by a fascinating set of experiments performed a few years ago by von Melchner et al. (2000), who showed that if the optic nerves from the eyes of a ferret (a small furry animal) are connected to the auditory cortex, the auditory cortex will gradually develop representations that are normally found in the visual system. The conclusion that von Melchner and his colleagues drew from this was that visual stimulation from the environment alters the way the auditory cortex, which is now receiving visual input, grows. This demonstrates not only the enormous plasticity of the nervous system, but also how its development is shaped through the interaction with the environment. The reason this point is important is that it shows how we might be able to investigate the evolution of learning. The fact that the block pushers' "brains" change in response to environmental signals allows us, as observers, to say that the block pushers are learning.

6.8 Self-Organization: The Powerful Ally of Mutation and Selection

One of the main arguments leveled against evolution is the question as to how certain complex structures, such as the mammalian eye, ever evolved in the first place. The eye is made up of many interdependent parts, and if any of them fail, the eye does not work. So how could evolution, which relies on random mutation and selection, have produced all of the right pieces, and put them together in the proper way to get the eye? Dawkins, in his book *Climbing Mount Improbable*, elaborates in detail that if cumulative selection is taken into account it is possible to explain the existence of eyes by the development of a series of increasingly better eyes, each produced by an accumulation of random mutations, from simple structures that only detect light intensity all the way up to those that capture crisp images. In other words, there is a gradual path, through many intermediate structures, to the full-featured eye. Put differently, evolution can climb "mount improbable" using only random mutation and selection, and no intelligent designer is required. However, the way in which mutations shape and organize the growing organism plays an important role in this process: they can exploit the self-organizing characteristics of the physical world. Recall that there are three driving forces of evolution: cumulative selection, variation (provided by random mutation), and self-organization. Let us inspect the latter one a bit more closely.

One of the intermediate structures on the way to a complete eye is, roughly speaking, a kind of pouch formed by transparent sheets of cells filled with a clear fluid such as water. This structure can be seen as the first traces of a lens. The question then becomes how such a lens could form during an evolutionary process. While thousands of cells will be involved in this process, it turns out that pouch formation, or "invagination," requires the cooperation of only very few genes; in other words, the genes kick off a series of physical processes that force invagination to occur. Eggenberger Hotz, whom we encountered earlier in this chapter, created a simulation that shows how this can happen. The idea is actually quite simple: evolution can rely on a "powerful ally," i.e., the self-organizing properties of the physical world (Eggenberger Hotz, 2003).

In his simulation there are two cell layers, each consisting of one type of cell. The cells are attached to one another by so-called cell adhesion molecules. Cell adhesion molecules determine the force by which the cells are held together or pulled apart: the larger the concentrations of the cell adhesion molecules on the surface of neighboring cells, the more strongly they attach to each other. Imagine now that there is a gene in each of these two types of cells that produces cell adhesion molecules if it is activated. Further imagine that a gradient of signaling molecules is produced capable of activating these genes so that they produce cell adhesion molecules. You can envision that the gradient is created by some point source in the environment, and that molecules diffuse out from this point. Near the source their concentration will be highest, and it will diminish with increasing distance from the source. If the signaling molecules happen to activate the proper genes so that they produce the cell adhesion molecules, in one layer the cells are pulled closer together; in the other they are pushed apart, and as a result a kind of pouch will be formed. All it takes in this case is that the cells in the two layers have genes that react to the signaling molecule by producing cell adhesion molecules (which then in one layer will pull the cells more together and in the other push them more apart). The specific form of the pouch is emergent from the physical forces acting between the cells. Thus, the specific shape of the pouch is not controlled directly, but it self-organizes according to the laws of physics. Note that this process works irrespective of the number of cells: even if there are thousands of them, we can employ exactly the same procedure. There is no need to control each cell individually. At the genetic level, only a few mutations would be required to start this self-organizing process of pouch formation.

This exploitation of physical forces and signals in the environment, of processes of self-organization, reminds us of the diversity-compliance issue: intelligent agents exploit their niche for their purposes, mostly without knowing that they do so. We are not claiming that the individual cells are intelligent, but once again we see that compliance—exploitation of the environment—can lead, relatively easily, to interesting behaviors. In this case, the behavior is the formation of a pouch, which could be used as a lens, which in turn could play a part in the evolution of eyes.

Let us briefly summarize some of the main points of this example. By modeling the interaction between genetic regulatory networks, cells, and physics—the ease with which good solutions such as eyes or wings can be evolved—we can greatly enhance the evolvability of complex structures, at least in the domain of artificial evolution. By setting up our evolutionary algorithms in this way, we may be able to evolve more complex agents than by using the more standard approach. Finally, it is not the structure of the organism which is encoded in the genome and manipulated by evolution. Rather, evolution tunes the way in which genes respond to their environment such that physics can be exploited for the benefit of the organism. Once again, neither evolution nor the organism (the pouch) knows anything about this!

6.9 Artificial Evolution: Where Are We and Where Do We Go from Here?

When mimicking natural evolution, researchers have to make enormous abstractions: for example, molecules, genes, and gene products are represented by numbers rather than modeled in detail; aspects of the structure of the organism are represented in the genome (as in Sims's virtual creatures) rather than the growth processes themselves; researchers define a fitness function rather than letting the agents simply mate and reproduce; often there is no distinction between genotype and phenotype (as in the "Methinks" example); the processes of ontogenetic development, if modeled at all, are reduced to the bare essentials (as in Bongard's block pushers); fitness testing is often performed in a simulation that leaves out many details of the real world; generations of individuals are assumed to be synchronized, i.e., there is a discrete sequence of generations; and so on.

In spite of all these simplifications, we have seen many examples in which artificial evolution has come up with truly creative ideas, and the common folklore that computers can only do what they are programmed for has been disproved many times. Also, artificial evolution is able to compete successfully with humans in certain engineering design tasks: just think of Rechenberg's pipes or the NASA antennas that have been designed automatically (or at least semi-automatically) using evolutionary methods. So, the goal of fully automated design is now one step closer, especially if automated manufacturing methods such as the ones used in Lipson's experiments are further developed. This is thrilling but of course also scary: while we have no problem letting machines take over tasks where muscle power is required, we resist emotionally when it comes to the taking over of intellectual tasks, tasks that require intelligence, such as robot design.

Futurists like Ray Kurzweil, CEO of a number of technology companies, Hans Moravec of Carnegie Mellon University, and Bill Joy, hero programmer and cofounder of Sun Microsystems, feel that the power of simulated evolution is unlimited because it is only Moore's law[2] that matters: the more computing power we have, the larger the virtual populations we can use, the longer we can let them evolve, and the better solutions we will eventually get. However, we have seen many times now that computation alone is not sufficient for achieving intelligent behavior, but that some interaction with the real world is also required. Now the question arises to what extent we can in fact simulate this agent-environment interaction in a sufficiently realistic way for artificial evolution to make progress. As we saw in the pouch example, we have to simulate intercell attraction, as well as the ability for genes to respond to signaling molecules, in order for the pouch to appear. This is an important research question, but we suspect that one of the reasons evolution in the real world worked as well as it did is because of the indefinite richness of the natural environment: there is always something to be exploited. For example, air can be used by flying animals to stay aloft, by trees for dispersing their seeds over a wide area, and by animals and humans for broadcasting sounds and language. And just think of how many ways water is exploited by different organisms! If air or water is not modeled in an evolutionary robotics simulation, then no artificial agent can evolve to exploit them. We have seen a bit of the power of artificial evolution when it is allowed to work in the real world, as, for example, in Thompson's experiments on evolving electronic circuits using FGPAs or in Bird and Layzell's study where a new sensor modality, a radio receiver, evolved.

Perhaps the connection between artificially evolved agents and the real world can be further intensified in the near future via connections between computational systems and chemical laboratories. One example of such an attempt is the Programmable Artificial Cell Evolution (PACE) project, a multinational project funded by the European Union under its long-term basic research initiative. The idea there is to evolve agents in a real-world chemical environment, rather than a simulated one. The PACE laboratories contain sophisticated microfluidic arrays, which are arrangements of tiny tubes whose operation can be electronically controlled in order to very precisely influence chemical reactions. The inventive guru of DNA computing and mastermind of the PACE project, John McCaskill, calls this setup the "Omega machine." The idea is to use this Omega machine to evolve an artificial cell from scratch. An evolutionary algorithm will be run on a computer, while the phenotypes—artificial cells or precursors of them—will be produced in the microfluidic arrays, where their fitness will also be tested. The fitness of an artificial cell is the extent to which it can sustain itself, i.e., to what degree it can metabolize food and whether it can reproduce or not. The goal is to make a cell which is increasingly independent of its computational support system, so to speak, over evolutionary time. Whatever happens, it will most certainly be fascinating to follow this line of groundbreaking research on artificial evolution.

Although we have not said anything directly in this chapter about how our artificial evolutionary systems can help us learn about biological evolution, it definitely is possible. For example, Eggenberger's simulations of invagination may, in the future, help us to better understand not only how complex structures form in response to genetic and environmental signals, but also how complex structures, such as the eye, evolved in the first place. The fun, but perhaps not particularly accurate figure 6.4 shows how artificial evolution could help us to better understand biological evolution, biological organisms, and the production of relatively sophisticated agents in the near future. It also shows some of the possible future results of combining the study of artificial evolution with the study of the nature of intelligence. What's next?

6.10 Summary: Design Principles for Evolutionary Systems

Let us now briefly summarize the principles that are most important to observe when designing evolutionary systems, but also when analyzing natural phenomena related to evolutionary processes.

Population principle First, we should always think about populations, not individuals, because populations are evolution's most valuable resources: the failure or success of one agent is not so important compared to the evolutionary change occurring in the entire population. And we must never forget that maintaining the diversity in the population is a prerequisite for keeping the population adaptive and for the evolution of interesting agents. If all the individuals in the population are identical,

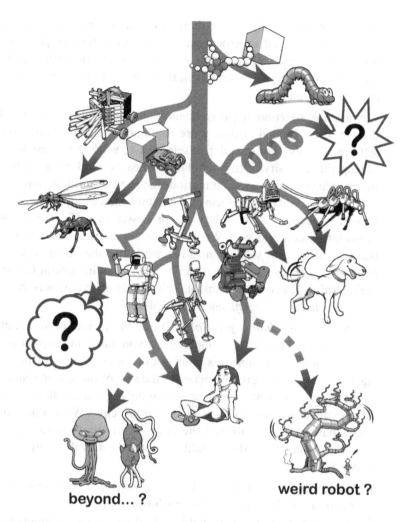

Figure 6.4
Artificial evolution: where do we go from here? This cartoon illustrates possible, hypothetical developmental paths for the future of artificial evolution. Will there ever evolve anything like real robots or even creatures resembling today's animals or humans, or will it lead to creatures that nature has not come up with so far?

and the environment changes, then all the agents may perform equally badly in the altered environment, and the evolutionary process leads nowhere. If they are all different, some agents may do better in the new environment than others, and evolution can continue. This is called the *population principle*.

Cumulative selection–self-organization principle Second, the basic driving forces behind evolution are cumulative selection, variation, and self-organization. For cumulative selection to work, a process for maintaining the diversity in the population must be implemented. Because the chance of several useful mutations happening simultaneously is very low, the probability of producing a completely new kind of structure from scratch is virtually zero, unless the processes of self-organization are taken into account as well. We have seen some examples of how selection, mutation, and self-organization work together to produce novel structures, such as a pouch that can be seen as an important first step in the direction of evolving a lens, and ultimately an eye. This is the *cumulative selection–self-organization* principle.

Brain-body coevolution principle Third, brain and body should be evolved together, which is apparent if you take an embodied view. While obvious, embodiment is often not taken into account when evolving agents because it greatly increases the size of the search space, compared to the case when only the neural network controller is evolved. This is called the *brain-body coevolution* principle. While this principle states that both the brain and the body should be evolved together, it does not specify how this should be done. That is the content of the next principle.

Scalable complexity principle Fourth, ontogenetic development must be incorporated into the artificial evolutionary process. In other words, the developmental processes that lead to the final agent, rather than the structure of the agent itself, should be encoded in the genome. This is not only desirable but necessary if we want to grow really complex structures. And these developmental processes are best modeled as genetic regulatory networks because of the generality of such networks. As nature has shown during the course of its evolution, an enormous variety of structures can be evolved in this way. Also, as we have seen, using genetic regulatory networks to grow agents allows more complex agents to evolve without requiring an increase in the number of genes to do so. For this reason, the fourth evolutionary design principle is called the *scalable complexity* principle.

Evolution as a fluid process principle Fifth, evolution should be modeled as a fluid process. *Fluid* means that agents should be made up of large numbers of units like cells, and that evolution should only make small modifications rather than large ones. If the agent is made up of only a few building blocks, then changing one or more of them will be highly disruptive; if the agent is made up of many, then changing a few here and there should not affect fitness too much, and some changes may be slightly beneficial. Sims's agents were built of about ten building blocks, Bongard's creatures from hundreds, and Eggenberger's agents from thousands. So the more units, the more fluid the evolutionary process can be. As simulation technology improves and computing power increases in the future, we should be able to play around with agents made up of hundreds of thousands or even millions of building blocks. We have termed this the *evolution as a fluid process* principle.

Minimal designer bias principle The sixth and final evolutionary design principle states that we should design as little into our systems as possible and let evolution do most of the work for us. Obviously, the less we put in, the less designer bias there will be and the more surprising and novel the potential solutions will be. And, as always, if we can show that one property or characteristic of an agent is emergent from another time scale, this constitutes scientific progress. For example, learning agents, e.g., agents making use of Hebbian learning to capture correlations, may evolve from nonlearning agents over generations. Finally, if we can show that cheap design or ecological balance results from evolution, we have corroborated those design principles. This is called the *minimal designer bias* principle.

In this chapter we have made a strong point that populations are crucial for evolution to work. We continue the population perspective in the next chapter by discussing collective intelligence, exploring groups of agents in which intelligent behavior arises from the interactions among the individuals in the population.

In 2002, at the Seventh International Conference on Intelligent Autonomous Systems in the beautiful town of Marina del Rey in the Los Angeles area, the young Danish engineer Kasper Støy surprised his audience with an unbelievable robot demonstration. First he showed a video of a robot consisting of several modules that could move very much like a snake. So far so good—snake robots are nothing new: they date back as far as 1972 (a long time ago when it comes to robotics) when the snake robot pioneer Shigeo Hirose of the Tokyo Institute of Technology, whom we introduced in chapter 2, developed the ACM-III robot, also known as the SnakeBot, the first fully functional snake robot (Hirose, 1993). But the snake demonstration was not all Støy had to show: after the snake had been crawling for a while, he picked it up and pulled it apart in the middle and put the two pieces back on the ground. And, the two smaller snakes started moving just like the big snake! If you are used to conventional, centralized control schemes, this may seem truly unthinkable. The audience was accordingly amazed. But the experiment was not yet complete. When he pulled the snake apart and put the modules together to mimic a four-legged creature, it started walking, leaving the participants in the conference stunned.

What Støy had in fact demonstrated (for more details see Støy et al., 2002 and Støy et al., 2003) was a modular robot: a robot consisting of a number of modules that can be arranged in different ways to perform different functions. His demonstration was proof, so to speak, that modular robotics, a field that can be traced back to the famous Cebot experiments by the robotics engineer Toshio Fukuda of the University of Nagoya in Japan in the 1980s, had finally come of age.

Støy had worked for several years at the University of Southern California before joining the HYDRA project, sponsored by the European

Union, at the University of Southern Denmark. This project had the futuristic title "'Living' building blocks for self-designing artifacts." The reason that the researchers involved, headed by principal investigator Henrik Lund, chose this name is that if you cut off large parts of the hydra (a tiny marine animal, a few millimeters to 1 cm or more in length, with a diameter of less than 1 mm and a mouth surrounded by tentacles), the part will simply regrow—a nice metaphor for this kind of research. The name is derived from Hydra, the monstrous serpent in Greek legend that had many heads and grew two more whenever one was cut off. The regenerative powers of hydra are truly remarkable: a single hydra may be cut into many pieces, and each piece will develop into a complete animal. If this facility for self-repair, which is the metaphorical goal of the hydra project, could be even partly reproduced in artificial systems, this would represent enormous progress. Perhaps, at some point, a robotic "hydra" will become possible, though at this moment we still seem to be a good distance away.

The behavior of Støy's original modular robot is an example of collective intelligence: several modules cooperate to achieve some global behavioral pattern (moving like a snake or walking on four legs). In this case, *global* refers to the behavior of the entire robot, which is the result of the interplay between the different individual modules and their environment. One inspiration for modular robotics comes from biology. In the hydra, the "modules" are its individual cells, which "cooperate" to generate behavior. Needless to say, the hydra has many more cells than Støy's robots have units, but the principle is the same. On the other hand, biological organisms, including the hydra, are limited in a way that robots are not: robots can reconfigure from one shape into a completely new one by changing the attachments of their individual units, i.e., they can "mutate" from a snake into a four-legged creature. Thus, modular robotics may have the potential to go beyond what is possible in biological systems—another instance of exploring "intelligence as it could be."

Modular robotics is a very promising and exciting way to exploit collective intelligence. Another line of development in collective intelligence deals with systems where the individual components are complete agents in their own right, rather than nonautonomous modules. Such systems are often referred to as multiagent systems. One example of a multiagent system is the Swiss robots: in that case the units of the collective system are the robots themselves.

In this chapter we will proceed as follows. First we will provide a number of reasons why one might want to pursue collective intelligence.

Then we will discuss the multiagent approach, starting with agent-based modeling in simulation. We will then digress into a short discussion comparing simulations and real robots, which will lead to a survey of research on collective intelligence using real robots. We will also briefly discuss the issue of cooperation, which turns out to be surprisingly controversial. We will then expand on the field of modular robots and consider the issue of scalability, i.e., what will happen—and what will become possible—if the next generations of robotic modules become much smaller. We will also follow up on the hydra-inspired questions of self-assembly and self-repair and discuss the so-called homogeneity-heterogeneity trade-off. We will then briefly touch upon the issue of self-reproduction, presenting a case study where real robots behave in a way that one might interpret as robots reproducing themselves. We will finish by summarizing the main insights developed in this chapter as a set of design principles for collective intelligence. Before we start we should perhaps mention that, depending on what we consider to be part of collective intelligence and modular robotics, the field can be extremely vast, so that here we had to select for inclusion those topics most closely related to our ideas about embodied intelligence.

7.1 Motivation

So far we have been talking about agents as individuals; in this chapter we will explore the possibilities of agents acting in groups. But we have already touched on the increased power of multiple agents: evolution always requires populations. Thus, at a theoretical level, it is important to understand behavior in groups, not only behavior of individuals in isolation.

A second motivation for studying collective phenomena is that because individuals can interact in groups, they can do things that individual agents cannot do on their own. For example, as we saw in chapter 2, ants can find the shortest path to a food source by depositing pheromones as they search for food and return from the food source, as well as following the pheromone trail with the highest concentration. This mechanism is extremely simple, but it only works if there are many ants. If the shortest path to the food source had to be found by a single ant, this would require considerable cognitive abilities (e.g., memory and comparing distances) and exploratory activity on the part of the individual, capacities beyond a single agent. Similarly, there are many tasks that a single agent could not physically achieve on its own, but that can be mastered by a group: ants, working together, can carry large objects such as leaves or sticks, which they could not possibly do alone.

An important part of the fascination of collective intelligence is emergence: global behavior patterns are not programmed into the individuals but emerge from their interaction. For instance, the ant trail formation process is emergent from so-called stigmergic[1] interactions: as mentioned in chapter 2, ants deposit pheromones and follow high pheromone concentrations. In other words, they follow purely local rules, but collectively, by individually applying these rules, they perform a complex optimization task—finding the shortest path between a food source and the nest—without realizing that they are doing so. The term *self-organization* is used to describe these kinds of processes because neither external or hierarchical control, nor directing influences are required for the global behavior patterns to occur (Camazine et al., 2001). Often, when self-organization can be exploited, the resulting solutions tend to be simpler and more robust.

Another reason for looking at groups of agents is redundancy. For example, if during a Mars mission there is only one robot and it breaks down, the mission is over, whereas if there are many, others can continue to do the job, which makes the multiagent approach more robust. Also, for many tasks it may be more efficient to have several agents. If a large territory on Mars needs to be searched for interesting rock samples, having multiple robots take care of different areas will speed up the process enormously. As a biological example, bees routinely perform food collection in an entirely distributed way, with hundreds of bees working in parallel. This is much more efficient than having only one agent collect food at a time. An additional advantage of a collective approach is that the individual agents can typically be much simpler: often a set of simple agents can perform the same task as one complex agent. And if they are to be manufactured, simple robots will typically be cheaper to produce.

But collective intelligence is not restricted to groups of individuals: it can be found in many other domains and at different levels. For example, groups of cells can assemble to form organs, and organs in turn make up entire organisms that are capable of performing tasks that individual cells could not achieve on their own, such as moving around by walking, running, flying, or swimming. Moreover, agents can achieve an increased level of adaptivity by changing their morphology: the deadly puffer fish *Fugu*, which we encountered in the previous chapter, can blow itself up to scare away predators; birds can spread their wings if they want to fly.

So, another motivation for collective robotics—and for modular robotics in particular—is that through morphological change the level of adaptivity can be significantly increased.

The goal of modular robotics is to design and build robots out of a number of modules such that the robot as a whole is capable of achieving various kinds of tasks that a nonmodular robot may not be able to. For example, one of the captivating abilities of modular robots, as we have seen in Kasper Støy's experiments, is that they can change their morphologies; for example, they can morph from snakes into walkers. The size of Støy's modules is on the order of 5 to 10 cm, and biological cells are much smaller, so, at the moment, the two types of systems are very different. However, that may change as the modules become smaller through technological development, in particular nanotechnology. If modular robots are made up of many more units in the future, the application possibilities become virtually unlimited: they will be able to take on any shape whatsoever and perform tasks that are currently hard to imagine (such as being injected into the bloodstream to clean out clogged arteries).

A last point of motivation, and perhaps the most futuristic one, concerns self-repair and self-reproduction. Modular robotics not only attempts to develop robots out of modules that can perform certain tasks, but also to build robots that can repair themselves, a characteristic that hydra possess to an amazing degree, but that is present to some extent in all species. Researchers in the field are also developing robots capable of reproducing themselves, an ability common to most biological organisms. Many cells or modules are necessary for self-repair and self-reproduction to work, but we will get to that later. Let us turn now to agent-based modeling.

7.2 Agent-Based Modeling

Josh Epstein and Rob Axtell, both with formal training in economics, public policy, and computing, in their thin but very compelling book *Building Artificial Societies: Social Science from the Bottom Up*, suggest using artificial life methods to do social science in general, and to study economics in particular. The results from the experiments performed using their "digital social science toolbox," one type of agent-based simulation, are intriguing and often surprising. One investigation they present in their book goes back to the influential Harvard University economist Thomas C. Schelling, who in the late 1960s was interested in racial segregation, because it was—and continues to be—an unresolved issue in many parts of the world. Using their agent-based simulation toolbox, Epstein and Axtell could define various preferences for their agents. The agents "live" on a two-dimensional grid-world, and they follow only one local rule of interaction: if the number of neighbors of a different color (red instead of blue) exceeds the agent's preference level, it moves to a different grid point. In one simulation, they assumed that the members of one race would prefer to have at least 25% like neighbors (but they did not care if, for example, 70% of the neighbors were different). Even with this very moderate preference the society becomes somewhat segregated, i.e., blue and red regions start to form, and the distribution of the agents is far from random. When they made the individuals slightly less tolerant and assumed a uniform distribution of the preferences between 25% and 50%—e.g., some individuals would move when there were more than 27% percent differently colored neighbors, others when there were more than 40%, etc.—the society gets highly segregated into very large blue and red areas. This result holds in spite of the fact that the individuals are still fairly tolerant, so to speak. What is surprising about these results is that apparently the very moderate preference not to live in a neighborhood completely surrounded by members of the other race will lead to segregation. Thus, the society as a whole looks very segregated, but the segregation is not a reflection of the beliefs of the individuals. The segregation is emergent from the simple local behavioral rule, i.e., a rule that takes only direct neighbors into account (for the original model, see Schelling, 1969; for a modern version of the model, see Epstein and Axtell, 1996, 165–171).

Note that the behavioral rule of the agents is highly abstract and does not take perceptual or sensory-motor processes into account, which implies strong assumptions about how social interactions can be modeled. In other words, the rule takes for granted that it is OK to ignore the details about the agent's perception. Most agent-based simulation models are built on such high-level social-interaction rules, which abstract away all the details of embodiment, including perception. In Charlotte Hemelrijk's dominance interaction model of artificial primates, she assumes a social-interaction rule called the dominance interaction rule, which increases or decreases the dominance values of the individuals depending on whether they win or lose the current dominance interaction (e.g., a fight). In the real world, such a dominance interaction is a complex social act requiring sophisticated perceptual and motor skills. The interesting fact is that in spite of these abstractions, fascinating insights can often be gained: in the Schelling model, the ease of segregation of a society could be demonstrated; in Hemelrijk's model, it was found that the individuals with high dominance values end up in the center of their living space, while the others are moved toward the periphery, very much like in groups of real primates (for details, see Hemelrijk, 2002). It will be interesting to see what kinds of emergent behaviors arise from future simulations (or real-world experiments) in which the sensory and motor abilities of the agents are modeled, but at the moment this line of research remains relatively untouched.

Another attractive possibility of agent-based simulation studies is to combine them with evolutionary methods. Epstein and Axtell proposed the so-called Sugarscape model, a grid-world where the grid points have sugar concentrations and the agents are characterized by two genetically determined parameters, vision (how far they can see), and metabolism (how rapidly they burn sugar), and a current state given by the amount of sugar they actually have in store. The agents follow a simple behavioral rule: look for the grid point with the highest sugar concentration in the field of vision, move to that point, and consume the sugar (i.e., add it to the store). The farther they can see, the more possibilities for finding a high sugar concentration, and the lower the metabolism, the less sugar they will burn. There is also a "sex rule" by which agents can reproduce and transmit their genetic attributes—vision and metabolism—to their offspring.

Assume now that there are seasonal changes in sugar concentrations. As one might expect, agents that can see far and have a low metabolism have a higher chance of survival. Thus, on an evolutionary time scale individuals with high vision and low metabolism will proliferate, which is fairly obvious. If an additional rule, an inheritance rule, is introduced—when an agent dies, its children will inherit its sugar in equal parts—the results are truly surprising: through inheritance, the selective pressure on vision drops and individuals with low vision that would, without inheritance, have been weeded out by evolution now have a chance of surviving. Thus, we see that a social rule, inheritance, has an influence on biological evolution. Now this result is, of course, a politically hot topic. According to Epstein and Axtell: "Interestingly some 'Social Darwinists' oppose wealth transfers to the poor on the ground that the undiluted operation of selective pressures is 'best for the species.' Conveniently, they fail to mention that intergenerational transfer of wealth from the rich to their offspring dilute those very pressures." (p. 68). Agent-based simulation opens up the possibility to study issues, e.g., the interaction of social conventions and biological evolution, that cannot be systematically studied in the real world.

As a last example of this type of simulation let us look at flocking behavior. Craig Reynolds, a computer scientist who is fascinated by nature's achievements, was already as a child intrigued by the question of how birds can fly in flocks. Many animals, such as insects, birds, and fish, form flocks, but so do mammals (bison and wild horses are but two examples). Reynolds created the "boids," computer simulations of agents that can flock (Reynolds, 1987). Reynolds stresses the point that the term *boids* has nothing to do with *birds* and that the "boids" exist in their own right as electronic creatures rather than being some sort of model of real birds. Such a stance is, by the way, often encountered in the artificial life community, and, alas, it reduces the appeal of the research. Nevertheless, the relation to biology or the real world suggested by the term is what makes this work truly fascinating: irrespective of how lovely Reynolds's boids fly in simulation, we cannot help asking how real birds might in fact do it: are they doing something similar to the boids?

The boids flock on the basis of three simple local rules of interaction: collision avoidance, velocity matching or alignment, and flock centering. Collision avoidance means that boids should not fly into other boids, so there is a kind of repulsion from other objects. A boid adjusts its velocity to match the average velocity of its neighbors, i.e., if they go faster it will speed up as well, and will start to fly in roughly the same direction as the others. Moreover, based on the location of its neighbors, the boid will move toward the highest local density of boids. The results of the simulations are truly amazing, given the simplicity of the rules. However, our experience, and the experience of many others, has been that—depending on the environment—the three simple rules need a bit of additional help. For example, the boids easily split when there are obstacles, and a default velocity—a velocity that they adopt whenever no other information is available—has to be introduced, otherwise the flock as a whole might not move at all but may instead stay in one place.

Although Reynolds's rules may not be accurate models of biological bird flocking, the resulting behavior looks so natural that variations of the algorithm have been widely applied in the entertainment industry to make the simulated movement of groups of animals or humans look natural. It has been used in a number of movies to model flocking of animals, e.g., penguins in Tim Burton's *Batman Returns*, herds of wildebeest stampeding together in Disney's *Lion King*, and different sorts of marine life swimming together in *Finding Nemo*.

Flocking also provides an interesting case study about the differences between simulation and real robots. So let us inspect this issue a little further.

7.3 Simulation versus Real Robots

In an agent-based simulation you can have two views: a situated one, where the only information available for controlling the behavior of the individuals is what the individuals can sense in their local environments; and a god's-eye perspective, where the programmer can use global information. For example, in a boid simulation the situated perspective implies that the only information the individual boids have is obtained through their own sensory systems, whereas from a god's-eye perspective, the programmer has access to the positions and velocities of all agents simultaneously. This information can be easily used, to calculate the local densities of agents in the neighborhood of a particular individual, information which is required to apply Reynolds's rules. Needless to say, the latter perspective makes the programmer's life much easier, and in fact most boid simulations benefit from this global information. In the situated perspective you have to simulate the sensory stimulation of the individuals, e.g., how other boids appear to a boid in its visual field. Extracting, for example, the velocity of neighboring boids from this visual information is a very difficult task.

The minute you start working with real robots, however, global information is no longer possible, unless you have a complicated setup, for example, with overhead cameras watching all the robots in the arena and a vision program for extracting the position of each robot (an arrangement which is sometimes used in robot soccer tournaments). Or, if you are running outdoor experiments, you can equip them with GPS. But if you are interested in natural systems, the only valid perspective is the situated one: real birds do not have a GPS. But working with local sensor information alone makes life difficult. How would you, as an agent, go about adjusting your velocity to that of your neighbors? How do you determine that they are moving faster or slower than you? How do you know in which direction they are moving? How do you even recognize a neighboring agent? Extracting this from sensors alone, e.g., from the visual system, is a nontrivial task, as we discussed when talking about computer vision in chapter 3. One way is to compare the relative position of an agent in the visual field at two different points in time and register any changes, taking into account your own motion during that time.

And then, this needs to be done for all neighbors. But which are the neighbors? Of course, solutions can be found, but they all have a sort of ad hoc flavor.

In the multiagent domain life is so much easier in simulation: first, you can run experiments for as long as you like, with as many agents as you like, and you do not need to deal with all the messiness of real-world interaction such as low resolution of images, noise on the sensors and the motor system, rapidly varying lighting conditions, power consumption, mechanical breakdowns, and the fact that the experiments take a long time. Moreover, in simulation there is the possibility of running evolutionary studies, which are currently possible in the real world only to a very limited extent, as we have seen in the previous chapter. On the other hand, we have mentioned several times now that it is very easy to gloss over details when running simulations only. "Do a dominance interaction" is easy to define in simulation, but hard to implement in robots in the real world. What sensors are used? How do the robots recognize each other? On the basis of what information do they decide to enter a dominance interaction? How do they interact? How long does the interaction last? What about battery charge? Clearly, there is a need to work at least in part with physical robots in order to truly investigate the relationship between sensor-motor processes and collective intelligence. So, let us turn to real robots now.

7.4 Groups of Robots

Each year the Neuroscience Center in Zurich stages a "Brain Fair" which has the general goal of communicating the latest research in the vast area of neuroscience to the general public. The center is a huge operation, which unites roughly a hundred research groups that, one way or other, work in the field, including brain researchers, medical doctors, pharmacologists, psychologists, computational neuroscientists, and last but not least artificial intelligence researchers and roboticists employing ideas from neuroscience in their experiments. Rolf's AI lab in Zurich takes part in this event on a regular basis and we typically stage robot demonstrations in order to illustrate ideas about embodiment. At the 1999 Brain Fair, Hanspeter Kunz, a physicist and computer scientist who is studying emergent phenomena in groups of robots together with Charlotte Hemelrijk, showed off an experiment on robot flocking using a small number of Samurai robots (about six). These are circular-shaped three-wheeled robots, about 30 cm in diameter and 30 cm high, equipped with a ring of infrared sensors, a wireless LAN card, and an omnidirectional camera with a 360° field of vision. Many animals, such as insects or rabbits, have almost 360° vision, so this is a biologically plausible setup for conducting biorobotics experiments. In order to illustrate the frame-of-reference issue to the visitors, Kunz projected information from one of the robots onto a very large screen for everyone to see: the raw camera image, the various stages of visual processing—extraction of edges, color, and identification of other robots—the state of the neural network that controls the robot, and the signals sent to the motors. This is a nice way to provide an intuition of what the world looks like from the perspective of the robot, i.e., the situated perspective. Furthermore, each robot was equipped with a version of Reynolds's rules.

Let us quickly describe the omnidirectional camera. Imagine that you have a curved mirror like a silver-coated lightbulb facing downward so that it reflects the environment all around it, and then you have a normal camera facing upward at this curved surface: this creates a 360° camera. While this setup is effective and simple, the design has a serious draw-back: The resolution is very low because a large portion of the environment—much larger than for a standard camera—is mapped onto the normal camera, which makes the visual analysis and thus the imple-mentation of the Reynolds rules difficult. Recognizing the other robots, which is a prerequisite for the flocking rules to work, also becomes very hard for this reason. In order to overcome this problem, Kunz put wide bands of brightly colored tape on his robots to make it easier for them to recognize other robots. And indeed, nice flocking behavior emerged in the laboratory and even in the arena at the site of the Brain Fair—an 8 × 8 meter square area delineated by panels about 20 cm high—when tested the night before the event. However, at the event itself the system often broke down, i.e., some of the robots took off toward the border of the arena rather than staying in the flock. Our analysis quickly revealed the problem: many of the children in the audience wore clothes of the same bright colors that the robots used to recognize the other robots. When Kunz's robots were alone in the arena, or surrounded only by aca-demics dressed in black, gray, and beige, the flocking worked fine, emerg-ing from the local rules of interaction. But later the robots, instead of flocking with respect to the other robots, took the children for robots! So much for visual processing in the real world. What to us, as human observers, seems almost ridiculously obvious—children are quite differ-ent from circular robots on three wheels with omnidirectional cameras—may not be obvious from the situated perspective of the robot. This example illustrates the low level of robustness of the behavioral system: slight changes in the environmental conditions cause the system to break down. All the more reason to admire the enormous robustness of natural systems!

Mind you, this difficulty did not come about because Kunz did not know what he was doing: he has a lot of experience with these sorts of experiments, and he has done his homework and studied the literature. A look at the literature on collective robotics is in fact very interesting: in spite of the enormous potential of collective intelligence, there seem to be a number of problems that may be indicators of deeper underlying issues. First, there are surprisingly few experiments on groups of real robots reported in the literature, but there are a lot of experiments in simulation. Second, the kinds of tasks reported are relatively limited in scope. Third, typically in these experiments only a few robots are used. Fourth, the scientific value of the experiments is hard to assess because they are typically not systematically done. Fifth, in many collective robotic experiments, emergence is not of interest. And finally, there are very few, if any, applications of collective robotics in the real world.

To be sure, there is a body of interesting experiments that deals with the emergence of global patterns in physical robots: robot clustering (e.g., Beckers et al., 1994, and Martinoli et al., 1999); robots splitting into individual subgroups (Holland and Melhuish, 1999); exploration (Hayes et al., 2000); the creation of division of labor (Ling at al., 2004); transportation and manipulation of large objects (Ijspeert et al., 2001; Groß and Dorigo, 2004); and communication networks that cover an arena (Ichikawa et al., 2003). This list is incomplete, but it is hard to find additional case studies on collective intelligence that are performed on real robots, and in which the functionality of the group as a whole is emergent from local rules. There are a few conferences specifically dedicated to collective intelligence such as DARS, the Conference on Distributed Autonomous Robotic Systems—but within DARS there is relatively little work on emergence—and SWARM, which is specifically devoted to large groups of agents, but there again most of the work involves simulation only.

But let us return to the problems revealed by the literature, such as it is, and speculate a bit about why there are so few physical studies. Hardware is often unreliable and costly, and its use requires researchers with a lot of hardware know-how, which is why normally only few robots are involved. Typically only 5, 10, or 20 robots are used, and, as far as we know, the record so far for the most physical robots used together is 100

(McLurkin and Smiths, 2004). The term *swarm intelligence*, which is sometimes used as a synonym for collective intelligence, suggests really large numbers of agents. The microrobotics specialist Joerg Seyfried of the University of Karlsruhe in Germany, one of the robotics hubs in Europe, is planning to use 1000 millimeter-high robots for exploration, cleaning, collection, and assembly tasks, in a large research project called "i-swarm" (Seyfried et al., 2005), sponsored by the European Union's IST-FET programs (Information Society Technology, Future and Emergent Technologies). In 2006 the experiments on real robots were still in the planning stage, but it will certainly be exciting to follow their progress.

Experiments with physical robots also take a long time because one has to deal with all the problems of the real world discussed in chapter 3; robots take time to move; and, because of the unreliability of the hardware, experiments often have to be repeated. The time and effort involved is orders of magnitude greater than in simulation studies.

When we survey the kinds of applications this branch of research is interested in, irrespective of whether real robots or virtual agents are used, we encounter, always, roughly the following behaviors in addition to the ones we just mentioned: dispersion (i.e., covering an area as completely and regularly as possible); foraging (looking for food, which may involve dispersion or finding the shortest path to a food source); map-building (forming a representation by exploring the environment); simple assembly tasks (such as the NASA Work Crew project, where a pair of robots cooperate to pick up and transport long metal beams to a construction site where they are then fitted into place [Schenker et al., 2003]); robot soccer (e.g., Kitano et al., 1997); cleaning; and object-collection tasks. And to our knowledge none of these have yet been turned into practical applications, which makes one wonder about when large-scale collective robotics will become practical.

Another reason—a psychological one—for the relatively limited number of applications is that we still do not seem to trust self-organization and emergence, because we do not have a sufficient understanding of how to design systems such that the desired functionality emerges from local rules. And whenever we do not trust self-organization, we tend to overcontrol our systems (i.e., we give our agents too much "brainpower") and the ghost of cognitivism creeps in. And, to speculate a bit more, a last reason might be that emergent behaviors and self-organization are useful for natural systems in the service of survival and reproduction, but may be less useful in environments where we, as humans, would like to get a specific task done by robots.

7.5   A Note on Cooperation

Before we move on to modular robotics, we should add a few comments here on cooperation. Cooperation is sometimes seen as the hallmark of intelligence: after all, it is ultimately through cooperation that our achievements as humans in science, technology, and society have been possible. However, given the current state of the art in artificial intelligence and robotics, we are nowhere near being able to design and build agents capable of similar accomplishments. Rather than trying to give a comprehensive review of research on cooperation, we will comment on the term itself, illustrate how it has been used in the field, and then point to a particularly promising area where cooperation plays an essential role, RoboCup.

What do we actually mean by cooperation? In some sense, the Swiss robots cooperate: they all do the same task, thus speeding up task completion. But do they really cooperate? The answer is far from clear. If you imagine only one Swiss robot performing the task, theoretically what will happen is exactly the same as what happens with several robots, only it will take much longer for piles to appear. But in practice it often happens that the robots get stuck somewhere in the arena. So, if there is only a single robot, it will remain stuck and not continue to work, thus leaving the arena cluttered. However, if other robots are around, they will—because the arena is closed—eventually pass nearby the trapped robot and "free" it, by bumping into it, so that it can continue its job. So, the robots help each other—they cooperate—but of course they do not know anything about their honorable behavior.

Similarly, ants depositing pheromones when searching for food cooperate—otherwise they would not find the shortest path to the food source—but they need not know that they are doing so. The question is whether the term *cooperation* is justified in the first place for the description of these behaviors. It is OK to use it, but we have to be aware of the fact that the cooperation is in our heads, as observers, rather than in the heads of the agents: the frame-of-reference issue strikes again!

What about ants carrying a large leaf? In this case we are more inclined to use the term *cooperation* because the behavior of the ants involved depends directly on the behavior of other ants. Likewise, if several robots are pushing a large object, we are inclined to call this cooperation. Of course, if we actually know that the agents are observing one another and basing their actions on the observed behaviors of other agents, then they are definitely cooperating.

Historically, a highly interesting experiment in robot cooperation was the "robot ecosystem" designed by Luc Steels and David McFarland in the mid-1990s (McFarland, 1994; Steels, 1997). Briefly, in this system there is a limited amount of total energy flowing into the system, which mimics the limited resources available in natural ecosystems. There are a few robots within an arena, a charging station that can supply varying levels of energy, and a few boxes with infrared lamps. The lamps are called "competitors" because they—like the robots—consume energy from the ecosystem; also, because the overall amount of electricity is limited, the robots have to compete with the lamps for the electricity. By banging against them, the robots can reduce the energy consumption of the lamps. Reducing their consumption dims the lights' output, and as a consequence more current will be available in the charging station. If the lamps are left alone, their lights will steadily get brighter again and consume more energy. In terms of cooperation we say that, in a sense, the robots that push against the lamps help the one in the charging station. In this setting, it would be interesting to study under what conditions this cooperative behavior could in fact be learned and what kind of feedback the robots would need. At the evolutionary time scale, given enough generations, the cooperative behavior might eventually emerge because the ones that do cooperate get more energy overall. For example, we could imagine a successful behavior evolving that is something like this: if a robot senses that another robot is in the charging station, it will find the closest lamp and bang against it. So far, however, evolving cooperation in embodied agents has not yet been tried, though there has been some preliminary work on evolution of cooperation in simulation (e.g., Spector et al., 2005).

One of the best examples of cooperation, and one that holds great promise for the field of artificial intelligence, is RoboCup, the by now famous Robot World Cup Initiative (Kitano et al., 1997) that we introduced in chapter 2. One player robot passing the ball to another so that it can kick it into the goal is undeniably, in any respect, an act of cooperation. In contrast to other cooperative tasks for which robots have been used, this one requires several sophisticated perceptual and sensory-motor skills: the robots must have the ability to move rapidly, dribble, kick the ball, avoid opponents, recognize the ball as well as the goals and the players of its own and the opponent's team, they must have the ability to predict the positions of the ball and of other players, etc. Cooperation is programmed into these robots, but even so, in the spirit of the synthetic methodology, a lot can be learned about the prerequisites of cooperation in this domain: under what conditions should the ball be passed to another player? When should the player continue its dribbling? When should it try to kick the ball directly into the goal? Needless to say, there is still a lot of basic research required to improve the sensory-motor skills of these robots to support these sophisticated behaviors. So far in RoboCup, mostly wheeled robots have been used, but recently a humanoid league has been established, where the players are humanoid robots. In that domain it will be highly challenging to achieve the requisite skills, since humanoid robots that can walk around on their own have been developed only recently. If the humanoid league truly gets off the ground, we can expect even more spectators at the world championships, compared to the 100,000 that showed up at the Fukuoka Dome in 2002.

Let us now turn to modular robotics, a field that spans robotics, artificial intelligence, and artificial life and which has been picking up a lot of momentum recently.

7.6 Modular Robots

Returning to the story at the beginning of the chapter, Kasper Støy surprised his audience with a modular robot equipped with distributed control: each unit acts on its own, instead of all the units being commanded by some leader module or off-board computer. Støy used the notion of "roles" to make it all work: the modules could autonomously detect how they were connected to their neighbors and, depending on the connectivity, determine their role in the system and react accordingly by activating the control program corresponding to that role. Without going into technical detail, if a module is connected to only one other module, it is at the end of a limb (or a snake). If it is connected to two modules, one at each end, it forms part of a limb or the body of the snake. If it is connected in a T shape, it is at a position where a leg joins the body, etc. If the right control programs are assigned to the right roles, useful behavior, such as locomotion, can be achieved.

We have seen that certain organisms, such as the puffer fish *Fugu*, can perform different functions by changing their morphology. Fumio Hara of the Science University of Tokyo coined the term *morphofunctional machines* for artifacts that can perform different tasks by changing their morphology (Hara and Pfeifer, 2003). This ability boosts their level of adaptivity compared to normal robots where adaptivity can only be achieved by changes in the control architecture. And changing morphology is one of the essential goals of modular robotics. To further illustrate this point let us look at another example.

M-TRAN

M-TRAN is a robotic system developed by Satoshi Murata at the Tokyo Institute of Technology, who is one of the recognized leaders in the field of modular robotics. He seems to have a sort of link into the future, as his first-class research has a definite science-fiction flavor. But in contrast to science-fiction stories, his ideas are actually implemented not only in simulation but also on actual hardware. Murata developed a module, the M-TRAN, with which he can achieve an unbelievable variety of behaviors. Although some of the basic principles are similar to Støy's approach, M-TRAN can, by contrast, autonomously attach to and detach from other modules without human intervention. While this sounds easy at first, on closer inspection it turns out to be far from trivial from a hardware perspective. One possibility would be to use electromagnets: when you want two modules to attach, the magnets are switched on by applying a current, and when the connection is no longer needed the current is shut off. The problem with this solution is power consumption and heat dissipation: the modules, when attached, continuously need to be powered, and this power has to somehow be supplied to all the modules; moreover, at least one side of every module will always be attached and thus every module requires current. As an alternative, we could use permanent magnets. They are easy to attach, and once they are attached no extra energy need be delivered. But how about detaching? If we want the modules to stick together well, so that they can, for example, support an "arm" with several M-TRAN modules sticking out—say, two or three—the "arm" will weigh between 800 and 1200 grams (given that each module weighs about 400 grams). Thus we need relatively strong magnets, which implies that detaching them will require even stronger forces. In the M-TRAN module this problem is resolved by having an ingenious detachment mechanism (the reader interested in the details is referred to Murata et al., 2004).

M-TRAN modules are quite complex. They consist of two semicubes—cubelike on one end, cylinder-like on the other—and each one is $6 \times 6 \times 6$ cm, connected by a link, and driven by a servo motor (see figure 7.1a). Each module is equipped with three connecting plates on the surface, a battery, a microprocessor chip, magnets with a detachment mechanism, and links for communication between neighboring modules. Self-reconfiguration is achieved by repeating the basic operations of detaching a surface from a neighbor, rotating a semicube, and

(a)

(b)

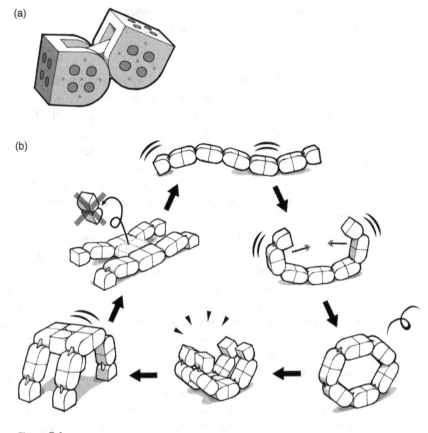

Figure 7.1
Self-reconfiguring robots: Satoshi Murata's M-TRAN system. (*a*) The individual module.
(*b*) Morphing process with intermediate steps.

reconnecting the surface to another neighbor. The basic problem in self-reconfiguration, then, is as follows: given a starting configuration A (a "snake," i.e., a linear arrangement of modules) and a goal configuration B (a four-legged walker), can configuration A be transformed into configuration B by a sequence of local operations? This is a hard computational problem, and Murata and his team developed an algorithm to do the job. Through this method, walkers can be transformed into snakes and rollers for locomotion purposes (see figure 7.1b). As mentioned earlier, the idea of self-reconfiguration here is that there is no need for a designer to take the structure apart and reassemble it, but it can, in a step-by-step manner, "morph" itself into the new structure. Thus, the creatures built from M-TRAN modules are prime examples of morphofunctional machines.

The algorithm for calculating the transformation sequence is run off-line on a separate computer, and then the modules are instructed to move in particular ways to achieve the shape transformation. In this sense it is a centralized control scheme, but the way in which the transformation comes about is decentralized: it is carried out by the combined actions of the individual modules. The generation of locomotion patterns is, of course, more difficult on such a system than on a robot with a given morphology, because each pattern has to be tailored to the different morphologies to which the system is capable of changing. In the M-TRAN–based robots, this is achieved by using an optimization method based on artificial evolution, as discussed in the previous chapter.

As always, we are interested in emergence, and one way to look at emergence is in terms of artificial evolution: the gait patterns—snake-like, legged, or roller movements—emerge from an evolutionary process carried out on an M-TRAN robot. The locomotion patterns are also in some sense emergent because they result from simple movements of the individual modules, which then, in the interaction with each other and the environment, produce a particular gait or other movement pattern. The reconfiguration process itself, however, is centrally controlled and thus not emergent because it does not rely on the module's interaction with the environment during reconfiguration.

"Slimebot"

In order to get a better feel for emergence let us look at one last example of self-reconfiguration in modular robots that has a clear focus on emergence. The roboticist Akio Ishiguro of Tohoku University in Japan is known for his nontraditional thinking and has had a long-standing interest in ecological balance, morphological computation, and neural-body coupling. For his latest robot he once again drew inspiration from nature. The "Slimebot" is motivated by the slime mold, a creature that has attracted the attention of many researchers in artificial intelligence and artificial life. The slime mold is—not surprisingly—slimy. It has no head, no real body, and no limbs. It consists only of one type of cell and has no neural system, but it has a highly interesting life cycle. The cycle consists of an animal-like phase in which it moves, eats, and digests—just like an animal—and a plantlike reproductive phase. Ishiguro was interested in slime molds because their many cells can produce locomotion patterns even though the organism does not have a neural system, let alone a brain.

He built a module, completely different in nature from the M-TRAN: it is a wheel-like structure, with eight spokelike parts that can each be actuated by so-called linear actuators (i.e., an actuator with a thinner tube moving inside one with a larger diameter, just like the pistons in a car engine). The "wheels" lie horizontally on the ground. For attachment to other modules, the circumference of the wheel is covered by Velcro, so that when it comes into contact with another Velcro-covered robot they stick together. To detach, the actuators push the units apart. Moreover, there is a mechanism for controlling the ground friction—high or low— which is used to generate locomotion: when the high-friction part is on the ground, it can be used to pull or push neighboring cells. Using a kind of oscillator, like those we have seen in "Puppy" and in the lamprey, and taking advantage of the mutual coupling of neighboring modules, a type of coordinated wave of neighboring modules is produced that travels through the entire cluster of more than 30 modules; and by exploiting this high-low friction control mechanism, the entire robot starts moving even though no one module can move on its own. Note that the waves traveling through the robot are a result of the interaction of neighboring modules and friction, and are not globally controlled; the movement is clearly emergent—it is a result of a process of self-organization.

In many of these modular robot approaches, one problem has been the mechanical issues involved in attaching, detaching, and moving modules, which requires considerable force and consumes a lot of power. But there may be easier means to achieve that, such as by taking advantage of the fact that in water or other liquids, properly designed modules can float. This was one of the ideas underlying the HYDRON modules developed in the context of the previously mentioned HYDRA project. While this approach alleviates the mechanical problems, one has to cope with the issues of operating in liquids. In any case, it will be interesting to see the results of this work in the future. Another solution might be to reduce the size of the individual modules, which would make them lighter and lessen (or at least change) the mechanical problems. This leads us to the question of scalability, which will become increasingly relevant if we want to approximate the abilities of natural systems, such as the ability to self-repair and self-reproduce.

7.7 Scalability, Self-Assembly, Self-Repair, Homogeneity, and Heterogeneity

The first physical robot that can be said to repair itself is presumably the "fracta" machine, also built by Murata. The fracta machine is a modular robot that works on the basis of the *identification-expulsion-replacement* principle. First, the faulty module is identified: the modules can detect whether one of their neighboring modules is faulty by measuring whether it is drawing power. If a faulty module is detected, it is expelled from the system. Expulsion may not be easy because the module might sit amid many others; clever reconfiguration procedures may need to be applied. Finally, the module is replaced: a new module is recruited from a repository of extra modules and moved into the proper position, which again requires a sophisticated algorithm.

While the fracta machine clearly constitutes a groundbreaking development, the approach has important limitations. The self-repair process is disruptive, so to speak, as an entire large-scale module is eliminated and replaced. Biological organisms such as the hydra work differently— their power for self-repair stems from the genetic regulatory networks that guide their growth and from their large number of cells. However, given the state of the art in technology concerning growth and differentiation of artificial modules or cells, we seem to be stuck with the identification-expulsion-replacement strategy for the time being. Nevertheless, this approach could be made much smoother if the size of the modules could be significantly trimmed down and their number substantially increased. However, for significant cuts in size to be possible, the nature of the modules will have to change fundamentally: rather than having sophisticated electromechanical and communication systems, different technologies will have to be applied (electrical motors, for example, cannot be made arbitrarily small).

In this context, technologies that allow the modules to become arbitrarily small are called scalable technologies. A somewhat complementary meaning of scalability in modular robotics implies that an approach can be applied not only to robots with 10, 20, or 100 modules but also to those with thousands. Of course, if we want to have very small modules, our technologies need to be scalable in both directions. Because we can no longer control the modules in the classical sense by programming a microprocessor, we have to rely more on their surface properties, on their shapes, and on self-organizing processes to guide their behavior. For example, the units will need to be able to move. This can be achieved with artificial muscles based on electroactive polymers that can change shape in response to electrical stimulation, a scalable technology; electroactive polymers are currently being investigated in various research laboratories around the world. Another alternative, the one chosen for the HYDRON modules, is to put them into a liquid environment.

Moreover, the surface properties of the modules might be exploited so that, by analogy to biological cells, a certain type of surface can connect only to a specific other type of surface, e.g., Velcro can attach only to Velcro (in biological systems, this kind of functionality is achieved in part by cell adhesion molecules). This way, the process of self-assembly could also be made less computationally intensive because the surface properties, together with the movement of the modules, perform a kind morphological computation. One could imagine having a box full of very small modules, with the energy supply required for the individual modules to move in order to attach to other modules provided by shaking the box. Even though this shaking process is random, the resulting structure will be nonrandom because of the various surface properties and forces acting on them. This idea has been demonstrated by Isao Shimoyama and his colleagues at the University of Tokyo, where the modules were formed like triangles and through shaking of the box, the pieces self-assembled into various shapes—hexagons having the highest probability of being created (Hosokawa et al., 1995). Generally speaking, if the modules get smaller and smaller, direct assembly becomes more and more difficult so that one will have to rely increasingly on processes of self-organization, as is well known from nanotechnology. The phenomenon of self-assembly has been demonstrated and exploited for applications at many levels, from nanometers to centimeters (Whitesides and Grzybowski, 2003). The details of how this works do not matter at this point, but we can expect these developments to have a significant impact on the field of modular robotics in the near future.

One of the important benefits that comes with shrinking the size of the modules is generality. The more you shrink the size of the modules, the more closely you can approximate any kind of shape: it is hard to build a dexterous hand from large, square bricks only, whereas if you have building blocks the size of biological cells, arbitrary shapes can be constructed. This leads us to another essential point in modular robotics.

A biological organism is not built from one type of cell, but from many different types. For example, as mentioned before, a human contains a total of roughly 10^{14} cells, differentiated into several thousand cell types, depending on what you count as a type. So, complex functions can only be achieved by having many different types of cells, at least in biological organisms.[2] Only through the joint effect of having very small cells (on the order of 10 micrometers) and many different cell types has it been possible for evolution to achieve the enormous biodiversity on this planet with its estimated 30 to 50 million different species (Erwin, 1988, 1997). So, being modular alone is not sufficient; there must also be diversity of cell types in order to achieve variety in functionality. Let us now see how these questions translate to the design of modular robots.

In modular robotics we have many design choices. We can build one single type of module that can perform a variety of different functions, which is essentially the approach taken by Støy, by Murata, by Ishiguro, and in the HYDRA project. These building blocks can communicate with their neighbors, they provide structural support, they can actuate their neighbors, they can attach and detach, they can sense their environments (e.g., they can detect light or chemical concentrations of sugar), and they can process sensory and motor signals. Using these kinds of "universal" building blocks implies that a lot of their functionality will not be used, for example, if blocks inside the organism are employed only for structural support, like bones. (We use the quotation marks here to indicate that in the real world there is no universality.) Such a design will be expensive and much of it is overkill. But the advantages of universal modules are the flexibility and the redundancy they provide: the one type of module can be applied everywhere, and if a module ceases to function it can be replaced by any other module. Also, for obvious reasons, self-reconfiguration will be made much easier if only one type of building block is used. Moreover, for mass manufacturing, producing only one type of module is certainly more economical.

So, again, one might want to think about using different types of modules and try to find a compromise: some modules only equipped with attachment possibilities (for structural support—no need for sensing, actuation, and processing); some specifically for actuation; some for sensing, etc. But that will require taking care that we have the right types of modules in the right place. Also, for self-repair, we will need a repository of extra copies of all the different types of modules. On the other hand, specialized structures can be built more cheaply if different types of specialized modules are available. There is no absolute best solution to this problem: depending on the specific task environment, the financial constraints of manufacture, and the amount of robustness needed, a compromise will always have to be found.

Now let us look at another capability of modular systems: self-reproduction.

7.8 Self-Reproducing Machines

There is a long history of trying to build self-reproducing machines, starting with John von Neumann, one of the inventors of the modern digital computer and one of the greatest mathematicians of the twentieth century, who made innumerable stunning contributions to many fields of mathematics. One of his many achievements was the invention of the cellular automaton—an abstract machine like the Turing machine—which he then used as the basis for describing a self-replicating mechanism. Von Neumann believed that biological organisms could be seen as machines—very sophisticated machines, but machines nonetheless, a thought that we have already encountered earlier. He also believed that the important part of an organism is not the matter from which it is made, but rather the information it contains. And he was especially interested in complexity, asking the question of how many components are needed for a machine to reproduce itself: von Neumann described a self-reproducing cellular automaton made up of 200,000 "cells," and each cell could be in one of 29 possible states. Since then, several other abstract machines have been developed, mathematically and in simulation, that can reproduce themselves using fewer units and fewer states. Von Neumann's demonstration was made around 1950, and it is interesting to note that when von Neumann devised his self-replicating machine, the replication mechanisms of DNA had not yet been discovered—that came only in 1953. DNA-based mechanisms are, of course, fully embodied physical systems, but they can also be analyzed in information-theoretic terms: how much information do they, or can they, contain?

Because we are interested in embodied systems rather than abstract simulations, we will not discuss all the simulations of self-reproduction but will describe just one approach to building real, physical, self-replicating machines. Interestingly enough, one of the most advanced self-replicating robot systems was built recently in Hod Lipson's laboratory at Cornell University. Remember that Lipson, as a researcher at Brandeis University, made a name for himself by demonstrating the first automated manufacture of evolved robot designs in the Golem project, as described in chapter 6.

Victor Zykov and Efstathios Mytilinaios of Lipson's lab built eight robot cubes that could attach and detach from each other (figure 7.2). In a sense, their system behaves somewhat like Murata's M-TRAN modules. The advance here is that a snakelike robot built from four of these cubes could move and grab onto additional blocks placed at "feeding stations," and it could attach these blocks together at another location to build a new, functioning, four-unit snake robot. The cubes have a "cut" through their middle: a motor can turn one half of the cube relative to the other half, so that the cubes attached to the free end rotate (see figure 7.2a). The cubes grab onto each other—and release each other—using electromagnets, which can be turned on and off by a microprocessor embedded in each cube (the processor also controls the

(a)

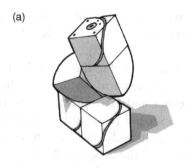

(b)

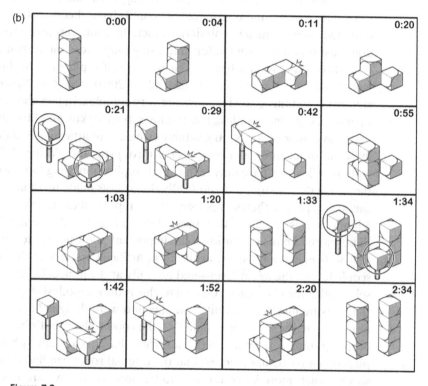

Figure 7.2
Self-reproducing robots: The Cornell system. (*a*) A four-unit snakelike robot. (*b*) The four-unit robot makes a copy of itself by taking new units from two "feeder stations" (the thin rods) and attaching them to the new robot. Units attach to and detach from each other using electromagnets embedded in the cubes' sides. Numbers indicate minutes and seconds. Note that the new robot (on the right) swivels its own units to help with its own construction.

motor). The robot, without any human intervention (except for the placement of the blocks at the feeding stations), is able to build a functional copy of itself: it self-replicates (Zykov et al., 2005).

Needless to say, this robot is much simpler than von Neumann's 200,000-cell self-replicator. Also, the sequence of motor commands that causes the first robot to pick up cubes and place them on the growing robot—and the one that causes the second robot to help with its own construction—were designed by Zykov himself. Each cube has a copy of the self-replication control program, and the cubes send signals to each other when they are connected, instructing each other on what to do next. Of course, these commands could have been automatically designed using artificial evolution. In fact, the same research group has done just this, but in simulation, and using only two-dimensional rather than three-dimensional blocks. The reason self-replication in this case works with so few units (four instead of 200,000 in von Neumann's studies) is that the individual units are very complex. In fact, the modules themselves are, more or less, functioning robots. Zykov and Mytilinaios's units have their own circuitry, actuation, means of attaching and detaching from other units, and computer control programs. Although Zykov and his colleagues have only realized self-replication using four modules, they have demonstrated theoretically that robots made up of more units can also replicate themselves using this setup: needless to say, however, a longer series of actions than those shown in figure 7.2b are needed for these more complex situations. The important point here is to illustrate that self-replication can be achieved in artificial systems at the macroscopic level—the agent level—and not only at the molecular level (as in self-replicating chemistry). Of course, this is only a modest step forward: the units themselves are quite complex and were designed and built by humans, energy has to be supplied to the robots, the robot's behavior is preprogrammed, the parts of the new robot have to be built by hand and placed in a particular place so that the original robot can find them, and so on. Much more work remains to be done before we are anywhere close to realizing true self-replicating machines.

7.9 Collective Intelligence: Where Are We and Where Do We Go from Here?

We have seen many fascinating illustrations of collective intelligence in simulation and on real robots: models of racial segregation, flocking algorithms that have been used in Hollywood movies, groups of robots that can optimally cover an area or cooperate to carry large objects, robots that can play soccer at an impressive level of competence, modular robots that can change their morphology from caterpillars to snakes and walking machines, self-repairing systems, and even robots capable of self-reproduction, that is, of making complete copies of themselves in the real world. Given the power and fascination of collective intelligence, and given that the ideas of emergence and collective phenomena have been around for a long time, it is somewhat surprising how little impact this research has had on our conception of intelligence, and how few systems have been turned into practical applications. Except for entertainment, there have been virtually no applications where emergence has played an essential role.

One decidedly successful development in collective intelligence is RoboCup: the initiative has achieved international visibility, attracted many creative researchers and spectators to both the technical meetings and competitions, and significantly advanced our understanding of robot cooperation and robot behavior in rapidly changing environments. Moreover, it has made its way into schools, where it is now widely recognized as a highly valuable educational tool. But up until now, the initiative has yielded no practical applications where robots collectively and autonomously perform tasks in the real world. The same is true of swarm intelligence, which is another thriving area in collective intelligence. In swarm intelligence, large groups of agents are studied, and emergence is an essential research goal. Although there have been many suggestions for fascinating applications, e.g., the idea of using ant algorithms for load balancing in computer networks, there are to date only a few truly distributed commercial applications where the individual agents (the electronic ants) interact locally with one another, but there are some interesting ones. Ant algorithms are now used to route trucks throughout Europe for the Swiss supermarket chain Migros and the Italian pasta maker Barilla. AirLiquid-USA has also employed such algorithms to solve various logistic problems. However, all of these applications use virtual agents rather than real-world robots. Swarm intelligence in the real world—large numbers of robots cooperating to perform tasks—has not been realized and put to daily use. The same can be said of modular robotics: to date there have been only very few, if any, applications where modular robots are in fact applied to perform everyday duties.

Even further removed from realization are self-reproducing robots. So far we have not come across any applications in the real world, although we can see enormous potential for their use in space exploration or in any kind of environment that is inaccessible to humans and where robots would have to survive a long time. The ability for self-reproduction will make the agents much more self-sufficient over the long run, at least at the group level. Progress in nanotechnology might lead the way toward practical realization of these ideas.

We have already listed several reasons why so few experiments have been conducted in the real world. We mentioned the unreliability and high cost of hardware, lack of trust and belief in emergence, and the general point that self-organization might be suitable for survival in biological systems but less useful for engineering tasks, where top-down, tightly controlled global behavior may in fact be better for multirobot systems than emergent, self-organizing behaviors. So, it seems that there are two categories of factors that are holding us back: technological and conceptual ones. Yet they are closely related to one another. Let us briefly inspect them here.

Unreliable hardware and high hardware costs are currently critical issues preventing rapid progress. In addition, robots produced in large numbers, because of the high cost, are typically simple and lack sophisticated sensory and motor skills. The relatively restricted setup of these robots may also be part of the reason we always see the same kinds of behaviors in the experiments—clustering, dispersion, cleaning, foraging, cooperative pushing, map-building, and simple assembly tasks. The robots employed in RoboCup tournaments are typically of limited sensory-motor complexity, and only a few are used to play the game—significantly fewer than in real soccer games. Unless the robots become available in large numbers at cheap prices—"agents for the masses," as we have called them earlier (Pfeifer and Scheier, 1999)—the field may not really take off. The true information society, with all its possibilities, only came into being once computers and networks became accessible to millions around the globe. We believe a similar social revolution will occur once physical machines enter our world in large numbers. Thus, the issue is not only technological but also economic.

We have already encountered some of the technological difficulties involved in modular robotics: the attachment-detachment mechanisms, the low strength of the actuators, the energy supply, the intricacies of controlling a large number of modules, and the issue of scalability. But several conceptual issues are also holding back this technology: there is a definite lack of understanding about collective intelligence, emergence, and self-organization. Of course, these are difficult concepts, much harder to grasp than top-down control. The lack of proper technology at the same time impedes conceptual progress: because we have not had the opportunity to experiment at a large scale with groups of robots or with modular robots consisting of very many tiny modules, we have not been able to build up a proper conceptual framework. And because we are not used to thinking in terms of emergence and new kinds of morphologies, it may be that we simply lack the imagination to conceive of what robots with completely different morphologies might be able to do—a situation that could change with future developments of the technology and with advances in evolutionary robot design. New kinds of robots acting in completely new ways may broaden our list of future commercial applications for these types of robots. Also, these developments might in fact lead to entirely new forms of intelligence.

In conclusion let us return to the title of this chapter: "Cognition from interaction." We have deliberately not talked much about cognition in this chapter, but rather about global behavior patterns. The term *global behavior pattern* refers either to a group of agents performing some collective task, or to an individual made up of cooperating modular units. The idea has been to achieve sophisticated behavior with minimal control by capitalizing on interaction, that is, by exploiting the potential of the group.

7.10 Summary: Design Principles for Collective Systems

All of the foregoing examples—collective systems, agent-based modeling, groups of robots, cooperation, modular robots, and self-reconfiguring and self-reproducing machines—should make it clear that we are not dealing with a unified or clearly delineated subject matter. Nevertheless, we will try to briefly summarize the essential principles that we should observe when designing collective intelligence, or that we might want to apply when analyzing biological systems.

Level of abstraction principle First, the term *collective intelligence* applies not only to groups of individuals (as in societies of social insects, animals, humans, or robots), but equally to any kind of assembly of similar agents, such as groups of cells, or groups of modules in modular robotic systems. Whenever talking about collective intelligence we must clearly identify the scale or level of abstraction at which we are investigating our agents: when talking about insect behavior, for example, we are abstracting away details of the organism's individual cells or molecules. This is called the *level of abstraction* principle.

Design for emergence principle   Second, we should focus on design for emergence so that the desired functionality—e.g., racial segregation in society, finding the shortest path to a food source in an ant colony, or the movement and the form of a flock in a group of birds—is not directly programmed into the agents but emerges from a set of simple rules of local interaction. Of course, interesting applications have been developed by directly programming robot groups, but design for emergence has a number of advantages. Because systems with emergent functionality rely on self-organizing processes that require less control, they tend to be not only more adaptive and robust but also cheaper. Emergent functionality requires us to think differently, for example, about social interaction, because much of what we may have thought would be under conscious control turns out to be the result of reflex-like local interactions. Another advantage of emergent designs is scalability: if global behavior is emergent from local rules, then more or fewer agents can be used without affecting the resulting global behavior. This is called the *design for emergence* principle. It directly relates to our general considerations on emergence, but we make a special point of it in the domain of collective intelligence because here it seems particularly difficult to come up with the local rules of interaction that lead to the desired global behavior. Applied to the analysis of biological systems, the principle states that we should look for the local rules of interaction that give rise to the global behavioral pattern that we are studying, such as flocking in birds.

From agent to group principle   Third, agent design principles (from chapter 4) can also be applied to groups of agents, not just individuals. For example, groups of agents are consistent with the principle of parallel, loosely coupled processes because each agent can be interpreted as a process and there are many of them. The agents are loosely coupled either through the environment, as in stigmergic interactions (depositing a pheromone trail), or by local rules of interaction (following other agents, aligning with other agents in a flock). The principle of cheap design can also be applied: often it is cheaper to design a multirobot system consisting of a bunch of simple agents to achieve a particular task than to use a single, very complicated robot, say, for moving large objects. The redundancy principle also applies to collective systems, since multiple agents provide redundancy in natural ways, often having largely overlapping functionalities. This is called the *from agent to group* principle, which, in essence, states that we can always try to translate the principles of agent design to the domain of collective intelligence.

Homogeneity-heterogeneity principle   Fourth, when designing a modular robotic system, a compromise has to be found between the extremes of having only one type of general purpose module and different specialized types of modules. This is more for technological reasons than conceptual ones, namely that we cannot have processes of cell division (or module division) and module specialization in the real world, at least not with existing technologies. We can simulate module specialization, for example by turning off certain components in a module, but then there will be a lot of unused resources "hanging around", and this will not conform to the principle of cheap design. But in terms of the redundancy principle, having one type of "universal" module is beneficial as any module can assume any functionality (within the possibilities of the design of the building block). Of course, this can also be applied to multi-robot systems, where we have to decide whether to use only one type of robot or a number of specialized ones. We call this the *homogeneity-heterogeneity* principle.

This completes the—somewhat heavy—theoretical part of the book. We now turn to the lighter part, part III, which outlines a number of applications of embodied intelligence and discusses how the properties and principles of intelligent agents developed in chapters 3 through 7 relate to these applications.

III   Applications and Case Studies

In this part of the book we will deliver on our promise to explore how the theory of embodiment as discussed so far changes the way we view ourselves and the world around us. Again, the issue is not so much how we can achieve the highest level of technological sophistication when building robotic or embedded technologies, but what we can learn and what sorts of insights about intelligence we can gain from these technologies and from our theoretical framework.

We will explore four very diverse areas: ubiquitous computing, management, the psychology of human memory, and robotic and artificial intelligence technologies in our everyday lives. We will show that the perspective of embodiment can shed new light on all these topics. The case studies are self-contained and can be skipped or read in any sequence. In previous chapters we tried to maintain a relatively systematic format. Because in what follows we will be looking at case studies from very diverse areas, our approach will be more exploratory and less rigidly structured. The reader who is interested primarily in the conceptual aspects or underpinnings of intelligence can skip this part and move directly to part IV, where the major insights from this book are discussed.

In chapter 8 we will look at ubiquitous computing, a new area of computer science that has gained a lot of momentum in recent years, where the primary goal is to empower the user by deploying technology out into the environment, rather than to develop intelligent systems per se. Although at the moment the fields of ubiquitous computing and artificial intelligence are relatively separate, we believe there is a lot of potential overlap and that much can be gained from applying our design principles for intelligent systems to ubiquitous technology.

Then, in chapter 9, we will look at ways in which the design principles could be used to help managers and entrepreneurs create and manage new businesses and companies that will be able to adapt and survive in the dynamic, uncertain, and competitive economic environments of the twenty-first century. What we find especially intriguing is that existing management theories can be seen in a new light, and that some important aspects of management have been largely neglected. The case study presented in chapter 9 also demonstrates that the application of the design principles is not a one-way street, but that the field itself—management and entrepreneurship—adds interesting issues to our theory of intelligence, i.e., to the design principles themselves.

In chapter 10 we will return to a subject that is very closely related to the study of intelligence: human memory. In that chapter we will see how a psychological function, memory, which is normally attributed to high-level cognition, can be understood much better when embodiment is taken into account. Again, we will see how the design principles can guide the study of human memory. We find this case study exciting for two reasons. On the one hand, the perspective of embodiment helps to explain why some classical notions of memory—e.g., the storehouse metaphor—are not appropriate. On the other it supplies the theoretical underpinning for alternative theories of memory, such as the ecological approach to memory, and memory as a dynamical system.

Finally, in chapter 11 we will briefly review the state of the art in robotics, focusing in particular on those robots that have moved out of the research laboratories and into the real world and have become— or will soon become—part of our everyday lives. Because these robots are out in the world and interact with humans and the physical environment, by definition they cannot be abstract, isolated "things," and therefore it is necessary and extremely helpful to take into account the design principles which deal with embodied systems. Again, we feel that if the theoretical insights captured by the design principles were employed, the field could make great strides forward.

Most of the case studies utilize the basic set of design principles as outlined in chapter 4, but the design principles for development, evolution, and collective intelligence are not so consistently applied. This is largely due to the fact that until now, there have been only very few robot implementations of these other approaches. Of course, there is evolutionary robotics, but although artificial evolution is often applied as an optimization method, the more advanced approaches of genetic regulatory networks have not yet been heavily employed for designing intelligent robots. Also, real-world robots have mostly been hand designed and built from a "here-and-now" perspective; except for short learning phases, development has not played a significant role either. And, as we have already seen, applications of collective and modular robotics in the real world—outside the research laboratory—have been rare to date. We suspect that in the future these more recent design principles will come to play an increasingly important role as developmental, evolutionary, and collective robotics applications become more commonplace. But for the time being, we feel that we can demonstrate the power and wide applicability of our theory using the basic set of design principles for the "here-and-now" perspective.

8 Ubiquitous Computing and Interfacing Technology

In 1984 the prophetic computer scientist Ken Sakamura of the University of Tokyo started thinking about the future of computing beyond the laptop computer, and he developed a vision that he called "computing everywhere." One of his ideas was that the number of laptop computers, which had only just reached the market, would never significantly exceed the number of people on the planet, whereas the number of embedded systems, i.e., systems equipped with sensor and actuation capability acting autonomously in the real world, most certainly will, with an average household incorporating at least 100 embedded microprocessors with appropriate sensors and actuators. This is when he started the TRON project, which stands for The Real-time Operating system Nucleus, and was intended to provide the infrastructure on top of which his vision could be realized. In 1988 Sakamura embarked on the "TRON Intelligent House" venture, a 330-square-meter house equipped with 380 computers and many sensors and actuators, in Tokyo's Nishi-Azabu district. It was completed in 1989: "Of course, the house was filled with computerized gadgets. All external information (from television, radio, telephone, etc.) and all internal information (from the audiovisual system, television door phone, intercom, security sensors, etc.) were funneled into display units available in each room. . . . The kitchen had a video disc system for recipes, and things were video recorded and stored out of sight in automated basement storage areas. The toilet was totally automated from door and lid opening to hand washing and drying." [1] An essential design issue in the TRON house was to make the technology behind all of this invisible, which was, at a time when miniaturization was not nearly at today's level, a nontrivial problem.

Around the time the TRON house was built, Mark Weiser of Xerox PARC, the Palo Alto Research Center of Xerox Corporation in

California, who had been thinking along similar lines, coined the term *ubiquitous computing*. Although Weiser is typically credited in the West as the "father of ubiquitous computing," in Asian countries and among insiders, it is Ken Sakamura. Presumably there is some truth to both positions. In any event, Sakamura recognized early on the importance of having the proper tools available if this dream of putting technology everywhere out into the real world is ever to materialize: the TRON project, in the meantime, has become a global success. The TRON operating system can be used in all sorts of everyday devices and gadgets like digital cameras, car engines, cell phones, and fax machines and shipped annually in an estimated two to three billion devices worldwide, whereas the Windows operating system is shipped with around 200 million computers a year.

The ideas of both Sakamura and Weiser were to put computing into the environment rather than augmenting the PC. Now, why is this development interesting in the context of this book? Even though researchers talk about intelligent buildings, intelligent rooms, intelligent chairs, intelligent cars, intelligent phones, intelligent clothes, intelligent everything, their goal, in contrast to that of researchers in artificial intelligence, is not so much to develop autonomous forms of intelligence or to understand natural intelligence, but to create environments and design objects—man-machine systems—that continuously adapt to the needs of the users. It is our hypothesis that if the real power of ubiquitous technology is to be exploited, the environments and the objects in them must have a certain level of autonomy, and must have agent characteristics.

In this chapter we will proceed as follows. We start with a short note on terminology. Then, because ubiquitous computing is about empowering the user by augmenting the environment, we will begin by inspecting ubiquitous technology from the viewpoint of the three-constituents principle and look at the importance of scaffolding. Next, we will discuss the properties of ubiquitous technology, similar to the agent properties introduced in chapter 4. This will be followed by an attempt to apply some of the design principles. And finally, we will talk about how humans interact with ubiquitous technology and what happens when we become completely intertwined with the technology, i.e., when we become cyborgs.

So before we continue, a note on terminology is in order. Researchers in the field have used many terms for the kind of application of computing they have in mind. Most of the expressions that are used, with some notable exceptions, have their origin in the United States. Here as elsewhere we will avoid terminological debates and treat all of the following expressions more or less synonymously: computing everywhere (Ken Sakamura, Tokyo, 1984), ubiquitous computing (Mark Weiser, Xerox PARC, 1988), calm computing (John Brown, Xerox PARC, 1996), universal computing (James Landay, Berkeley, 1998), invisible computing (G. Barriello, University of Washington, 1999), pervasive computing (Academia, IBM, 1999, SAP 2000), context-based computing (Berkeley/IBM, 1999), hidden computing (Toshiba, 1999), ambient intelligence (European Commission, FP5), everyday computing (Georgia Tech, 2000), sentient computing (AT&T, 2002), autonomous computing (IBM, 2002), and amorphous computing (DARPA, 2002). (All of these were taken from the introductory lecture by Alois Ferscha given at the Ubiquitous 2004 conference.) In this chapter we will use the term *ubiquitous computing* or—in order to stress the fact that we are talking not only about abstract computation but also sensors, actuators, etc.; in short, embodied artifacts—*ubiquitous technology*. Now we will explore how we can relate our ideas about intelligence to this field.

8.1 Ubiquitous Technology as Scaffolding

The field of ubiquitous computing is a fascinating, creative, multifaceted research area that cannot be easily and clearly delineated. Also, the field has raised many new research topics, such as how the functionality of objects can be augmented with microprocessors and sensor-actuator technology, how we can interface with them, how they can be networked to augment their power, and so forth (see figure 8.1). While some aspects of ubiquitous computing do relate to artificial intelligence—the fact that the systems under development are physically embedded in the real world, have some agent characteristics, and are partly situated with a certain level of autonomy—other aspects are separate—they do not concern artificial intelligence directly—for example, networking issues, sensor-range issues in radio frequency identifier tags (RFIDs), and server infrastructure.

Recall for a moment what we said in chapter 4 about the three-constituents principle. We can fix two constituents and try and design the third. For example, given an agent and a set of desired behaviors, how can we structure the environment such that the agent can perform those tasks? Note that this is actually an unusual view to take on design, but it is one commonly adopted in ubiquitous computing. For example, in order to improve car safety, cars and roads can be equipped with

(a)

(b)

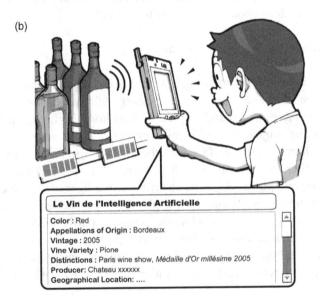

Figure 8.1
Examples of ubiquitous computing technology. (*a*) Wearables. (*b*) Radio frequency identification (RFID) tags for displaying detailed information about wine (including its history,
its geographical position, its fabrication process, and food it goes with).

technology to support the driver. In this case the agent is the driver (which is given), the task is to drive safely (which is also given), and the environment consists of the car, the roads, and the traffic lights, which in this case are considered to be the subject of design. This is the idea of scaffolding that we have encountered a number of times before. By structuring the environment through the creation of artifacts of all kinds, autonomous or nonautonomous, and deploying them around ourselves, we can augment our abilities. We put direction signs into the environment, which help us find our way when driving without the need to know anything about the geography—i.e., we can off-load cognitive tasks to the environment. Assume that for some reason you happen to be in Switzerland and you want to drive from Zurich—the country's economic stronghold—to Berne—the country's capital. All you need to do is follow the signs saying "Berne" and this will get you there eventually, especially in a country like Switzerland where such systems are implemented with great perfectionism; absolutely zero geographical knowledge is required. This perspective puts the user at center stage and aims at augmenting the capabilities of the joint user-artifact or user-environment system by providing whatever technology is required to achieve the goal.

Of course, this way of thinking has been around since the beginnings of civilization, and has been the incentive behind the development of all sorts of artifacts. One of the major differences between this standard view of augmenting the capacity of humans by putting regular objects (pans, hammers, wheels, and signs) into the environment, and ubiquitous computing is that now, with the power of the microprocessor (as well as novel sensor and actuator technologies), the possibilities of designing potentially useful artifacts have skyrocketed, moving artifact design into entirely new dimensions. Another major difference is—and this is Sakamura's main point—that you cannot network pans and hammers, but you can network communication devices. We will take up the idea of the power of networking shortly.

In the next section we will focus on ubiquitous technology: how do we design and deploy technology out into the environment to maximally empower the user?

8.2 Ubiquitous Technology: Properties and Principles

As just mentioned, passive objects—objects that can neither sense nor act on their own—can support and help users to achieve their tasks, which is the idea of scaffolding. In this section we are going to investigate what happens when we consider artifacts with increasingly more agent properties. As pointed out at the beginning of the book, intelligence is not an all-or-none property, and neither are agent properties. So, an object can be more or less like a complete agent, depending on the extent to which the properties discussed in chapter 4 are present. First, let us look at objects that can only sense but not act. This was in fact one of the original ideas of ubiquitous computing. As a first step, sensors were put everywhere, into rooms (mostly cameras and motion detectors to monitor the overall situation), floors (e.g., pressure sensors to detect the position of individuals), objects such as cars (for automatic driving), chairs (to know if they are free or occupied), beds (to monitor if someone is awake, sleeping, or no longer moving), but also cups (to detect the level and temperature of the content), mobile phones (to determine how they are used), and clothes (to measure physiological data such as pulse rate, blood pressure, or skin resistance), and so on. Augmenting environments and objects with all sorts of sensors is still one of the major research areas of the field. However, objects that only sense, although extremely useful, have limitations. For example, if there is some dangerous situation, the only thing that a technology that senses but cannot act can do is to warn a human operator about the danger; it cannot take any action on its own. To use the terminology we introduced earlier, such technology has only limited agent characteristics.

But ubiquitous computing has not only considered artifacts that sense, but also those that act. Buildings that automatically adjust the blinds given certain temperature and lighting conditions, cars that automatically apply their brakes if the distance to the car in front gets too small, or cameras that automatically adjust their focus and exposure time depending on the distance to the objects in the center of the camera's field of vision have been developed. As we have stressed throughout this book, one of the fundamental discoveries in artificial intelligence is that the close coupling between sensory and motor systems is essential (see chapter 5). In ubiquitous computing this insight is slowly making its way into the community but has not been widely recognized.

Let us explore this idea a bit further. Endowing ubiquitous technology with sensors and/or actuation raises lots of interesting possibilities. For example, rather than focusing only on the standard functionalities used in artificial intelligence such as vision, haptics, audition, vestibular sensors (for keeping one's balance), and proprioception, we as engineers can—in the mode of exploring "life as it could be"—think of introducing new kinds of sensors not found in biological organisms, such as infrared sensors, radio sensors, laser distance sensors, GPS sensors, phone-signal sensors, etc. The same applies to actuation possibilities. A telephone, for example, will need a sensor for the telephone signals, which typically requires the presence of some kind of antenna, and a microphone to pick up the audio signals from the user. However, a phone does not necessarily require vision, although phones are beginning to be equipped with cameras that could also be used as input devices, e.g., to transmit the speaker's image. Actuation in a phone clearly consists of a loudspeaker that physically puts pressure waves into the environment, a vibrator—for the silent vibration mode—and a noise generator for the ringing tone and key press tones. Legs or wheels, though, will typically not be necessary—although we could imagine a walking telephone, however questionable its utility. Also, manipulators will not be necessary, since phones, in general, are not expected to be able to grasp cups and other objects. Normally, phones are parasitic on humans for moving about and do not need their own locomotion system, i.e., they let themselves be carried around. Recalling diversity-compliance, we know that compliance implies exploitation of the ecological niche; mobile phones are doing a good job at this. We also know that in order to exploit the niche the agent doesn't have to know that it is doing so: although it is anti-intuitive to think this way, phones exploit their users by hitching a lift with them! Other examples of objects that have both sensing and actuation capabilities include fuel injection systems in car engines, which have sensors for detecting the concentration of fuel, the temperature, and the position of the accelerator and, based on these measurements, inject a fuel-air mixture, which is the actuation part. Washing machines have sensors for detecting how dirty the laundry is, the kind of fabric, and the weight; and the output is heat to warm the water, the dosage of detergent, and the kind of physical manipulation of the laundry—heavy shaking or gentle turning—required. These kinds of systems, with their own sensory and motor abilities, can be considered *embedded systems*. They are also ubiquitous, and the markets for these products are estimated to be much larger than, for example, the market for personal computers as alluded to earlier. Ubiquitous computing goes an important step further by not only putting microprocessors that are embedded in sensory and actuation systems into household appliances, consumer electronics, and cars, but into everything that surrounds us—rooms, walls, floors, windows, furniture, clothes, shoes, objects like cups, pens, toys, plates, books, magazines—anything we can possibly think of.

Now that we are considering ubiquitous technology with agent characteristics—i.e., artifacts that can sense and act in the environment—the technologies we are looking at will possess the agent properties discussed in chapter 4. Furthermore, we can apply the agent principles to these technologies. These ideas will be explored in the following section.

Properties

Recall from chapter 4 that the mere fact that they are physically embodied systems implies that agents are subject to the laws of physics (they fall down, their operation and their movement requires energy); that through motion, or generally through interaction with the real world, they generate sensory stimulation; that through behavior they affect the environment; that because they are complex dynamical systems they will have attractor states; and that they perform morphological computation. Locomotion requires energy and so does sensing, although to a lesser degree. Unlike mobile robots, ubiquitous computing devices—wearables, cups, personal digital assistants (PDAs), intelligent rooms, smartboards, mobile phones, etc.—do not move autonomously, but many of them do move by being parasitic on other devices (e.g., navigation systems move by being mounted in cars) or on humans (mobile phones, PDAs, and intelligent shoes or T-shirts move by being carried around or worn by humans). As we have seen, this is a clever way for such technologies to exploit the environment for their own "purposes." We use quotation marks here because the devices themselves do not know that they are piggybacking on other agents: the purpose is entirely in the eyes of the designers and the users. And because they are moved around by users, these devices will generate sensory stimulation—depending, of course, on the types of sensors they have. A wearable head-mounted camera will record moving images wherever the person carrying the camera goes or looks; acceleration sensors embedded in shoes will produce different data depending on whether the person walks, runs, sits on a chair, or rides in a car; a car navigation system will receive signals depending on where it is driven; and a mobile phone receives signals from the network delivering the strongest signals, and maybe from a GPS satellite, depending on where its owner takes it.

Another characteristic of complete agents, as noted in chapter 4, is that as complex dynamical systems they have attractor states: washing machines have their own rhythms depending on the particular programs and loading conditions, and one can view a mobile phone that is ringing as being in a particular attractor state. More interesting will be the emergence of new attractor states as a characteristic of the joint artifact-human system. Through the interaction of humans with artifacts, the number of attractor states (of the artifact-human system), and of the transitions between them, will be increased because now the human has many more possibilities to act. For example, a mobile phone allows him or her to dial numbers, talk and listen (sensory-motor coupling), and to play computer games, all activities that can be viewed as attractor states and transitions between them. Again, this is an instance of how ubiquitous technology can scaffold the user's environment.

The last property of complete agents is that they perform morphological computation. After surveying the kinds of ideas that researchers are pondering, we have not seen much that reflects anything like morphological computation in embedded devices. An exception might be video cameras in which the light-sensitive cells are more dense toward the center of the field of vision, a configuration whose main advantage is that the amount of data is reduced enormously with none or only very little loss of functionality. This is because toward the periphery, where motion detection is important, significantly fewer pixels are required. Before moving on, it is worth pointing out that the properties of complete agents will become much more apparent in these technologies in the future, when their sensing and actuation abilities are increased. Let us now move on to the principles of agent-like ubiquitous technologies.

Design Principles

There are a number of reasons why we feel that ubiquitous computing represents an excellent field of application for our design principles. First, ubiquitous computing systems are by definition embodied, and so, at least to some extent, the principles do apply. Second, these systems can be seen as natural extensions or variations of real physical robots, which is why we also like to call them robotic devices: they have sensory and (at least limited) motor abilities, and so they do have definite agent characteristics. Third, although perhaps less relevant from an engineering perspective, there is a lot of talk about the intelligence of these devices, which calls for a clarification of the underlying concepts. Calling embedded devices "intelligent" may not only be misleading but may also create unnecessary fears about this kind of technology, which could in turn lead to resistance and thus prevent progress. And finally, we feel that by broadening our own thinking, by going beyond the perspective of embodied intelligent systems—i.e., by considering more than just animals and robots—we may gain further insights about life, or intelligence as it could be. Also, as we will discuss in the last chapter, we may be able to develop novel perspectives on how we perceive ourselves and the world around us.

We talked about the three-constituents principle when we outlined the kinds of design issues in ubiquitous computing, so let us apply a few more of the design principles to ubiquitous technology.

The Principle of Sensory-Motor Coordination   Note that the sensory-motor coupling is very limited in ubiquitous technology devices because their potential for actuation—for autonomously influencing the world—is very limited. We have also seen that categorization, perception, and concept development, which are essential for agents interacting with the real world, all require sensory-motor coordination. If it is indeed the case that higher-level cognition emerges from a developmental process based on sensory-motor coordination, as we argued in chapter 5, then it will be hard to achieve higher levels of intelligence in such devices. Also, we saw in chapters 4 and 5 that sensory-motor coordination can reduce the computational demands placed on an agent, thus leading to more balanced systems capable of real-time response to the environment. If there is no sensory-motor coordination in ubiquitous technology, we can expect increasing difficulties, because we will be confronted with unstructured data and we will have to rely more on internal computation. For example, if the goal is to recognize faces in order to determine whether the person is allowed to use the mobile phone, instructions have to be given by the device that simplify the task, such as to hold the phone in front of the person's face in good lighting conditions—and no beard-growing allowed!

One could, however, imagine important applications involving video capture. If you have ever seen footage from wearable cameras, you know that it is often almost impossible to watch without feeling disoriented, because the images are not stabilized in any effective way. One could imagine an image-stabilization mechanism inspired by the VOR, the vestibular-ocular reflex. The VOR is a reflex eye movement whose main function is to stabilize the visual images on the retina during rapid head movements, by moving the eye in the direction opposite to the head movement. Needless to say, this requires sensory-motor coordination. The jitter-cancellation systems found in modern digital video cameras can deal only with relatively small disturbances, whereas the movement of running, for example, cannot be canceled out as it is in humans and animals. However, researchers have begun to investigate this issue.

Koppel et al. (2005) have proposed an algorithm that uses video flow to infer the motion of the camera and to compensate with respect to the movement. Although the approach seems promising, the algorithm does not yet use other information, such as acceleration, to infer the camera's motion.

However, in general, because the goal is not to achieve autonomously intelligent systems but rather symbiotic systems, the lack of sensory-motor coupling may not be a problem; we simply have to be aware of it. Perhaps the principle of sensory-motor coordination can give us an indication as to how the intelligence of the entire human-machine system can be augmented. Conceivably, the sensory-motor coupling does not have to be achieved autonomously, but rather once again the ubiquitous computing agents can exploit the fact that they are parasitic on humans. Yoichi Takebayashi's group at Shizuoka University in Japan is investigating how information, from acceleration sensors captured during karate practice can be exploited for teaching purposes (Takahata et al., 2004). In their experiments, Takebayashi and his students attached acceleration sensors to new karate students and hooked the sensors up to speakers, so that the students could literally hear the acceleration of their movements during training. After ten months, it was found that this process actually enhanced learning, as well as the enjoyment of the sport, according to the new students. This first study demonstrates the possibility of combining ideas from embodiment with embedded devices to enhance human capability. Think, for example, of a hand prosthesis driven by electromyographic (EMG) signals taken from an amputee's arm, like the one developed by Tokyo University professor Hiroshi Yokoi. The actual movement of the hand provides visual and tactile feedback when the user picks up a bottle, and this feedback can be exploited by the individual to generate other—better—EMG control signals for the hand. In addition, the "Yokoi hand" performs morphological computation (see figure 8.2). Because of the morphology of the hand, the elastic tendons, and the deformable materials, very coarse EMG signals are sufficient to allow it to grasp medium-sized objects of virtually any shape (Yokoi et al., 2003). So, even though the artifact itself—the prosthetic hand—does not have the ability for sophisticated sensory-motor coupling, the joint human–prosthetic hand system does.

The practice of providing feedback from physiological measurements to enable people to exert additional control over normally unconscious body functions—to alter blood pressure, for example, or to prevent migraine headaches or epileptic seizures—started in the 1960s in

Figure 8.2
Cyborgs: The Yokoi artificial hand. The hand, developed by Hiroshi Yokoi and Alejandro Hernandez, is controlled by EMG signals from the arm.

medicine and has had considerable success (Hatch and Riley, 1985). With the advent of wearables and their improved sensory and processing abilities, such biofeedback could be continuous and permanent rather than confined to treatment sessions at a doctor's office or at home. Constant monitoring of body processes is critical for the management of medical conditions such as diabetes, various heart conditions, and high blood pressure. Having continuous measurement and instantaneous feedback anywhere, anytime will increase the autonomy and thus the quality of life for possibly millions of people. This kind of technology will definitely be a boon to the elderly and those with chronic illness. However, we do not want to produce a society of hypochondriacs who continuously need to monitor all of their physiological functions, so we must consider and react to the social changes that might come about as cheap, precise, embedded devices become more prevalent—more ubiquitous—in our society.

The Redundancy Principle Let's say we want to measure and record data about vital functions from people living in a home for the elderly. We can imagine a T-shirt for measuring pulse rate, or perhaps blood sugar levels for diabetic patients. According to the redundancy principle, it is important to have different physical systems providing partially overlapping functionality. So in addition to the pulse rate measurement, we might think of installing a camera system that analyzes motion, or detects if there are any movements during the night. Thus, if the pulse rate measuring system ceases to function, e.g., because the person took off the T-shirt containing the measuring device before going to bed, there is still the camera system, which, while perhaps less precise, would still provide some information about the person's status by indicating whether he or she is still moving. We could also envision embedding pressure sensors in the bed that would provide movement information. This is a nice illustration of the redundancy principle, because all the sensors are based on different physical processes and deliver different types of signals, but there is still an overlap because one sensory modality can be partially predicted from the other. If the pressure sensors in the bed record no movement, then the camera system is likely also to signal no movement.

Ecological Balance At the moment the principle of ecological balance can only be applied in a limited extent to current ubiquitous technology, because, as mentioned earlier, up until now actuation has not been emphasized in this domain. Recall that the principle of ecological balance has two parts. The first concerns the complexities of the sensor, motor and control systems, and the second involves the possibility of a task distribution between morphology, materials, control, and system-environment interaction. Let us look at an example.

Despite the incredible practicality and usefulness of many embedded systems applications such as intelligent food (devices shipped with food to record temperature histories and "shock histories"), most likely the engineers that are designing these systems are not yet considering the principle of ecological balance as it applies to their problems. For example, intelligent food agents do not have actuator possibilities, and their morphology does not affect their sensing ability, but probably these systems do not need these properties to get the job done.

However, we can imagine many situations in which morphological considerations, or ideas about actuation, could augment the power of ubiquitous technology. Consider an intelligent room with sensors distributed in a particular way throughout the floor, walls, and ceiling. If people now walk through the room, the pattern by which pressure sensors in the floor are activated gives us information about where the people are without any further computation. Note that this is an example of morphological computation: the physical placement of the sensors in the environment (an aspect of the room's morphology) is exploited, and reduces the computational load for calculating people's positions. Imagine, in contrast, extracting all this information from a single surveillance camera!

Imagine further that this position information causes doors to open and close, and directional signs to change. This actuation on the part of the room changes where people go, and, in a sense, changes the stimulation of the pressure sensors in the floor. Although this exploitation of the principle of ecological balance is not as strong as, for instance, the induction of optic flow in a robot or insect, it does point the way toward applying these principles in future ubiquitous technology applications.

Parallel, Loosely Coupled Processes   What about parallel, loosely coupled processes? One of the essential ideas of ubiquitous computing, according to Sakamura—and many in the field agree—is that there will be very many agents: millions and even billions, not just hundreds or thousands. This is not unrealistic if you think about RFID tags that can now be put virtually everywhere: food can carry nutrition information and warn about allergies; a bottle of wine can be tagged with detailed information on where it comes from, how long it should be stored before drinking, and foods the wine goes well with; children's books can show animations; car tires can provide information about their history and the proper air pressure required; and so on. The great thing about RFID tags is that they require no power of their own. The power is supplied by a reading device that sends out a radio signal, which is exploited by the RFID chip to power its circuitry and to send the requested information back to the reading device. In order for this mechanism to work, RFID chips must be equipped with an antenna. The RFID tags can be made really small: Sakamura and his collaborator Noboru Koshizuka, a professor at the University of Tokyo, developed an RFID chip which is $0.4 \times 0.4\,\text{mm}$. If you put 50 to 100 of them into a little flask, they look like dust— computational dust! RFID tags are interesting from the point of view of diversity-compliance: they exploit the ecological niche in extremely clever ways, off-loading the power supply to the external world, just as parasites exploit other agents for energy supply or locomotion. In contrast to bar codes, RFID tags can be updated by the reading devices, thus providing, in some sense, a bit of behavioral diversity: next time around, they will react differently to the reading device.

Given the massive amount of parallelism that becomes possible with these technologies, it is obvious that the individual agents, e.g., the RFID tags, can no longer be strongly coupled, because no architecture could support the communication overhead needed to synchronize all of the components involved. Moreover, once we have that many agents, even if their energy supply is minimal, energy demand does become a problem. The extent to which the interaction with the environment is exploited for coordination is minimal (but it is exploited—for example, for energy supply). Thus it makes little sense to view the entire network as one single agent—as we would an animal, a human, or a robot—because the latter are physically organized into one entity through their embodiment. In a ubiquitous computing network, the coupling is much looser. For example, in the case of the RFID tags, coupling is realized through the reading devices and the social and organizational system in which they are embedded. Similar arguments apply to mobile phones, PDAs, temperature measurement modules, airflow control systems, or other intelligent objects. It is interesting to speculate about the kind of intelligence that might emerge in an enormously distributed and parallel system, just as many people like to speculate about the brainlike intelligence of the Internet. The major difference is that the individual agents in the Internet have much more powerful processors and they lack real-world sensors or actuators. Also, the Internet is small compared to the potential of ubiquitous computing networks, Sakamura-style, in ten years' time, hard as that may be to believe. Of course, it seems likely that embedded devices will be integrated with the Internet, so that both types of systems will support and empower each other. If our intuition tells us that such ubiquitous networks have a certain level of intelligence, we might want to extend the set of design principles in the future to capture these specific characteristics as well.

8.3 Interacting with Ubiquitous Technology

Before moving to the last and most provocative topic of this chapter, cyborgs, let us briefly inspect the interaction of humans with autonomous or semiautonomous systems, which is a standard feature of ubiquitous technology.

Interacting with Ubiquitous Environments

Artifacts are never entirely autonomous, even if we call them "autonomous agents"; we always interact with them in one way or other: we have to set the thermostat, we have to put the clothes into the washing machine, we have to answer the phone, talk into it, dial numbers, we have to push the accelerator in the car to trigger the fuel injection system, or we have to somehow set the sound level of the stereo system and tell it what music to play. You might argue, as people in ubiquitous computing would, that the intelligent room should figure out by itself where to set the thermostat, depending on outside temperature, the physical condition of the person entering the room, and perhaps the task the person has to perform. If the person is to do physical exercise, the temperature might be set lower than if he or she is going to relax and watch TV. But then still, the designer has to define the interaction between the user of the room and the room itself, for example, by connecting to a T-shirt that measures body temperature and to a camera system installed in the room that provides the information about the task the person is involved in. Even if the artifact we are interacting with is an autonomous robot, we have to tell it, at some level of detail, what to do. Now, the interaction with some of the devices will be relatively archaic, e.g., with a laptop computer where we have to use a keyboard and a mouse, or a mobile phone where we also have to push buttons. But we can imagine much smoother and more sophisticated forms of interaction. With robots, for example, we assume that they will, like us, communicate with us via vision, gestures, facial expression, and of course, natural language. But as engineers we have many additional possibilities, so we can exploit all sorts of other means that are not normally employed in the interaction between people (except perhaps during a doctor's appointment). For example, we can measure skin resistance, pulse rate, blood pressure, acceleration, etc. And all these measurements can be used to control other robots and our environments, i.e., they can all be made part of a human-environment interface.

An interesting point to add, perhaps, is that the more we exploit the environment for our purposes the more we are dependent on it, as demonstrated by the principle of cheap design. So, in this sense, we are becoming more and more intertwined with the technology and the environment around us. But we can push this tight coupling even further—by becoming cyborgs.

8.4 Cyborgs

The term *cyborg* was created in 1960 by the technologically minded medical doctor Manfred Clynes, at a NASA conference on space exploration, where he suggested that not only should environments be adapted to human needs, but that the human himself could be modified to survive in space. Clynes coined the term *cyborg* to designate "self-regulating man-machine systems," which is short for the combination of *cybernetic* and *organism*. The idea of cybernetics in turn was created somewhat earlier, in 1947, by the MIT professor Norbert Wiener, one of the greatest mathematicians of the twentieth century. At a number of conferences in the 1940s on control and communication in animal and machine, the commonalities of these worlds—in particular the idea of feedback loops—were identified (Wiener, 1948).[2] So the suggestion that there are important commonalities between natural and artificial systems that also underlie the field of artificial intelligence is not a new one; it dates back at least to the publication of Wiener's book.

In his thoughtful book *Natural-Born Cyborgs* (Clark, 2003), the AI philosopher Andy Clark points out that we have all become cyborgs and that the process started long ago, as humans became dependent on artifacts. Now, there are various levels of "cyborgness." Early tools such as knives, sticks, arrows, bows, bowls, etc., all have in common that they do not have agent characteristics. More interesting tools have a certain level of autonomy in that their operation is partly automatic, such as mills that grind automatically, watches that automatically display the time, or engines that keep turning without human intervention. Although for most of human history, tools were about mastering the physical environment, more interesting scaffolding possibilities have emerged over time. One of the most significant examples was the invention of the printing press in 1436 by Johannes Gutenberg, an invention that boosts our cognitive abilities by allowing us to off-load and communicate ideas out into the environment. Its importance for today's art, science, technology, and social organization can hardly be overstated. However, these possibilities were surpassed by the introduction of the modern digital computer, providing potential ways of interacting with the environment that have yet to be thought of: the Internet revolution is only the beginning. And the next step—ubiquitous computing networks—is in the making. Humans are obviously adopting all sorts of ways of augmenting their own functionality, as so aptly described by Andy Clark. According to Clark's hypothesis, humans are constructed such that they have a natural tendency to welcome and incorporate any kind of technology into their daily routine, and to make the technology part of themselves, so to speak, thus creating a strong interdependency.

But back to the degrees of "cyborgness." One dimension is autonomy. Objects out there in the world such as a pan, a shoe, or a wheel are not very threatening. If they function to some extent autonomously they are more interesting, but perhaps also a bit more threatening because we do not so much like to be dependent on independent machines. On the other hand, we can get a lot more leverage from machines than from "dead" tools. "Cognitive machines" like computers are yet more useful, but again, one level more threatening because their functionality comes closer to what we like to think only humans can do. The other dimension of cyborgness is how close—literally—the technology is to us: the closer and the more intense the potential interactions, the more threatening the technology may seem and the stronger our dependency upon it. We are enormously dependent on our cars, our mobile phones, our laptops—and the closer and more intense the interaction, the more we are dependent on them. Mobile phones, watches and wearables, and any other thing that we wear directly on our body or that we always carry with us are literally very close to us, and, for some, they are too close for comfort. But again, because wearables are so close they provide signals that more remote technologies cannot deliver, e.g., the measurement of physiological variables, and we can react to these measurements immediately. We can go one step further and put under the skin what was outside of the skin earlier. This is the step that for many signals the "real" cyborgs: cochlear implants, for example, which replace a part of the human auditory system, have been successfully used in human patients who have lost the ability to hear; retinal or cortical implants are intended to give people back a certain level of vision. Along with heart pacemakers and other implanted devices, these are all versions of cyborg technology that reside inside our body. For many of us, this kind of technology is threatening.

But this is what real cyborgs are all about, the direct connection of biological neural tissue to technology, in particular to digital chips. And prostheses are an obvious version of this technology. So let us look at a few examples of these kinds of cyborgs where neural substrate is connected directly to digital systems. Remember the creepy eel-like fish from chapter 5, the lamprey? The engineer and neuroscientist Fernando Mussa-Ivaldi, one of the leaders in neural interfacing technology, conducted a science fiction–like experiment in which he connected a lamprey's brain to a Khepera robot, the circular 5 cm robot that we have encountered several times already (Reger et al., 2001). The connection, which is mediated by a neurorobotic interface, goes both ways: from the lamprey's brain—or, more precisely, the lamprey's reticular formation—to the robot; and from the robot to the lamprey's brain. The reticular formation is a region in the brain stem that controls a number of functions such as the animal's level of arousal, cardiac reflexes, attention, and—especially relevant for this experiment—movement. The reticular formation combines sensory signals from almost anywhere in the body—visual, tactile, and vestibular—with motor commands, and uses this information to change the motor output of the spinal cord (which is heavily involved in motor control). The lamprey is a good subject for such a cyborg experiment because of the easy maintainability of its brain stem, i.e., it can be kept alive easily for a long time, and because there are especially large neurons in this region that make recording relatively easy.

Mussa-Ivaldi and his students focused on those regions that normally combine vestibular signals with motor commands to stabilize orientation during swimming. They inserted four electrodes into the reticular formation: two for recording and two for stimulating. The stimulation was provided by a frequency pulse generator whose activation was determined by the right and left light sensors on the robot: the higher the light sensor reading on the robot, the higher the stimulation provided on that electrode to the lamprey's brain. To determine the motor control signal for the robot a recording was taken from those centers in the reticular formation corresponding to the movement system. This recording was converted by the interface into voltages that were then supplied to the electrical motors of the Khepera robot. The results of these experiments are staggering: the robot starts behaving very much like a Braitenberg vehicle driven by a simple artificial neural network: it moves toward certain stimuli and away from others, and so on. The structure of this neural network, so to speak, can be changed by placing the electrodes into different parts of the reticular formation, e.g., by switching between left and right. Depending on the placement, the robot moves reliably toward a light source or away from it. Moreover, the researchers could demonstrate some basic adaptation of the neural network (we will leave out the details of these experiments here). Because it is exactly known what is happening in the robot and the interface, this setup can be used to study the neural circuits of the lamprey brain, whose functionality is much less well known. From this groundbreaking experiment it can be seen that biological and artificial systems can cooperate smoothly, and that we can use robots or other kinds of artifacts to better understand the functioning of biological neural systems.

The neuroscientist Steve Potter of the Georgia Institute of Technology in the United States, who is a pioneer in cyborg technology, had a truly avant-garde idea. Not only did he want to build a cyborg, but, in addition, he wanted to use the cyborg to produce art. Moreover, he wanted the art to be created over the Internet. Potter's declared goal is "to create fundamentally different types of artificial intelligence" (Bakkum et al., 2004, p. 130).

In contrast to Mussa-Ivaldi, who uses animal brains, Potter took neurons—tens of thousands of them—from rat brains and cultivated them in a small dish. In this dish was a so-called multielectrode array,

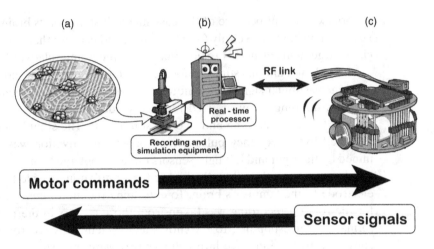

Figure 8.3
Cyborgs: connecting robots and biological brains. Steve Potter's neurally controlled mobile robot. (*a*) Neural tissue cultivated in a dish. (*b*) Recording and simulation equipment, including real-time processor. (*c*) Robot controlled by biological brain.

essentially a computer chip with 60 electrodes to which the neurons could attach themselves. Then he had to decide how to connect this partly organic, partly electronic "brain" to the robot, and the robot to the "brain" (the setup of the experiment is depicted in figure 8.3). The activity of the 60 electrodes was determined by the activity of the neurons that had grown and attached to them, but the electrodes could also be stimulated, which in turn stimulated the attached neurons. Potter's goal was to have a robot that could follow another robot, i.e., it had to maintain a given fixed distance to an object. Potter and his colleagues connected the robot to the neural network as follows. They stimulated the network at two different electrodes with a certain delay in between, leading to a certain overall response of the neurons. When the delay between the two stimulations was large, the neural response was high. The response was minimal at a delay of 150 msec, but when the delay was even shorter than that, there was a maximum overall response.

The delay was determined by the distance of the robot to the object, which can be roughly measured by infrared sensors, as we have seen before: if the robot was distant from the object, the delay between the signals was large, which led to a high overall activation. This high overall activation was translated into a "move forward" signal sent to the robot. Whether the robot moved left or right was determined by which of the two electrodes was stimulated first, which in turn was determined by whether the robot received the sensory stimulation on the left or the right. If the distance to the object was just right, it was mapped onto a delay of about 150 msec, leading to very low overall activity, which was mapped onto a "no movement" command to the robot. A very close distance to an object was mapped onto a short delay, which then led to a maximum stimulation, which in turn was mapped onto a "move back" signal for the robot. Potter used two robots, one controlled by the biological network and one controlled by a computer. The neurally controlled one had to follow the one that was computer controlled. Indeed, it managed to do so! This is again a beautiful demonstration of smooth cooperation between biological neural systems and robots. There is even some preliminary evidence that some behavior changes occur over time, which may be traced back to mechanisms of neural plasticity. What is nice about this setup in contrast to Mussa-Ivaldi's is that here the activity of the neurons, because they are in a dish, can be much more easily measured during behavior. Also, thanks to the multielectrode array, hundreds of neurons can be recorded from simultaneously, offering a new and unique method for investigating brain function.

But Potter did not stop there: as we said before, he not only connected the neural substrate to a mobile robot, but because he wanted to create art, he also connected the neural substrate in the dish via the multielectrode array and the Internet to a robot arm. The arm held a pen, and depending on incoming motor commands could draw upon paper placed under it. The robot arm was located in Perth, Australia, while the "brain" controlling it was located in Atlanta, Georgia, some 12,000 miles away: the brain and body were located half a world away from each other! There was an overhead camera "watching" the drawing, from which feedback to the 60 electrodes on the array was calculated. Of course, the "artwork" created, i.e., produced by the movements of the arm, strongly depends on how these camera images are fed back to the network and how the new movements are generated. This is work in progress, but certainly is fascinating research. And the drawings themselves are not simply random scribbling—many people would be happy to be able to produce such drawings (Bakkum et al., 2004).

Mussa-Ivaldi and Potter both fully endorse the perspective of embodiment, i.e., the idea that if we really want to understand the function of the neural system, it must be fully embodied. But of course it is also of interest to compare the functionality of neurons in a disembodied and an embodied state, as we did when discussing the lamprey central pattern generators and how they function very differently in a disembodied and an embodied condition. By studying neural systems in both states, we can investigate how brains and bodies interact with each other to produce intelligent behavior. But aside from the conceptual advantage of studying brains in this manner, cyborg technology has many practical uses. One of the central goals of the research of Mussa-Ivaldi and Potter is a better understanding of how biological and artificial systems can be connected, in particular with a view toward medical applications, namely prostheses, power-assisting devices, support suits, or anything that can help make the lives of people with physical or mental impairments easier. We will speculate about these problems a bit in chapter 11 when discussing robots in our everyday lives.

8.5 Summary and Conclusions

In this chapter we investigated a new area of computer science that comes with many labels—computing everywhere, ubiquitous computing, or pervasive computing—and we inspected to what extent the design principles would apply to this field. In its current state, the field is thriving and highly innovative but definitely lacks a theoretical underpinning. But if we adopt Feyerabend's somewhat anarchistic view of how science works, or should work, for a moment, as pointed out in chapter 3, the absence of rules implies that there is potentially a lot of progress, new ideas, and rapid developments. Still, the design principles for intelligent systems might help to manage this creative chaos and organize our thinking about how best to design embedded technologies. On the other hand, because of the new agent architectures—and here it is important to note that ubiquitous computing networks are conceptually and practically much more than another kind of Internet—the design principles may in fact have to be extended to incorporate potential new kinds of intelligences that might emerge. The reason we are stressing the point that these systems are different from the Internet is that they are embodied; they have sensory and motor abilities and can autonomously interact— at least partially—with their environments without human intervention. Of course, in this short overview it is impossible to do justice to the richness of the field. Nevertheless we have tried to sketch out in this chapter how the future of ubiquitous devices holds much promise, not just in terms of practical application but also for shedding light on the nature of intelligence. In the next chapter, we will bring the intuitions we have developed so far about complete agents to bear on another field that is even less directly connected to artificial intelligence: the corporate world.

9 Building Intelligent Companies

Simon Grand and Rolf Pfeifer

What is the essence of management? When Chester Barnard retired as the CEO of New Jersey Bell Telephone, he recorded his insights about management in his book *Functions of the Executive*, which was published for the first time in December 1938 and has since gone through 39 editions. Barnard, who is now widely recognized as one of the founding fathers of general management as a field or discipline, argued that management is concerned—or should be concerned—with those activities in a company or an organization that cannot be delegated because they are inherently uncertain and complex. This uncertainty and complexity, according to Barnard, has its origin in the distributed nature of the activities and processes in the organization. This contrasted sharply with the widely held belief that the essence of management was understanding and controlling manufacturing, sales, administrative, and organizational activities, which can in fact be precisely defined and could thus be easily delegated, whereas strategy and innovation, because of their inherent uncertainty and complexity, cannot. Even though the statement by Barnard represents a key insight into managerial practice, most contributions to the management discipline failed to take it seriously and have mainly focused on those aspects that can be clearly delineated. Barnard died in 1961, but his ideas are still alive and well, and especially in recent years have regained currency with the emergence of the strategic management research community.

In previous chapters we have demonstrated that the design principles for intelligent systems, and the general approach of embodied systems, can be used for the creation of artificial systems—computer simulations, robots, and embedded devices—and for the analysis of biological systems. Remember the challenging properties of real-world environments: acquisition of information takes time and is always incomplete and inaccurate, which implies that it is intrinsically uncertain and thus predictable only to a very limited extent. At the beginning we surmised that the design principles will not only shed light on robotics, artificial intelligence, and cognitive science, but will impact the way we see ourselves and the world around us. In this chapter we would like to explore to what extent we can exploit this approach to learn something novel and interesting about an entirely different domain, namely that of management and entrepreneurship. We will try to cash in on this claim in this chapter.

We will proceed as follows. First we will briefly scan the management literature for its interpretation of the goals of entrepreneurship and management. Then we will argue that companies can be viewed as embodied agents and that the design principles for intelligent systems can be translated to the domain of building companies in uncertain environments. In some respects, management has surprising similarities with engineering: not so much traditional engineering, but rather engineering of adaptive systems, systems that have to function in rapidly changing environments (see figure 9.1). We will then review the synthetic approach, diversity-compliance, frame of reference, and emergence in the managerial domain. We will continue with a discussion of some of the key design principles and summarize their implications for this field of study. We will conclude by talking about how these principles could be supported in a management context.

9.1 Management and Entrepreneurship: Decision and Action under Uncertainty

The interest in management as decision and action under uncertainty has emerged again as a key theme with the growing interest in true entrepreneurship in the last two decades. In 1911, the controversial economist Joseph Schumpeter published his famous book *Theory of Economic Development*, where he introduced the entrepreneur into the analysis of economic and technological development as their key driver. He concludes that if we are to understand how creative entrepreneurial initiatives can turn into successful businesses—current examples would be biotech-based drug development or ubiquitous computing, and how successful companies like Genentech and Microsoft operate in the context of technological innovation and continuously changing competition—we must investigate decision and action under uncertainty. In addition, we learn from Chester Barnard that these processes are not mystical and

(a)   (b)

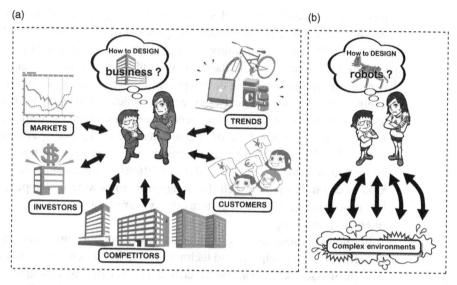

Figure 9.1
A company as an embodied agent having to act under conditions of high uncertainty. Because the situation of and a company doing business in an economic environment (*a*) a biological or robotic agent performing tasks in an ecological niche (*b*) are very similar, it is plausible metaphorically to view a company as an intelligent embodied system and to apply the design principles to building new companies and businesses.

the purview of a few gifted individuals, but that a scientific understanding is indeed possible and necessary.

If this is true, Peter Drucker, the author of many visionary books and probably the most influential management authority in the 20th century, was right in arguing that innovation and entrepreneurship must be conceived as tasks that can in fact be organized and thus can be methodically investigated. While scientific and technological disciplines like physics, biology, or engineering have evolved organically over time, understanding of management and entrepreneurship has never reached a similar level of comprehensiveness. Or to use Drucker's words from his 1985 book *Innovation and Entrepreneurship*, "As a useful knowledge, a techne [i.e., a technology], management is the same age as the other major areas of knowledge that underlie today's high-tech industries, whether electronics, solid-state physics, genetics, or immunology" (p. 14). However, if it is to contribute to our knowledge of the processes underlying the creation and development of companies, businesses, and innovations, the discipline of management will have to consist of more than just philosophical approaches and general rules. It will have to incorporate tangible principles and concrete techniques that support decision and action by addressing the question of how to decide and act under conditions of uncertainty. In this perspective, management can be seen as a new technology in itself, or, we could say, it constitutes an engineering discipline in need of design principles. Note that we do not mean engineering per se, classical engineering, which focuses on precision, speed, controllability, cost-effectiveness, and optimization. Rather, we are interested in a new kind of engineering, the kind we are pursuing in this book, which has to do with adaptivity, learning, and autonomy, i.e., systems that have to operate under conditions of uncertainty. It is this kind of engineering for which the design principles were developed, and it is precisely these types of systems that we are targeting in the context of entrepreneurship.

In line with these insights, we suggest viewing management and entrepreneurship as a discipline and technology—to build new companies and new businesses, which can be described as a set of basic, tangible, and consistent principles. We stress the requirement that the principles be consistent, since this is often not the case in the management literature. In fact, it is only a slight exaggeration to compare the reaction of the management discipline to the actions of the drunk under the lamppost who searches for his keys where the light is best and not where he has lost them: rather than tackling the issues of uncertainty that constitute the actual core of the discipline, the field has, for the most part, avoided the truly hard questions by focusing on the safer, better known, and more clearly defined issues such as logistics and marketing. From the approach to artificial intelligence and cognitive science that we have developed in this book so far, we will try to transfer basic ideas and major principles for the design of intelligent embodied systems to management, arguing that companies can indeed be understood as intelligent embodied systems. In what follows, we will argue—even though we do not yet have firm empirical evidence—that this transfer is not only plausible but leads to interesting insights and often surprising conclusions that might not have been reached otherwise.

9.2 Companies as Embodied Systems

One of the most exciting areas in which true entrepreneurship and management skills are required is the creation of new companies and businesses. Technology corporations like IBM, Sony, Siemens, or Genentech constantly create new technological opportunities in their laboratories (e.g., new memory and processor chip technologies or new ways of controlling the expression of genes) which have to be translated into new products (e.g., cheap storage media with large storage capacity and minimum energy requirements or new drugs and therapies), new solutions and businesses (e.g., a new generation of mobile phones or integrated health care solutions), new business units, ventures, patents, and partnerships. Scientific research laboratories in universities and private research institutions create new business opportunities for biotechnology, computer science, artificial intelligence, and information technology in general. It is interesting to note that the term *venture* itself reflects the intrinsic uncertainty of starting a new business, at the stage where it remains to be seen whether the result will be a product, a company, an investment opportunity, or only an unrealized idea or unfinished project.

While the organization of research and development processes in the pharmaceutical industry—"Big Pharma" in the jargon of management insiders—or the operational management of established technologies in information technology corporations—genetic engineering methodologies, mobile phone infrastructures, and network services for financial transfers—are well covered in the literature on management and entrepreneurship, the construction and establishment of new companies, businesses, and markets, including the question of how the opportunities provided by research and development can be translated into successful products and services, has not been equally explored.

The Emergent Nature of New Technologies and Businesses

There are many illustrative case studies and historical accounts of particular industries and of products like bicycles and mainframe computers that demonstrate the complex and emergent nature of new technologies and businesses, which often show unexpected patterns of development. Today's booming bicycle industry, for example, emerged from the complex interaction of technological developments (new materials, components, and manufacturing methods), design trends (many choices, "cool" appearance, customization through "modding"), societal developments (high-tech hobbies, active recreation, fitness), scientific research (safety, speed, sports medicine), and perhaps competition with other transportation and sports vehicles and devices, developments that were simply not possible to anticipate. Or take the mainframe computers that, a few decades ago, seemed to be the way in which computing would evolve. Just recall the vision developed in the 1960s in Stanley Kubrick's cult movie *2001: A Space Odyssey*. The superintelligent computer HAL 9000 was essentially a huge mainframe computer stowed within a spaceship (if the characters in HAL are shifted by one position in the alphabet it becomes IBM). But mainframes have largely lost their importance and have been replaced by powerful networked personal computers, as we all know, a development that nearly ruined IBM in the early 1980s, when it was by far the largest computer technology giant on the planet. And now it seems that after the initial distributed overshoot, so to speak, there is a certain rebound, with mainframe computers—at least temporarily—finding a moderate but still important role in the market between supercomputing, server infrastructure, and fully distributed systems.

Given the highly emergent nature of these developments, it is difficult if not impossible for individual managers or companies to anticipate what will happen if a certain action is taken, for example, if a new business is established or a new product or service is launched. Clearly, an individual company cannot enforce a specific development or new technology on the market. Moreover, it is infeasible for an individual player (company or individual) to define and develop a new technology on its own: new technologies emerge from the dynamic interaction of various technology corporations, new ventures, potential customers and competitors, and political institutions. For example, mobile communication cannot be viewed as a single "technology"; rather, it is emergent from a rapidly changing technology environment in which many actors are involved: companies, consumer organizations, and even states or countries; companies provide computer chips, processors, digital cameras, server infrastructure, battery technology, display screens, networking services, roaming contracts, and automatic payment; consumer organizations promote regulations to protect the health of the consumers; countries provide the basic legal frameworks for the roaming contracts; and so forth.

As these examples suggest, when establishing new technologies and businesses in today's economic environment, one is confronted with situations that are inherently uncertain, ambiguous, dynamic, and complex. They are uncertain with respect to future developments and with respect to the activities and competencies that will be required for survival; ambiguous because alternative opportunities can always be assumed to exist and to be justified; dynamic in terms of the continuous coevolution of many actors and artifacts; and complex because of the nonlinear structure of interactions, which implies that the result of the interactions cannot be predicted, at least not in the long term. Recall that sensitivity to initial conditions is an intrinsic property of complex dynamical systems, which means that the evolution of the system crucially depends on the initial conditions, so that if there is the slightest deviation, the system can develop in a completely different direction.

But the situation is even more perplexing. Not only are developments unpredictable, but also even in hindsight cause and effect may not be clear. There is often great controversy as to what has actually happened and who had been doing what. An example is the conflict-ridden discussions that surrounded the introduction of UMTS (Universal Mobile Telecommunications System, a third-generation mobile communication system) in Switzerland: nobody seemed to know why some companies suddenly "lost interest" in the licenses. Another is the question of what the long-term business impact of open-source software development will be, because the underlying processes are highly distributed and largely self-organized, and it is only partially known which companies influence open-source development.

Two Strands of Development in Management

After this discussion it should come as no surprise that the management field has separated into two clearly distinguishable strands. The traditional one concentrates on the well-defined aspects of a company as outlined earlier. The modern one faces the challenge of uncertain environments, focusing on true entrepreneurship: the ability to identify, evaluate, and exploit new opportunities, and map them onto concrete actions based on experience, intuition, creativity, and vision. The traditional position—represented by key figures like Kenneth Andrews, known for the SWOT analysis (strengths, weaknesses, opportunities, and threats; Andrews, 1987) and Igor Ansoff, sometimes called the father of strategic planning (Ansoff, 1965)—which tries to apply methods from traditional engineering to the strategic management of companies, has been strongly criticized by Henry Mintzberg (1994). Mintzberg, whose somewhat anarchistic views led to heated debates in the 1970s, rose to become one of the most influential management gurus in the 1990s. He stressed the emergent nature of strategy, i.e., the idea that management cannot be planned in a top-down manner but must instead rely on the many strategic initiatives and activities of employees lower in the company hierarchy, which eventually emerge into overall patterns of behavior through their interaction with the environment. For example, the strategy of a Big Pharma corporation is not deliberately defined by the senior management only, but emerges from the complex interaction between internal research activities, new scientific insights, feedback from clinical studies, competitive moves, and value created through partnerships, all of which substantially shape the overall direction of the corporation.

It is typically easier, of course, to describe top-down processes than to explain emergent phenomena, which may be another reason why many people are more comfortable with top-down approaches, along with the feeling that they are more controllable. This is illustrated by the fact that the authors of this chapter—Simon and Rolf—in fact had a hard time explaining exactly what Mintzberg meant when he stressed the "emergent nature of strategy." The distinction between the more traditional strategy school on the one hand and the more recent emphasis on emergence and interaction on the other is surprisingly analogous to that of classical control engineering—which dominates industrial robotics, where it has been extremely successful—versus intelligent robotics, where new kinds of principles such as the ones proposed in this book are required. With these principles we are in a sense defining a new kind of engineering: rather than designing from the top down, we are engineering for emergence, as discussed in chapter 4.

If we want to create successful companies geared toward establishing new technologies and businesses like third-generation mobile telecommunications or next-generation software development, it is fundamental for the field of management to have principles or methods at hand to work out the measures needed for the company to remain innovative over extended periods of time, to create ideas, to decide and act under conditions of uncertainty, and to find productive ways of thinking about business creation and company design.

Given the characteristics of the real economic world, which strongly resembles the situation of intelligent agents trying to survive in their ecological niche, it makes perfect sense to view companies as adaptive structures; as embodied systems. We think that this perspective enables us to address the particular conceptual and practical challenges of management under these conditions by applying the design principles described in earlier chapters. In summary, we hope to demonstrate that understanding companies as embodied intelligent systems, and thinking about company creation in a synthetic, design-oriented, principle-based way creates fundamental new insights for entrepreneurial and managerial practice.

Before we continue, a short note on terminology is necessary. As we just explained, the environments in which entrepreneurs have to act are inherently uncertain, ambiguous, dynamic, and complex. In the remainder of this chapter we will often refer to such situations simply as uncertain, rather than always listing all four characteristics.

9.3 A Synthetic Approach to Management

We thus argue for an embodied perspective on management and entrepreneurship as a particular way of asking questions and interpreting managerial practice as a particular thinking style. Similar to engineering, management is defined as shaping and designing organizations and structuring business activities; for example, for a new biotech venture, a new service exploiting third-generation mobile communication infrastructure, or a business unit dedicated to functional food within a large nutrition corporation. Most academic research on management is descriptive and analytical only, analyzing under what conditions strategies are successful without considering the inherent complexity of managerial practice. And most of the popular literature is very philosophical and suggests simplistic rules for company success, independent of any particular context and situation. It is then left to management itself to integrate these various insights into their particular practice and turn them into concrete actions. We feel that we can provide the "missing link" with our design principles, and we also believe that they will not only be useful for managers, but will also help investors to assess the prospects of their potential investments.

It is clear that the embodied perspective on companies is to be taken metaphorically, because companies are social constructs and are, as such, virtual entities rather than physical ones. The fact that some aspects of companies—buildings, infrastructure, and people—are physical does not change the picture. Nevertheless, companies can, as a whole, sense their environment and act upon it in intelligent ways. It is important that in what follows we keep the company as a whole in mind rather than the intelligent agents that constitute it: the managers, the employees, and the staff. Let us now go through some of the theoretical considerations that we suggested in chapter 3—the synthetic methodology, diversity-compliance, frame of reference, and emergence.

Diversity-Compliance and Exploration-Exploitation
In chapter 3 we introduced the notion of diversity and compliance and pointed out that it reappears in various guises and under various labels in the literature on cognitive science: plasticity-stability in learning and development, and exploitation-exploration in an evolutionary context.

In organizational learning and evolutionary theories of market and company development, exploration-exploitation is the predominant framework for thinking about the behavior of managers. For companies to survive in a complex and dynamic environment, given their limited resources—financial, personnel, production facilities, information and communication technology infrastructure—it is essential on the one hand to establish the necessary diversity to be able to react appropriately to potential opportunities and challenges and explore whether they could and should be turned into concrete projects. On the other hand, it is equally important to optimally exploit those opportunities—technologies, businesses, and projects—already present in the company. For example, features can be added to a product that has been successful, or additional services can be offered to a well-defined group of loyal customers.

It is important for emerging new companies to establish a clear, well-defined focus; indeed this is one of the core evaluation criteria that investors use when deciding whether to invest or not. But uncertain environments imply that there are many possible actions and directions in which the company could move. For software ventures, for example, the selection of the appropriate technology platform (hardware and software), the identification of the right business model (customer-oriented projects versus software products), the definition of efficient software development methods, and the creation of a market understanding (e.g., what kinds of products the market wants, how fast it changes, and how other products, the general economic situation, and politics influence the market) are all open, not well understood, and thus initially undefined areas. For biotech ventures, defining a clear focus is even more challenging, given that it can take up to fifteen years until it becomes clear whether a pharmaceutical product, a chemical substance, a drug, or a vaccine is to be successful on the market. Therefore, proper allocation of limited resources is at the same time very important and impossible: managers are faced with a very real trade-off, whether they like it or not.

Focusing too narrowly on one particular direction can be dangerous. For software ventures it might well be that the technological platform used for their development moves them in unforeseen directions—for example, the hardware company that supplies the platform is losing market shares—the market is not emerging as planned, perhaps because the remote monitoring market for which the software was developed did not catch on—or the business model does not work or is not understood by the market. For biotech ventures, resolving the conflict or trade-off between exploration and exploitation is one of the toughest problems as venture capital firms try to define clear plans and milestones for the companies in which they invest (exploitation), while at the same time knowing that the directions of their ventures will shift and change over time and that the plans will have to be adjusted accordingly (exploration). For bioinformatics companies, for example, which operate at the borderline between biotechnology and information technology, the fact that the uncertainties inherent in both fields multiply, so to speak, makes the search for a balance between diversity and compliance even harder. So finding the right position in the trade-off between defining a clear focus in order to exploit new opportunities, and structuring the company in such a way that it is flexible enough to explore and react to changing technology and business environments, is absolutely fundamental.

Frame of Reference and Mimetic Behavior

For management and entrepreneurship, the frame-of-reference issue is of particular importance: entrepreneurs and managers learn by observing the behavior of their colleagues in their own and in competing companies; by reading success stories published in newspapers and magazines; by observing leading-edge companies and trying to make sense of what they are doing; and by studying management gurus who promote certain rules of success. We know from management theory (e.g., Gomez and Jones, 2000) that managers and entrepreneurs tend to engage in mimetic behavior whenever there is uncertainty; and when they are confronted with the problem of creating a new business or building a new company, there will always be a lot of uncertainty. By mimetic behavior we mean that managers largely imitate the behavior of others rather than pursuing their own course of action. In our perspective, it is important for entrepreneurs and managers to understand that what they see and read does not explain how the behavior of the company and the managers involved came about. Very often, managers generalize from particular cases without considering the specific environment and the historical evolution of the cases they observe. As we know, by observing behavior alone, we cannot draw firm conclusions about the underlying mechanisms that bring the behavior about. Remember our discussions of building a walking and running robot: capturing the movements, of the joints of a biological organism and trying to reproduce them does not lead to proper walking. The better approach is to try and understand the mechanisms underlying the walking process rather than trying to reproduce the actual joint movements, because those movements were a result of very specific environmental conditions—flat, tilted, or bumpy surfaces.

Moreover, given that the behavior of the company emerges from its interaction with the environment, it is important to design the company for both emergence and interaction, and not to simply try to replicate the behavior of another company. For example, there are different methods and practices for developing high-quality software, which implies that simply replicating the software practices of a successful competitor does not necessarily yield the same or similar results. The specific cultural, organizational, technical, or ideological backgrounds that go with the software engineering process, and which constitute an essential component of the underlying mechanisms, must be considered as well. But because these practices have often developed over years and are highly distributed throughout the company, their replication is virtually impossible. In other words, what we observe is the global, overall behavior of the company, not the underlying mechanisms. In order to replicate the behavior, we would need to understand and implement the specific local rules of interaction that lead to the global behavior: the multiplicity of parallel activities and processes not visible to the general public— and, as we have seen a number of times, inferring these rules and processes only from observation of the global behavior is next to impossible. An additional difficulty is that there is often a vast discrepancy between what is written up in the official software development manuals, and the actual software development practice. Thus, studying the manuals will not help much either.

9.4   Design Principles for Building Intelligent Companies

Starting from these basic reflections and first illustrations, as well as the agent design principles developed in earlier chapters, we will try to deduce a series of implications for the actual creation, development, and establishment of successful companies and businesses.

As illustrated in chapter 4, the design principles form a consistent set, which implies that they should not be considered in isolation. For example, the principle of cheap design, taken alone, might be misleading because it does not refer to redundancy, which is absolutely essential to achieve robust adaptive behavior. Having said that, as in the other chapters on the application of the design principles we will not give a systematic account by going through all of the principles, but rather we will pick some that we feel can contribute interesting novel insights in this domain. To this end we will inspect the three-constituents principle, the complete agent principle, the principle of sensory-motor coordination, the principles of cheap design and redundancy, and the value principle.

The Three-Constituents Principle

Business creation and company building in an embodied systems perspective first and foremost imply an in-depth understanding of what it means to create and sustain a company within a particular dynamic and complex environment, or ecological niche, to use the biological metaphor. As suggested by the three-constituents principle, it is important for any entrepreneur or manager when creating a new company or establishing a new business to think about the following three questions, corresponding to the basic constituents of the agent design process: definition of the ecological niche, the desired behavior and tasks, and the agent itself.

1. *Ecological niche*   What do I know (and not know) about the particular niche and environment (economic, financial, technological, institutional, cultural) in which I would like to do business?

2. *Desired behaviors and tasks*   What do I know about the particular characteristics of my intended behavior (interaction with the environment) as a company to succeed in this niche?

3. *The agent itself*   What do I know about the particular setup of my company and business activities, in terms of structures, processes, competencies, and culture?

First, there are fundamental differences between, for instance, creating a new company or business in biotechnology and creating a new software engineering company. The development of new drugs, as mentioned earlier, takes on average more than a decade, and sometimes up to 15 years, and may cost hundreds of millions of dollars. There is also a lot of inherent uncertainty with respect to whether the drug will be successful, because the field of biotechnology is undergoing rapid change. Such change may alter the very basis on which the product idea was developed, for example because of the availability of new technologies from genetic engineering. In software development, the basic underlying technologies are very different and the development times are much shorter, a fact that has strong implications for business practices. For example, software companies can typically generate revenue in a much shorter period than biotech enterprises. But, as in the biotechnology area, the ecological niche is characterized by high uncertainty, albeit considerably less so because of the much shorter time frame.

Second, it is very important for any company to think about its desired behaviors and tasks. For example, is the company pursuing a path of high growth or one of moderate growth? Is a biotech company focusing on basic research or working toward product development? A software company's desired behaviors might include working in a product-oriented or in a project-oriented manner toward customized solutions (e.g., developing text-processing systems or search engines to be commercialized and sold in the market versus creating customized software). These different kinds of behaviors require completely different sorts of resources and design decisions. Obviously, the intended behavioral patterns of the company, the relevant economic and technological environment, and the criteria of success for this specific company must be aligned. For example, if the market is too small and there is too much competition within the ecological niche, a product-oriented approach might not be feasible.

And third, the company itself—its organizational structures and processes—must be designed. This requires the use of the remaining agent design principles that we discuss in this chapter.

The major challenge for the creation and establishment of new companies and businesses lies in the alignment and interaction of these three dimensions: the understanding of the relevant environment and its characteristics (what environment are we in?), the structures and competencies of the company (what are the characteristics of our company?), and—often neglected or taken for granted in entrepreneurship and management—the intended behaviors (how do we intend to act as a company?). This implies that the following points need to be clearly worked out and defined: (1) what is known about the environment, the company, and its intended behavior? And (2) to what extent are the environment, the company, and the intended behaviors aligned or matched? The three-constituents principle can be used as a heuristic to reflect on the design problem: if two of the three constituents are given, the third one is emergent. For example, if the ecological niche, i.e., the economic environment, and the agent, i.e., the company structures and processes, are given, the behavior emerges from the interaction of the agent with the environment. Alternatively, if the desired behaviors and tasks and the economic environment are given, conclusions about the structure of the company can be drawn. In the third case, given the agent and its behaviors, what are the environments in which it will function properly? This latter case might occur when a company is looking for new markets.

There are many standard schemes in the management literature for discussing and analyzing issues and questions related to the environment and the company. Perhaps the three most prominent ones are these: evaluation of strengths, weaknesses, opportunities, and threats—the SWOT analysis—put forward by the Harvard Business School business policy professor Kenneth Andrews in the 1970s (e.g., Andrews, 1987), which proposes, in essence, a systematic analysis of the company structures and its potential interactions with the ecological niche in which it is to operate; the five forces and competitive strategy concept by Michael Porter, also of Harvard University, in the 1980s (Porter, 1980); and the extended discussion around core competencies started by Gary Hamel (owner of Strategos, a consulting firm specializing in strategy and innovation) and C. K. Prahalad of the University of Michigan in the 1990s (Hamel and Prahalad, 1994). Interestingly, in all of these proposals there is a strong focus on the company and its environment, but it seems that they underestimate the importance of understanding that the behavior of the company is emergent from continuous interactions between the environment, the ecological niche, and company structures. This focus also implies that insufficient consideration is given to the alignment of all three constituents.

The Complete Agent Principle

The complete agent principle states that when designing an agent we have to think about the complete agent behaving in the real world. One of the important implications is that we must never design one part of the system in isolation. For example, we should never design the sensory systems without thinking about the motor systems, because of the couplings between the two. In a corporate context we should always try to determine the kind of information the company might need—for example, for deciding whether to try and launch a particular project—and think in terms of the potential actions the company has at its disposal to extract the required information from its environment (see also the principle of sensory-motor coordination, below). But this "sensing of the environment" is not arbitrary; it must be directed toward keeping the company profitable in the long term. Remember that the agents that are of particular interest for us, as outlined in chapter 4, are the ones that are autonomous and self-sufficient, i.e., that can sustain themselves over extended periods of time without, or with only little help from, other agents.

Thus, the major challenge of any company is the establishment of a sustainable organizational structure, a structure that enables the company to survive over extended periods of time. Sustainability in particular implies resource autonomy, which means that the company, in the long run, should be able to generate its own resources so that it will not always have to depend on others. This explains why the discussion and analysis of the business model of any company is so important: where exactly do the necessary resources come from—from the company's own sales, or from investments of other companies? How will the investments be allocated, e.g., into development of infrastructure, hiring external expertise, acquiring know-how by purchasing other companies, etc.?

In the Internet hype and technology bubble of the late 1990s there was a heated debate about whether the mechanisms of resource generation and allocation for traditional companies would still hold for new ventures in a networked economy: the notorious dot-com companies. In the meantime we know that those companies that survived had a clear business model in terms of resources: eBay, Amazon, and Google all have a simple and straightforward idea of where the revenues would come from in the short and in the long run—e.g., in the initial phase a high percentage of revenues should come from investors while steadily increasing revenue should come from sales of real products and services (books, auction, and advertisement platforms) later on. If such an idea can be realized, a company can sustain itself over time and become autonomous. By contrast, companies that managed to get a lot of venture capital and realized initial public offerings (IPOs)—i.e., they went to the stock exchange—without a clear-cut understanding of the resource flow and of how financial liquidity and business development could be ensured, did not survive. A great example is the now defunct company govWorks.com, which was highly celebrated and intensely covered by American television, and featured in the documentary film *startup.com*.

In this perspective, it is important for managers and entrepreneurs to view their companies and business activities as complete agents, for which self-sufficiency and autonomy play a critical role: we not only have to work out and define clearly what the necessary resources are for our company, but also to determine where they come from, now and in the future. And given the competition for resources in the ecological niche, how can a constant resource flow be ensured? And what resources need to be allocated to allow for resource generation in the future? Moreover, in this resource discussion the focus should not be on one particular part but on the entire agent: all aspects of the company must be considered.

For example, often the vision problem in a robot can be drastically simplified if it is given the ability to move around: the agent can move closer to the to-be-investigated object, can move around it and view it from various angles and distances. Thus, fewer resources have to be invested into vision if we account for the motor system as well, rather than trying to solve the vision problem in isolation. In a similar perspective, Mintzberg emphasizes that instead of relying on extended strategic information gathering and strategic planning activities in the corporate headquarters at the top of the organization, most managers actually prefer to communicate with the people who are directly involved in specific initiatives and local activities at the ground level of the organization, as a way to actively probe for information.

No company or business activity can become sustainable without taking into account that the generation and allocation of the necessary resources itself requires a substantial investment of resources. Interestingly, there is a prominent, but rather specific management tradition—largely initiated by Harvard and Stanford University professors—of discussing the importance of understanding resource dependence in order to achieve proper resource allocation. This line of argument started with Joseph Bower (Harvard University) in the 1970s and continued with Robert Burgelman (Stanford University) in the 1980s and Clayton Christensen (Harvard University) in the 1990s. Basically, they contend that much more emphasis should be placed on understanding how the company depends on internal and external resources, and how it can potentially achieve a certain degree of autonomy in the market. A more specific feature of this principle is that one should never analyze one component in isolation, but that we should always look for complete sensory-motor loops, as illustrated in the principle of sensory-motor coordination that we discuss next.

The Principle of Sensory-Motor Coordination
One of the most important and surprising insights comes from an in-depth understanding of the principle of sensory-motor coordination, which, in essence, states that through the interaction with the environment, sensory stimulation is induced in different sensory channels, and that the sensory data thus generated are highly structured and contain correlations, both within one sensory channel and between channels. Again, this insight can be translated into a management context. One of the key challenges for managers and entrepreneurs is to deal with an enormous variety and complexity of information, as well as with

interpretations of financial and economic data and production figures, all of which are potentially relevant for the company. At the same time, as pointed out previously, entrepreneurship and management face inherent and fundamental uncertainty due to lack of information and understanding of their environment, as well as of their own position, i.e., how the environment will react to what the company does.

We know from research and practice that successful managers and entrepreneurs act in a particular way when facing uncertainty. Instead of waiting for additional information, which might allow them to better understand and represent the current situation, they proactively interact with the environment in order to provoke concrete reactions, feedback, and learning opportunities—which, of course, reflects precisely the content of the sensory-motor coordination principle. As entrepreneurs present their business plans to potential customers and investors, they generate feedback and reactions which allow them to further develop and specify their business cases; technology corporations develop their new products in close cooperation with potential lead users in order to clarify the particular features and characteristics the new product should have in order to become successful.

Furthermore, from the perspective of the principle of sensory-motor coordination, it is important to understand how, through these interactions with the environment, correlations in the data are induced and what the nature of these correlations is, in order to assess the quality of the data thus generated. It is essential that new ventures or new initiatives by established companies stimulate feedback and input from particular sources: from experienced investors who really understand a particular business case; or from potential customers for this newly developed product, whose reactions can be used to draw conclusions about the potential of the product. This activity of provoking, of generating information by acting on the environment, is essential for gaining an overview of the market situation; and, as we know from exploration-exploitation, we must invest a certain amount of resources in exploration in order to survive in the long run.

These considerations contrast with the predominant perspective in the management literature, which emphasizes the importance of the appropriate identification, evaluation, and exploitation of new external opportunities and potential strategies as a precondition for successful business creation: this view places all its emphasis on sensing, and little or none on acting. By contrast, the principle of sensory-motor coordination suggests that before we can identify and evaluate we must act in order to generate the required information. This can be summarized by the following questions: What sorts of feedback and insights would be most valuable to identify a new business opportunity? This in turn entails the question of what—proactively initiated—interactions will yield the necessary information.

It is not surprising that this line of argument is almost entirely absent in the management literature, with the exception of a few rather dissident positions. On the one hand this minority view has been upheld by practitioners who have experience with the entrepreneurial reality of developing a new company or a new business in the context of high uncertainty—including the former Macintosh "evangelist" Guy Kawasaki, in his book *Rules for Revolutionaries* (Kawasaki, 1999)—and on the other hand from creative scholars such as Michigan University's Karl Weick, whose idea of enactment can be crudely paraphrased as "How do you know what you think, before you see what you do?" (Weick, 1995).

The Principle of Cheap Design

The principle of cheap design is in essence about exploiting whatever happens to be present in the niche for one's own purposes. Given the limited resources available to realize new products, create new companies, and launch new initiatives, it is important to think about exploiting existing mechanisms in the environment or the company to increase efficiency (i.e., doing things with minimum resources) and effectiveness (achieving one's goals).

One area of rapidly increasing importance is communication. We know that for most companies and businesses, a major challenge is not so much the development of new products and services themselves, but how to communicate about them to the players in the market, including potential customers, business partners, and competitors, which is an essential prerequisite for establishing the product in the market. Remember our discussion of how market developments emerge from complex interactions: this process of communication constitutes one aspect of this complex dynamics, and the market may or may not react to it. It is thus important to structure the communication about the new products and services as effectively as possible. Many companies have started to exploit media that they already use to do business for these purposes. For example Dell and Amazon are exploiting their presence on the Web, which they employ as their major business channel, for the purpose of communicating about their products and services. Nokia exploits its own product, mobile phone networks, for precisely the same purpose. Finally,

Swatch communicates through its choice of locations. For example, in 2004 the company acquired a multistory building in Tokyo's elegant Ginza district, which is known for its posh shopping areas and luxury goods, where it will build its flagship store. By placing its facilities among the prime outlets for fashionable labels, the company communicates the view of "Swatch as cheap, but top design" indirectly. The message is conveyed for free, so to speak, since the building, though expensive, obviously serves other fundamental purposes. This way, by piggybacking onto existing resources—in this case the clustering of high-end businesses within the Ginza district—the company can achieve both high visibility and strong impact for its new products while investing a limited amount of resources in the communication process.

Another important way in which existing resources can be exploited is through systematic reliance on dispersed expert networks, often coordinated via the Internet. We know that today many communities constantly evaluate and communicate about new developments and opportunities. Such communities may be organized as newsgroups directed by influential opinion leaders (note also the importance of web logs in this context). If a company succeeds in getting supportive evaluations in such a networked context, it can expect enormous leverage, almost for free. For example, people using a search engine like Google automatically contribute to this process. By linking their page to certain web pages they—indirectly—change the order of the search results, and they do not need to be paid for their "service"! It is obvious, however, that the same publicity can also go in a negative direction, leading to potentially disastrous consequences for any new company or business. This raises an interesting issue, namely that of the stability of the mechanisms exploited in a cheap-design framework, and points to the potential dangers of exploiting such resources. An analogy from biology would be that animals living in the sea can exploit the streams in the ocean to cheaply—i.e., with minimal energy expenditure—reach their destinations, but exploiting these streams may occasionally lead to disasters, such as dolphins being stranded on the beach.

For managers and entrepreneurs it is thus essential to work out and define which internal and external processes, mechanisms, and media can be exploited in order to economize with limited resources, and to assess carefully the implications of using such mechanisms for the perception and evaluation of the company or business in the market.

There are many interesting individual case studies that illustrate how entrepreneurs turn the fact that they must work with limited resources into an advantage by exploiting particular processes and mechanisms, documented in individual success stories (e.g., the Google search engine) or in rulebooks for building new companies and businesses. However, it is worthy of note that to our knowledge there are no systematic accounts of these mechanisms.

The Redundancy Principle

We know from recent insights into operational efficiency—i.e., the cost-effective handling of logistics, sales, coordination, organizational learn-ing, and knowledge management—that if we want to build companies capable of surviving major perturbations of the skittish economic markets, redundancy is extremely important. The university professor and top manager Ikujiro Nonaka, called "Mr. Knowledge" by the *Economist* magazine and author of *The Knowledge-Creating Company* (Nonaka and Takeuchi, 1995) is one of the most prominent "spiritual leaders" in knowledge management. He emphasizes the importance of redundancy for the creation and development of new knowledge. Only if many different people and companies use, evaluate, adapt, and sys-tematize experiences and knowledge in many different contexts and by resolving different tasks, according to Nonaka, does this knowledge establish itself and become generally accepted.

As we learned in the context of the principle of sensory-motor coor-dination, the proactive confrontation of particular customers and impor-tant investors with new ideas and insights provokes the necessary feedback to evaluate and strengthen those ideas and the related expert-ise of the company. This means a substantial investment of time and resources. We mentioned that companies need redundancy to achieve stability so that there are alternative ways of working if something breaks down. In the course of the 1990s, many such redundancies were system-atically reduced in order to make companies more lean and focused—outsourcing and concentration on core competences were the buzzwords at the time. However, the elimination of these redundancies made the companies very vulnerable and unstable. If key people leave the company, lack of redundancy leads to major problems; if core processes break down in the organization, redundancy is a precondition for con-tinuing the company's operation; if one particular new development does not work out well, it is important that parallel, related developments are there to fill the gap. The redundancy principle, as introduced in chapter 4, says more than just that there must be redundancy—it tells us, to some extent, what kind of redundancy to look for. Mere duplication of skills is only one form of redundancy, and it is often necessary but not sufficient for success. More interesting is redundancy through partial overlap in functionality. Employees with overlapping but different kinds of expertise make the company more adaptive. If two employees have related but differing knowledge, their knowledge obviously covers a wider range, which can only be beneficial. If one of them leaves the company, some of the knowledge is lost, but because there is partial overlap the company can continue to function. Since the 1960s we know from Herbert Simon (again!) and his former student Jim March that slack resources, i.e., resources that have not been dedicated to a particular purpose, are essential for companies and businesses to survive in innovative and dynamic markets; the slack resources are necessary—they provide the required redundancy—for experimentation and for engaging in exploratory activities (March and Simon, 1993).

For managers and entrepreneurs, the tough task is to strike a balance between cheap design and redundancy. On the one hand they must look for existing resources that can be exploited in order to minimize resource consumption. Having a lean organizational structure to some extent relies on the prediction that the environment will remain as is. On the other hand they have to work out what kind of redundancies should be introduced into the company, while taking into account the partial overlap of functionality. This balancing act creates an obvious tension in most new companies and businesses. Only limited resources are available, while at the same time there is the need to provide the required redundancy to make the company adaptive so that its developments and activities lead to sustainable business over extended time periods.

The Value Principle

The last principle that we will discuss here is the value principle, a principle that is crucial for any intelligent system, but is also hard to understand and implement in concrete situations. As mentioned throughout this chapter, entrepreneurs and managers face fundamental uncertainty and ambiguity in the form of many sorts of questions. For example, what exactly is the technological, economic, cultural, and institutional environment in which they try to succeed? What exactly are the appropriate structures and priorities for the company to effectively develop its products and services? To what extent will it be possible to successfully launch the new business among customers and investors?

We know from empirical research and personal accounts that most entrepreneurs and managers are able to make decisions, evaluate opportunities, or interpret developments only if they rely on clear, basic values to guide their thinking and acting. If they know what their business stands for (leading-edge technology development, customer intimacy, moral beliefs and values, environmental concerns, etc.) and what is really important to them (financial success, interesting projects, intelligent people, etc.), it is often quite obvious whether a particular development or a new opportunity is of any relevance for them. We know from a long tradition of research on culture and identity how important this value perspective is.

This also implies that there is no such thing as a global, objective reference for a value structure that holds for all companies and businesses. Financial success has a very different meaning for a venture capital–financed company, a family-held company, a publicly traded company, or an individually owned company; relevant technology takes on completely different meanings for an innovation-driven, leading-edge technology company and for a company focused on established products and solutions; and cultural and societal issues have a different impact on companies depending on their ideological orientation. For managers and entrepreneurs, the task then is to work out and define a set of values that hold independently of any development of the company and its business, and to identify the major implications of those values.

The value system, as introduced in chapter 4, is responsible for telling the organism what is beneficial to it. For biological organisms, value—at least *basic* value—is related to physiological parameters such as blood sugar level, level of dehydration, or oxygen content, and any behaviors that keep these parameters within acceptable ranges are considered beneficial. In this sense, value is rather objective. However, for a company it is hard to define objectively the equivalent of a company physiology, and thus there is a certain arbitrariness in the value systems for companies. However, there are some very basic, almost "physiological" values, namely that the financial basis is sound and the company engages only in legal practices. Beyond these obvious values, it is up to the individual company to decide what is of value to itself and what is not.

9.5 Corroborating the Speculations

We hope that we have been able to demonstrate that the general theory and design principles for intelligent systems yield interesting results and insights if applied to the area of business creation. Although we believe that we have made great strides toward a better understanding of the "design principles" of companies, the final proof will lie, of course, in applying the principles to the construction of actual, physical companies in the real world. Indeed, this is an idea that the authors of this chapter plan to pursue in the near future, in order to put these ideas to a tough test. Another exciting form of feedback will be generated if some readers feel inspired by these ideas and apply them in their own managerial and entrepreneurial environment whenever new businesses, products, companies, or technologies need to be developed. Of course, as we are dealing with the real world where people, markets, and large amounts of money are involved, the possibilities for free experimentation will be limited compared to experimentation with robots and simulations. Also, aiming for reproducible experimental results can no longer be the goal, so we have to apply more pragmatic criteria related to the success of companies where entrepreneurs have been applying these principles. Last but not least, these criteria should be evaluated with respect to the question of what we have learned and what new questions the results create.

9.6 Summary and Conclusions

One of the main insights from this application of the design principles to business has been that in many respects the environments—the ecological niches—for intelligent embodied systems and companies are very similar and share numerous features, but in particular they are both intrinsically uncertain and unpredictable. Given this background it seems promising to transfer the design principles that have been developed for intelligent systems to an economic context, and in particular to company design. Because of this similarity, some of the topics raised by the design principles have been taken up. Others, in some of the more recent literature on management however, such as the frame of reference in mimetic behavior or the proactive generation of information, have to date been largely ignored. The major advantage of the design principles is that they constitute a consistent and comprehensive set, something that as far as we can tell has been missing from the management literature.

10　Where Is Human Memory?

In December 2004, on a foggy, cold morning at the weekly dynamical systems meeting in the Artificial Intelligence Laboratory of the University of Zurich, the brilliant young theoretical physicist and robotics engineer Simon Bovet gave a presentation about what he called a "minimal cognitive architecture" for one of his robots. As a robot he used the Artificial Mouse, which we met in chapter 4. The provocative title of his presentation was "Delayed Reward Learning without Memory." Delayed reward learning refers to situations in which the subject—an animal or robot—has to make a particular decision, e.g., whether to turn left or right in a maze, but the feedback as to whether the decision was right or wrong is provided only later, when the reward is given or not (the rat finds the cookie in the maze or it does not). Bovet's work is provocative indeed: the difficulty for the agent in delayed reward learning is to recognize at what point the correct or incorrect decision has been taken, a problem sometimes called the credit assignment or blame assignment problem. In order to solve this problem, the rat (or robot) must remember its decisions—there can be absolutely no doubt about it. Therefore, delayed reward learning requires memory. Or does it?

Bovet's experiment works as follows. The Artificial Mouse is equipped with whiskers for touch (the tactile sensor), a camera for vision, and a special "reward sensor" for detecting the reward. The task of the Artificial Mouse is to learn how to find the reward—an electronic cookie, which in this case is simply an electrical signal—in a so-called T-maze, a very simple arrangement of corridors in the shape of a T lying on the table. As it enters the T-maze through the center corridor (the base of the T), the problem for the robot is whether to turn left or right when it reaches the junction; the reward is at the end of either the left or the right arm. At one of the corners of the junction, there is a tactile cue (a vertical stick) that can be detected with the whiskers. If the tactile cue is on the left, the reward will always be at the end of the left arm of the T-maze; if it is on the right, the reward will be at the end of the right arm. But the robot does not know about this, otherwise the task would be trivial and it would not have to learn anything. Also, the inside of the wall of the horizontal bar of the T is colored red along its entire length, so that when the robot enters the T-maze it is facing this red wall. During the experiment, the position of the tactile cue, together with the reward, is randomly switched from left to right, and each time the robot is given a chance to find the reward.

What happens in the experiment is that after a number of trials, during which the positions of the tactile cue and the reward have been randomly switched, the robot consistently starts making the correct choices, i.e., when the cue is on the left it turns left, and vice versa.

Now, how does that work? In order for the robot to learn this task, we would expect it to retain a memory of the decisions it has taken so that as it reaches the reward it "knows" whether the cue had been on the left or on the right, and whether it had turned left or right. It could then use this memory, together with the presence or absence of the reward, to update the connections in its neural network—its "brain"—appropriately so that next time around it had a better chance of turning in the correct direction. However, this is not what happens—a result that caused jaws to drop among the audience in Bovet's seminar: if there is no memory of the decisions and the situations in which they were taken, how could the robot successfully learn to make the correct decisions? How is this possible? The answer is that it works because the "memory function" is off-loaded into the environment, and this is enabled by a particular, very simple neural network architecture.

Let us first briefly look at this architecture. For each sensor modality, there is one set of "neurons" (nodes) representing the state of the sensor, and another that represents the change in the same sensor. For the camera, one set of neurons represents the intensity and color values of the camera pixels, while another set indicates change in these values. Similarly for the whiskers—the tactile system—there are neurons for detecting touch and change in touch (from nontouch to touch, or vice versa). There is also a neuron for the reward sensor. In the motor system there are neurons for direction and change of direction. All these groups of neurons are mutually connected to each other by synapses. There is a simple Hebbian learning mechanism which reinforces all the connections between neurons that are simultaneously active. In other words, it picks up instantaneous correlations, i.e., correlations between the sensory and motor signals at a particular instance in time, or correlations between different sensor modalities. We stress this point, because only events (sensors and motors being stimulated) happening at the same time can be associated in this way; it is not possible that a current event can be associated with one in the past.

Here is roughly what happens. At the beginning, the reward neurons are stimulated by the experimenter, mimicking the idea that the Artificial Mouse "wants" to get the reward. As long as the synaptic connections are weak—no associations have been formed—there is no effect of this stimulation on the behavior of the robot. If it now enters the T-maze and moves to the junction, it senses the tactile cue on either its left or right side, and makes a turn in an initially random direction. Through the Hebbian learning mechanism, the tactile neurons, the motor neurons, and the vision neurons (which detect the red wall) become more closely associated, i.e., the connections between them are strengthened. Assuming that, by chance, the decision has been correct, the robot will somewhat later detect the reward and because at the same time it will see the red wall on one side of its visual field (e.g., on the right), it will associate "red wall on the right side" and "reward." Indirectly then, the information about the turn the robot has taken previously is contained in the current situation, i.e., that the red wall is detected on the right side implies that the robot had turned left before. In the next trial, assuming the same arrangement of the cue and the reward, the stimulation of the reward sensors will—because of what has been previously learned (reward associated with red wall on right)—already provide some activation in one side of the visual field (red wall on right), which in turn is associated with the proper turning direction (turning left). The requirement for this procedure to work is that the same arrangement occur for two trials in a row (and this will always happen if we wait long enough). (This description presents the key ideas from the experiment, but the actual architecture and the network dynamics are somewhat more complicated; the interested reader is referred to Bovet and Pfeifer, 2005). So, in essence, the robot performs delayed reward learning without possessing an explicit memory of the relevant events and decisions taken!

So we see that in some sense the Artificial Mouse exploits the interaction with its environment, in this case the red wall, to achieve the task. It is interesting to note that this works in spite of the fact that the red wall is entirely neutral with respect to the task, i.e., it provides absolutely no information whatsoever about the location of the reward. Of course, it makes perfect sense to attribute something like memory to the robot, but once again, this is a frame-of-reference issue: memory is attributed to the robot by an external observer; there is no box or explicit representation in the system providing the memory function (see the discussion later in this chapter of Ross Ashby's notion of memory.) Of course, the robot's "history" is partly represented in the neural network because through Hebbian learning, the synaptic strengths have been changed. But there is no explicit memory in the robot's brain about the decisions it has taken in the past.

In this chapter, we will start with some introductory comments on memory. Then we will present the storehouse metaphor, which views memory as a place where "things" are stored, and discuss some of the problems of this view. Next we will provide an overview of the different kinds of memory concepts that are used in the literature. We will then introduce Ashby's perspective on memory, which serves well as a foundation for any discussion about learning and memory. This will be followed by examples of developments in the area of human memory research, and we will apply our design principles to them, as we have in previous chapters. We will see that the embodied perspective often leads to interesting insights and changes our views about memory. Finally, we will discuss some implications for memory research in particular and for research on cognition in general.

10.1 Introduction

Throughout the book we have encountered memory, and it is indeed hard to imagine an intelligent agent without it. Additionally, learning is a core ability of intelligent systems, and learning is directly coupled to memory. Human memory is considered a high-level cognitive function, and is directly related to abilities like natural language and tasks such as an expert solving a hard problem, a student taking a test, a grandfather telling stories to his grandchildren, a teenager recognizing a piece of music, a child reciting a poem, a waiter taking an order in a restaurant, a taxi driver figuring out a route to the customer's destination, and so on. All of these activities involve memory one way or other. The goal of this chapter is to demonstrate that memory cannot be sensibly conceptualized purely as an abstract entity within the brain; but that embodiment must also be included in our considerations.

Earlier we mentioned that psychology, the discipline dealing with the most complex known system, the human, is carved up into subdisciplines like perception, language, problem solving, learning, *memory*, development, emotion, and social behavior. We suggest that these subfields are not so much concerned with the search for the particular modules in the brain responsible for the corresponding set of behaviors, but rather that they constitute different ways of viewing a complete agent with many behavioral capabilities: memory represents an important perspective on the same physical system, the human subject. For example, in the psychology of perception the human subject is systematically exposed to stimuli, such as familiar and unfamiliar faces under various conditions (front view, side view, bright, dark), and depending on whether subjects recognize the face as familiar or not, they are asked to perform a particular behavior, such as pushing a button on a computer keyboard. The experimental methods in the psychology of emotion are similar, except for the nature of the stimuli and the expected responses. One might present a story that induces a happy or sad emotional state in the person, or show them a video of a sexually arousing scene, and measure physiological variables such as adrenaline, skin resistance, pulse rate, and blood pressure. Alternatively, a particular emotional state is induced and the subjects have to solve a problem and then the experimenter makes an assessment of the quality of the solution. In memory research, the basic experimental arrangement is similar, but again, the contents of the stimuli and required responses are different. The typical materials are lists of words which have to be remembered and then recounted later on, or stories which subjects read and are then later tested for how well they remember the plot or certain details. Depending on the perspective of the research discipline—e.g., perception, emotion, memory—models for most of these functions have been proposed. For memory, the most prominent one has been the storehouse metaphor (for a review, see, for example, Koriat and Goldsmith, 1996) which suggests that memories are stored in particular locations from where they are later retrieved.

So far so good. So, where is the problem? Or is there a problem? Well, there are a number, in fact. They can briefly be summarized as follows. First, the storehouse metaphor fails to explain certain important phenomena related to memory. Second, a large number of different memory types are described in the literature, which raises the question of how these types of memory differ and whether there are any unifying concepts that underlie all of them. Third, in many reports externally observable behaviors and the mechanisms underlying them are not clearly distinguished. And fourth, in spite of a rapidly increasing interest in embodiment, memory is still often conceptualized as an abstract entity isolated from the body.

There is a huge and very rich literature on memory in psychology and neuroscience, and it is not possible in this short chapter to do justice to all the outstanding research that has been done in this area. What we will try to do instead is to present a novel viewpoint on memory—an embodied perspective—that has not been systematically adopted in the field, although ideas of embodiment are rapidly gaining interest and acceptance.

Before we continue, a note on terminology is necessary because the word *memory* can mean two things. First, it is the "thing" to be remembered, for example a memory of a wonderful dinner at a girlfriend's house, the memory of the fish smell in a small port in Okinawa, the memory of the taste of an excellent Australian Chardonnay, or the memory of an extremely embarrassing situation. The other meaning is the more abstract, theoretical one; the "vehicle," so to speak: the set of processes that are responsible for and underlie changes in behavior. This latter meaning is intended in the titles of textbooks on the subject, for example Neath and Surprenant's *Human Memory* (2003), and in this chapter.

10.2   The Storehouse Metaphor and Its Problems

If cognition is viewed as computation, as in the traditional perspective, then the storehouse metaphor comes very naturally. In this view, there is a certain input which is somehow processed, represented, and stored in some kind of memory, from where it can be retrieved if needed at a later point in time. But the computer analogy, as assumed in the cognitivistic paradigm, is misleading because in a computer there are actual storage locations, and data is entered, stored, and later retrieved; while in the brain the mechanisms are of an entirely different nature. The NASA computer scientist and author of the influential book *Situated Cognition*, Bill Clancey, called this perspective "memory as stored structures (or representations)" (Clancey, 1997). However, there are many very familiar phenomena that are hard to explain using this idea. We provide only a short summary here; for a more detailed perspective, the reader is referred to chapter 15 of Pfeifer and Scheier (1999). For example, when listening to an unfamiliar rendition of a particular piece of music, we can quickly recognize it even though the particular sounds—possibly different instruments, a different key, a different tempo—are new to us. Or take the question that Israel Rosenfield asks in his provocative book *The Invention of Memory*: "When we speak of a stored mental image of a friend, *which* image or images are we referring to? The friend doing what, when and where?" (1988, p. 163). Is it the one from last week, from two years ago, with a hat, without a hat, shaven or unshaven, with short hair, sunglasses, with different clothes, in bright sunlight or shade, etc.? Or let us take tennis. How can we explain, in a stored-structures conception of memory, the fact that every stroke is different from previous strokes, in other words that every stroke is unique?

It is with remembering as it is with the stroke in a skilled game. We may fancy that we are repeating a series of movements learned a long time before from a text-book or from a teacher. But motion study shows that in fact we build up the stroke afresh on the basis of the immediately preceding balance of postures and the momentary needs of the game. Every time we make it, it has its own characteristics.

This passage, which has a very modern flavor to it, comes from the eminent psychologist F. C. Bartlett in his famous book *Remembering*, published in the first half of the last century (Bartlett, 1932). It reminds us of the principle of ecological balance, where part of the task is off-loaded into the morphology and the interaction with the environment. This off-loading, in addition to being economical—only relatively little information needs to be stored in the brain—makes the system intrinsically adaptive and responsive to the needs of the situation. (But we will say more about that later.) Finally, generally speaking, the storehouse metaphor entails all the problems of the classical cognitivistic paradigm, such as the symbol grounding problem: if memories are stored as discrete and separable entities in the brain (like symbols), where are they stored? How are they related to the original, remembered event? Is there one memory for each remembered event, or many? How do memories relate to each other?

In summary, there are a number of problems with the storehouse metaphor, and alternative perspectives are needed. If confronted with the question, even the most conservative researchers would presumably not endorse a strict storehouse view of memory. Yet, Koriat and Goldsmith, in their seminal paper on memory metaphors, point out that "although perhaps no investigator today would endorse such an extreme version, it is important nonetheless to confront its implicit logic, which still pervades much contemporary research and thinking about memory" (1996, p. 169). In other words, even though most researchers would reject a strict storehouse view, there is still, at least implicitly, the underlying assumption of "memory as stored structures." And this seems to hold even today.

10.3 Concepts of Memory

If we browse the literature on human memory we immediately realize that memory is not a simple, unified concept. Rather, it is a multifaceted and complex phenomenon whose presentation depends upon the interests and research paradigms of the authors. Perhaps it is not even a phenomenon, but rather many different phenomena that need to be accounted for, and for which different experimental paradigms have been developed. In order to explain this host of phenomena, different memory concepts have been proposed. For example, in classic experiments on list learning, where subjects are presented with a list of, say, ten, twenty, or thirty words, it has been found that there is a tendency for the items at the end of the list to be very well recalled if tested immediately after the experiment, a phenomenon termed the recency effect. However, after a brief delay in testing, e.g., 15 or 30 seconds, the recency effect disappears, while performance on earlier items in the list is relatively unaffected by the delay (e.g., Baddeley, 1997). So, it was natural to postulate that there are two different kinds of memory and to call them short-term memory, or STM, and long-term memory, or LTM. This is a distinction that has been elaborated in great detail over decades of memory research. STM is invoked to explain the fact that the items from the end of the list are well remembered shortly after the list has been presented. The time scale, i.e., the retention period of STM, is on the order of seconds to minutes, whereas LTM is anything from minutes to hours to years, up to an entire lifetime.

Additional strong evidence for separate STM and LTM memory systems comes from studies of brain-damaged patients, e.g., H. M., a patient who around 1966 had a substantial amount of brain tissue removed from his temporal lobes and hippocampus in order to treat his epilepsy. "Although H. M. could recall incidents from his earlier life, his capacity for acquiring new information was drastically reduced. He was unable to learn to recognize new people, had no recollection of ongoing events, and could repeatedly read the same magazine without it seeming familiar. . . . In spite of this dramatic impairment in the capacity to learn new material, his immediate memory span was quite normal" (Baddeley, 1997, p. 42). This suggests a defective LTM system but a normal STM system. While there is very solid evidence for the existence of these two types of memory systems, their roles, in particular the role of STM in cognition, have been widely debated. Atkinson and Shiffrin (1968), two influential cognitive psychologists, have argued that STM acts as working memory, while the memory researcher Alan Baddeley, author of the standard memory textbook *Human Memory* (1997), and his students have argued for a more complicated multicomponent structure with a controlling central executive system and a number of subsidiary slave systems that specifically relate to vision and hearing. Even though Baddeley explicitly points out that the computer metaphor can be misleading because human memory functions very differently from a computer, the terminology employed is highly computational, suggesting a cognitivistic perspective.

So far, we have come across the terms STM (also called primary memory), LTM (also called secondary memory), and working memory. These terms designate aspects of the complex human memory system. But many more have been proposed: for example memory for vision and acoustics, and memories at different time scales (sensory buffers for very short-term storage, short-term, and long-term memory). Similar distinctions are sometimes made for other sensory modalities such as haptic, olfactory, and taste, but they are only rarely treated in textbooks. Within LTM there are additional distinctions such as episodic memory (for personal experiences), semantic memory (for general knowledge), propositional memory (similar to semantic memory, for facts, objects, and people), autobiographical memory (recollections making up one's personality), flashbulb memory (specifically vivid memories, typically from emotionally charged situations), prospective memory (concerned with when something should be remembered, as in making a mental note) and retrospective memory (concerned with what should be remembered),[1] procedural memory (for know-how, programs on how to do things), memory for sensory-motor skills such as driving a car, playing tennis, and juggling (which is related to procedural memory), declarative memory (for facts), and so on and so forth. These various types of memory are strongly intermixed. For example, a person's memory of the sight and sound of a Yamanote Line train in Tokyo (sensory memory) is associated with the memory of that person's last visit to Tokyo (episodic memory), which in turn makes up part of the individual's personality (autobiographical memory), and the meaning of the term Yamanote Line train (semantic memory).

Additional distinctions are based on the assumed format in which the memories are stored. An interesting debate concerns whether visual memory is propositional—in the form of logical expressions or symbol structures—or pictorial in nature. Another conception of memory, schema-based memory, maintains that memory is built out of certain types of schemas, structures that strongly resemble record structures from standard computer technology. In the mid-1980s, distributed memory models based on neural networks—connectionist models—started to become popular (see later in this chapter). Yet further distinctions concern memory access, e.g., explicit memory, where performance requires deliberate recollection or awareness, versus implicit memory, where performance does not require the individual being aware of it. Another characteristic is whether the memories are unconscious (or subconscious) or conscious, a distinction especially made in the clinical literature dealing with neurotic symptoms that are believed to be based on unconscious memories.

Literally thousands of experiments investigating these different types of memories have been conducted. While some of the distinctions are well founded not only in terms of psychological experiments but also physiological evidence, such as the STM-LTM distinction, or the sensory buffers whose very short time characteristics are due to the special neural structures underlying their operation, other distinctions seem to be more geared toward "explaining" experimental findings that occur in very specific experimental situations, and as such they are nearly always limited to the data they are intended to "explain." We put "explain" between quotation marks because there may be a frame-of-reference issue involved, a point that we will discuss in the next section. Although there is nothing intrinsically good or bad about having many concepts in a research field, this enormous number makes one wonder whether there is perhaps a better way of approaching the question of memory.

10.4 The Frame-of-Reference Problem in Memory Research: Ashby's Proposal

As pointed out many times, behavior and its underlying mechanisms are often confounded. In order to develop a better understanding in the context of memory, let us inspect a quotation from the great cybernetician Ross Ashby's excellent book *An Introduction to Cybernetics*:

Suppose I am in a friend's house and, as a car goes past outside, his dog rushes to a corner of the room and cringes. To me the behaviour is causeless and inexplicable. Then my friend says, "He was run over by a car six months ago." The behavior is now accounted for by reference to an event of six months ago. If we say that the dog shows "memory" we refer to much the same fact—that his behavior can be explained, not by reference to his state now but to what his state was six months ago. If one is not careful one says that the dog "has" memory, and then thinks of the dog as having something, as he might have a patch of black hair. One may then be tempted to start looking for the thing; and one may discover that this "thing" has some very curious properties. Clearly, "memory" is not an objective something that a system either does or does not possess; it is a concept that the observer invokes to fill in the gap caused when part of the system is unobservable. (1956, p. 117)

Let us translate Ashby's example to a situation in a memory experiment. Assume that during the test phase the subject is asked to recall as many items as possible from a list. Of course, in this situation it is obvious that the behavior of the subject in the current situation, the recall phase, is explained by reference to a situation in the past, namely the learning phase. The subject's internal state is, to the experimenter, completely unobservable (although with modern brain imaging techniques, one might get a small glimpse of it), and the experimenter will explain the subject's behavior in the current situation by reference to an event from the past, namely the learning phase. The notion of memory is invoked in order to link the subject's current behavior to that earlier situation, which is assumed to have somehow influenced the subject in such a way that he or she now behaves differently than he or she would have, had it not been for the previous situation. Note that we are not saying anything about *how* this connection is achieved, we are only saying *that* it is, and that this is what we call memory. In other words, we are not saying anything about the underlying mechanisms, but there is no doubt that the behavioral change—the way in which the earlier situation has exerted its influence—is ultimately achieved by mechanisms of neural plasticity. However, the two levels, the one of behavior and the one of underlying mechanism, need to be clearly separated: as we mentioned in chapter 3, confounding the two would amount to what is known in philosophy as a category error.

By varying the experimental situation—for example, by making the list longer, by presenting it to the subjects in different sensor modalities (acoustic, visual), by introducing interfering tasks (such as counting backward from 100 in steps of 7 after the learning phase to prevent rehearsal), by limiting the time for learning and for reproducing the items on the list, etc.—we can explore the mechanics of the underlying processes that connect the two situations, learning and recall. In all this, it is important to realize that the human subject is always a complete agent interacting with the real world: the subject must read or listen to the words on the list and then somehow pronounce them or write them down, all of which require sensory-motor processes. In other words, there is always sensor stimulation induced by the agent-environment interaction, i.e., there is always sensory-motor coupling involved in memory. In this sense, memory cannot be dissociated from the embodied agent, and this interaction is somehow part of the "mechanisms underlying memory," even if we do not—yet—know the details. Thus it might be inaccurate to conclude from experiments of this kind that memory is organized as a "storehouse," where memories are separated from sensory-motor processes and then stored in the brain. A long-standing bias toward this view of memory can be found in the literature, and it is therefore hard to eradicate. Unfortunately, as we all know, the naive view of science as an unbiased process does not quite reflect the realities of research.

Let us pursue this issue a little further. In our list-learning task, the behavior of the subject changes in very concrete and specific ways: the agent reproduces some of the items that had been on the list previously presented. And this is the only aspect of the agent's behavior that is taken into account, even though his or her behavior encompasses more than the task at hand: looking around the room and at the experimenter (perhaps a pretty woman), the interior (maybe drab and dull), fidgeting on the chair (which may be very uncomfortable), thinking about the experimental situation (will I do a good job or will I fail?) and about himself (do I have a good memory?), looking at the computer equipment (maybe out of date), realizing that he had forgotten to go to the bathroom (how long will the experiment take? or should I ask for a bathroom break now?), etc. From a complete agent perspective, all of these processes are taking place simultaneously, and the resulting behavior on the experimental task (the presentation of the list in the learning phase, and the request to recount the items on the list in the test phase) will be the consequence of—will be emergent from—a complex combination of mechanisms underlying the subject's behavior. It is interesting that in spite of all these factors, which vary significantly from individual to individual and that potentially influence the performance of the subject, the experimental results are surprisingly consistent. And so it is understandable that in order to explain this consistency "a system for storing and retrieving information" (Baddeley, 1997, p. 9) is proposed: a certain structure in which the list with the items is stored and from which it is retrieved. But taking the frame of reference into account, we have to be aware that the way the subjects' behaviors come about might in fact be much more complicated. Another way of looking at this is that what appears like a structure to the outside observer might be dynamically created, just like a water fountain whose bell-shaped appearance is not stored as a structure inside the fountain, but is emergent from the interaction of the shape and direction of the jets, the pressure at which the water is ejected, the surface tension of the water, and gravity acting on the water: it looks like a structure but is continuously created; it isn't "stored" anywhere.

Interestingly, Ashby's proposal is entirely compatible with the opinion of Neath and Surprenant, who argue that "Memory is never directly observed . . . rather, its existence is inferred from some particular behavior or some change in level of performance." (2003, p. 4). In Ashby's example, the observed behavior was the strange actions of the dog as the truck passed by; in the list-learning experiment it is the reproduction of words by the human subject from the list presented previously. In both cases, the notion of memory is invoked to connect events from the past with the present behavior.

In what follows, we will investigate how embodiment can be used to shed new light on some of the issues in memory research by applying the design principles to this field.

10.5 The Embodied View of Memory: Applying the Design Principles for Intelligent Systems

We should perhaps start with a methodological comment. We could have organized the chapter by either following the general structure of memory research, which would yield sections such as "the ecological approach," "reconstructive memory," and "memory as a complex dynamical system," or we could use the design principles, which give a different "cut" through the field. We chose the latter approach because we have used that structure throughout the book, but also because there is a surprising level of compatibility between the design principles and modern—embodied—research on human memory.

In chapter 4 we argued that an embodied agent, as soon as it interacts with the environment, will generate sensory stimulation and that there will typically be correlations in the sensory data so that their processing is made easier; learning is in fact enabled in this way. It is interesting that this view corresponds to the more ecological perspective of memory, which was originally proposed by the grand old man of cognitive psychology and memory research, Ulrich Neisser, in 1978. The question to be asked, he suggested, was how people use memory in everyday situations. The psychologist Arthur Glenberg, director of the Laboratory for Embodied Cognition at the University of Wisconsin–Madison—the name of the laboratory itself tells an important story—in an often-quoted article entitled "What Memory Is For," argued that memory has not evolved for the purpose of learning lists of words on memory tasks in the laboratory, but rather in the service of behavior; of perception and action (Glenberg, 1997). Because of the increasing recognition of the importance of embodiment, agents' actions have caught the interest of memory researchers. Asher Koriat, for example, stated in a recent paper on motor behavior, "Interest in memory processes underlying motor behavior has also been spurred by the notions of embodied cognition and situated cognition, which have been gaining impetus in recent years, driving a conceptual framework in which cognitive processes are seen to be deeply rooted in the body's interactions with the world" (Koriat and Pearlman-Avnion, 2003, p. 435). And they continue a bit later: "the growing interest in embodiment phenomena in diverse psychological domains . . . brings action to the forefront of cognitive theory" (p. 435).

In an embodied perspective of memory, the interaction with the environment plays a central role, which is perhaps somewhat counterintuitive for many people who associate memory function with conscious recall and our ability to reexamine the past. However, a number of researchers have argued that although conscious recall is interesting in itself, it is probably relatively infrequent compared to those memory phenomena not under conscious control (e.g., Bridgeman, 2003; Karn and Zelinsky, 1996; Kolers and Roediger, 1984). The fact that unconscious processes influence behavior was established a long time ago through studies of the phenomenon of implicit memory, which demonstrated that regardless of whether subjects could recognize a particular passage as one they had read before, they read previously encountered passages more rapidly the second time (e.g., Jacoby and Dallas, 1981). And the idea that unconscious memories influence our behavior is, of course, the essence of the psychoanalytic theory of neurosis in clinical psychology and psychiatry, as so brilliantly outlined by the father of psychoanalysis, Sigmund Freud, in the early twentieth century.

The Three-Constituents Principle and the Complete Agent Principle: The Ecological Approach

Let us briefly look at the three-constituents principle and the complete agent principle in the context of memory. The three-constituents principle tells us that that there are always three components to take into account: the desired behaviors and tasks (or, in the case of natural systems such as human subjects in memory research, the observed behaviors we are trying to explain); the environment; and the agent itself. It seems that the experimental memory research in the laboratory tradition of the German scholar Hermann Ebbinghaus, the acknowledged founder of experimental investigation of higher-level cognitive functions, focuses on the agent's behavior and tries to very precisely control environmental influences. By contrast, the ecological approach to memory research, Neisser-style, capitalizes on the interaction of the agent with the environment by investigating the function of memory in real-world situations. The intention of the laboratory research is interesting and important: by tightly controlling the environmental conditions, it can be uncovered what the "pure memory function" is about, without it being mixed up with other factors. However, this goal assumes that there is something like a "pure memory function," an assumption that, given Ashby's argument of memory as a theoretical construct, is at least not obvious. Rather, as we have said, memory is one way of carving up the behavior of a complete agent, and memory research, in this perspective, is about finding interesting connections between agent behaviors, as well as ways in which the behavior of agents changes depending on the situations they have experienced.

One of the problems in memory research is the strong context dependency of memory as revealed by studies on autobiographical memory and eyewitness testimony. For example, the accuracy of a witness's response to a question is extremely sensitive to the witness's choice of whether or not to volunteer a response, and also to how precisely the response must be reported (Fisher, 1996). From a complete agent perspective, context dependency of memory may simply be an indication that the conception of memory as a place where items are stored and later retrieved is inappropriate. According to the influential psychologist Fergus Craik, "Clearly something in the system must change as a result of experience, but the changes may be diffuse and widespread modifications of the whole cognitive system so that the system now interacts with aspects of the environment in a different way, rather than events being recorded specifically and discretely like events on a video recorder" (Craik, 1983, p. 356; cf. Koriat and Goldsmith, 1996). In other words, memory manifests itself through changes of the behavior of the individual. We, as observers, might want to describe these behavioral changes by invoking the concept of memory, which is precisely Ashby's idea. The ecological approach, by studying humans in complex real-life situations outside the laboratory where there are many influences, focuses on individuals as a whole and studies how they adapt to their environment. Although it provides a more realistic view, the ecological approach itself does not dismantle the storehouse metaphor; it does, however, make the idea harder to maintain.

Complete Agents, Sensory-Motor Coordination, the Situated Nature of Memory, and Memory as Recategorization

This discussion already indicates that in the ecological approach to memory, given all the factors potentially influencing the subject's behavior in real-world situations, it will be harder to produce scientifically sound and reproducible results. It is this difficulty that led Baddeley to argue about Neisser's book *Memory Observed* that it "is well worth browsing through, but it does, I am afraid, tell us more about Neisser's enthusiasm and tastes than about how human memory should be studied" (Baddeley 1997, p. 2). But perhaps all is not lost; the design principles may help provide a focus. For example, complete agents, whenever they act, generate sensory stimulation, and this sensory stimulation typically contains correlations that can be exploited in various ways. For instance, when we overhear some snatch of a song from the radio but cannot remember the whole song, and repeatedly hum the overheard part, the rest just might come to us automatically. Typically this sensory-motor-coordinated action will support the recall function. Reproducing part of the sensory-motor sequence, i.e., humming a certain passage of a tune by moving the muscles of the vocal tract, generates sound waves in the environment and induces sensory stimulation in the agent; you hear your own humming, which helps you recall the rest of the song. If we argue with Glenberg, we would of course have to explain where the "goal" to call up this song comes from in the first place. Well, there need be no goal; simply a sequence of behaviors is triggered by the piece of music played on the radio. This anecdotal example illustrates the principle of sensory-motor coordination, namely that through a sensory-motor-coordinated action—the humming—sensory stimulation is induced that has highly specific effects on behavior.

Because memory is directly related to sensory-motor coordination rather than acting as internal storage only, we have to interact with the environment in particular ways to activate memory functions, so to speak—and this is what we call the situated nature of memory: its strong dependence on the interaction with the world and the current situation. And normally, as we have pointed out above, memory seems not often to be a conscious act. But then, much less needs to be stored because part of the work is taken over by the system-environment interaction. Take the example of Josh, one of the authors, who, while studying at the University of Zurich, walked down a ramp at Zurich's main train station. All of a sudden he was reminded of an episode from his childhood in Canada, where, when attending a doctor's appointment, he had to walk down a very similar ramp at the front of the building—an episode that he had long ago "forgotten"—even though the environment was, visually speaking, entirely different. Apparently, the sequence of sensory-motor signals thus generated evoked the particular memory. Or take Bovet's Artificial Mouse—although not human—where the interaction with the red wall, and the exploitation of that interaction, was crucial for the success of the delayed reward learning task.

Let us elaborate a little further on the principle of sensory-motor coordination with respect to memory. In previous chapters, in particular in chapter 5 on development, we argued for the importance of sensory-motor coordination for categorization, and we have used the notion of attractors to designate sensory-motor states corresponding to categories. Psychological research makes a clear distinction between categorization and memory. In the literature on categorization, such concepts as prototypes and exemplar-based models, are introduced to explain the ways in which subjects respond, for example, when asked to classify pictured objects as "animal," "fruit," or "furniture." Memory research, on the other hand, is concerned with the concepts we have discussed such as LTM, STM, episodic memory, etc. It seems that these distinctions refer more to experimental paradigms than to underlying mechanisms; again, it may be that these are not two separate processes taking place in the brain, but rather two different ways of viewing human behavior.

From a complete agent perspective at least, the two concepts—categorization and memory—are virtually indistinguishable because in the real world, no two things are ever alike, so, when we recognize a person, we have to make an abstraction anyhow (as argued earlier): even though it may be the same person, the way he or she appears, and the sensory stimulation he or she evokes will be very different on each encounter.

Consider another quote from Rosenfield's *Invention of Memory*:

We recognize people despite changes wrought by aging, and we recognize personal items we have misplaced and photographs of places we have visited. We can recognize paintings of Picasso as well as adept imitations of Picasso. When we recognize a painting we have never seen as a Picasso or as an imitation, we are doing more than recalling earlier impressions. We are categorizing: Picasso and fakes. Our recognition of paintings or of people is the recognition of a category, not of a specific item. People are never exactly what they were moments before, and objects are never seen in exactly the same way. (1988, p. 163)

Rosenfield's observation can, on the one hand, be taken as an argument against the storehouse metaphor: if we were just pulling up specific items from memory, they would never match the one we currently see. Thus, remembering must be seen as a form of categorization, not of simple matching. This is compatible with Gerald Edelman's perspective, which views memory as an ability to organize the world into categories: "Memory is the enhanced ability to categorize or generalize associatively, not the storage of features or attributes of objects as a list" (Edelman, 1987, p. 241). This is a behavioral characterization and does not imply specific mechanisms. Memory, in Edelman's view, is a property attributed to complete systems: "It is the entire sensorimotor system and its repetitive activity and responses coordinated with the function of classification couples in global mappings that leads to memorial response" (1987, p. 266). (Classification couples are specific neural structures involved in categorization.) This excerpt expresses the fact that we are dealing with a complete agent involved in sensory-motor processes that can show behavior for whose description we use the term memory. Once again, remembering, like categorizing, thus is not the activity of a module inside the brain, but rather involves the agent as a whole.

There is an additional point of crucial importance here, briefly alluded to by Rosenfield when he mentions that "objects are never seen in exactly the same way." In chapter 3, we mentioned Steven Grossberg's ART theory, the adaptive resonance theory. An essential feature of ART is that with every act of categorization the categories themselves, and thus the interpretations of the sensory stimuli, are somewhat modified: either the existing categories are adjusted to match the current sensory stimulation or new categories are formed. While ART represents a disembodied perspective, it illustrates the idea of recategorization. The attractiveness of Edelman's approach to recategorization is that not only is it fully embodied, but in addition, he comprehensively maps out the neural systems involved in sensory-motor coordination and thus in recategorization. So, we can see that when we consider the sensor-motor processes involved in recognition, memory and categorization become indistinguishable; they are likely not separable modules residing somewhere in the brain, but rather different ways of viewing the same process—a process resulting from embodied behavior.

Diversity-Compliance, Cheap Design, and Ecological Balance: Scaffolding

Let us briefly inspect a few more of the ideas from our theory—diversity-compliance and the design principles of cheap design and ecological balance—with respect to memory research. Recall that diversity-compliance is about exploiting the ecological niche, cheap design tells us that intelligent agents must exploit the givens of the niche in order to optimize resources, and ecological balance is about how this can be achieved, namely through morphological computation. The morphology and the intrinsic dynamics of the physical embodied agent, in themselves, provide a memory function: behavioral sequences need not be stored internally but they simply take their course, so to speak. Remember the episode of Josh, who while walking down a ramp was reminded of an episode from his childhood; there was no need to explicitly store this sequence in detail, but the relevant sensory stimulation was generated when he walked. In some sense, this task was off-loaded into the system-environment interaction, which reduced the need for internal storage to a bare minimum. In this sense, physical embodiment provides a memory function because the physical dynamics can be exploited for this purpose.

More sophisticated ways in which the interaction with the environment can be exploited have to do with the general notion of scaffolding. A well-documented way in which people support their memory function is by manipulating and structuring their environments in ways to facilitate later interactions, as elaborated in chapters 5 and 8. Stigmergic interactions, such as depositing pheromone trails or putting traffic signs into the world, are one way of scaffolding the environment. Scaffolding is all around us in the modern, literate world: people take notes, keep diaries for their appointments, and use sticky-note pads and PDAs to support their memories. As Andy Clark put it, "Our brains make the world smart so that we can be dumb in peace! Or, to look at it another way, it is the human brain plus these chunks of external scaffolding that finally constitutes the smart, rational inference engine that we call mind" (Clark, 1997, p. 180). This notion is entirely compatible with the ecological perspective on memory.

Another fact that adds validity to this idea of off-loading memory tasks into the environment is that recognition is usually better than recollection. It is much easier to recognize a person than to imagine what the person actually looks like. Also, it is generally much easier to judge whether an item on a list has been seen before than to recall the items on the list. It seems that humans are "economizing" by not representing unnecessary detail—these details need not be represented because they are there in the environment anyhow. This is reminiscent of Rodney Brooks's provocative statement: "The world is its own best model" (Brooks, 1990, p. 6). Moreover, if we were to represent a lot of detail in our memories, it would be much harder to keep track of the changes that might occur because the world continuously changes (people change clothes, they get haircuts, and acquire wrinkles) this information would soon lose its value for adaptive behavior.[2] In Bovet's experiment, the Artificial Mouse also off-loaded memory onto the environment by exploiting the incidental presence of the red wall that could be used to connect two associations separated by time: between the tactile cue, the turning, and the red wall on the one hand, and the reward and the red wall on the other.

There is ample anecdotal evidence that the sensory-motor—or, more generally, the embodied—nature of memory and the design principles can be readily applied to provide explanations about behavioral change. However, sound experimental evidence from the laboratory would make a much stronger case. Unfortunately, there are relatively few experiments to date providing empirical support for the embodied nature of memory. We suspect that one reason there are so few, in comparison with the thousands of experiments on the disembodied notion, has to do with methodological difficulties: for a disembodied memory experiment, in essence only a computer screen is required, whereas in order to capture the sensory-motor aspects of memory more sophisticated equipment, additional sensors (touch, torque, joint angle), and recording facilities such as motion capture equipment might be required. Moreover, it is difficult to integrate current brain imaging technologies into sensory-motor tasks where individuals have to move around, because current equipment requires the subject to remain still. If the tasks are "purely cognitive" and therefore require no movement, experimentation is straightforward and standard procedures can be employed.

Frame of Reference and the Principles of Parallel, Loosely Coupled Processes and Redundancy: Constructive Memory, Dynamics, and Attractors

It is obvious that in all of what we have discussed so far in this chapter, the brain, and specifically neuronal plasticity, plays an essential role; but we have deliberately put the focus on the design principles—on the interaction with the environment, on scaffolding, and on sensory-motor coordination—because often in the neuroscience-oriented memory literature only brain processes are discussed and the complete agent is largely ignored. So, let us now, for a moment, focus on the brain processes involved in memory. Additional evidence from the brain sciences might shed additional light on the processes under investigation. We briefly looked at the STM-LTM distinction, where there is clear evidence from neuroscience (from physiology and anatomy) that these are at least partially distinct systems at the brain level. As pointed out above, Edelman very nicely mapped out the neural structures underlying categorization—or rather recategorization—behavior. The brain researcher Walter Freeman, in the 1980s, in a classic series of investigations on the smell organ of rabbits, studied the brain mechanisms underlying the ability of these animals to identify odors (see Freeman, 1991, for a summary of these experiments), as we briefly mentioned in chapter 3. Let us now look more closely at these experiments because they provide an interesting perspective on memory.

Freeman recorded electroencephalograms (EEGs) simultaneously from about 60 different locations on the surface of the skull situated above the olfactory bulb—the brain region responsible for smell—of the rabbits. The recordings of the EEGs reflected the activity of groups of thousands of neurons just below where the electrodes were attached. A rabbit was trained to respond to the smell of sawdust by licking or chewing, and when it did respond, an EEG recording was taken. Then it was trained to respond to the smell of banana and when it responded correctly, a second EEG recording was made. Finally, it was reconditioned to respond only to the smell of sawdust and a third recording was taken. To Freeman's great surprise, although the rabbit clearly identified the sawdust during the third stage, the EEG pattern was totally different than when sawdust was presented the first time! In other words, the exposure to banana somehow affected the neural system such that the dynamics recorded during the second exposure to sawdust (the third stage) no longer matched those from the first one. From this experiment we can conclude that the categories for the smells are not represented at the level of brain dynamics only, or at least not those portions that were measured by the EEG. The invariances—corresponding to the smell categories "banana" and "sawdust"—we are seeking are not to be found at the level of EEG patterns, or, to use the jargon we have developed in this book, at the level of internal mechanisms only, but rather in the behavioral response of the complete agent (which is how the researchers knew which smell the rabbits had identified in the first place). This is another instance of the frame-of-reference problem: if we look at the behavior of the entire agent we get the same (or similar) response to sawdust in the first and the third trial, whereas if we look at brain dynamics only (the EEG patterns), the first and the third situation are clearly distinct.

Generally speaking, many researchers—including Walter Freeman, Scott Kelso (author of *Dynamic Patterns*), Esther Thelen and Linda Smith (authors of *A Dynamic Systems Perspective on Development of Cognition and Action*), and Kunihiko Kaneko and Ichiro Tsuda (authors of *Complex Systems: Chaos and Beyond*), to mention but a few prominent examples—consider the brain as a dynamical system, and have proposed pertinent models of brain dynamics, i.e., models of how the activity of the brain changes over time. Many of them propose that memories may exist in the brain as attractors (see focus box 4.1). However, once again we caution that brains should not be viewed in isolation: sensory-motor processes play an important role in creating and influencing the attractor states and the transitions between them.

Freeman, who was one of the pioneers in dynamical brain theory, suggested that specific memories could be viewed as chaotic attractors. Recall that a chaotic attractor is a region in phase space that is bounded but whose trajectory cannot be predicted in detail. In other words, even if the brain settles into a (chaotic) attractor, the brain patterns will differ to a certain extent. Freeman speculated that "chaos underlies the ability of the brain to respond flexibly to the outside world and to generate novel activity patterns" (1991, p. 78). For each smell the organism can discriminate, there is a chaotic attractor, and whenever a new one becomes meaningful (can be distinguished), a new attractor is created. In Freeman's model of the olfactory bulb, remembering is achieved by jumping between different chaotic attractors—one for sawdust, one for banana, etc. The attractor into which the rabbit's brain will jump and into which it settles is determined by the particular smell presented (and which it has learned to recognize). Going back to the sawdust-banana experiment, because of the high variability of the patterns, it is not obvious when two different EEG plots belong to the same chaotic attractor. Viewing memories as attractor states has also been suggested by a number of people in the artificial neural networks community (see Amit, 1989, for an excellent overview).

This way of theorizing about memory is perhaps somewhat speculative, but it is intuitively very appealing, and if it helps researchers develop new ideas for experiments and theoretical concepts, then it has real value regardless of whether it turns out in the end that the dynamical system metaphor is a good one to understand brain function. To close this discussion of brain dynamics and memory we should mention that there is a lot of exciting (but, alas, somewhat complicated) formal, mathematical research going on that further explores the possibilities of this framework (e.g., Kaneko and Tsuda, 2001).

A number of conclusions can be drawn from the work on the dynamical systems approach to memory. First, as most scientists working in the field will probably agree, much basic research will be required to achieve a deeper understanding of the brain dynamics underlying human memory. Second, what is emerging from the work done so far is that memory cannot be conceptualized as passive—stored—structures but that there are dynamic processes involved. This is precisely what makes memory—and, by extension, human behavior in general—so enormously adaptive. And third, behavior is not stored in the brain, but rather emerges as the agent interacts with its environment. If in this interaction behavior arises that is comparable to that in earlier, similar situations, we say that the system has remembered the situation. Because the "memories" are not sitting inside the system, but are dynamically constructed during interaction with the world, we say that memory is constructive. There is also loose coupling through the interaction with the environment: the neurons in the olfactory bulb "cooperate"—they are loosely coupled through the interaction with the environment—to settle into a patricular chaotic attractor state when exposed to a particular smell. Finally, the constructive nature of memory is a consequence of the complete agent perspective and the situated nature of agents, a view that is in line with that of situated cognition (e.g., Clancey, 1997). In the situated cognition perspective, knowledge is not internal to an agent, but is created as the agent interacts with the real world. (We prefer the term *constructive* memory over *reconstructive* memory because the latter suggests that there are components stored somewhere and that the current memory is constructed from these parts. Thus reconstructive memory would be compatible with the storehouse idea; it is just that the stored chunks would be smaller.)

To wrap up this section, let us link this discussion back to the more classical field of neural networks. In the 1980s and 1990s many memory models based on connectionist networks were developed, and they continue to be refined, especially in psychology, as can be seen in such texts as *Connectionist Psychology*, published in 1997 and written by two of England's leading psychologists, Richard Ellis and Glynn Humphreys; and *Rethinking Innateness* by Jeff Elman and his colleagues, which outlines the connectionist perspective on development. Remember our discussion in chapter 2 about the "landscape of artificial intelligence," where we introduced connectionism as a special type of neural modeling and a popular way of investigating psychological and biological functions. Because the knowledge in these networks is stored in the strengths of the connections between the artificial neurons, we cannot figure out what knowledge is actually encoded in them by merely looking at the connectivity matrix: it is largely distributed and not stored in a particular location. Now remember that embodied agents must perform some kind of action in order to generate sensory stimulation. Since most connectionist models are disembodied, they cannot, of course, behave, and thus they cannot generate sensory stimulation. So, the experimenter must provide the sensory stimulation to the networks in order to get something out of them, and this sensory stimulation must be carefully prepared. While embodied agents can generate "good" sensory stimulation on their own through interaction with the world, disembodied systems must be given the right input in order to yield useful output. Connectionist models are a starting point for developing models of memory that go beyond simple storehouse ideas. However, connectionist models, although they can learn, typically are static in the sense that there is no intrinsic dynamics: input is provided, the signals are propagated through the network, and a certain output is produced. And then the next input has to be provided. Recall that in chapter 2 we noted that the trend in psychological modeling and in neuroinformatics is toward more dynamical models. This is also happening to some degree in connectionist research: as we have mentioned, a popular extension of neural network models is the spiking networks, where the timing and the propagation of the spikes, the action potentials, play an important role. Only if this timing is taken into account can there be interesting dynamics. The models by Freeman, Kelso, Kaneko and Tsuda, and others, are all highly dynamic, but much more research is required to gain a better understanding of how dynamic neural networks work, especially when they are used by embodied agents.

10.6 Implications for Memory Research: Summary and Speculations

What can we learn from our application of the design principles to issues in memory research? We started by describing a robot experiment that had a surprising result: the robot could learn a delayed reward task by only picking up on instantaneous correlations. We could say that the Artificial Mouse does not need to remember the decisions and the situations in which they were taken for its task, even though this kind of memory seems to be required for delayed reward learning. We then reviewed the storehouse metaphor, which is so intuitively compelling—what else could human memory be?—and hard to eradicate, and we listed some of its problems. We also saw the frame-of-reference issue cropping up in memory research: although behavior in a list-learning experiment can be appropriately described by an observer as storage and retrieval, we should not take this as the basis for a model of the mechanism underlying the behavior. This would be, to borrow one of Bill Clancey's analogies, like describing a camera's workings by the photographs it produces (Clancey, 1991). The clearest statement of the frame-of-reference problem in the context of memory research has been given by Ashby, who defined memory as a theoretical construct invoked to connect the observed agent's current behavior with events that have happened to it in the past. We also expressed our puzzlement over the sheer number of different memory concepts that have been described in the literature. The complete agent perspective suggests that all of these concepts are actually different perspectives on a complete agent, and that we should not look for a "thing," memory, inside the agent.

Next we applied our design principles to issues in memory research. The three-constituents principle and the complete agent principle are directly related to the ecological approach and to the strong context dependency of memory. We then looked at sensory-motor coordination, i.e., the way in which sensory stimulation is generated through interaction with the world; the situated nature of memory, i.e., the strong dependence of memory on the current situation; and the idea of memory as recategorization, which is an alternative model of memory proposed by Edelman. We also investigated how diversity-compliance, cheap design, and ecological balance, which lead to the notion of scaffolding, tie into the idea of off-loading aspects of memory into the environment, a phenomenon that further supports the notion that memory is not a "thing" inside the head of an agent but is something that spans both the agent and its environment. Finally, we looked at frame of reference (once again!) and the principles of parallel, loosely coupled processes and redundancy, which led us to the notion of constructive and distributed memory, dynamics, and attractor models.

To conclude we will speculate a bit about the potential insights and research topics that might be generated from applying the design principles to guide research in the field.

First, we may be able to learn a lot about memory from the synthetic methodology, i.e., from experimenting with robots. Just take Bovet's Artificial Mouse experiment, which revealed a truly surprising phenomenon. Although we have to be careful when transferring insights from robot experiments to humans or to biological systems in general, at some abstract level it is often possible to find principles that can indeed be applied to biology. The idea of off-loading part of the memory function to an accidental, neutral environmental property can in principle hold for robots, animals, and humans.

Second, in the title of this chapter we have asked the question, Where is memory? It is a question that has attracted a lot of attention. The complete-agent perspective together with the frame-of-reference idea suggests that different memory concepts such as episodic, working, semantic, and autobiographical memory—but also other psychological functions such as attention, perception, planning, problem solving, and reasoning—are simply different views on the complete agent, rather than separate "systems" that can be found in the brain. Recent brain imaging studies using fMRI (functional magnetic resonance imaging) and PET (positron emission tomography) have demonstrated, for example, that there is a strong overlap of brain activation in tasks that are assumed to involve attention, working memory, episodic memory, and consciousness (e.g., Naghavi and Nyberg, 2005); these results also support the complete agent hypothesis. Moreover, for example, fMRI studies have shown that episodic memory retrieval tasks have a strongly distributed nature and cannot be localized to one particular brain region, again suggesting that there is no "episodic memory box" inside the brain, but that the term episodic memory refers to a particular view on a set of behaviors of the complete agents—the subjects—investigated in these experiments. While the brain areas involved in behaviors related to episodic memory are distributed, there is also a certain localization, i.e., some brain areas seem to be more heavily involved in episodic memory tasks than, for example, in reading tasks. In chapter 5 we discussed the hippocampus in the context of experiments with rats' place and head-direction cells, and we pointed out that the hippocampus is believed to be central to the formation of memories. However, insights change, and recently "more and more researchers are suggesting that the role of the hippocampus has been overestimated" (Neath and Surprenant 2003, p. 195), a statement that is corroborated by recent brain imaging studies.

This backtracking makes clear that we should be careful not to overinterpret results from brain imaging studies. On the one hand, what we do see is the difference between a neutral condition (e.g., the subject has no specific task), and an experimental condition (e.g., the subject has to perform a list-learning task), and this difference is, depending on the particular method, a maximum of 5%. The remaining 95% of the activation is at the same high levels under both conditions! Naghavi and Nyberg (2005) also caution against too much enthusiasm in their extensive review article on brain imaging studies of attention, memory, and consciousness by stating that "functional neuroimaging techniques can at best specify the coincidence of regional brain activations with specific cognitive demands. These methods cannot determine which brain regions are essential for a specific cognitive process."

But where is memory, then? Neath and Surprenant: "The fundamental question of where memory is located remains unanswered. However, it seems likely that a combination of local and distributed storage will provide the ultimate solution" (2003). We would add that we may not be asking the right question here: If memory is a theoretical construct rather than a "thing," the search for it may in fact be futile. What is called memory is about change of behavior, and its underpinnings are not in the brain only. The change of behavior results from changes in brain, body (morphology, materials), and environment. So when we ask, Where is memory? we should perhaps be looking not only inside the brain but at specific relationships between the agent, its task, and its environment. Bovet's Artificial Mouse robot learns the delayed reward task—it changes its behavior in interesting ways. In order to do so it uses the red wall in the environment as scaffolding. Take away the red wall, and the robot will no longer "remember" the solution. Thus, the Artificial Mouse's "memory" in this experiment not only consists of the synaptic change in the neural network, but also includes the system-environment interaction.

Third, related to the previous point, throughout the book we have stressed the sensory-motor nature of intelligence and behavior. The tasks that are typically investigated in the field of memory research and with brain imaging techniques are so-called cognitive tasks, tasks that are somehow assumed to be happening "inside" the subject and therefore require only minimal interaction with the real world. In other words, there is no interesting kind of sensory-motor coupling necessary to perform the tasks. This is partly due to current technological limitations and partly due to the particular theoretical framework employed in memory research and in cognitive psychology in general. It would be fascinating to have mobile brain imaging technology such that recordings could be made as the subjects perform real-world tasks. Moreover, if recordings were made simultaneously, of body movement using motion capture equipment, or of physiological data using ubiquitous computing technology, interesting correlations might be discovered.

Fourth, ubiquitous computing equipment will most likely be used more extensively for memory experiments in the near future. Consider, for example, the work of the futurist Jim Gemmell of Microsoft Research: his MyLifeBits Lifetime Store (Gemmell et al., 2006), can record virtually everything recordable from a person's life—e.g., web pages viewed, telephone conversations, music, television, and physiological data—using wearables. This would make an excellent setup for studying autobiographical memory, in particular with respect to accuracy. With this material, one would have access not only to the person's recollection—and possibly other people's reports—but also to the individual's data, recorded from his or her situated perspective!

The research area of human memory is vast, and it is not possible to do justice to all the important work that has been done in the field. We have tried to bring the ideas from many pertinent fields—psychology, neuroscience, brain imaging, dynamical systems, robotics, and artificial intelligence—to bear on the study of memory, but our framework still lacks the conceptual clarity of the storehouse metaphor. Nevertheless we prefer to continue with an idea that, although vague, holds promise, rather than with one that—though conceptually clear and simple—has proved inappropriate in many respects.

Robotic Technology in Everyday Life

In October 2004, in the Hitotsubashi Conference Hall near the Imperial Park in the center of Tokyo, Yoshio Tsukio, a former Tokyo University professor, one of the leading technological visionaries in Japan, outlined some of the major problems facing humankind in the twenty-first century in his opening lecture to the conference "Living with Robots—Symbiosis of Robots and Human Beings." Two of the main challenges he pointed out were an aging population (particularly in Japan where, starting in 2020, more than 25% of the population will be over 65) and global warming. He suggested a number of ways, and a number of scientific disciplines that could be employed, for tackling these problems: information technology, nanotechnology, brain science, and what he called the "symbiosis frontier." The symbiosis frontier, which focuses on humans living together with the world of artifacts—in particular, information technology and robots—was the core topic of the conference.

Just about a month later, Takashi Matsuyama of Kyoto University organized the Second International Workshop on Man-Machine Symbiotic Systems. According to the conference Web site, "The purpose of this workshop is to discuss the latest advances in novel man-machine interaction technologies that realize multi-modal and dynamic interaction between human beings and machines." Again, the goal was to explore the possibilities of humans living in an even closer relationship with technology, specifically information technology and robots, than we do now. For many people in the West this idea is somehow uncomfortable because it implies a strong dependency of humans on technology, whereas in Japan novel technology tends to be viewed positively. To be sure, this dependency on technology has a long history, and has grown very strong over the past century: think how our lives would be different without e-mail, cell phones, television, cars, or radio. But perhaps with intelligent robotics, the relation between humans and technology will enter a qualitatively new dimension. We have already started discussing symbiosis—the smooth interaction of humans with the world of artifacts—in the context of ubiquitous computing, but we will look at it from another perspective in this chapter: how humans will relate with robots in the near future.

Our goal in this chapter is not so much to make forecasts—we leave that to others who feel more confident about predicting the future (we side with the physics Nobel laureate Niels Bohr: "It's hard to predict—especially the future.") Rather we want to demonstrate how the design principles for intelligent systems can be applied to provide some theoretical grounding to the galloping field of robotic technology. It seems that the technology of intelligent robots that has been the major focus of this book, together with the groundbreaking communication concepts of Ken Sakamura that we discussed in chapter 8, will provide the foundation for a symbiotic, man-machine society of the future.

In this chapter we will proceed as follows. First we will give an overview of the field of intelligent robotics and we will argue that robots have long become part of our lives; that it is not a question of whether they will become so or not: it has already happened. Then we will discuss a few applications where we, as normal human beings, directly encounter robotic technology in the form of specialized robots designed for household purposes. We will then switch to entertainment and pet robots and make a short digression into medical, therapeutic, and rescue robots. This is followed by a discussion of the most challenging issue in intelligent robotics: creating humanoid companion robots capable of social communication as well as facial and bodily expression. We will also look at our design principles vis-à-vis some of the most advanced robots around. We will conclude with a theoretical note on sophisticated robots as models of human or animal behavior.

11.1 Introduction: Everyday Robots

The field of intelligent robotics is enormously rich and varied, and it will not be possible to give anywhere near complete coverage. So, we have been highly selective, trying to choose representative examples illustrating important issues, and viewing current robots from the perspective of the design principles. Also, it is virtually impossible to categorize the field, because there are so many different ways of carving it up. For example, we can classify robots intuitively in terms of their seeming degree of intelligence (i.e., how diverse their behavior is and how fully they exploit their environment), or in terms of how much they resemble humans. These categories would be dominated by humanoid robots, many of which we have encountered already in the chapter on developmental robotics. Or we could classify robots according to the task they are designed for, such as industrial robots (especially manufacturing, assembly, and packaging) or service robots (mail and meal delivery, sewage pipe inspection, or assistance in homes and hospitals). Companion robots are related to service robots, but unlike service robots they not only perform household chores (cleaning dishes, vacuuming, preparing and serving meals, doing laundry) but also hold conversations, remind the person of his medication and exercise, suggest entertainment programs and outdoor activities, propose meals and offer refreshing drinks, etc. Another related class of machines are medical robots, such as prostheses (artificial limbs), orthoses, or power-assist devices (devices used for supporting or improving weak or deformed parts of the body). Companion robotics is also related to entertainment robotics, which is, interestingly, probably the oldest branch of robotics: people since the middle ages have tried to reproduce human- or animal-like behavior in machines. Famous European examples are the mechanical duck and the flute-playing robot of Jacques de Vaucanson, and the writing and drawing robot developed by Pierre Jaquet-Droz and his son Henri-Louis in the eighteenth century in La Chaux-de-Fonds in Switzerland. Both are now on exhibit at the Museum of Neuchatel, also in Switzerland. An interesting detail about Vaucanson's duck is that it was capable of picking up grains, digesting them, and getting rid of them at the end of its digestive tract. In Asia, the Karakuri Ningyo—the traditional craft of building mechanical entertainment dolls—was developed in Japan mainly during the Edo period (1603–1867) through commissions from rich merchants. The Karakuri Ningyo, like Vaucanson's creations, were purely for entertainment purposes.

To be sure, robots will—or already have—become part of our lives. Whether we accept this statement as true or not depends, of course, on what we mean by robots. Obviously there are no intelligent humanoid robots interacting with humans on a day-to-day basis yet, but devices with more and more intelligent-agent properties can be found all the time. As we made clear when we discussed ubiquitous technology and cyborgs, the term *robot* cannot—and should not—be precisely defined; still, we must have some idea about how to use it. Rather than giving a definition, it is more interesting to analyze the extent to which a given robot has agent properties and how well it conforms to the design principles.

To illustrate this point let us look at two examples of robots, industrial robots and embedded systems. Industrial robots have restricted agent capabilities because they typically have only a limited number of sensors, they do not exploit their physical environment much, and they are simply preprogrammed to perform certain tasks, such as assembling car engines from basic parts at an assembly line, mounting electronic components on a printed circuit board, or putting candy into boxes. In other words, they have little ability to exploit their morphological constraints, and their behaviors are created by a human designer rather than emerging from a developmental or evolutionary system. Embedded systems, such as air-quality monitoring systems in buildings, fuel-injection systems in cars, control systems for washing machines and other household appliances, etc. (discussed in chapter 8) are another type of robotic device. Although they do have agent characteristics in the sense that they are equipped with sensory systems and have means to influence the environment, they are less robotlike because their motor systems—and therefore their manipulation abilities—are very constrained: they do not have arms like industrial robots and they do not move like autonomous, mobile robots. Therefore, they are limited in how they can exploit the physics of the real world. Consider the difference between a wall-mounted fire detector and the relatively rich sensory-motor mechanisms of Puppy. Intuitively, the more agent characteristics embedded devices acquire, the more we consider them to be robots rather than just artifacts.

Robots and robotic devices, by any definition, are clearly on their way into more and more areas of our lives. According to World Robotics 2004, an Internet publication of the United Nations Economic Commission for Europe, there are roughly 800,000 industrial robots worldwide (about half of them in Japan), a million household service robots (mostly for vacuuming and lawn mowing), and another million entertainment and toy robots. The predictions of the report state that there will be almost 5 million robots performing domestic tasks by the end of 2007, and roughly 3 million acting as entertainers. The report also claims that there will be comparatively few (75,000) professional service robots in agriculture, professional cleaning, inspection, construction and demolition, medicine, and firefighting, and roughly 25,000 humanoid robots by the end of 2007. "Robots are taking over—can't anyone stop the robots!" proclaimed reporter John Soat in reaction to the World Robotics 2004 report in an Information Week article from 2004. We will not evaluate here the desirability of this development, but rather we will discuss various examples of existing robots in the light of our design principles for intelligent systems. We feel that if these principles are fully taken into account, our understanding of intelligence in general will be augmented and the rate at which robots are designed, manufactured, and introduced into daily life might in fact be accelerated.

11.2   Vacuum Cleaners: Roomba, Trilobite, and Similar Species

As pointed out in chapter 1, the original meaning of the word *robot* implies that they were meant to do work for humans. The Roomba, produced by Rodney Brooks's company, iRobot, and the Trilobite, manufactured by Electrolux, one of the world's largest producers of appliances, are vacuuming robots. They are reported by consumers to be extremely useful and they do a lot of work for their owners, especially those who own fur-shedding pets like cats or dogs. Roomba, when turned on via remote control, will start moving in a spiral pattern, cleaning as it goes, spending more time on dirtier spots, until it finishes its task. It will automatically return to the charging station when its battery level is too low and will go back out to clean when charged, so that it is continuously operational, just as you would expect from a self-sufficient agent. The Trilobite, although different in detail, shares some characteristics with Roomba. Both robots have important agent properties: they have some sensing abilities—they can sense dirt, find the charging station, avoid obstacles, measure the level of battery charge—and they also influence their environment, i.e., they remove dirt and they produce noise. Although these machines achieve a certain level of autonomy, the container bag for the dust is small and needs to be replaced frequently by a human operator.

Roomba has received a lot of media attention because it is looked upon as one of the first robots to be really useful in people's homes, and therefore as one that might trigger a real robot revolution. We should not underestimate the potential of these little beetle-like creatures: they will continue to improve and will become more interesting and useful over time. However, the agent characteristics of Roomba and similar robots are very limited. Their ecological niches and task environments will always remain highly confined (which is why they can be designed relatively cheaply, at least in the case of Roomba). Robots designed to perform only simple and specific cleaning tasks will not require overly complex morphologies or rich behaviors, according to the principle of ecological balance. Because Roomba and its kin are commercial products, their inner workings are not well known, so it is not clear which of the design principles they instantiate, and to what degree, so we will no longer pursue their discussion here. But it should be mentioned that for the first time we have mobile robots sharing their living space with humans and performing useful day-to-day tasks.

11.3   Entertainment Robots

Although Roomba and Trilobite can be very entertaining, they are designed to be useful. Entertainment robots, on the other hand, have value by their mere existence. A host of entertainment robots have been developed, with mixed results, and it seems worthwhile to look at them from the perspective of the design principles. Although they are extremely interesting, we will not discuss very simple toys like Tamagochi (virtual pets that grow and live inside simple, very small hand-held computers) or Furby (an animatronic toy) because their agent characteristics are so limited. Instead we will focus on more complex ones like AIBO, which is a representative example among many entertainment robots.

The Pet Robot AIBO

"Remarkably intelligent, highly entertaining, and extraordinarily skillful," runs the slogan on Sony AIBO's home page. And indeed, looking at the highly varied behavior of this roughly 20-centimeter-high, doglike robot one cannot help but be very impressed: it recognizes objects in its environment, it moves around in interesting ways, and it interacts with the user in an engaging manner. For the most part, users find these interactions pleasant and enjoyable, and so we can expect this style of robot to become increasingly popular. AIBO was born in 1999 as "the first ever entertainment robot" and has since been successively improved and reached an impressive level of sophistication. Let us briefly view AIBO from the perspective of the design principles.

AIBO has about ten degrees of freedom of actuation and a number of sensors: a color camera, infrared sensors, touch sensors on the back of the head, on the back, under the chin, on the paws, as well as stereo microphones on each side of the head, and there is a powerful processor. Perhaps the easiest approach is to discuss AIBO in comparison to Puppy, as both are four-legged robots. The advanced version of Puppy has pressure sensors on its feet like the sensors on the paws of AIBO. Puppy has three degrees of freedom on each leg, but the kinds of movements it can perform are much less sophisticated than those of AIBO. However, because of Puppy's "artificial muscles"—the springs—it can better exploit the dynamics of interaction with the environment for rapid locomotion: Puppy can move considerably faster than AIBO. In this respect, Puppy performs much more morphological computation in its motor system than AIBO. In other words, the motion patterns of Puppy's legs are much more complex than the commands being sent to the motors; AIBO's legs, on the other hand, are completely controlled by the microprocessor. When AIBO moves, it generates sensory stimulation on its paws, in its acceleration sensor, in its camera, and in its "ear" sensors, and this stimulation, especially from the feet, might potentially be exploited to adjust its gait pattern. Puppy, with its very simple control and its morphology with artificial muscles, is therefore more ecologically balanced than AIBO. AIBO's behavioral diversity, on the other hand, is decidedly higher: it can perform more and different kinds of behaviors. AIBO does not make substantial use of its niche because its body dynamics, although it has many degrees of freedom, are hardly exploited: all the movements are preprogrammed, self-stabilization is not used, and control is top-down. All this requires a lot of computation. Since it has a varied sensory setup—cameras, IR sensors, acceleration sensors, audio sensors—it can, for example, compensate for loss of vision by exploiting its infrared sensors, at least for obstacle avoidance—there is much potential for AIBO to apply the redundancy principle: AIBO could be enabled to continue functioning even when it loses some of its sensor channels. It should be clear from this discussion that there is no obvious "better" or "worse"; the utility of a robot depends on the goals pursued by the designers. Puppy, on the one hand, is designed for rapid locomotion and self-stabilization, whereas AIBO should provide entertainment for children (and perhaps even adults). Even if naturalistic locomotion isn't the primary goal, the design principles could be used to greatly enhance the capabilities of entertainment robots. For example, AIBO's gaits, which are somewhat unnatural though they might seem cute to some, could be improved by exploiting morphological computation.[1]

The reason that the most advanced robots—in terms of complying with the design principles for intelligent systems—are in the entertainment domain is that it does not matter too much if they malfunction or break down. A breakdown might even be considered entertaining, whereas robots designed for useful tasks must function reliably, for example in medical applications, in factory environments, or during rescue operations, even if their actions are routine and dull.

The Therapeutic Robot Paro

A few years ago, the award-winning roboticist Takanori Shibata from Japan's gigantic AIST research institute in Tsukuba Science City, about an hour's trip from Tokyo, had a great idea. More to the point, he combined two great ideas. It is well known, he reckoned, that pets improve people's moods, especially residents of homes for the elderly or children in hospitals. In addition, he surmised that if robots can entertain people, and entertainment is generally considered beneficial for people's moods, then we should be able to employ robots for entertaining the people most in need of some cheering up. Moreover, because of hygienic considerations such as danger of infection or allergies, real pets often cannot be used for this purpose, so artificial pets, in the form of entertainment robots, might in fact be the solution. With his characteristic determination he pursued his goal. Starting at the MIT Artificial Intelligence Laboratory he designed and built a simple tail-wagging robot and tested, together with psychologists, the effect the tail-wagging had on people: despite the incredible simplicity of the robot, the tail made it seem relatively natural, and evoked positive emotions in many of the subjects.

One of the problems with a robot like AIBO is that it is intended to resemble a dog, and since most of us are very familiar with the behavior of dogs, we know what sorts of behaviors and reactions to expect from them. So if a doglike robot doesn't act like a dog, we are quick to notice it. According to Shibata this is one of the reasons AIBO has not achieved true popularity. Shibata himself, earlier on, had developed an entertainment robot in the form of a cat, Tama, which was, he admits, somewhat of a failure: people were frustrated at the reactions of the cat because it failed to fulfill their expectations. So he looked for an animal that everybody knows and likes, but whose behavior is not so well known, so he developed a baby seal robot, Paro. And Paro has turned out be a considerable success (see figure 11.1a).

Paro has achieved world fame as a cuddly little creature, with two degrees of freedom in the neck, one for each of its two front and two rear flippers, and independent movements of the eyelids. Paro is covered with white fur, produces certain noises, reacts to touch on its head, and moves in engaging ways. It is also equipped with light sensors, microphones, and touch sensors. Whiskers act as additional touch sensors similar to those of the Artificial Mouse, discussed in the previous chapter. Like AIBO, it is equipped with a speech recognition system. But Paro has no vision, only simple light sensors, and no infrared sensors. Shibata was not only passionate about his project, but also systematic. He put his

Figure 11.1
Gentle robots. (*a*) The seal baby robot Paro, by Takanori Shibata, which is used in homes for the elderly and hospitals as a stress- and boredom-relieving tool. (*b*) The attractive female robot Actroid.

robot through much careful testing. Residents in a home for the elderly could volunteer to participate in experiments with Paro: they could play with the robot twice a week for about an hour, over a period of several months. He then gave them a questionnaire to assess their subjective mood states, and he found that those who had participated in the experiment rated themselves considerably higher in terms of well-being than those who had not. Shibata also had physiological measurements taken, such as urine and blood tests, and, to his great surprise, the health of the participants was also improved. Impressive! We believe that because the Japanese are enthusiastic about robots anyhow, they will welcome them into their daily lives to a much greater extent than will Europeans or Americans. Nonetheless, Shibata, like a kind of missionary, travels all over the world to spread the word about Paro. He has visited exhibitions, and has convinced managers of homes for the elderly and hospitals to try using Paro as an entertainment and therapeutic tool. Overall, the reaction has been overwhelmingly positive, and Shibata even received a design award from Japan's prime minister.

When we asked Shibata why Paro is not used in homes for the elderly and children's hospitals all over the world, he pointed out that the robots are now for sale via the Internet and sold worldwide, and soon, so he hopes, everyone will be using them: according to Shibata, it is only a matter of time. Of course, technical improvements will be necessary, but the basic idea is there. What needs to be investigated from a theoretical perspective is whether the beneficial effects—and there is no doubt that many of them must be attributed to Paro—are in fact due to the intelligent agent properties of the robot, or whether they result from the introduction of something new and interesting into the relatively uneventful lives of elderly home residents and long-term hospital patients. Shibata is convinced that Paro, although much less sophisticated than AIBO, faces the brighter future because of its fundamentally different design. And he plays very cleverly on McFarland's idea of "anthropomorphization, the incurable disease": people warm to the robot because the furry, cuddly, cute appearance causes them to attribute lifelike properties to this admittedly simple device.

Shibata is also exploiting the three-constituents principle in smart ways: he focuses not only on the design of the robot itself but on its task environment and on its potential interactions with people. For example, he is capitalizing on the fact that people will do things with it, stroke it, put it on their laps, talk to it, etc. So, perhaps the robot itself does not have to do all that much to achieve the design goal of entertaining the owners. If the morphology and the materials are chosen properly—and the baby seal–like shape and the fur seem to play an essential role—they will do much of the "work" as people interact with it. Or very broadly speaking, the robot's body will perform morphological computation by exploiting the interaction with its environment. Thus, depending on the robot's task environment, maximizing its autonomy may not always be the best strategy.

Shibata's goal has never been to develop a truly intelligent robot; he was more concerned with the sorts of emotions robots could evoke in humans. And his project has been successful. Only the future will tell whether this approach will ultimately pan out, but there is a lot of evidence that pets are a great comfort to elderly people, so maybe pet robots will be as well. Shibata also has no plans to replace human caretakers with robots, but for him it was always obvious that pet robots could support people emotionally, in addition to family and caregivers. The idea of using robots for therapeutic purposes—to support the elderly, the physically challenged, and the ill—has inspired many engineers all over the world. Developing robots is fun, and if they are useful to those in need, developing them is even more rewarding.

11.4 Therapeutic, Medical, and Rescue Robots

Many researchers besides Shibata have pursued the idea of developing robots for medical and therapeutic purposes. The range of applications is wide: there are teddy bears that collect physiological data (pulse rate, blood pressure, skin resistance, blood sugar level) from patients; devices that carry heavy bags and support elderly people as they go on errands; robots that help people get out of bed, take a shower, and go to the toilet; prostheses that can be controlled directly by the person's neural system; robots that assist in surgical operations; and so on. Again, the purpose of this kind of application is not so much to replace human beings but rather to provide as much autonomy to the user as possible. It is so much more convenient, for example, to use an elevator than having someone carry you up the stairs! The grand old man of Japanese robotics, Hirochika Inoue, a former professor of engineering of the University of Tokyo and director of the huge Japanese Humanoid Robotics Program that we mentioned earlier, sees this not only as a physical issue, but a mental one. If people can maintain their autonomy—if they can move independently without the help of others—this will free their minds. This is an interesting thought that might change the predominantly negative attitude of Europeans and Americans toward this type of technology.

Our purpose is not to outline the social implications of robotics, but rather to understand how best to design intelligent systems. And in many domains of robotics, intelligent systems may not be the primary goal. For example, in medical robotics—precision surgery would probably be a better term—what is needed is high-precision control and teleoperation rather than autonomy or other agent characteristics. To be sure, we probably do not want surgical robots that come up with new procedures on their own; rather, we want these robots—these devices—to do exactly what we tell them to do. That said, however, there are many applications for intelligent robots in the medical domain. For example, humanoid robots are used to bring medication to patients, to remind them when to take what pills, to show them the exercises they should be doing, to support them when taking a walk, and to entertain them when nothing is happening. Human-friendly robot companions are used not only in households but also in hospitals and homes for the elderly, and such uses are bound to become more common.

Another area of real-world robotics, related to the medical domain, is search and rescue. Hours after hearing about the attack on the World Trade Center on September 11, 2001, the engineering professor Robin Murphy at the University of South Florida drove the eighteen hours to Manhattan with three of her graduate students and about eight different robots. Although they did not directly find any survivors, they were able to send their robots into holes that were too small or dangerous for humans or dogs. Several other research groups with their robots were called in to the disaster site, including Tom Frost and his team from iRobot, the same company that produces the Roomba. iRobot's ATRV2 robots, used at the World Trade Center site, are another example of biologically inspired robots. The ATRV2 is like a kangaroo, in that a larger robot carries a set of smaller "baby" robots in its pouch, and only sends out the smaller robots to crawl down into small holes to search for victims when the "mother" robot can go no further.

Six years earlier, in 1995, a Richter Scale 7.2 earthquake—the Kobe earthquake—hit south-central Japan, killing over 5,000 people and injuring more than 26,000. This further motivated Japanese researchers to design and build robots that could help people. One result was the development by the Tokyo Fire Department's Fire Science Laboratories of a line of robots that can walk up stairs or climb walls. One model has arms to pick up human casualties. So it seems fitting that the most recent international workshop on safety, security, and rescue robotics was held in Kobe in 2005. Shigeo Hirose (whom we know as the one who started "snake robotics," so to speak) and Kan Yoneda are developing rugged snake robots in their joint laboratory at the Tokyo Institute of Technology. The task of these robots is not so much to transport or treat disaster victims, but to use their long, narrow bodies to move through the thin cracks and holes at a disaster site. This is yet another example of how careful design of a robot's body can allow it to better achieve the desired task. However, to the best of our knowledge these Japanese rescue robots are still in the experimental stages and have not yet been used for actual search and rescue operations (Davids, 2002).

Almost all of the rescue robots used in actual disaster sites lack autonomy: they are controlled remotely by a human operator and so the concept of behavioral diversity cannot really be applied to them; the diversity comes from the operators rather than the robots themselves. Thus we would not intuitively consider most rescue robots to be highly intelligent at this point. But then, the truly hard research questions in the field concern the technologies of moving within disaster sites while performing rescue tasks, and so intelligence has been a minor issue. But once the basic technological problems of search and rescue robots have been solved, it may be of interest to also augment their agent characteristics, i.e., to add more sensory and autonomous action capabilities. Given the speed of development we can expect rescue robots to become part of our lives in the not too distant future.

Aside from the snakelike rescue robots and petlike entertainment robots, another class of robots has already entered our environment, although many of us have not actually seen one "in the flesh" before—the humanoid robots.

11.5 Humanoid Companion Robots

We have encountered humanoids already in many places throughout this book, in particular in chapter 5 where we discussed developmental robotics. In this section we will look at a few particularly attractive instances from this "species." The terms *humanoid* and *android* are used for a wide variety of robots, from doll-like toys to sophisticated robots such as Asimo, H-7, or Qrio. We have already discussed a number of robots that resemble—to a greater or lesser extent—animals rather than humans, e.g., Puppy, Paro, and AIBO, but there are many more in this class that we will not list here. Let us now look briefly at some robots from the large collection of humanoids, which are also used mainly for entertainment (although some are employed for research purposes as well). There is Hoap-2, a 30-centimeter-tall martial arts humanoid robot produced by Fujitsu Corporation (Japan); FII-RII of Takara Toys (one of Japan's largest toy manufacturers), a stylized robot that can connect to the Internet so that its owner can remotely monitor his or her home; and iRobot's "My Real Baby," which resembles a real baby and mimics many of its behaviors. The Utah-based Sarcos corporation builds high-performance human-sized robots, some of which are remote controlled; and the awesomely realistic Marilyn Monroe animatronic robot was invented by Shunichi Mizuno of Cybot Corporation (Japan). The attractive talking robot Actroid by Kokoro Dreams (Japan), built jointly with Osaka University, is probably the most lifelike humanoid robot today (figure 11.1b). And then there is the BN-7 entertainment robot by Bandai Corporation, the Japanese toy company made famous by their widely popular Tamagochi toys; the Japanese computer giant NEC's Papero, which is billed as a "friendly walking, talking, personal robot with human-like characteristics"; the "Hyperkinetic Humanoid H-2 Robot" by Faustex Systems Corporation, a martial arts robot that is supposed to be faster than any human; and many others. We find the robots in the above list particularly interesting, either because their designs—explicitly or implicitly—take the principles of intelligent systems into account, or because they have in fact been tested over extended periods of time in environments with humans. We will not discuss each of these robots in turn; the list is given to provide a feel for the diversity of humanoid robots that are out there. Instead, we will focus on only a few: the communication robot Robovie, developed jointly by Osaka University and ATR, a famous research institution in Kyoto; the flute-playing robot WF-4; and the HRP-2, which has been designed specifically for human-robot interaction and for supporting people in hospitals and homes.

If we are designing a companion robot, it should definitely have some capacity with regard to culture, entertainment, and music. Waseda University of Tokyo, one of the leading universities in humanoid robotics, has led the way in the development of music-playing robots. In the early 1980s, researchers there began working on the Wabot-2, the organ-playing robot that we mentioned in chapter 5, which was completed in 1984. The task of the Wabot-2 was to play a keyboard instrument, since an artistic activity such as playing an organ or a piano ought to require some amount of humanlike intelligence and dexterity. With a camera in its head, Wabot-2 could read normal musical scores and play them if they were of an intermediate level of difficulty; it (or he?) could perform up to 15 keystrokes per second. It could also accompany a singer, which requires considerable interaction skills: the robot had to "listen" and adapt to the singer's rhythm and pitch. Wabot-2 was certainly a milestone in the history of humanoid robotics, as the kinds of skills it exhibited are normally considered indicative of a substantial level of intelligence. However, no one would claim that the Wabot-2 possessed human-level intelligence. Sensory-motor coordination served an important role in its playing, but there was relatively little self-generated sensory stimulation. The robot's hands were dexterous, but the movements of its body and thus the sensory stimulation generated through its behavior were quite limited. Because the task was relatively constrained, however, this did not matter.

Musical robots enjoy a long history. Pierre Jaquet-Droz and his son Henri-Louis developed an organ-playing robot in the eighteenth century in Switzerland. However, the organ that the robot was able to play was specifically designed for it, whereas Wabot-2 could, essentially, play any kind of organ. Thus Wabot-2 had richer behaviors and was more adaptive than these historical robots; it exhibited more diversity and compliance. Because of its ability to play along—to interact—with a singer, Wabot-2 can also be considered a true milestone in the development of a "personal robot" or robot companion.

Very recently one of the leaders in humanoid robotics, Atsuo Takanishi, engaged in the development of a new class of music-playing robots, the robot flutist WF-4. Takanishi is at the same time a visionary and a practitioner: he not only has big ideas, he also quickly turns them into practical applications. For example, realizing that one of the main limitations of wheelchairs is that their ecological niche is, in essence, limited to flat surfaces, he built a walking chair together with the leading Japanese robotics company Tmsuk, with the goal of enlarging these devices' ecological niche.

But back to robot "musicians." Just like robots that can play the organ, flute-playing devices have their origins in the eighteenth century. Jacques de Vaucanson, after becoming famous for his mechanical duck, developed a sophisticated flute-playing robot as well as a drummer, but again, the flute and the drum were made specifically for the robot. Let us now look at WF-4 in more detail. The technological makeup of this robot is awe-inspiring, and in its relevant parts it is highly anthropomorphic. There are two "lungs"—two cylinders that hold roughly the same amount of air as the lungs of an adult male; there is a neck with four degrees of freedom to allow for humanlike head movements; there are two hands with fingers that together total twelve degrees of freedom; it can open and close the valves of the flute up to eight times per second; and there is a three-degrees-of-freedom lip mechanism to shape the beam of outgoing air, which is essential to creating sound with the flute. And finally there is a vibration mechanism so that the robot can reproduce vibrato, an essential part of any accomplished flute performance. There is a musical performance system which includes a MIDI interface so that WF-4 can play, for example, an entire quartet. As the Wabot-2 organ-playing robot could accompany a human singer, WF-4 can play along with a human flutist. For this purpose there are a number of interface sensors. A microphone is used to pick up the flutist's playing, but there are also several sensors attached to the (human) flutist: an acceleration sensor detects the person's arm movements; another sensor measures his stomach contractions; and another is embedded in conductive rubber on the ground to measure his foot motions. Interestingly, it seems that a greater emphasis is placed on the sensors in the robot's environment than on the sensors placed on or in the robot itself.

Before going through some of the design principles as they apply to WF-4, let us consider its agent properties. Of course, the robot is subject to the laws of physics; in this case, the properties of air are of particular relevance. The agent is definitely affecting its environment through its behavior in interesting ways by producing pressure waves that, when they interact with the environment—the flute—produce audible, and hopefully pleasant, sounds. WF-4 is definitely a complex dynamical system, and there are many attractor states corresponding to the tune played on the flute: air blown through the flute sets up vibrations that settle into attractor states corresponding to particular sounds. If the robot changes the air flow or moves its fingers, the vibrations change, producing a new sound. Moreover, there is a truly ingenious way in which WF-4 performs morphological computation: the morphological properties of its lips—their material and shape—and the material properties of the vibrato mechanism are exploited to produce the proper air beam. In this sense the robot exploits, at least to some extent, ecological balance, i.e., the fact that the materials and morphology provide control properties.

While WF-4 does exploit ecological balance, other design principles are applied to a much lesser degree. For example, sensory-motor coordination that leads to structured sensory stimulation could potentially be used. One could argue that because the robot holds the flute and puts it to its lips, it could potentially produce sensory stimulation that it could then exploit to adjust the shape of its lips and the air flow. Clearly, hearing what one plays and sensing the vibrations produced is one of the most basic mechanisms for learning how to play an instrument, but learning was not the goal in this case. And, so far as we can tell, WF-4 does not listen to its own music or sense its own actions. With respect to the developmental and evolutionary design principles, all of the processes that WF-4 exhibits take place in the "here and now." Takanishi and his coworkers wanted to understand and build the actual mechanisms themselves, rather than to use learning or evolutionary methods to design them. And they did a wonderful job at that: the music WF-4 produces is enchanting. With respect to diversity-compliance, there is little exploitation of the robot's ecological niche, though as we have mentioned, it does make use of the dynamical properties of air. While there is a lot of behavioral diversity, in the sense that the robot can essentially play any musical piece, even the high-speed "Flight of the Bumblebee" by Nicolay Rimsky-Korsakov, it has to be programmed to perform these pieces. But the diversity of WF-4's behavior could be easily expanded by giving it score-reading abilities like those of the Wabot-2.

The intention of the WF-4 project was to explore a single ability, music playing, rather than to develop a complete robot companion with many abilities. From the complete-agent perspective it would be interesting to investigate the relation between several abilities, such as playing music and speaking, within, for example, a developmental context: what sensory-motor capacities need to be in place before an agent can perform these difficult tasks? The lungs and the lip mechanism might also, at least partially, be used for speech and facial expression. There are already several robots capable of speech, and in some of them the actual vocal tract is physically modeled for producing sound, rather than using a digital sound chip. What kind of developmental mechanisms would allow the robot to learn how to use its lungs, vocal tract, and lips to produce speech or to create music? It appears that the developmental design principles could be usefully applied in this context. For example, it seems clear that the "development as an incremental process" principle will come into play here: the robot would probably first have to learn how to produce basic sounds using simple movements, and only when it has succeeded at that should it begin to use more and more degrees of freedom in its lips and fingers to produce subtle changes in tone.

Because emotional expression is also important for playing the flute, there could be an interesting transfer of what has been learned from building musical robots to the creation of facial expression robots where emotions play a focal role (we will discuss this class of robots below). For example, WF-4 might be able to use its lips to communicate happiness or sadness. Another question that immediately comes to mind is whether WF-4, because it knows how to play one musical instrument, could learn how to play another one more quickly, as is the case in humans. Again, this relates to the developmental design principles: learning one skill should help bootstrap the learning of another. Musical robots have been developed for a number of instruments: MIT's Matt Williamson further elaborated the Cog robot so it could play the drums (Williamson, 1999); Toyota Motor Company has developed a trumpet-playing robot; and the young roboticist Koji Shibuya is building a violin-playing robot, in which *kansei*, the Japanese word for sensitivity and feeling, plays an essential role. From the complete-agent perspective, the question also arises as to what extent the ability to walk and move in complex ways and the ability to produce speech—and the large variety of sensory-motor competences required for these abilities—are essential for learning how to play the flute. This kind of consideration is rarely taken into account but is immediately obvious from a complete agent perspective. And this brings us, as so often, back to McFarland's anthropomorphization warning: the fact that WF-4 displays certain admittedly impressive skills does not imply that it has other humanlike abilities as well.

Before we go on to robots that have social skills, let us briefly inspect some other famous humanoids: Asimo, Qrio, HRP-2, and Cogniron. We have encountered Asimo a number of times in this book. Originally the main goal for this robot was to develop walking behavior, but now, as its walking has substantially improved, other behaviors have been included, as discussed in chapter 3 (waving, carrying packages, walking up and down stairs, dancing, shaking hands, conversation, visual abilities such as recognizing faces, connecting to the Internet, etc.), increasing its potential as a companion robot. Qrio, Sony's version of a humanoid although only 58 cm tall, is more designed for entertainment than for doing household chores, but it has, generally speaking, similar characteristics and it can exhibit a wide range of behaviors. The HRP-2, 154 cm tall and weighing 58 kg, one of the HRP robots developed during the Japanese Humanoid Robotics Program (thus its name), was designed and built by Kawada Industries. One of the main design goals of the HRP robots was to cooperate with humans. For example, they should be able to assist people in hospitals, show them how to do their exercises, walk around with them, talk to them, and bring them their meals. HRP-2 has some special and very impressive skills: it can stand up again when it falls down, and, together with a human, it can carry a large panel, a delicate cooperation task that requires sophisticated sensory-motor skills.

Even though all three robots, Asimo, Qrio, and HRP-2, exhibit considerable behavioral diversity and therefore conform to one part of diversity-compliance, they only exploit their environments to a very limited extent in order to achieve those tasks. For example, to date they do not exploit passive dynamics. Nor has the idea of morphological computation—of exploiting material properties, by using artificial muscles to take over part of the control—been incorporated (yet) and so most of their behaviors are actually preprogrammed. But given the technological challenges involved in developing humanoid robots, the achievements are truly impressive. Still, there is a long way to go before we will have companion robots that truly deserve the name. They will not only need to improve their sensory-motor, but also their social interaction skills.

While the origins of companion robots have been almost exclusively Japanese, the "wave" has recently reached America and Europe. For example, the Cogniron project—the name stands for "cognitive robot companion"—is also focused on building humanoid robots capable of sharing their living space and interacting naturally with humans. Cogniron is a large, European Union–supported project, and about ten research laboratories from all over Europe are working together on this initiative. The stated goal of the project is to study what perceptual, reasoning, and learning skills an embodied robot must have in order to function in human-centered environments: an ambitious goal indeed! It is exciting to contemplate how their robots will conform to the design principles and what such robots can teach us about intelligence.

11.6 Robots Capable of Social Communication

Robots with social skills are what visionaries such as Atsuo Takanishi (WF-4), Hirochika Inoue (H-7), Hiroshi Ishiguro (Robovie), Fumio Hara and Hiroshi Kobayashi (the "face robot"), and companies such as Honda (Asimo), Toyota (Partner Robot), Sony (Qrio), Kawada (HRP-2), and Kokoro Dreams (Actroid) have in mind when they develop their research programs. To what extent social skills can be realized on robots with very limited sensory and motor systems is an open question. Language is a crucial part of social communication, and the exclusively human capacity for natural-language processing may in fact require an enormously complex sensory-motor system to provide the proper grounding for the rich conceptual structures that can be communicated (this relates back to the symbol grounding problem discussed in chapter 5). To what extent this is the case is an open question that is being studied in the field of evolution of language. Many robots talk, i.e., they have some basic conversational skills, but for the most part these abilities are entirely ungrounded and do not relate to the basic embodiment of the robot itself, i.e., they are programmed into the robot rather than acquired through its own sensory and motor system. In addition, in general, the capacity of robots for verbal communication is very limited. Even pre-programmed, highly limited language competence impresses people, but this is due to our universal weakness for anthropomorphization. This phenomenon has already been demonstrated in the 1960s by Josef Weizenbaum's well-known computer program Eliza (Weizenbaum, 1966). Eliza, a virtual psychiatrist, worked on the basis of elementary pattern-matching algorithms that would rearrange the sentences people typed in and output them as questions, so that the user got the impression that the program understood them, even though the term *understanding* is clearly inappropriate here by anybody's standards. To what extent robots will need to have sensory-motor abilities that resemble those of humans in order to develop humanlike natural language abilities is still an open research issue.

Robovie, the famous communication robot specifically designed for interaction with humans, was developed by Hiroshi Ishiguro of Osaka University and members of the ATR research laboratories in Kyoto. The name "Robovie" has been adopted from the French word "vie," meaning life, so Robovie literally translates to "robot life." Although the intention was to develop a humanoid—the shape of the torso is very roughly human, and the robot has two arms, a head, vision and speech systems, and "ears" (microphones)—it also makes use of technologies not available to nature, such as wheels for locomotion, an omnidirectional camera, sonar sensors for determining distance, RFID tag readers, and a wireless connection to the Internet.

The recognition and expression of feelings has been a major design goal in many humanoid robotics projects. The underlying assumption is that these two abilities will be required for smooth interaction between robots and humans, a hypothesis that is still awaiting long-term testing. On a routine basis, humans interact very smoothly with machines, such as our cars, our stereos, and household appliances, and we seem to be perfectly happy that they are machines with no emotions whatsoever. Testing how humans interact with socially skilled robots over extended periods of time is necessary, as an experiment by the ATR researchers in a grammar school in Japan clearly demonstrated. When Robovie was first introduced at the school, the students interacted with it frequently, but after two weeks the interaction frequencies were significantly lower, a phenomenon that we have already discussed in the context of entertainment robots in general. Often, the novelty of a complex device wears off quickly, especially if the device does not learn and exhibit new behaviors.

Let us again try to apply some of the design principles to these robots. One of the principles that the Robovie developers relied on, whether explicitly or implicitly, was the three-constituents principle: rather than putting everything inside the robot, they modified the robot's environment, thus exploiting environmental scaffolding effects in original ways. For example, by putting RFID tags into the environment and onto students, Robovie could deal with groups of students crowding around it, something that would have been hard to cope with using vision, audition, and touch only. In this sense, it also complies with the principle of cheap design: technologies placed in the environment often allow the robots themselves to be much simpler. Placing artifacts and sensors on humans, rather than just on robots, brings us back to cyborgs: perhaps robots in the future will be better able to interact with humans if humans wear—or contain—technology.

This idea also combines the synthetic methodology with the goal of studying life as it could be: new forms of "life," or at least new types of interaction partners, will provide many new possibilities for contact and communication (see also our discussion of ubiquitous computing in chapter 8). The redundancy principle also applies to Robovie: the RFID tags placed on the students provide partially overlapping functionality with the vision-based face-recognition system, and perhaps with the speech recognition system as well. We will not discuss the other design principles here, because they do not strongly apply to Robovie's current design. Generally speaking, designing a robot for interaction may turn out to be simpler than designing a solitary robot because properties of interaction can be exploited and the participants can provide scaffolding for each other's actions: if a human asks a specific question, it shapes what kinds of answers the robot should provide and vice versa. This idea of conversation as a scaffolding tool is inspired by Simon Garrod's paper, "Why Is Conversation So Easy?" (Garrod and Pickering, 2004), in which he argues that the thought processes of both participants are mutually aligned and supported by conversation, thus making it much easier than, for example, giving a speech.

11.7   Robots Capable of Facial and Bodily Expression

Body posture, gestures, and especially the face play a crucial role in communication. For this reason, recognizing faces and facial expression have become important research topics in the field of intelligent robotics. Robotics projects on facial expression started in the early 1990s with the construction of the "face robot" by Fumio Hara (whom we mentioned in chapter 7 as the coiner of the term *morphofunctional machine*) and his student Hiroshi Kobayashi. The "face robot" is a robot head with 24 degrees of freedom, capable of a large variety of facial expressions, including the so-called basic emotions: happiness, sadness, disgust, anger, surprise, and fear. The face robot's expressions are based on the Facial Action Coding System (FACS) developed by the psychologists Paul Ekman and Wallace Friesen at the University of California at San Francisco in the 1980s. Because facial muscles cannot be individually innervated, FACS uses the concept of so-called action units, i.e., groups of muscles that act together to produce an expression. A wonderful illustration of the face robot can be found on the cover page of the book *Robo Sapiens*, by Peter Menzel and Faith d'Aluisio. Early on, Hara and his students realized that the material properties of the robot's face would be essential for realizing realistic expressions. In human facial expression, the facial tissue itself provides much of the underlying machinery, in addition to the facial muscles. For example, in order to produce a smile, only very few action units are necessary, and the rest is taken care of by morphological computation, so to speak. Using the FACS system as a design basis was a clever move, as it provided a guide for how to control the robot: in order to produce a full set of expressions, many of the required action units from the human face were reproduced using the actuators in the robot. But note that action units work only because they exploit the material properties of facial tissue. Thus the face robot is a nice example of the principle of ecological balance: not only the actuators and controllers for the robot were taken into account, but also the properties of the face material.

But the face robot is not a complete agent: it is only a head with no body, arms, or legs; it was meant to be a case study in facial expression only. The Waseda "Eye" robot (which was specifically developed for facial expression) and Actroid have, in addition to a head capable of facial expression, a torso and arms that they can use for making gestures. In both cases, much attention has been paid to materials, and Actroid uses artificial muscles in the form of pneumatic actuators, which substantially adds to the realism of its facial expressions. Actroid has an additional feature that is important in social interaction: it (or she?) is very attractive, an attribute that may play an increasing role in future humanoid robotics (see figure 11.1b).

The social communication and facial expression robot Kismet (Breazeal, 2002) that we introduced in chapter 4, is an odd-looking, puppetlike creature that also consists only of a head. Nevertheless, in addition to a set of basic reflexes, it is endowed with a sophisticated model of human emotions and emotional expression. Recall from chapter 4 that the collection of simple reflexes—turning toward loud noises, tracking slowly moving objects, retracting the head when something enters its "personal space," getting "bored" when an activity lasts too long (habituation)—which are coordinated largely through the interaction with the environment, make it behave in ways that resemble social competence to a surprising extent—a nice illustration of the principle of parallel, loosely coupled processes. In addition, it can express the basic emotions of anger, happiness, surprise, etc., and many mixtures of these, which makes its repertory of facial expressions relatively diverse and realistic. The facial expressions are even more convincing because they arise from the robot's current social interaction, and it is known that the ability to recognize emotions in facial expression is highly context-sensitive, i.e., it depends on the participant's current interaction. This fact is also exploited by Kismet: it can "count on" the fact that the people it interacts with are aware of the social context and so they will "recognize" the proper emotion in Kismet even if its means of expressing them are relatively crude (it has much fewer degrees of freedom in the face than humans). For example, if there is a sudden loud noise, the likely emotions will be surprise or fear. Once again, in the spirit of morphological computation, aspects of the task are off-loaded into the environment—in this case the social context provides information—thus the process of displaying the proper facial expression is greatly simplified.

Most people cannot help but to fall into the trap of anthropomorphization when they come into contact with Kismet. This raises the serious question of whether human social behavior might not largely be the result of simple, reflexlike behavioral rules rather than sophisticated cognitive processes. How do we know that what goes on in humans during social interaction is so much more advanced or high-level than what goes on in Kismet? The hypothesis that behavior might be largely controlled by simple reflexes is, as we have already mentioned, corroborated by Simon Garrod's idea of mutual alignment in conversation, and

by the psychologist John Bargh's deliberations on "the unbearable automaticity of being" (Bargh and Chartrand, 1999), in which he argues that
our social actions are actually driven by automatic reflexes much more
than we would think or would like to think. To be sure, reflexes certainly
do not explain all of human behavior, but it is nevertheless amazing, and
perhaps disconcerting to some, how robot behavior that looks very realistic, sophisticated, and social can be achieved in very simple ways.

11.8   A Theoretical Note

In this chapter we have described several robots that look like humans
or animals, or mimic some specific behaviors like playing music, holding
a conversation, or expressing emotion using facial expressions. As engineers we could be happy with these accomplishments, which are indeed
impressive, but as scientists we are also interested in what we can learn
from all of these unbelievably rich and diverse developments. So we may
want to ask to what extent the humanoid or animal-like robots that we
have seen can actually be used as models of humans or animals. Take,
for example, a robot that mimics human walking, like the passive
dynamic walker we encountered in chapter 4. Now, there is a fundamental difference between an abstract model of human walking—e.g., a
model of the dynamics of the neuromuscular system of the human—and
a physical robot that has to walk in the real world. While the abstract
model is only about humans, the real robot has its own intrinsic dynamics, which, because of the different morphology, may in fact deviate significantly from those of humans. The passive dynamic walker has oddly
shaped, wide feet, and its arms are attached immediately to the hip. The
robot, in order to achieve walking, must comply with its own dynamics,
not those of a human. As we know from our discussion of the lamprey,
the dynamics of the central pattern generators must be tuned to the
dynamics of the animal's body. This implies that we cannot simply transfer models of human neural systems, such as what is known about control
of walking, to humanoid robots, and we cannot directly draw inferences
about human neural control from control architectures that work well
on humanoid robots. In this sense, what we can say about human walking
directly may indeed be limited. However, we can say a lot about general
principles of behavior (e.g., about the dynamics of locomotion), and
these general principles apply to artifacts as well as to humans. And for
a general theory of intelligence, it is those abstract principles that we are
after. Two examples of such abstract principles in the case of locomotion

are the exploitation of the passive forward swing of the leg during walking, and the elastic properties of the muscle-tendon system.

A similar case can be made for emotions and facial expression. In humans and animals, emotions and facial expression are tightly coupled to their specific embodiment (the shape of the face, the facial tissue, the action units) and physiology (limbic system, hormones, arousal system, pain and pleasure). Also, the facial expressions should correspond to some sort of attractor state of the joint physical-neural system, in other words to the particular dynamics of the facial expression system. Again, this is obvious and unproblematic. The trouble only starts when we use robots as models of human expression of emotion. It is important to keep the question in mind of what we can learn by implementing models of emotional expression on robots. What we can learn is, for example, that if we focus on the control of facial expression by exploiting material properties, we can achieve realistic expressions with relatively simple control. What we can also learn is how people react to robots that can display facial expressions (which is, of course, a very different story). What we cannot learn, simply by studying what works in robots, is how humans control facial expression. Also, if we transfer models of human emotional expression directly to robots, the neural control will certainly not match the dynamics of the robotic system in terms of its physical dynamics, and therefore the expressions and/or emotions will not be grounded—will not be meaningful—for the robot. This is the same line of reasoning we followed in chapter 5, where we argued that symbols that have meaning for the robot—grounded symbols—can emerge only from the particular dynamics of the robot itself. If we were to relate emotions to the physiology and physical dynamics of the robots, e.g., their energy supply system and their physical setup, or if we used a developmental or evolutionary process to allow for the emergence of such emotions, we might be able to create a system of "robot emotions"; grounded emotions. This is a tantalizing future possibility for socially capable and expressive robotics.

There is one last aspect that we would like to raise briefly here; that of ethics. The more sophisticated this kind of robot technology gets, the more directly it will enter our lives, and the more ethical considerations will become relevant. We have alluded to some of the issues when discussing medical robots used in hospitals and homes for the elderly, topics that become increasingly vital as the level of intelligence of the robots increases. Do we want to let these robots into our lives? Do we want to let them take over important tasks and even responsibilities? If they are capable of learning on their own, developing their own concepts and ideas, can we let them function autonomously in our environments? We feel that all of us can have an informed opinion on these topics. So, rather than trying to impose our own views, we have established a Web site where these subject matters can be debated. Also, we hope that the ideas raised in this book will stimulate discussion in related mailing lists and other online forums.

11.9 Summary and Conclusions

The intention of this chapter has been to illustrate on the one hand the highly diverse and creative research and development work that is going on at the "symbiosis frontier," where robots have either entered into everyday interaction with humans or may soon do so. On the other hand, we have used the ideas developed in this book so far to point out the issues to be resolved before smooth interactions between humans and robots will actually be possible. An important point, as always, is the notorious frame of reference: merely building robots that reproduce human or animal behaviors will not suffice. We have to develop an understanding of the robot's own embodiment because it is this embodiment that will ultimately determine the grounding and thus the level of understanding and communication that is possible between humans and robots. In chapter 5 we described how a robot might use its own morphology to generate grounded symbols. In a similar way, we have argued in this chapter that a robot's body will also allow it to ground its emotions and communicate them to other robots and humans. Service robots for clearly defined tasks such as vacuuming, mowing the lawn, or carrying heavy items when shopping are unproblematic because we consider them as mere machines, and expect them to achieve their task to the satisfaction of the user. Robot companions are more challenging because we expect them to share our own knowledge and intuitions about the world, which, because of their different embodiment, will be possible only to a limited extent. Understanding these constraints will lead to much smoother and more beneficial interaction.

We have described how the agent design principles apply to entertainment, companion, and socially competent robots. However, we have said little in this chapter about developmental, evolutionary, or collective design principles. Most obviously, the developmental design principles will be very important in this particular field of robotics, because social interaction is a major part of development, and robots that participate in human society must interact well with humans, animals, human devices like cars and telephones, and other robots. So the social interaction design principle will play an important role in the development of future robots for everyday life. The design principles for collective robots will also come into play: if there are many robots involved in daily human environments, they must cooperate with each other, as well as with humans, to get their jobs done. So we must think about these robots from a population perspective rather than an individual perspective and ask how they should behave as a group. More important, how will humans and robots cooperate as a group? This will necessitate the application of the "from agent to group" collective design principle. The reader is encouraged to think about how the other design principles might be useful in designing robots for everyday life.

As for the future, it is an entirely empirical question—one that needs to be tested in the real world—to what extent these robot technologies will be accepted and endorsed by humans. We may find that we learn a lot about human nature, not only by reproducing human behavior in robots but by presenting humans with a unique social situation: robots in everyday life. So, the creative experimentation and robot construction that is currently under way must, by all means, continue, and be complemented by studies such as those of Takanori Shibata and other socially minded researchers. Only the future will tell us whether the robots we develop will be successful as partners in human society. We also hope that the theoretical considerations, based on the design principles outlined earlier, will provide guidelines for future research.

IV   Principles and Insights

Part IV, the last part of the book, consisting of chapter 12, summarizes the main points of our theory and provides a concise review of the design principles. We will not repeat them all, because they have been discussed in detail throughout the book, but we will simply provide an overview table. We will then present a list of selected highlights that together contain an overview of the key insights we have tried to convey in this book. Coming back to one of the central goals, we will close by presenting a collection of examples illustrating how things can always be seen differently.

Unfortunately, chapter 12—just like the previous ones—will not provide any solid answers to all the issues raised in chapter 1, such as the mind-body problem. But we feel that although we have not been able to bridge the gap between understanding the physiological basis of consciousness and knowing how this leads to subjective experience—and maybe we never will, as suggested by Dubois-Reymond's famous quote "Ignoramus, ignorabimus" (Focus box 1.1)—we still have made great strides toward a better understanding of natural intelligence and the different forms it can take, and we now know much better how to build artificially intelligent systems.

But before we get to the last chapter, this may be the place to add some anecdotal evidence. Often, when we explain our theory and our insights to an audience of nonexperts in artificial intelligence, many people respond, Yes, of course, it sounds very plausible—e.g., the idea of an agent structuring its own sensory information through interaction with the real world. Often, the individual points we have to make about embodiment strikes people as obvious. We feel that this is a good thing, because the intuitive appeal of the arguments implies that they are plausible. More important, the revolutionary nature, if you like, of the new view of intelligence presented in this book becomes apparent only when all of the insights are considered as a whole. We are also frequently asked why it has taken us—the entire research field—so long to form a coherent theory of intelligence, i.e., about 20 years since Brooks's introduction of embodied intelligence back in the mid-1980s. We would like to point out here that, like any new scientific view, it has emerged after a large amount of slow, hard work. But there is much more to be done.

At the 1991 International Joint Conference on Artificial Intelligence in Sydney, Australia, Rodney Brooks, whom we have already encountered many times throughout the book, received the prestigious "Computers and Thought" prize, which is awarded to young scientists with extraordinary achievements in the field of artificial intelligence. It was surprising that he received the award because his ideas, at the time, ran completely against the mainstream in the field. On the other hand, it was clear that there was a dire need for innovation, and Brooks was just the right person for this. At the same conference he presented the lecture "Intelligence Without Reason," mentioned in chapter 2. The title contains a pun with two messages hidden in it. First, there is no reason why there should be anything like intelligence in the first place, but it is there anyhow, as we all know; this is probably the usual reading of the sentence. Second, intelligence or intelligent behavior comes about without the need for rational thought. Here it is interesting to remember that one of the important research areas in classical artificial intelligence was—and still is!—problem solving and reasoning. Although one of the first papers on the alternative approach, the subsumption architecture (recall our discussion of the design principle of parallel, loosely coupled processes in chapter 4) was published five years earlier (Brooks, 1986), this lecture in 1991 represented a symbolic turning point, signaling the emergence of a new paradigm, which has given rise to much of the work described in this book. In his lecture, presented to an audience that mostly adhered to the classical paradigm, Brooks outlined the major differences between "computer-based" intelligence and biological forms of intelligence. And, of course, he made clear how important it is for intelligence to be "embodied."

Since Brooks's seminal lecture the field has dramatically expanded, as sketched in chapter 2, and the ideas have matured. We hope that the overview given in this book provides testimony to this claim. This chapter will summarize its major ideas and insights. We particularly want to show how the implications of embodiment have led to change, not only in the way we view biological intelligence and how we build artificial systems, but more generally in the way we view ourselves and the world around us.

We first summarize the ways in which the body shapes the way we think, by providing an overview of the theoretical ideas outlined in part II. But rather than giving a systematic account of all the design principles, which would be largely repetitive, we will instead provide an overall summary of what this theory consists of. Then we will highlight a number of insights that have resulted from our own and others' research, insights that we find particularly exciting and that demonstrate the power of these new ideas. Next, we will broaden the context and discuss how new insights gained through progress in science in general have shaped the way we think about the world and ourselves. So, before we start with the highlights, let us tackle the task of summarizing the theory.

12.1   Steps Toward a Theory of Intelligence

Our theory is perhaps not as compact as other scientific theories, because of the ill-defined nature of intelligence and also because the field is highly interdisciplinary and relatively immature. In its current state the theory consists of three components. First, there is a set of meta-considerations that provide the general context for the theory (chapter 3). Second, there is a characterization of real-world environments and of basic properties of agents as they interact with those environments (chapter 4). Third, and most important, there is a set of design principles for intelligent systems, whose discussion is organized around the three time scales: "here and now" (chapter 4), ontogenetic (chapter 5), and phylogenetic (chapter 6). An additional set of principles revolves around collective intelligence (chapter 7).

So, let us start by summarizing the first component of the theory, the general context. What we intuitively consider to be intelligent, and what is also reflected in some of the definitions that we have looked at, can be characterized by diversity-compliance: diversity implies that the agent has a large number of behaviors available so that it can react appropriately to the requirements of the particular situation. Learning is a powerful method for increasing the behavioral diversity of an agent over time. Compliance implies that the agent must follow the rules of its ecological niche, but it can also exploit them for its own purposes (e.g., exploiting friction and gravity for walking). The frame-of-reference issue has been mentioned so many times that the reader hardly needs this summary: (1) we must clearly define the standpoint from which we view behavior, i.e., the agent's (the situated view), the observer's, or the designer's; (2) behavior is always the result of a system-environment interaction—it is emergent—and thus can not be directly programmed into the agent; and (3) apparent complexity of behavior does not necessarily imply complexity of underlying mechanism (and vice versa, that seemingly simple behavior does not entail simple mechanisms). Although the synthetic methodology, "understanding by building," is deeply ingrained in artificial intelligence, the idea of conducting synthetic experiments is becoming increasingly popular in other scientific disciplines (e.g., drug testing in simulation in order to minimize animal experiments). A comprehensive explanation of intelligence always necessitates three time perspectives—"here and now," ontogenetic, and phylogenetic—that can also be applied to the design of intelligent agents. Finally, there is the central concept of emergence, which manifests itself in three main guises: behavior of an individual, global behavioral patterns in groups of agents, and behavior across the time scales (e.g., exploitation of passive dynamics resulting from an evolutionary process that has shaped the morphology and material properties of the legs).

The second component of the theory concerns the properties of physically embodied agents acting in the real world. Because the real world is very different from virtual ones, real-world agents have a number of properties that most virtual agents do not. In this book we have identified the following properties, which we should keep in mind both for design and analysis: Embodied agents are subject to the laws of physics, they generate sensory stimulation as they interact with the real world, they affect their environments, they are complex dynamical systems, and they perform morphological computation.

These properties have important implications. For example, because real-world agents are situated and move around, not only do situations change continuously from the perspective of the agent, but objects in the environment always appear at varying distances, orientations, and lighting conditions, which dramatically increases the difficulty of perception. Another consequence of the situated nature of real-world agents is that information acquisition not only takes time but is always very limited, since physical devices—in contrast to virtual ones—are always subject to noise and malfunction. Because the real world is infinitely rich, there is always more to be known and it is impossible to have complete information about it. Herbert Simon coined the term *bounded rationality* for decisions that have to be taken under these conditions. Moreover, because the real world has its own dynamics—things happen even if we do not do anything—and is a nonlinear dynamical system, the predictability of the environment will always be very limited. As we discussed in chapter 9 on building intelligent companies, because of these properties the utility of building detailed models is limited and increasing their precision is not very helpful. Given the "prediction mania" that exists in companies and in the financial world, and given the prevailing attitude in Western culture that everything is controllable, we feel that recognizing the properties of real worlds, in contrast to virtual ones, is an essential message that can provide many useful insights.

The third component, and by far the heaviest, concerns the design principles. Rather than going through all of them again, let us just emphasize some of the essential issues; the details can be taken from the overview table 12.1. The design principles help us to meet the three main goals of artificial intelligence, i.e., finding general principles of intelligent behavior, building intelligent artifacts, and understanding biological systems. More specifically, the design principles *are* in fact the general principles that we are looking for. But they can also be employed as heuristics for actually designing and building artificial agents. Finally, we can interpret these principles as descriptions of the properties of biological systems.

The principles all apply to biological and artificial systems, even though some have more of an engineering flavor than others. For example, the biological interpretation of the "design for emergence" principle is that we should look for the local rules of interaction that give rise to the global behavioral pattern that we are studying, such as flocking in birds. The engineering interpretation is that we should design a set of local rules that cause a desired global behavior such as the clustering of objects, as in the case study of the Swiss robots.

As mentioned above, the design principles are grouped into four categories: The first three correspond to the three time scales. The fourth one presents a different perspective, based on populations rather than individuals. The design principles overlap: The first set is the most general. Although it is mostly geared toward the "here-and-now" time scale, some of these principles are also applicable to the other perspectives. For example, the three-constituents principle, the complete agent principle, and the value principle also apply to the developmental

Table 12.1
Overview of the design principles

Name	Description
Agent design principles	
Three constituents	Ecological niche (environment), tasks, and agent must always be taken into account
Complete agent	Complete agent must be taken into account in design, not only isolated components
Parallel, loosely coupled processes	Parallel, asynchronous, partly autonomous processes, largely coupled through interaction with environment
Sensory-motor coordination	Behavior sensory-motor coordinated with respect to target; self-generated sensory stimulation
Cheap design	Exploitation of niche and interaction; parsimony
Redundancy	Partial overlap of functionality based on different physical processes
Ecological balance	Balance in complexity of sensory, motor, and neural systems; task distribution between morphology, materials, control, and interaction with environment
Value	Driving forces; developmental mechanisms; self-organization
Design principles for development	
Integration of time scales	Many time scales need to be integrated in one agent
Development as an incremental process	Start simple, build successively on top of what has already been learned
Discovery	The agent must have the ability to explore and evaluate, which implies that the agent can discover through its own activities
Social interaction	Sensory-motor coordination together with social interaction provides most powerful engine for development
Motivated complexity	Why complexity increases during ontogenetic development
Design principles for evolution	
Population	Population is the prerequisite for evolution to function
Cumulative selection and self-organization	Cumulative selection will produce interesting results only if the evolutionary process exploits processes of self-organization
Brain-body coevolution	"Brain" (neural control) and body must be evolved simultaneously
Scalable complexity	In order for complex organisms to be achieved, the ontogenetic developmental processes must be encoded in the genome
Evolution as a fluid process	Agents should be modeled with a large number of cells; evolution should make only small modifications
Minimal designer bias	Design as little as possible and let evolution do as much work as possible

Table 12.1
(continued)

Design principles for collective systems	
Level of abstraction	Proper level of abstraction must be chosen, and the implications must be clearly kept in mind
Design for emergence	Find local rules of interaction that lead to desired global behavior patterns
From agent to group	Agent design principles can often be applied to collective systems
Homogeneity-heterogeneity	A compromise has to be found between systems using only one type of module or robot, and employing several specialized types

perspective: agents are always complete and dynamical systems, irrespective of time scale. The principle of parallel, loosely coupled processes—with a slight reinterpretation of processes as complete agents—applies to collective intelligence as well. As a final example, the value principle from the "here-and-now" set is closely related to the motivated complexity principle from the developmental category, and the cumulative selection principle from the evolutionary one. All of these principles relate to motivation, e.g., the autotelic principle for development and the fitness function for evolution.

Let us now turn to a number of highlights among the things we have learned while developing this theory.

12.2   Selected Highlights

The following collection features those ideas and insights that we feel are exciting, unexpected, and thought-provoking while clearly illustrating the importance of embodiment. This loose collection starts with a few theoretical highlights, and the rest are roughly ordered using the three time scales.

Through Engineering to Science

Engineers sometimes have a bit of an inferiority complex because others often see them as "only building things" and not doing "real science." This is in spite of one definite advantage of engineering over the analytical sciences: analytical science is confined to the study of natural systems whereas engineers can build whatever they like, and they can use any kind of material, irrespective of whether it exists in nature or not. But with the synthetic methodology, "understanding by building," which capitalizes on the set of design principles, we achieve a kind of symbiosis between engineering and science. Design is about construction, about building, the business of engineers. Science is more about analyzing and understanding existing systems—in our context animals (for biology), humans (for psychology), and more specifically brains (for neuroscience). Although the analytic sciences have been enormously successful in the past, with the more powerful tools now available—including computer and robot technology—many sciences, not only artificial intelligence, have become more synthetic, employing simulation and using computational models that reflect the underlying physical processes. Because of the engineering perspective artificial intelligence has become even more interdisciplinary and, as discussed in the "landscape" chapter, now includes, in addition to computer scientists, biologists, psychologists, and neuroscientists, also electrical and mechanical engineers, biomechanicists, and dynamical systems and material science researchers. The synthetic approach, by engineering real-world agents, draws all of these different kinds of researchers together.

Intelligence as It Could Be

We have talked many times now about the artificial life motto "life as it could be." With the synthetic approach there is the exciting possibility that we can explore intelligence as it could be. Robots, of course, are a form of "life" that we do not find in nature. Recall our discussion of, for example, modular robots in chapter 7: what kinds of intelligent behaviors will a self-reconfiguring robot exhibit, given that self-reconfiguration of this kinds does not exist in natural systems? Or imagine that Bongard's block pushers are put into more challenging task environments. Block pushers of the Bongard type do not exist in nature. What will happen if they further evolve to perform more complex tasks, what kinds of bodies and brains will they have? Will they all have centralized nervous systems as most biological organisms do, or will there be an entirely different neural organization? Or consider the huge networking capabilities of ubiquitous technology which might at some point lead to entirely unexpected forms of intelligence that are not found in nature.

Broad Applicability of the Theory

One of the surprising results of applying the theory in different areas is that our ideas about intelligence do not remain confined to particular technologies. Wherever agent characteristics can be identified, there is a potential for application. For example, we have seen that the devices used in the field of ubiquitous computing so far have only limited agent characteristics, often restricted to sensory inputs with no or very little actuation possibility, thus strongly limiting their level of intelligence. But if these systems are endowed with agent capabilities (actuation in addition to sensing), their utility could skyrocket. Already, the market estimates for ubiquitous technology are astronomical: just about 2% of all the microprocessors manufactured go into PCs; all the rest go into systems embedded in the real world. In chapter 9, coauthored by the strategic management expert Simon Grand, we have looked at the creation of new businesses and companies, where a company can be interpreted as an agent. Extrapolation from companies to other social organizations such as cities or countries might present another field of application. For example, like the market, political consensus is an emergent phenomenon, where only very limited control can be exerted.

Information Self-Structuring through Sensory-Motor Coordination

The real world poses challenges that are very hard to deal with using only a computer program. Remember our example of computer vision. While the sometimes very complex and sophisticated algorithms that have been developed work fine in highly constrained factory environments, they break down if applied in real-world situations where, for example, the distances between objects and the camera are rapidly changing. However, agents can physically interact with the real world to turn these challenges into opportunities. For example, there is the obvious—but so far almost entirely neglected—point that through physical interaction with the real world, sensory stimulation is induced in different sensory channels. Depending on the particular kind of interaction, correlations are induced, e.g., moving the fingers over the edges of a coffee cup will generate correlations in the haptic, the visual, and the proprioceptive sensor modalities. As a result, the brain gets good—that is, correlated—raw material for further processing, so to speak. If, in addition, the sensors are positioned in morphologically "clever" locations, the control for acquiring the sensory data and generating the correlations will be simple. The touch sensors on the fingertips, where they are densely spaced, are easily stimulated when the hand is simply closed around an object. Put differently, the easy generation of "good" data is a result of the morphology of the hand. This process is further enhanced because the deformable and elastic properties of the hand tissue and the muscle-tendon system enable the fingers to smoothly close around objects of any shape.

With the "strategy" of sensory-motor coordination combined with proper morphology two goals can simultaneously be achieved. First, rich sensory stimulation is acquired with little effort, and second, the complexity of sensory stimulation is significantly reduced through sensory-motor coordination. Note that this "information reduction" is achieved through the physical interaction with the environment. A surprising insight indeed, and one of the most significant imports of embodiment.

Morphological Computation

One of the most essential implications of embodiment is that in order to achieve their tasks—walking, running, swimming, recognizing and manipulating objects, flying and avoiding obstacles—agents not only can but must off-load some neural processing into their morphology and the environment: for running, the elastic properties and the energy-storage capacity of the muscle-tendon system must be exploited; for flying and avoiding obstacles, insects have to exploit the morphology of their compound eyes to compensate for motion parallax; for recognizing objects in the real world, agents have to achieve data reduction through sensory-motor coordination, thus inducing correlations; for object manipulation we have to exploit the morphology—the anatomy—of the hand and its material properties, i.e., the deformable fingertips and the elasticity of the muscle-tendon system.

Specific morphologies and materials have to be selected when designing an artifact anyhow, so why not make wise choices that can be exploited for morphological computation? However, one of the problems seems to be that these design decisions constrain the possibilities of the agent. One possibility to reduce the constraining nature of morphological and material design decisions is to introduce changing morphologies and material properties. Because the brain can control the stiffness and elasticity of the muscles, the material properties can be adapted to the needs of the particular phase during running. For example, the stiffness needed when impacting the ground is different from that needed during the flight phase. The biomechanics expert Steven Vogel, although he does not explicitly call it morphological computation, discusses many examples in his engaging book *Cats' Paws and Catapults* (1998). Change of morphology enables agents to perform different functions depending on the situation. Achieving morphological change is one of the important goals of modular robotics, as discussed in chapter 7.

In spite of its high intuitive appeal, the concept of morphological computation still awaits quantification: how much computation is really done by a spring in the joint or a change in morphology? Or perhaps this is not the right question. Even if we do not yet know what the question is, we now have, as a start, concrete case studies to think about.

The Brain Does Not Control the Body

It is obvious that the brain controls the body; how else could it be? When neuroscientists talk about motor control, they mean neural control. When roboticists talk about control, they mean a microprocessor that runs the control program, which then controls motors which in turn actually move the limbs of the robot. So what's the problem? Well, the body has its own intrinsic dynamics and the dynamics of the neural system has to match the dynamics of the body system. As Sten Grillner showed with his lamprey experiments, the frequencies at which the central pattern generators operate when they are part of the isolated spinal cord are different from their frequencies when integrated normally into the body of the animal. This implies that it is not the neural oscillators alone that determine the behavior of the body, but the body just as much determines the frequency of the neural circuits. In other words, there is mutual coupling, or to use dynamical systems jargon, there is mutual entrainment.

At the more anecdotal level, when you are running on flat terrain at a certain pace and the path starts going downhill, you automatically run faster, but not necessarily because you—or the brain—give the commands to the muscles to move faster, but because the body is pulled downward by gravity, leading to a speedup which in turn will accelerate the neural oscillators in the brain (or spinal cord). It seems that the classical notion of control needs to be fundamentally reconceptualized. The idea that the brain is not in complete control once again goes against our traditional Cartesian thinking: the physical substrate of the mind is the brain and so the brain should be in control. We will return to the subtle relation between the mind and the brain-body system, i.e., to the notorious mind-body problem, below.

Exploiting Intrinsic Dynamics

One especially interesting form of morphological computation is provided by the intrinsic dynamics of the physical system, i.e., its attractor dynamics. Exploiting this dynamics can lead to the achievement of tasks entirely "for free," with no control. The passive dynamic walker is a prime example: it demonstrates how a system self-stabilizes while walking as long as its morphology and environment are appropriate, or to use dynamical systems jargon, as long as it is in the basin of attraction of the attractor for walking. The quadruped robot Puppy also nicely demonstrates self-stabilization. One might think that putting rubber pads on its feet to increase friction would be a good idea, because the agent will not slip as much, compared to having only bare aluminum on the feet. But if you do that the robot is more likely to fall over, because the slippage from the aluminum is needed for self-stabilization to occur. Or to use, once again, dynamical systems lingo, the slippage extends the basin of attraction that corresponds to a stable gait pattern.

Another fascinating way that intrinsic dynamics can be exploited is for learning. Because the agent's dynamics is natural to the system itself, the learning mechanisms should capitalize on it; this is what biological organisms seem to do, and so we might want to exploit this idea for robotics as well. Assume that you have a passive dynamic walker, i.e., a biped walker capable of walking down an incline without control and actuation. If you now put it on a flat surface and provide very little actuation, its movements will be near an attractor state—i.e., in the basin of attraction—corresponding to a "natural" gait pattern, because it is exploiting its own intrinsic dynamics. If the agent is in one of these basins of attraction, it is, so to speak, doing almost the right thing, and only slight modification to the neural control will be required to make it walk smoothly on level ground. This effect is precisely what was exploited in the recent experiments by Steve Collins and his colleagues (Collins et al., 2005), in which a robot learned how to walk on a flat surface by approximating its performance on an incline (which corresponds to its intrinsic dynamics).

Embodiment as a Prerequisite of Cognition

In chapter 5 we saw that development is an incremental and continuous process. Incremental means that what the organism currently does builds on what it has learned earlier. Continuous means that there are no discrete stages where particular abilities such as cognition "kick in." According to Thelen and Smith (1994), continuous sensory-motor development enables the child to categorize and generally to perceive the real world and to learn increasingly sophisticated distinctions. Even though the development is continuous, the ability to make novel distinctions sometimes occurs suddenly. Applying the dynamical systems metaphor, we could explain this sudden emergence as the discovery of a new attractor state.

Categorization is one of the most basic cognitive abilities, on top of which all other, higher-level abilities, including thinking and ultimately consciousness, build. When talking about sensory-motor processes, cognition, and thinking from a developmental perspective, it becomes obvious that no clear boundaries can be drawn between them—it is all fuzzy and fluid. But this is not so important. What does matter is understanding the mechanisms underlying development. Using the example of body schema, in chapter 5 we provided some idea about how we might envision the emergence of cognition during ontogenesis. This idea of cognition as emergent from a developmental process has been pushed even further. According to the Lakoff-Núñez hypothesis, even very abstract mathematical concepts ultimately have their origin—i.e., they are grounded—in bodily experiences, which are reflected in a body schema. These experiences, in turn, are a result of the intrinsic complex neural-body dynamics. Lakoff and Núñez use the notion of conceptual metaphors (which have their origin in linguistics), e.g., warmth for affection, as in "warm regards" or "he was really cold toward her," to support their claim. They argue that what makes this a good metaphor is that the "inferential structure" is preserved: if warm means affection, then warmer means more affection. Because these kinds of metaphors build on bodily experiences and ultimately something like a body schema, they are, in a sense, embodied. We will not further pursue the idea of metaphors—it is a huge field in itself.

In summary, it is hard to imagine how abstract thinking could ever come about during an individual's lifetime without the body providing the proper sensory stimulation, the raw material for the brain to process. Again it seems compatible with the Lakoff-Núñez hypothesis that thinking has its origin in our body and is shaped by it. We might also want to say that the body, or rather embodiment, is a prerequisite for high-level cognition.

Symbol Grounding through Complex Dynamics

The issue of symbol grounding is directly connected to the previous insight that thinking requires a body. But instead of arguing about the prerequisites of cognition and where it comes from, we start from the assumption that there *is* a body and ask the question of how it is possible that abstract symbols, which are discretely identifiable entities (a symbol is, by definition, either a symbol or not) come about within the continuous dynamical system that constitutes the agent. One of the striking insights has been that the introduction of complex sensory-motor systems, which enable complex body dynamics in agents, forms in fact a prerequisite for symbol grounding. Put differently, "going down" is an enabler of "going up": working on locomotion and low-level sensory-motor processes in general opened up the opportunity for symbol grounding, so to speak. We strongly suspect that complex sensory-motor coordination, because it enables complex categorization in the real world, will turn out to be the foundation for higher-level cognition, and to date we do not have evidence to the contrary. However, proving this with robot experiments and further research on animal behavior remains to be done.

We are grateful to a number of people working in dynamical systems, especially from the University of Tokyo, who drew our attention to this issue—namely, Yasuo Kuniyoshi, Yoshihiko Nakamura, and Masafumi Okada, whom we introduced in chapter 5. Although we have taken only a few initial steps by showing how something like a body schema might be acquired and used by an agent, we feel that the idea of relating attractor dynamics to symbol processing has much explanatory power.

To be sure, the approach proposed here is different from the one of Stevan Harnad, who originally articulated the problem. Harnad starts from the assumption that there is a symbol-processing system and discusses how this might be connected to the outside world. The approach taken here comes at the problem from a different direction: rather than assuming a symbol-processing system, the goal is to find aspects of dynamical systems that can be interpreted as symbol processing by an outside observer but also by the agent itself. We suggested that attractor dynamics might be a promising way to proceed.

Artificial Evolution in the Real World

Karl Sims's evolved entertaining creatures undoubtedly constituted a landmark development in artificial evolution: they were embodied agents, and their fitness was accordingly tested in a physics-based simulation. We know that evolution potentially exploits everything there is in the world. If the world consists of a simulation, it will contain only what we actually put there. By contrast, because the real world is infinitely rich, there is always, in a sense, a playground where evolution can "seize opportunities." Thus, if we want to unleash the full power of artificial evolution, we have to link it to the real world. We have seen fascinating examples of this where real-world properties that the designers were unaware of were exploited. Recall the experiments by Adrian Thompson, who evolved amazingly simple electronic circuits that exploited subtle electromagnetic interactions between unconnected components. Even more dramatic was the experiment of Jon Bird and his colleagues, where the goal was to evolve an oscillatory circuit without using the internal clock. To everybody's surprise, the circuit evolved into a radio receiver, which captured the clock signal from a nearby desktop computer! Cheating, you might say, on the part of the evolutionary algorithm, but it was very "clever" cheating: it exploited the signal already present in the air. The radio receiver can be seen as a new kind of sensor modality, a beautiful example of the compliance idea (exploiting the givens of the ecological niche). In some cases, artificial evolution even outperformed human engineers at a design problem: just recall Ingo Rechenberg's strangely curved pipe and the NASA satellite antenna (see chapter 6).

Finding Solutions to "Impossible" Problems

Remember Bernstein's problem about learning to control a complex body with very many degrees of freedom, or the problem of evolving an eye: they are both extremely hard. The answer that nature has "chosen" in both cases is to start with an imperfect solution, which is then incrementally refined and elaborated. More specifically, the initial solution works to some extent and later solutions then build upon what was there before—this is the incremental process. In human development, the baby initially has only very coarse control over his limbs and low resolution in his sensory systems. But this is enough to acquire a basic kind of sensory-motor coordination capacity. Once the latter is in place, the precision of the motor control and the resolution of the sensory systems can be successively increased (the story is more complicated, but this is the basic idea). Similarly, if during evolution something rudimentary has come about, e.g., light-sensitive cells—not nearly as good as a full-fledged eye, but better than having no way of reacting to light—this provides a definite advantage and the organism has a higher probability of living long enough to pass on the associated genes to its offspring. These types of agents will proliferate, increasing the probability that evolution will be able to improve on what is already there, and so on.

If very complex designs or behaviors are pursued without constraints, the probability of ever finding a solution will be virtually zero, i.e., the problem is "impossible." For example, imagine these two very improbable events: a baby suddenly coordinating all the degrees of freedom in his upper body, arm, hand, and fingers to pick up a bread crumb; or a set of simultaneous mutations that shape a group of cells into a sophisticated, fully functional eye in one generation. With the incremental approach of development and evolution, however, solutions can be found.

12.3 Seeing Things Differently

Science, since its very beginnings, has continually changed the way we see ourselves and the world around us. Often this is a gradual process, but in some cases it is sudden and dramatic. For example, Nicolaus Copernicus (1473–1543) showed that the Earth revolves around the sun rather than the other way around. This had a profound effect on how we as humans see our place in the universe. Another fundamental change in our thinking was wrought by Darwin's development of his theory of natural selection, in the nineteenth century. The fact that man was not created, fully formed, in God's image, but rather shares a common ancestor with chimpanzees and is likewise a product of evolutionary forces, altered how we view our relationship to God and to the other species on Earth. Hardly ever in science has there been a discovery with so many implications not only for science but for the world at large. Around the turn of the twentieth century, Sigmund Freud in essence claimed that our behavior can be driven by forces not under conscious control. If Freud's hypothesis, which underlies the psychoanalytic theory of neurosis, is indeed true, there are enormous implications for the concept of free will (see also focus box 1.1). In the middle of the twentieth century, James Watson and Francis Crick discovered that deoxyribonucleic acid, DNA, carries life's hereditary information, for which they (along with Maurice Wilkins) were awarded the Nobel Prize in 1962. This discovery confirmed that we have much more in common with all forms of life—including flatworms and yeast—than many of us would like to admit. Theoretically, this insight, once again, reduces the degree to which humans can really feel special or unique. The next stirring finding was just around the corner—one of the important insights of the Human Genome Project discussed in chapter 6, namely the relatively small number of genes contained in the human genome, 20,000 to 25,000 instead of the previously estimated 100,000. For scientists, the implications of this finding was that very complex phenotypes like humans (with their large and complex brains) can be grown by relatively few genes. As we mentioned, the flatworm *C. elegans* has about the same number of genes as we do, but we have about 100 billion neurons in our brains whereas *C. elegans* only has 302.

All of these discoveries have caused us, as humans, to see things differently. At a much smaller scale we would now like to present a few illustrations that have to some degree transformed our ideas about intelligence, in particular the mechanisms underlying behavior. Because we have discussed all of these examples earlier, we will only give a very short account here.

In order to clean up—to arrange distributed Styrofoam cubes into clusters—a robot first has to find a cube, perhaps using a camera, it has to move up to the cube, pick it up somehow, look for the nearest cluster, transport it to the cluster, and dump it there. How else could it be? The "Swiss robots" can clean up without recognizing what they have to clean up and without searching for the clusters where they have to deposit the cubes. They achieve this by exploiting the constraints of their particular ecological niche: closed arena, the size, shape, and weight of the cubes, and the proper positioning of the sensors.

Walking requires precise control of the trajectories of the joints, otherwise how would walking be possible? The passive dynamic walkers, by exploiting their intrinsic dynamics and their own morphology (wide feet, counterswing of the arm, passive swing of the leg) can walk without any control at all down an incline, or on flat ground with very little control.

Rapid locomotion in robots requires extremely fast electronics because of the high real-time demands of the sensory feedback loops. The quadruped robot Puppy can run with stable gait patterns with hardly any electronics and without any sensors whatsoever. By exploiting its own complex intrinsic dynamics as determined by the frequency of the oscillation, the weight distribution on the robot, the elasticity of the passive springs on the joints, and the deformability of the materials, it will settle into a stable gait pattern, an attractor state. As long as Puppy's variables are within a basin of attraction (i.e., it is near a natural gait pattern), it will self-stabilize, so that its movements become steady without explicit control.

If six legs need to be coordinated for walking, there must be a central global controller. It has been found that in insects there is in fact no such global central control; rather, there are largely independent local controllers for the legs (for forward swing, backward push, and up and down movement). How then, is coordinated walking possible? There *is* global communication between the legs, but it is through the embodiment and the interaction with the environment rather than via the neural system. Recall from chapter 4 that if the insect pushes back with one leg, the joint angles of the other legs on the ground will change accordingly. So all that is needed for global communication among the legs are angle sensors to complete the loop through the environment. And the insects do have these angle sensors.

In order to learn a delayed-reward task, the agent has to memorize its previous decisions in order to analyze which ones were right and which wrong. One of the fundamental problems in machine learning is credit or blame assignment: The agent receives the signal, the reward in a maze learning task, long after it has had to decide which way to turn. If it does not get the reward, then it has to figure out which one of its decisions was incorrect. Obviously, in order to be able to do that, it must have a certain memory capacity in order to remember its sequence of decisions. But Simon Bovet's Artificial Mouse can learn a delayed reward task in a T-maze without an explicit memory of its past actions, by only learning instantaneous associations between sensory and motor neurons. This is possible because the memory function is off-loaded into the environment (scaffolding), i.e., the agent exploits its interaction with the real world.

Social competence requires sophisticated perceptual skills to recognize another individual's internal state, but also common sense and a good understanding of the social rules of interaction. In other words, it requires high-level cognitive skills. The social-interaction robot Kismet achieves social competence in interaction with humans—or at least what looks like it to an outside observer—via a number of basic reflexes that are triggered and coordinated largely through its interaction with the environment: sound localization (turning the head toward a loud noise), turning toward quick movement, following slowly moving objects, and habituation (ceasing an activity after a while if there is no change in the environment). If the robot Kismet is engaged in a "conversation" and someone enters the door (loud noise), it turns its head (sound localization), follows the person that has entered for a while (following slowly moving objects), gets bored (habituation), and turns back to the previous "conversation": just as you would expect from a socially competent person!

If you want to find the shortest path to a particular location, you must have a notion of distance, or at the very least you must have a way of comparing two distances in order to tell which one is shorter. But ants can find the shortest path to a food source, without having the slightest notion of distance, by simply depositing pheromones wherever they go and following the highest pheromone concentrations. If a food source is nearby, the ant will return to the nest after a short period of time and the pheromones will have had less time to evaporate than if the source is more distant. The greater concentration of pheromones will attract other ants, which will in turn deposit their pheromones, etc. This is a process of self-organization that makes the seemingly impossible very easy. Again, the ants do this by exploiting their interaction with the environment.

Computers cannot be creative. How could they be, a computer is only a calculating machine! In this book we have discussed many sophisticated and innovative artifacts that were "designed by a computer": Rechenberg's hunched pipe, NASA's evolved antennas, Jon Bird's radio receiver, and Bongard's block pushers. As we have seen, computers can be creative when they use evolutionary systems for design—especially if they are also connected to the real world. Thus it is time to dismiss the myth of the computer as a mere number cruncher.

We could continue this list almost indefinitely, but the examples given here should suffice to illustrate the point that things can always be seen differently. To conclude, let us briefly return to the mind-body problem. As we have seen, Rodney Brooks suggested that, possibly, human intelligence and even human consciousness might be a bit like the simple, coglike mechanisms employed in the humanoid robot Cog (and its successor Kismet). The implication of Cog, and the many other robots that we have discussed in this book, is that intelligence or consciousness emerges from the interplay of many simple, largely autonomous, reflexlike processes, in a purely mechanical way. Needless to say, if Brooks and the other researchers following in his footsteps are right, this will profoundly change how we view ourselves and the relationship between mind and body.

12.4 Epilogue

In the outstanding novel *Confessions of a Taoist on Wall Street*, David Payne tells the story of a little boy, Sun I, who is born of a Chinese mother and an American fighter pilot in China. His mother dies at birth and his father returns home to the United States; he is left alone and grows up in a monastery. His mentor and teacher is the chef, Wu, who takes good care of him. The monastery is on a high rock upon a river. One of their daily chores is to carry water from the river to the monastery up a rocky path. The boy remembers that whenever they arrived at the top of the rock his buckets were empty, all the water spilled, whereas Wu's were always full. Here are Sun I's thoughts:

It was true. By some extraordinary luck or skill Wu never seemed to lose a drop, though he hurried along the treacherous stair at twice my pace. (I tried to cut my losses by moving slowly, plotting my course in advance and picking each footrest with deliberate care.)

"I don't understand it," I confessed to him. "You must know some kind of trick. Explain your method."

... "You haven't yet caught on. It's precisely this—excess of method—that confounds you, leaves the buckets nearly empty ..."

"If you're so smart, how do you do it then?"

"How do I do it? ... I close my eyes and think of nothing. My mind is somewhere else. My legs find their way without me, even over the most uneven ground. How can I tell you how I do it? ... I can't even remember myself!" (Payne, 1984, pp. 18–19)

Notes

Chapter 2

1. Machine learning is a field related to artificial intelligence, but it tends to focus exclusively on computational models of learning, whereas artificial intelligence is concerned with all aspects of human cognition.

2. Actually we should not say "controlling," because this suggests that there is the brain, the controller, and the body, the controlled. As we will argue later, both brain and body influence each other; they are mutually coupled.

3. *Spatiotemporal* means that the patterns change in space and in time: if you observe one area on the grid, there will be change, but local patterns also move over the grid.

Chapter 4

1. This term is used in other scientific disciplines where it has different meanings. For examples and a more technical treatment of our usage of the term, see (Lichtensteiger and Solomon, 2000; Paul, 2004; and Matsushita et al., 2005).

2. Of course, mere duplication is useful it some situations: having 200 feathers can keep an animal warmer than having only 100 feathers, but this point is unrelated to robustness.

Chapter 5

1. In the literature a distinction between body image and the closely related concept of body schema is often made. According to the neuroscientists Haggard and Wolpert [2005], "Body schema refers to a representation of the positions of body parts in space, which is updated during body movement. . . . Body image refers to a conscious visual representation of the way the body appears from the outside." (When it comes to Puppy, we can clearly identify the structures that are built up as it interacts with the environment, but whether we would want to call these structures body schema or body image is largely arbitrary and not so important—in particular because it is unclear what it would mean for Puppy to have a "conscious visual representation." What *is* important is that we always be able to pin down exactly what we are talking about. Thus, from the perspective of the synthetic methodology it is not necessary to go more deeply into this discussion; the interested reader is referred to the collection of papers entitled "Body Image and Body Schema" by De Preester and Knockaert, 2005).

2. In gait pattern diagrams, we can determine the state of the input layer by drawing a vertical line at a particular point in time and seeing whether any of the four lines crosses the

vertical line: if a line does cross, then that foot was on the ground at that instant; if it does not cross, then it was not.

3. There is an extremely rich literature in neuroscience that can be seen as contributing in one way or another to our understanding of body image (or body schema), e.g., Penfield and Boldrey, 1937; Edelman, 1987; Morasso and Sanguinetti, 1995; Jeannerod, 1997; Maravita and Iriki, 2004; Graziano and Gross, 1998; Ramachandran and Hirstein, 1998; Gallagher, 2005a, b; Haggard and Wolpert, 2005, to mention but a few.

Chapter 6

1. Rechenberg's major works are published in German; for those interested in more details about the history of evolutionary computation, including Rechenberg's contributions to it, we suggest Fogel, 1998.

2. Moore's law states that computational power within a standard computer doubles roughly every 18 months.

Chapter 7

1. Stigmergic interactions are those in which agents communicate indirectly with each other by altering the environment, such as by depositing pheromones or urinating in order to mark territory.

2. As mentioned above, the slime mold manages to do a lot with only one cell type, but its behavior, compared to that of organisms with different cell types, is very limited.

Chapter 8

1. Text taken from the TRON Intelligent House Web site, http://tronweb.super-nova.co.jp/tronintlhouse.html

2. The book was written in 1947 and published in 1948.

Chapter 10

1. According to Baddeley (1997) prospective memory has a very low information content: you need to remember to meet someone, or to take a cake out of the oven, but need not remember in great detail what you plan to say, or how to bake a cake. In contrast, retrospective memory tends to be concerned with the amount of information recalled.

2. Baddeley (1997, p. 271) points out that the statement "recognition is better than recall" is too categorical because it is not clear what is actually compared; but the general phenomenon certainly remains true.

Chapter 11

1. In January 2006 Sony announced that, as part of their restructuring effort, they would no longer produce and support AIBO. What effect this development will have on the future of entertainment robots remains to be seen.

References

Anderson, J. (1983). *The Architecture of cognition.* Cambridge, MA: Harvard University Press.

Andrews, K. R. (1987). *The concept of corporate strategy.* 3rd edition. Burr Ridge, IL: Richard D. Irwin.

Ansoff, I. H. (1965). *Corporate strategy.* New York: McGraw-Hill.

Arleo, A., and Gerstner, W. (2000). Spatial cognition and neuro-mimetic navigation: A model of hippocampal place cell activity. In Navigation in Biological and Artificial Systems, special issue of *Biological Cybernetics*, 83:287–299.

Asada, M., MacDorman, K. F., Ishiguro, H., and Kuniyoshi, Y. (2001). Cognitive developmental robotics as a new paradigm for the design of humanoid robots. *Robotics and Autonomous Systems*, 37:185–193.

Ashby, W. R. (1956). *An introduction to cybernetics.* London: Chapman and Hall.

Atkinson, R. C., and Shiffrin, R. M. (1968). Human memory: A proposed system and its control processes. In K. W. Spence, ed., *The psychology of learning and motivation: Advances in research and theory.* Vol. 2. New York: Academic Press, 89–195.

Autumn, K., and Peattie, A. M. (2002). Mechanisms of adhesion in geckos. *Integrative and Comparative Biology*, 42(6): 1081–1090.

Autumn, K., Sitti, M., Peattie, A. M., Hansen, W., Sponberg, S., Liang, Y. A., Kenny, T., Fearing, R., Israelachvili, J. N., and Full, R. J. (2002). Evidence for van der Waals adhesion in gecko setae. *Proceedings of the National Academy of Science*, 99(19): 12252–12256.

Ayers, J. (2004). Underwater walking. *Arthropod Structure & Development*, 33(3): 347–360.

Babloyantz, A., Nicolis, C., and Salazar, M. (1985). Evidence for chaotic dynamics during the sleep cycle. *Physics Letters A*, 111:152.

Baddeley, A. (1997). *Human memory: Theory and practice.* Revised edition. East Sussex, UK: Psychology Press.

Bakkum, D. J., Shkolnik, A. C., Ben-Ary, G., Gamblen, P., DeMarse, T. B., and Potter, S. M. (2004). Remove some "A" from AI: Embodied cultured networks. In F. Iida, R. Pfeifer, L. Steels, and Y. Kuniyoshi, eds., *Embodied artificial intelligence.* Berlin: Springer, 130–145.

Balakrishnan, K., Bousquet, O., and Honavar, V. (1999). Spatial learning and localization in rodents : A computation model of the hippocampus and its implications for mobile robots. *Adaptive Behavior*, 7(2): 173–216.

Banzhaf, W., Nordin, P., Keller, R. E., and Francone, F. D. (1998). *Genetic programming: An introduction.* San Francisco: Morgan Kaufmann.

Bargh, J. A., and Chartrand, T. L. (1999). The unbearable automaticity of being. *American Psychologist*, 54:462–479.

Barnard, C. I. (1938). *Functions of the executive.* Cambridge, MA: Harvard University Press.

Bartlett, F. C. (1932). *Remembering.* Cambridge: Cambridge University Press.

Basar, E., ed. (1990). *Chaos in brain function.* Berlin: Springer.

Beckers, R., Holland, O., and Deneubourg, J.-L. (1994). From local actions to global tasks: Stigmergy and collective robotics. In R. Brooks and P. Maes, eds., *Artificial life IV: Proceedings of the Fourth International Workshop on the Synthesis and Simulation of Living Systems.* Cambridge, MA: MIT Press, 181–189.

Beer, R. D. (2003). The dynamics of active categorical perception in an evolued model agent. *Adaptive Behavior,* 11(4): 209–243.

Bernstein, N. (1967). *The co-ordination and regulation of movements.* London: Pergamon.

Best, P. J., White, A. M., and Minai, A. (2001). Spatial processing in the brain: The activity of hippocampal place cells. *Annual Review of Neuroscience,* 24:459–486.

Bird, J., and Layzell, P. (2002). The evolved radio and its implications for modeling the evolution of novel sensors. In *Proceedings of the 2002 Congress on Evolutionary Computation.* Piscataway, NJ: IEEE Press, 1836–1841.

Blickhan, R., Wagner, H., and Seyfarth, A. (2003). Brain or muscles? *Recent Research Developments in Biomechanics,* 1:215–245.

Bonabeau, E., Dorigo, M., and Theraulaz, G. (1999). *Swarm intelligence: From natural to artificial systems.* Santa Fe Institute Studies in the Sciences of Complexity. Oxford: Oxford University Press.

Bongard, J. C. (2002). Evolving modular genetic regulatory networks. In *Proceedings of the 2002 Congress on Evolutionary Computation.* Piscataway, NJ: IEEE Press, 305–311.

Bongard, J. C. (2003). Incremental approaches to the combined evolution of a robot's body and brain. PhD thesis, Faculty of Mathematics and Science, University of Zurich.

Bongard, J. C., and Pfeifer, R. (2001). Repeated structure and dissociation of genotypic and phenotypic complexity in artificial ontogeny. In L. Spector et al., eds., *Proceedings of the Genetic and Evolutionary Computation Conference.* San Francisco, CA: Morgan Kaufmann, 829–836.

Bovet, S., and Pfeifer, R. (2005). Emergence of coherent behaviors from homogenous sensorimotor coupling. *The 12th International Conference on Advanced Robotics* (ICAR 2005), 324–330.

Bower, J. L. (1970). *Managing the resource allocation process: A study of corporate planning and investment.* Cambridge, MA: Harvard Business School Press.

Braitenberg, V. (1984). *Vehicles: Experiments in synthetic psychology.* Cambridge, MA: MIT Press.

Breazeal, C. (2002). *Designing sociable robots.* Cambridge, MA: MIT Press.

Bremermann, H. J. (1958). The evolution of intelligence: The nervous system as a model of its environment. Technical report 1, contract no. 477(17), Department of Mathematics, University of Washington, Seattle, WA.

Bridgeman, B. (2003). Is mental life possible without the will? A review of Daniel M. Wegner's *The Illusion of Conscious Will. Psyche,* 9(13). http://psyche.cs.monash.edu.au/

Brighton, H. (2004). *Introducing artificial intelligence.* New York: Totem Books.

Brooks, R. A. (1986). A robust layered control system for a mobile robot. *IEEE Journal of Robotics and Automation,* 2(1): 14–23.

Brooks, R. A. (1990). Elephants don't play chess. In P. Maes, ed., Designing autonomous agents: Theory and practice from biology to engineering and back. Cambridge, MA: MIT Press, 3–15.

Brooks, R. A. (1991a). Intelligence without reason. In J. Myopoulos and R. Reiter, eds., *Proceedings of the International Joint Conference on Artificial Intelligence.* San Mateo, CA: Morgan Kaufmann, 569–595.

Brooks, R. A. (1991b). Intelligence without representation. *Artificial Intelligence*, 47:139–160.

Brooks, R. A., and Stein, L. A. (1994). Building brains for bodies. *Autonomous Robots*, 1(1): 7–25.

Burgelman, R. A. (2002). *Strategy is destiny: How strategy-making shapes a company's future*. New York: Free Press.

Burgess, N., Donnett, J. G., Jeffery, K. J., and O'Keefe, J. (1997). Robotic and neuronal simulation of the hippocampus and rat navigation. *Philosophical Transactions of the Royal Society B*, 352:1535–1543.

Camazine, S., Deneubourg, J.-L., Franks, N. R., Sneyd, J., Theraulaz, G., and Bonabeau, E. (2001). *Self-organization in biological systems*. Princeton, NJ: Princeton University Press.

Carpenter, G. A., and Grossberg, S. (2002). Adaptive resonance theory. In M. A. Arbib, ed., *The handbook of brain theory and neural networks*, 2nd edition. Cambridge, MA: MIT Press.

Cartright, B. A., and Collett, R. S. (1983). Landmark navigation in bees. *Journal of Comparative Physiology*, 151:521–543.

Ceci, S., and Williams, W., eds. (1999). *The nature-nurture debate: The essential readings*. Oxford, UK: Blackwell.

Chalmers, D. (1997). *The conscious mind: In search of a fundamental theory*. Oxford: Oxford University Press.

Christensen, C. M. (1997). *The innovator's dilemma*. Cambridge, MA: Harvard Business School Press.

Clancey, W. J. (1991). Review of *The invention of memory* by Israel Rosenfield. *Artificial Intelligence*, 50:241–284.

Clancey, W. J. (1997). *Situated cognition: On human knowledge and computer representations*. New York: Cambridge University Press.

Clark, A. (1997). *Being there: Putting brain, body, and world together again*. Cambridge, MA: MIT Press.

Clark, A. (2003). *Natural-born cyborgs: Minds, technologies, and the future of human intelligence*. Oxford: Oxford University Press.

Collins, S. H., Wisse, M., and Ruina, A. (2001). A three-dimensional passive-dynamic walking robot with two legs and knees. *International Journal of Robotics Research*, 20:607–615.

Collins, S., Ruina, S., Tedrake, R., and Wisse, M. (2005). Efficient bipedal robots based on passive-dynamic walkers. *Science*, 307:1082–1085.

Craik, F. I. M. (1983). On the transfer of information from temporary to permanent memory. *Philosophical Transactions of the Royal Society of London B*, 302:341–359.

Crick, F., and Koch, C. (2003). A framework for consciousness. *Nature Neuroscience*, 6(2): 119–126.

Crockett, L. J. (1994). *The Turing Test and the frame problem: AI's mistaken understanding of intelligence*. Norwood, NJ: Ablex.

Cruse, H. (1990). What mechanisms coordinate leg movement in walking arthropods? *Trends in Neurosciences*, 13:15–21.

Czikszentmihalyi, M. (1990). *Flow: The psychology of optimal experience*. New York: Harper and Row.

Damasio, A. (1995). *Descartes' error: Emotion, reason, and the human brain*. New York: Quill.

Darwin, C. (1859). *On the origin of species by means of natural selection, or the preservation of favoured races in the struggle for life*. London: John Murray.

Dautenhahn, K., and Nehaniv, C. L., eds. (2002). *Imitation in animals and artifacts*. Cambridge, MA: MIT Press.

Davids, A. (2002). Urban search and rescue robots: From tragedy to technology. *IEEE Intelligent Systems*, 17(2): 81–83.

Dawkins, R. (1986). *The blind watchmaker: Why the evidence of evolution reveals a universe without design*. W. W. Norton.

Dawkins, R. (1996). *Climbing mount improbable*. W. W. Norton.

Deneubourg, J.-L., and Goss, S. (1989). Collective patterns and decision making. *Ethology, Ecology, and Evolution*, 1:295–311.

Dennett, D. C. (1997). Cog as a thought experiment. *Robotics and Autonomous Systems*, 20:251–256.

De Preester, H., and Knockaert, V., eds. (2005). *Body image and body schema: Interdisciplinary perspectives on the body*. Amsterdam: John Benjamin.

Descartes, R. (1637). *Discourse on method*. Trans. L. LaFleur. New York: Bobbs Merrill, 1960.

Dewey, J. (1896). The reflex arc in psychology. *Psychological Review*, 3(1896): 357–370. Reprinted in J. J. McDermott, ed., *The Philosophy of John Dewey*. Chicago: University of Chicago Press, 136–148.

Dorigo, M., and Stützle, T. (2004). *Ant colony optimization*. Cambridge, MA: MIT Press.

Dorigo, M., Di Caro, G., and Sampels, M., eds. (2002). *Ant algorithms: Third International Workshop, ANTS 2002*. Berlin: Springer.

Drucker, P. F. (1985). *Innovation and entrepreneurship: Practice and principles*. New York: Harper and Row.

Dürr, V., Krause, A. F., Schmitz, J., and Cruse, H. (2003). Neuroethological concepts and their transfer to walking machines. *International Journal of Robotics Research*, 22(3–4): 151–167.

Edelman, G. (1987). *Neural Darwinism: The theory of neuronal group selection*. New York: Basic Books.

Eggenberger, P. (1997). Evolving morphologies of simulated 3d organisms based on differential gene expression. In P. Husbands and I. Harvey, eds., *Fourth European Conference on Artificial Life*. Cambridge, MA: MIT Press, 205–213.

Eggenberger, P. (1999). Evolution of three-dimensional, artificial organisms: Simulations of developmental processes. PhD dissertation, Medical Faculty, University of Zurich.

Eggenberger Hotz, P. (2003). Genome-physics interaction as a new concept to reduce the number of genetic parameters in artificial evolution. *Proceedings of the 2003 Congress on Evolutionary Computation*. Piscataway, NJ: IEEE Press, 191–198.

Eliasmith, C. (2005). A unified approach to building and controlling spiking attractor networks. *Neural Computation*, 17(6): 1276–1314.

Ellis, R., and Humphreys, G. W., eds. (1999). *Connectionist psychology: A text with readings*. Hove, UK: Psychology Press.

Elman, J. L., Bates, E. A., Johnson, H. A., Karmiloff-Smith, A., Parisi, D., and Plunkett, K. (1996). *Rethinking innateness: A connectionist perspective on development*. Cambridge, MA: MIT Press.

Epstein, J. M., and Axtell, R. L. (1996). *Growing artificial societies: Social science from the bottom up*. Cambridge, MA: MIT Press.

Erwin, T. L. (1988). The tropical forest canopy: The heart of biotic diversity. In E. O. Wilson, ed., *Biodiversity*. Washington, DC: National Academy Press, 123–129.

Erwin, T. L. (1997). Biodiversity at its utmost: Tropical forest beetles. In M. L. Reaka-Kudla, D. E. Wilson, and E. O. Wilson, eds., *Biodiversity II*. Washington, DC, Joseph Henry Press, 27–40.

Fend, M., Yokoi, H., and Pfeifer, R. (2003). Optimal morphology of a biologically inspired whisker array on an obstacle-avoiding robot. In W. Banzhaf, T. Christaller, P. Dittrich, J. T.

Kim, and J. Ziegler, eds., *Advances in Artificial Life: Proceedings of the Seventh European Conference on Artificial Life* Berlin: Springer, 771–780.

Ferber, J. (1999). *Multi-agent systems: An introduction to distributed artificial intelligence.* Harlow, UK: Addison-Wesley.

Feyerabend, P. (1975). *Against method: Outline of an anarchistic theory of knowledge.* London: Verso.

Fisher, R. P. (1996). Implications of output-bound measure for laboratory and field research in memory. *Behavioral and Brain Sciences*, 19:197.

Fogel, D. B., ed. (1998). *Evolutionary computation: The fossil record.* Piscataway, NJ: IEEE Press.

Fraser, A. S. (1957). Simulation of genetic systems by automatic digital computers. I. Introduction. *Australian Journal of Biological Science*, 10:484–491.

Freeman, W. J. (1991). The physiology of perception. *Scientific American*, 264:78–85.

Freeman, W. J. (2000). *Neurodynamics: An exploration of mesoscopic brain dynamics.* London: Springer.

Fukuda, T., and Nakagawa, S. (1988). Approach to the dynamically reconfigurable robotic system. *Journal of Intelligent and Robotic Systems*, 1:55–72.

Gallagher, S. (2005a). Dynamic models of body schema processes. In H. De Preester and V. Knockaert, eds. (2005). *Body image and body schema: Interdisciplinary perspectives on the body.* Amsterdam: John Benjamin.

Gallagher, S. (2005b). *How the body shapes the mind.* Oxford: Oxford University Press.

Gallese, V., Fadiga, L., Fogassi, L., and Rizzolatti, G. (1996). Action recognition in premotor cortex. *Brain*, 199:593–609.

Gardner, M. (1970). Mathematical games: The fantastic combinations of John Conway's new solitaire game "Life". *Scientific American*, 223(October 1970):120–123.

Garrod, S., and Pickering, M. J. (2004). Why is conversation so easy? *Trends in Cognitive Sciences*, 8(1): 8–11.

Gaussier, P., Revel, A., Banquet, J., and Babeau, V. (2002). From view cells and place cells to cognitive maps: Processing stages of the hippocampal system. *Biological Cybernetics*, 86:15–28.

Geim, A. K., Dubonos, S. V., Grigorieva, I. V., Novoselov, K. S., Ahukov, A. A., and Shapoval, S. Y. (2003). Microfabricated adhesive mimicking gecko foot-hair. *Nature Materials*, 2:461–463.

Gemmell, J., Bell, G., and Lueder, R. (2006) MyLifeBits: A personal database for everything. *Communications of the ACM*, 49(1): 88–95.

Gleick, J. (1987). *Chaos: Making a new science.* New York: Viking Penguin.

Glenberg, A. M. (1997). What memory is for. *Behavioral and Brain Sciences*, 20:1–56.

Goldberg, D. E. (1989). *Genetic algorithms in search, optimization, and machine learning.* Reading, MA: Addison-Wesley.

Goleman, D. (1997). *Emotional intelligence.* New York: Bantam Books.

Gomez, P. Y., and Jones, B. C. (2000). Conventions: An interpretation of deep structure in organizations. *Organization Science*, 11(6): 696–708.

Graybiel, A. M. (1990). Neurotransmitters and neuromodulators in the basal ganglia. *Trends in Neuroscience*, 13(7): 244–254.

Graziano, M. S., and Gross, C. G. (1998). Spatial maps for the control of movement. *Current Opinion Neurobiology*, 8:195–201.

Gregory, R. L. (1987). *The Oxford companion to the mind.* Oxford: Oxford University Press.

Grillner, S. (1996). Neural networks for vertebrate locomotion. *Scientific American*, 274: 64–69.

Groß, R., and Dorigo, M. (2004). Cooperative transport of objects of different shapes and sizes. In M. Dorigo, M. Birattari, C. Blum, L. M. Gambardella, F. Mondada, and T. Stützle, eds., *Ant colony optimization and swarm intelligence*. Berlin: Springer, 106–117.

Guan, L., Kiemel, T., and Cohen, A. V. (2001). Impact of movement and movement-related feedback on the lamprey central pattern generator for locomotion. *Journal of Experimental Biology*, 204:2361–2370.

Guha, R. V., and Lenat, D. B. (1990). Cyc: A midterm report. *AI Magazine*, 11(3): 32–59.

Haenny, P. E., Maunsell, J. H., and Schiller, P. H. (1988). State dependent activity in monkey visual cortex. II. Retinal and extraretinal factors in V4. *Experimental Brain Research*, 69:245–259.

Hafner, V. V., and Möller, R. (2001). Learning of visual navigation strategies. In M. Quoy, P. Gaussier, and J. Wyatt, eds., *Proceedings of the Ninth European Workshop on Learning Robots*. Springer: Berlin, 47–56.

Haggard, P., and Wolpert, D. (2005). Disorders of body scheme. In H.-J. Freund, M. Jeannerod, M. Hallett, and R. Leiguarda, eds., *Higher-order motor disorders: From neuroanatomy and neurobiology to clinical neurology*. Oxford, UK: Oxford University Press.

Hamel, G., and Prahalad, C. K. (1994). *Competing for the future*. Cambridge, MA: Harvard Business School Press.

Hara, F., and Pfeifer, R. (2000). On the relation among morphology, material and control in morpho-functional machines. In J. A. Meyer, A. Berthoz, D. Floreano, H. L. Roitblat, and S. W. Wilson, eds., *From animals to animats 6: Proceedings of the Sixth International Conference on Simulation of Adaptive Behavior*. Cambridge, MA: MIT Press, 33–40.

Hara, F., and Pfeifer, R., eds. (2003). *Morpho-functional machines, the new species: Designing embodied intelligence*. Tokyo: Springer.

Harnad, S. (1990). The symbol grounding problem. *Physica D*, 42:335–346.

Hatch, J. P., and Riley, P. (1985). Growth and development of biofeedback: A bibliographic analysis. *Biofeedback and Self Regulation*, 10(4): 289–299.

Haugeland, J. (1985). *Artificial intelligence: The very idea*. Cambridge, MA: MIT Press.

Hayes, A. T., Martinoli, A., and Goodman, R. M. (2000). Comparing distributed exploration strategies with simulated and real autonomous robots. In L. Parker, G. Bekey, and J. Bahren, eds., *Proceedings of the Fifth International Symposium on Distributed Autonomous Robotics Systems*. Berlin: Springer, 261–270.

Hebb, D. O. (1949). *The organization of behavior*. New York: Wiley.

Hemelrijk, C. K. (2002). Self-organsation and natural selection in the evolution of complex despotic societies. *Biological Bulletin*, 202:283–289.

Herrnstein, R., and Murray, C. (1994). *The bell curve: Intelligence and class structure in American life*. New York: Free Press.

Hertzberg, J., Jaeger, H., and F. Schonherr (2002). Learning to ground fact symbols in behavior-based robots. In F. van Harmelen, ed., *Proceedings of the Fifteenth European Conference on Artificial Intelligence*. Amsterdam: IOS Press, 708–712.

Hirose, S. (1993). *Biologically inspired robots: Snake-like locomotors and manipulators*. Oxford: Oxford University Press.

Hofstadter, D. R. (1985). *Metamagical themas: Questing for the essence of mind and pattern*. New York: Basic Books.

Holland, J. H. (1992). *Adaptation in natural and artificial systems*. Cambridge, MA: MIT Press.

Holland, O., and Melhuish, C. (1999). Stigmergy, self-organization, and sorting in collective robotics. *Artificial Life*, 5:173–202.

Hosokawa, K., Shimoyama, I., and Miura, H. (1995). Dynamics of self-assembling systems: Analogy with chemical kinetics. *Artificial Life*, 1:413–427.

Hunt, K. D. (1996). The postural feeding hypothesis: An ecological model for the evolution of bipedalism. *South African Journal of Science*, 92:77–90.

Huxley, J. S. (1942). *Evolution, the modern synthesis*. London: Allen and Unwin.

Ichikawa, S., Miyamae, T., and Hara, F. (2003). Emerging of group formation: Morphological configuration of multi-robot system. In F. Hara and R. Pfeifer, eds., *Morpho-functional machines: The new species*. Tokyo: Springer.

Iida, F., and Pfeifer, R. (2004). Self-stabilization and behavioral diversity of embodied adaptive locomotion. In F. Iida, R. Pfeifer, L. Steels, and Y. Kuniyoshi, eds., *Embodied artificial intelligence*. Berlin: Springer, 119–129.

Iida, F., Dravid, R., and Paul, C. (2002). Design and control of a pendulum-driven hopping robot. In R. Siegwart and C. Laugier, eds., *Proceedings of the 2002 IEEE/RSJ International Conference on Intelligent Robots and Systems*. Madison, WI: Omni press, 2141–2146.

Iida, F., Pfeifer, R., Steels, L., and Kuniyoshi, Y., eds. (2004). *Embodied artificial intelligence*. Berlin: Springer.

Ijspeert, A. J. (2001). A connectionist central pattern generator for the aquatic and terrestrial gaits of a simulated salamander. *Biological Cybernetics*, 84(5): 331–348.

Ijspeert, A. J., Martinoli, A., Billard, A., and Gambardella, L. M. (2001). Collaboration through the exploitation of local interactions in autonomous collective robotics: The stick pulling experiment. *Autonomous Robots*, 11(2): 149–171.

Inamura, T., Toshima, I., Tanie, H., and Nakamura, Y. (2004). Embodied symbol emergence based on mimesis theory. *International Journal of Robotics Research*, 23(4): 363–378.

Ishiguro, A., and Kawakatsu, T. (2003). How should control and body systems be coupled? A robotic case study. In F. Iida, R. Pfeifer, L. Steels, and Y. Kuniyoshi, eds., *Embodied artificial intelligence*. Berlin: Springer, 107–118.

Ishiguro, A., Fujii, A., and Eggenberger, P. (2003). Neuromodulated control of bipedal locomotion using a polymorphic CPG circuit. *Adaptive Behavior*, 11(1): 7–17.

Ito, M., and Tani, J. (2004). On-line imitative interaction with a humanoid robot using a dynamic neural network model of a mirror system. *Adaptive Behavior*, 12(2): 93–115.

Jacoby, L. L., and Dallas, M. (1981). On the relationship between autobiographical memory and perceptual learning. *Journal of Experimental Psychology (General)*, 110:306–340.

Jaeger, H., and Christaller, T. (1998). Dual dynamics: Designing behavior systems for autonomous robots. *Artificial Life and Robotics*, 2:108–112.

Jeannerod, M. (1997). *The cognitive neuroscience of action*. Oxford, UK: Blackwell.

Kaas, J. H. (1995). The reorganization of sensory and motor maps in adult mammals. In M. S. Gazzaniga, ed., *The cognitive neurosciences*. Cambridge, MA: MIT Press/Bradford Books.

Kaneko, K., and Tsuda, I. (2001). *Complex systems: Chaos and beyond. A constructive approach with applications in life sciences*. Berlin: Springer.

Karn, K. S., and Zelinsky, G. J. (1996). Driving and dish washing: Failure of the correspondence metaphor for memory. *Behavioral and Brain Sciences*, 19(2): 198.

Kauffman, S. A. (1993). *The origins of order: Self-organization and selection in evolution*. Oxford: Oxford University Press.

Kawasaki, G. (1999). *Rules for revolutionaries: The capitalist manifesto for creating and marketing new products and services*. New York: HarperCollins.

Kelso, J. A. S. (1995). *Dynamic patterns: The self-organization of brain and behavior*. Cambridge, MA: MIT Press.

Kimura, H., Tsuchiya, K., Ishiguro, A., and Witte, H., eds. (2006). *Adaptive motion of animals and machines*. Tokyo: Springer.

Kitano, H., Asada, M., Kuniyoshi, Y., Noda, I., Osawa, E., and Matsubara, H. (1997). RoboCup: A challenge problem for AI. *AI Magazine*, 18(1): 73–85.

Klaassen, B., Linnemann, R., Spenneberg, D., and Kirchner, F. (2002). Biomimetic walking robot SCORPION: Control and modeling. *Robotics and Autonomous Systems*, 41(2–3): 69–76.

Kolers, P. A., and Roediger, H. L., III (1984). Procedures of mind. *Journal of Verbal Learning and Verbal Behavior*, 23:425–449.

Koppel, D., Wang, W. F., and Lee, H. (2005). Robust and real-time image stabilization and rectification. In *IEEE Workshop on Applications of Computer Vision*, Piscataway, NJ: IEEE Press, 350–355.

Koriat, A., and Goldsmith, M. (1996). Memory metaphors and the laboratory/real-life controversy: Correspondence versus storehouse views of memory. *Behavioral and Brain Sciences*, 19:175–227.

Koriat, A., and Goldsmith, M. (1997). The myriad functions and metaphors of memory. *Behavioral and Brain Sciences*, 20:27–28.

Koriat, A., and Pearlman-Avnion, S. (2003). Memory organization of action events and its relationship to memory performance. *Journal of Experimental Psychology (General)*, 132:435–454.

Koza, J. R., and Rice, J. P., eds. (1992). *Genetic programming: On the programming of computers by means of natural selection*. Cambridge, MA: MIT Press.

Koza, J. R., ed. (1994). *Genetic programming II: Automatic discovery of reusable programs*. Cambridge, MA: MIT Press.

Koza, J. A., Andre, D., Keane, M. A., and Bennett, F. H. (1999). *Genetic programming III: Darwinian invention and problem solving*. San Francisco: Morgan Kaufmann.

Koza, J. R., Keane, M. A., Streeter, M. J., Mydlowec, W., Yu, J., and Lanza, G., eds. (2003). *Genetic programming IV: Routine human-competitive machine intelligence*. Nonwell, MA: Kluwer Academic.

Krumlauf, R. (1994). Hox genes in vertebrate development. *Cell*, 78(2): 191–201.

Kuniyoshi, Y., Yorozu, Y., Inaba, M., and Inoue, H. (2003). From visuo-motor self learning to early imitation: A neural architecture for humanoid learning. *Proceedings of the 2003 IEEE International Conference on Robotics and Automation*, Piscataway, NJ: IEEE Press, 3132–3139.

Kuniyoshi, Y., Yorozu, Y., Yoshiyuki, E., Terada, K., Otani, T., Nagakubo, A., and Yamamoto, T. (2004). From humanoid embodiment to theory of mind. In F. Iida, R. Pfeifer, L. Steels, and Y. Kuniyoshi, eds., *Embodied artificial intelligence*. Berlin: Springer, 202–218.

Kunz, H., and Hemelrijk, C. K. (2003). Artificial fish schools: Collective effects of school size, body size, and body form. *Artificial Life*, 9:237–253.

Kurzweil, R. (2000). *The age of spiritual machines: When computers exceed human intelligence*. New York: Penguin Putnam.

Kuwana, Y., Nagasawa, S., Shimoyama, I., and Kanzaki, R. (1999). Synthesis of the pheromone-oriented behavior of silkworm moths by a mobile robot with moth antennae as pheromone sensors. *Biosensors and Bioelectronics*, 14(2): 195–202.

Lachman, R., Lachman, J. L., and Butterfield, E. C. (1979). *Cognitive psychology and information processing*. Hillsdale, NJ: Erlbaum.

Lakoff, G., and Johnson, M. (1980). *Metaphors we live by*. Chicago: University of Chicago Press.

Lakoff, G., and Núñez, R. (2000). *Where mathematics comes from: How the embodied mind brings mathematics into being*. New York: Basic Books.

Lambrinos, D., Möller, R., Labhart, T., Pfeifer, R., and Wehner, R. (2000). A mobile robot employing insect strategies for navigation. *Robotics and Autonomous Systems*, 30:39–64.

Langton, C. G. (1995). *Artificial life: An overview*. Cambridge, MA: MIT Press.

Libet, B., Gleason, C. A., Wright, E. W., and Pearl, D. K. (1983). Time of conscious intention to act in relation to onset of cerebral activity (readiness-potential): The unconscious initiation of a freely voluntary act. *Brain*, 106:623–642.

Lichtensteiger, L., and Salomon, R. (2000). The evolution of an artificial compound eye by using adaptive hardware. In *Proceedings of the 2000 Congress on Evolutionary Computation*. Piscataway, NJ: IEEE Press, 1144–1151.

Ling, L., Martinoli, A., and Abu-Mostafa, Y. S. (2004). Learning and measuring specialization in collaborative swarm systems. *Adaptive Behavior*, 12(3–4): 199–212.

Lipson, H., and Pollack, J. B. (2000). Automatic design and manufacture of artificial life-forms. *Nature*, 406:974–978.

Lohn, J. D., Hornby, G. S., and Linden, D. S. (2004). An evolved antenna for deployment on NASA's Space Technology 5 mission. *Genetic Programming Theory and Practice II*. Kluwer, chapter 18.

Lovejoy, C. Owen. (1981). *The origins of man. Science*, 211:341–348.

Lungarella, M. (2004). Exploring principles towards a developmental theory of embodied artificial intelligence. PhD thesis, University of Zurich, Switzerland.

Lungarella, M., Metta, G., Sandini, G., and Pfeifer, R. (2004). Developmental robotics: A survey. *Connection Science*, 15(4): 151–190.

Lungarella, M., Pegors, T., Bulwinkle, D., and Sporns, O. (2005). Methods for quantifying the informational structure of sensory and motor data. *Neuroinformatics*, 3(3): 243–262.

Mapping, B. (1994). Penfield's homunculus. *Journal of Neurology, Neurosurgery, and Psychiatry*, 56(4): 329–333.

Maravita, A., and Iriki, A. (2004). Tools for the body (schema). *Trends in Cognitive Sciences*, 8(2): 79–86.

March, J. G. (1994). *Primer on decision making: How decisions happen*. New York: Free Press.

March, J. G., and Simon, H. A. (1993). *Organizations*. 2nd edition. Oxford, UK: Blackwell.

Maris, M., and te Boekhorst, R. (1996). Exploiting physical constraints: Heap formation through behavioral error in a group of robots. In *Proceedings of the IEEE/RSJ International Conference on Intelligent Robots and Systems*. Piscataway, NJ: IEEE Press, 1655–1660.

Martin, P., and Bateson, P. (1993). *Measuring behavior: An introductory guide*. 2nd edition. Cambridge: Cambridge University Press.

Martinoli, A., Ijspeert, A., and Mondada, F. (1999). Understanding collective aggregation mechanisms: From probabilistic modeling to experiments with real robots. *Robotics and Autonomous Systems*, 29:51–63.

Matsushita, K., Lungarella, M., Paul, C., and Yokoi, H. (2005). Locomoting with less computation but more morphology. In *International Conference on Robotics and Automation*. Piscataway, NJ: IEEE Press.

McCarthy, J., Minsky, M. L., Rochester, N., and Shannon, C. E. (1955). Dartmouth Artificial Intelligence Project Proposal. (webpage) http://www.-formal.stanford.edu/jmc/history/dartmouth/dartmouth.html

McCorduck, P. (1979). *Machines who think*. San Franscisco: W. H. Freeman.

McCulloch, W. S., and Pitts, W. H. (1943). A logical calculus of the ideas immanent in nervous activity. *Bulletin of Mathematical Biophysics*, 5:115–133.

McDermott, J. J. (1981). *The philosophy of John Dewey*. Chicago: University of Chicago Press.

McFarland, D. (1994). Towards robot cooperation. In D. Cliff, P. Husbands, J.-A. Meyer, and S. W. Wilson, eds., *From animals to animats 3: Proceedings of the Third International Conference on Simulation of Adaptive Behavior*. Cambridge, MA: MIT Press, 440–444.

McFarland, D., and Bösser, T. (1993). *Intelligent behavior in animals and robots.* Cambridge, MA: MIT Press.

McGeer, T. (1990). Passive dynamic walking. *International Journal of Robotics Research,* 9:62–82.

McLurkin, J., and Yamins, D. (2005). Dynamic task assignment in robot swarms. In S. Thrun, G. S. Sukhatme, and S. Schaal, eds., *Robotics: Science and systems.* Cambridge, MA: MIT Press.

McMahan, R. A. (1984). *Muscles, reflexes, and locomotion.* Princeton, NJ: Princeton University Press.

Miki, N., and Shimoyama, I. (1999). Study on micro-flying robots. *Advanced Robotics,* 13(3): 245–246.

Minsky, M. (1985). *The society of mind.* New York: Simon and Schuster.

Mintzberg, H. (1994). *The rise and fall of strategic planning: Reconceiving roles for planning, plans, planners.* New York: Free Press.

Moor, J. H., ed. (2003). *The Turing Test: The elusive standard of artificial intelligence.* Dordrecht, Netherlands: Kluwer Academic.

Montefiore, A., and Noble, D. (1989). *Goals, no-goals and own goals: A debate on goal-directed and intentional behaviour.* London: Unwin Hyman.

Morasso, P., and Sanguinetti, V. (1995). Self-organizing body schema for motor planning. *Journal of Motor Behavior,* 27(1): 52–66.

Murata, S., Kamimura, A., Kurokawa, H., Yoshida, E., Tomita, K., and Kokaji, S. (2004). Self-reconfigurable robots: Platforms for emerging functionality. In F. Iida, R. Pfeifer, L. Steels, and Y. Kuniyoshi, eds., *Embodied artificial intelligence.* Berlin: Springer, 312–330.

Nadel, J. (2002). When do infants expect? *Infant Behavior and Development,* 7:517–522.

Nagai, Y., Hosoda, K., Morita, A., and Asada, M. (2003). A constructive model for the development of joint attention. *Connection Science,* 15(4): 211–229.

Naghavi, H. R., and Nyberg, L. (2005). Common fronto-parietal activity in attention, memory, and consciousness: Shared demands on integration? *Consciousness and Cognition,* 14(2): 390–425.

Neath, I., and Surprenant, A. M. (2003). *Human memory.* 2nd edition. Belmont, CA: Wadsworth/Thomson Learning.

Neisser, U. (1978). Memory: What are the important questions? In M. M. Gruneberg, P. Morris, and R. Sykes, eds., *Practical aspects of memory.* London: Academic Press, 3–24.

Newell, A. (1990). *Unified theories of cognition.* Cambridge, MA: Harvard University Press.

Nolfi, S., and Floreano, D. (2004). *Evolutionary robotics: The biology, intelligence, and technology of self-organizing machines.* Cambridge, MA: MIT Press.

Nonaka, I., and Takeuchi, H. (1995). *The knowledge-creating company.* Oxford: Oxford University Press.

Norman, D. A. (1980). Twelve issues for cognitive science. *Cognitive Science,* 4:1–32.

Núñez, R. (2004). Do real numbers really move? In F. Iida, R. Pfeifer, L. Steels, and Y. Kuniyoshi, eds., *Embodied artificial intelligence.* Berlin: Springer, 54–73.

Okada, M., and Nakamura, Y. (2004). Design of the continuous symbol space for the intelligent robots using the dynamics–based information processing. In *Proceedings of the IEEE International Conference on Robotics and Automation.* Piscataway, NJ: IEEE Press, 3201–3206.

O'Keefe, J., and Dostrovsky, J. (1971). The hippocampus as a spatial map: Preliminary evidence from unit activity in the freely moving rat. *Brain Research,* 34:171–175.

O'Regan, J. K., and Noë, A. (2001). A sensorimotor account of vision and visual consciousness. *Behavioral and Brain Sciences,* 24:939–1031.

Paul, C., Dravid, R., and Iida, F. (2002). Control of lateral bounding for a pendulum driven hopping robot. In P. Bidaud and F. B. Amar, eds., *Proceedings of the International Conference of Climbing and Walking Robots.* Suffolk, UK: Professional Engineering Publishing, 333–340.

Paul, C. (2004). Morphology and computation. In S. Schaal, A. J. Ijspeert, A. Billard, S. Vijayakumar, J. Hallam, and J.-A. Meyer, eds., *Proceedings of the Eighth International Conference on the Simulation of Adaptive Behavior.* Cambridge, MA: MIT Press, 33–38.

Payne, D. (1984). *Confessions of a Taoist on Wall Street.* New York: Ballantine Books.

Penfield, W., and Boldrey, E. (1937). Somatic motor and sensory representation in the cerebral cortex of man as studied by electrical stimulation. *Brain,* 37:389–443.

Pfeifer, R., and Glatzeder, B. (2004). Visualizing intelligence: The aesthetics of engineering (in German: Intelligenz sichtbar machen: die Aesthetik des Engineering). In C. Maar and H. Burda, eds., *Iconic Turn: Die neue Macht der Bilder.* Cologne, DE: DuMont.

Pfeifer, R., and Scheier, C. (1999). *Understanding intelligence.* Cambridge, MA: MIT Press.

Pfeifer, R. (2000). On the role of morphology and materials in adaptive behavior. In J.-A. Meyer, A. Bertoz, D. Floreano, H. Roitblat, and S. W. Wilson, eds., *Proceedings of the Sixth International Conference on the Simulation of Adaptive Behavior.* Cambridge, MA: MIT Press, 23–32.

Pfeifer, R., Bongard, J., and Iida, F. (2005). New robotics: Design principles for intelligent systems. *Artificial Life,* 11(1–2): 99–120.

Piaget, J. (1952). *The origins of intelligence in children.* New York: International University Press.

Piaget, J. (1963, 2001). *The psychology of intelligence.* New York: Routledge.

Pinker, S. (1997). *How the mind works.* New York: W. W. Norton.

Poli, R. (2001). Exact schema theory for genetic programming and variable-length genetic algorithms with one-point crossover. *Genetic Programming and Evolvable Machines,* 2(2): 123–163.

Popper, K. R. (1935). *Logik der Forschung.* Wien: Springer.

Popper, K. R. (1959). *The logic of scientific discovery.* London: Hutchinson.

Port, R. F., and van Gelder, T., eds. (1995). *Mind as motion: Explorations in the dynamics of cognition.* Cambridge, MA: MIT Press.

Porter, M. E. (1980). *Competitive strategy.* New York: Free Press.

Prigogine, I., and Stenger, I. (1984). *Order out of chaos: Man's new dialogue with nature.* Boston: Shambhala.

Ramachandran, V. S., and Hirstein, W. (1998). The perception of phantom limbs: The D. O. Hebb lecture. *Brain,* 121(9): 1603–1630.

Reber, A., ed. (1995). *The Penguin dictionary of psychology.* 2nd edition. London: Penguin.

Rechenberg, I. (1994). *Evolutionsstrategie '94.* Stuttgart: Friedrich Frommann.

Reger, B. D., Fleming, K. M., Sanguineti, V., Alford, S., and Mussa-Ivaldi, F. A. (2001). Connecting brains to robots: An artificial body for studying the computational properties of neural tissues. *Artificial Life,* 6:307–324.

Reynolds, C. W. (1987). Flocks, herds, and schools: A distributed behavioral model. *Computer Graphics,* 21:25–34.

Ridley, M. (2003). *Nature via nurture: Genes, experience, and what makes us human.* New York: HarperCollins.

Russell, S. J., and Norvig, P. (1995). *Artificial intelligence: A modern approach.* Upper Saddle River, NJ: Prentice Hall.

Sakamura, K. (1984). TRON—Total architecture. In *Proceedings of Architecture Workshop in Japan '84.* Tokyo: Information Processing Society of Japan, 41–50 (in Japanese).

Sakamura, K. (1990). TRON-concept intelligent house. *Japan Architect*, 65(4): 35–40 (in Japanese).

Schelling, T. C. (1969). Models of segregation. *American Economic Review (Papers and Proceedings)*, 59(2): 488–493.

Schenker, P. S., Huntsberger, T. L., Pirjanian, P., Baumgartner, E. T., and Tunstel, E. (2003). Planetary rover developments supporting Mars exploration, sample return and future human-robotic colonization. *Autonomous Robots*, 14(2–3): 103–126.

Schumpeter, J. A. (1984). *Capitalism, socialism, and democracy*. Fourth edition. New York: HarperCollins.

Searle, J. R. (1980). Minds, brains, and programs. *Behavioral and Brain Sciences*, 3:417–424. Reprinted in J. Haugeland, ed., *Mind design*. Montgomery, VT: Bradford Books, 1981.

Seyfried, J., Szymanski, M., Bender, N., Estana, R., Thiel, M., and Wörn, H. (2005), The I-SWARM project: Intelligent small world autonomous robots for micro-manipulation. In E. Sahin, ed., *Swarm robotics*. Berlin: Springer, 70–83.

Simon, H. A. (1969). *The sciences of the artificial*. 2nd edition. Cambridge, MA: MIT Press.

Simon, H. A. (1976). *Administrative behavior: A study of decision-making processes in administrative organization*. 3rd edition. New York: Free Press.

Sims, K. (1994a). Evolving virtual creatures. *Computer Graphics*, 28:15–34.

Sims, K. (1994b). Evolving 3D morphology and behavior by competition. In R. Brooks and P. Maes, eds., *Artificial Life IV: Proceedings of the Fourth International Workshop on the Synthesis and Simulation of Living Systems*. Cambridge, MA: MIT Press, 28–39.

Skarda, C., and Freeman, W. J. (1987). How brains make chaos in order to make sense of the world. *Behavioral and Brain Sciences*, 10:161–195.

Sloman, A. (1978). *The computer revolution in philosophy: Philosophy, science, and models of mind*. Brighton, UK: Harvester Press.

Smith, L. B., and Thelen, E. (2003). Development as a dynamic system. *Trends in Cognitive Sciences*, 7(8): 343–348.

Spector, L. C. (2004). *Automatic quantum computer programming: A genetic programming approach*. Boston: Kluwer Academic.

Spector, L., Klein, J., Perry, C., and Feinstein, M. (2005). Emergence of collective behavior in evolving populations of flying agents. *Genetic Programming and Evolvable Machines*, 6(1): 111–125.

Sporns, O., and Alexander, W. H. (2002). Neuromodulation and plasticity in an autonomous robot. *Neural Networks*, 15:761–774.

Steels, L. (1991). Toward a theory of emergent functionality. In J.-A. Meyer and S. W. Wilson, eds., *From animals to animats: Proceedings of the First International Conference on Simulation of Adaptive Behavior*. Cambridge, MA: MIT Press, 451–461.

Steels, L. (1997). A selectionist mechanism for autonomous behavior acquisition. In R. Pfeifer and R. Brooks, eds., Practice and future of autonomous agents. Special issue, *Robotics and Autonomous Systems*, 20:117–132.

Steels, L. (2001). Language games for autonomous agents. *IEEE Intelligent Systems*, 16(5): 16–22.

Steels, L. (2003). Evolving grounded communication for robots. *Trends in Cognitive Sciences*, 7(7): 308–312.

Steels, L. (2004). The autotelic principle. In F. Iida, R. Pfeifer, L. Steels, and Y. Kuniyoshi, eds., *Embodied artificial intelligence*. Berlin: Springer, 231–242.

Storm, C., and Freeman, W. J. (2002). Review of *Complex systems: Chaos and beyond. A constructive approach with applications in life sciences*, by K. Kaneko and I. Tsuda. *Engineering Applications of Artificial Intelligence*, 15(1): 117–119.

Støy, K., Shen, W.-M., and Will, P. M. (2002). Using role-based control to produce locomotion in chain-type self-reconfigurable robots. *IEEE/ASME Transactions of Mechatronics*, 7(4): 410–417.

Støy, K., Shen, W.-M., and Will, P. (2003). A simple approach to the control of locomotion in self–reconfigurable robots. *Robotics and Autonomous Systems*, 44(3–4): 191–199.

Strogatz, S. H. (1994). *Nonlinear dynamics and chaos*. Cambridge, MA: Perseus Books.

Suh, N. P. (1990). *The principles of design*. New York: Oxford University Press.

Takahata, M., Shiraki, K., Sakane, Y., and Takebayashi, Y. (2004). Sound feedback for powerful Karate training. In Y. Nagashima and M. J. Lyons, eds., *New interfaces for musical expression*. Hamamatsu, JP: Shizuoka University of Art and Culture, 13–18.

Thelen, E., and Smith, L. (1994). *A dynamic systems approach to the development of cognition and action*. Cambridge, MA: MIT Press.

Thelen, E., Schöner, G., Scheier, C., and Smith, L. B. (2001). The dynamics of embodiment: A field theory of infant perseverative reaching. *Behavioral and Brain Sciences* 24(1): 1–34.

Thompson, A. (1996). Silicon evolution. In J. R. Koza, D. E. Goldberg, D. B. Fogel, and R. L. Riolo, eds., *Proceedings of Genetic Programming 1996*. Cambridge, MA: MIT Press, 444–452.

Tinbergen, N. (1963). On aims and methods of ethology. *Zeitschrift Tierpsychologie*, 20:410–433.

Toda, M. (1982). *Man, robot, and society*. The Hague: Nijhoff.

Tononi, G., Sporns, O., and Edelman, G. M. (1994). A measure for brain complexity: Relating functional segregation and integration in the nervous system. *Proceedings of the National Academy of Science of the United States of America, USA* 91:5033–5037.

Tononi, G., Sporns, O., and Edelman, G. M. (1996). A complexity measure for selective matching of signals by the brain. *Proceedings of the National Academy of Science of the United States of America, USA* 93:3422–3427.

Triantafyllou, M. S., and Triantafyllou, G. S. (1995). An efficient swimming machine. *Scientific American*, 272:64–70.

Trullier, O., and Meyer, J.-A. (1997). Place sequence learning for navigation. In W. Gerstner, A. Germond, M. Hasler, and J. Nicoud, eds., *Proceedings of the Seventh International Conference on Artificial Neural Networks*. Berlin: Springer, 757–762.

Turing, A. (1950). Computing machinery and intelligence. *Mind*, 59:433–460. Reprinted in E. A. Feigenbaum and J. Feldman, eds., *Computers and thought*. New York: McGraw-Hill, 11–35.

Turing, A. (1952). The chemical basis of morphogenesis. *Philosophical Transactions of the Royal Society B*, 237:37–72.

Van Gelder, T. J. (1995). What might cognition be, if not computation? *Journal of Philosophy*, 91:345–381.

Vogel, S. (1998). *Cats' paws and catapults: Mechanical worlds of nature and people*. New York: Norton.

Von Holst, E. (1943). Über relative Koordination bei Arthropoden. *Pflügers Archiv*, 246:847–865.

Von Melchner, L., Pallas, S. L., and Sur, M. (2000). Visual behavior mediated by retinal projections directed to the auditory pathway. *Nature*, 404:871–875.

Von Neumann, J. (1966). *The theory of self-reproducing automata*. Edited and completed by A. W. Burks. Urbana: University of Illinois Press.

Walter, W. G. (1950). An imitation of life. *Scientific American*, 182(5): 42–45.

Webb, B. (1996). A robot cricket. *Scientific American*, 275(6): 94–99.

Webb, B., and Consi, T. R., eds. (2001). *Biorobotics: Methods and applications*. Cambridge, MA: MIT Press.

Wegner, D. M. (2002). *The illusion of conscious will.* Cambridge, MA: MIT Press.

Wehner, R., Michel, B., and Antonsen, P. (1996). Visual navigation in insects: Coupling of egocentric and geocentric information. *Journal of Experimental Biology,* 199:129–140.

Weick, K. E. (1995). *Sensemaking in organizations.* London: Sage Publications.

Weiser, M. (1991). The computer for the twenty-first century. *Scientific American,* 265(3): 94–104.

Weizenbaum, J. (1966). ELIZA: A computer program for the study of natural language communication between man and machine. *Communications of the ACM,* 9(1): 36–45.

Weng, J., McClelland, J., Pentland, A., Sporns, O., Stockmann, I., Sur, M., and Thelen, E. (2001). Autonomous mental development by robots and animals. *Science,* 291(5504): 599–600.

Wheeler, P. E. (1991). The thermoregulatory advantages of hominid bipedalism in open equatorial environments: The contribution of increased convective heat loss and cutaneous evaporative cooling. *Journal of Human Evolution,* 21:107–115.

Whitesides, G. M., and Grzybowski, B. (2003). Self-assembly at all scales. *Science,* 295: 2418–2421.

Wiener, N. (1948). *Cybernetics; or, Control and communication in the animal and the machine.* Cambridge, MA: MIT Press.

Williamson, M. (1999). Robot arm control exploiting natural dynamics. PhD thesis, Department of Electrical Engineering and Computer Science, Massachusetts Institute of Technology.

Winograd, T., and Flores, F. (1986). *Understanding computers and cognition.* Reading, MA: Addison-Wesley.

Wood, L. (2002). The world in a box. Little fanfare greets the coming out of a pivotal AI project. *Scientific American,* 286(1): 18–19.

Yerkes, R. M., and Dodson, J. D. (1908). The relation of strength of stimulus to rapidity of habit-formation. *Journal of Comparative Neurology and Psychology,* 18:459–482.

Yokoi, H., Hernandez Arieta, A., Katoh, R., Yu, W., Watanabe, I., and Maruishi, M. (2003). Mutual adaptation in a prosthetics application. In F. Iida, R. Pfeifer, L. Steels, and Y. Kuniyoshi, eds., *Embodied artificial intelligence.* Berlin: Springer, 146–159.

Yoshikai, T., Mizuuchi, I., Sato, D., Yoshida, S., Inaba, M., and Inoue, H. (2003). Behavior system design and implementation in spined muscle-tendon humanoid "Kenta." *Journal of Robotics and Mechatronics,* 15(2): 143–152.

Yoshikawa, Y., Asada, M., and Hosoda, K. (2004a). Towards imitation learning from a viewpoint of an internal observer. In F. Iida, R. Pfeifer, L. Steels, and Y. Kuniyoshi, eds., *Embodied artificial intelligence.* Berlin: Springer, 278–283.

Yoshikawa, Y., Tsuji, Y., Hosoda, K., and Asada, M. (2004b). Is it my body? Body extraction from uninterpreted sensory data based on the invariance of multiple sensory attributes. In *Proceedings of the 2004 IEEE/RSJ International Conference on Intelligent Robots and Systems.* Piscataway, NJ: IEEE Press, 2325–2330.

Zykov, V., Mytilinaios, E., Adams, B., and Lipson, H. (2005). Self-reproducing machines. *Nature,* 435(7038): 163–164.

Index

Printed in the United States
by Baker & Taylor Publisher Services